MY 16 '07	DATE DUE		
5-18-07			

Bowling, Beatniks, and Bell-Bottoms

Pop Culture of 20th-Century America

Bowling, Beatniks, and Bell-Bottoms

Pop Culture of 20th-Century America

Volume 4
1960s-1970s

Sara Pendergast and
Tom Pendergast, Editors

Detroit • New York • San Diego • San Francisco • Cleveland • New Haven, Conn. • Waterville, Maine • London • Munich

THOMSON

GALE

Bowling, Beatniks, and Bell-Bottoms: Pop Culture of 20th-Century America

Sara Pendergast and Tom Pendergast, Editors

Project Editors
Lawrence W. Baker, Allison McNeill

Editorial
Sarah Hermsen

Permissions
Kim Davis

Imaging and Multimedia
Leitha Etheridge-Sims, Luke Rademacher, Robyn Young

Product Design
Jennifer Wahi

Manufacturing
Rita Wimberley

Composition
Evi Seoud

LIBRARY OF CONGRESS CATALOGING-IN-PUBLICATION DATA

Bowling, beatniks, and bell-bottoms : pop culture of 20th-century America / Sara Pendergast and Tom Pendergast, editors.
    p. cm.
Summary: Recounts the enduring products, innovative trends, and fun fads of the past ten decades. In 5 volumes. Includes bibliographical references and indexes.
  ISBN 0-7876-5675-5 (set : alk. paper)
1. United States—Civilization—20th century—Miscellanea—Juvenile literature. 2. Popular culture—United States—History—20th century—Miscellanea—Juvenile literature. [1. United States—Civilization—20th century. 2. Popular culture—History—20th century.] I. Pendergast, Sara. II. Pendergast, Tom.
  E169.1 .B7825 2002
  306'.0973'0904—dc21
                                       2002001829

ISBN 0-7876-5675-5 (set); 0-7876-5676-3 (v. 1); 0-7876-5677-1 (v. 2); 0-7876-5678-X (v. 3);
0-7876-5679-8 (v. 4); 0-7876-5680-1 (v. 5)

Printed in the United States of America
10 9 8 7 6 5 4 3 2 1

CONTENTS

Volume 1

1900s

Commerce

Volume 2

Volume 3

Volume 4

Volume 5

1980s

Commerce

Fashion

Film and Theater

The Way We Lived

1990s

Commerce

Fashion

Film and Theater

Contents

ENTRIES BY ALPHABETICAL ORDER

A

Bold type indicates volume numbers.

C

J

K

L

N

O

P

S

Z

ENTRIES BY TOPIC CATEGORY

Commerce

Bold type indicates volume numbers.

Fashion

Film and Theater

Print Culture

TV and Radio

ADVISORY BOARD

Special thanks are due to U•X•L's Bowling, Beatniks, and Bell-Bottoms advisors for their invaluable comments and suggestions:

Catherine Bond, Department Chair, Library and Media Services, Conestoga High School, Berwyn, Pennsylvania

Cathy Chauvette, Assistant Regional Branch Manager, Fairfax County Public Library, Fairfax County, Virginia

Nancy Schlosser Garabed, Library Media Specialist, Council Rock High School, Newtown, Pennsylvania

Ann West LaPrise, Junior High/Elementary Media Specialist, Huron School District, New Boston, Michigan

Nina Levine, Library Media Specialist, Blue Mountain Middle School, Cortlandt Manor, New York

CONTRIBUTORS

Timothy Berg. Visiting assistant professor, Western Michigan University. Ph.D., History, Purdue University, 1999.

Charles Coletta, Ph.D. Instructor, Department of Popular Culture, Bowling Green State University. Contributing writer, *St. James Encyclopedia of Popular Culture* (2000).

Rob Edelman. Instructor, State University of New York at Albany. Author, *Baseball on the Web* (1997) and *The Great Baseball Films* (1994). Co-author, *Matthau: A Life* (2002); *Meet the Mertzes* (1999); and *Angela Lansbury: A Life on Stage and Screen* (1996). Contributing editor, *Leonard Maltin's Movie & Video Guide*, *Leonard Maltin's Movie Encyclopedia*, and *Leonard Maltin's Family Viewing Guide*. Contributing writer, *International Dictionary of Films and Filmmakers* (2000); *St. James Encyclopedia of Popular Culture* (2000); *Women Filmmakers & Their Films* (1998); *The Political Companion to American Film* (1994); and *Total Baseball* (1989). Film commentator, WAMC (Northeast) Public Radio.

Tina Gianoulis. Freelance writer. Contributing writer, *World War I Reference Library* (2001–2); *Constitutional Amendments: From Freedom of Speech to Flag Burning* (2001); *International Dictionary of Films and Filmmakers* (2000); *St. James Encyclopedia of Popular Culture* (2000); and mystories.com, a daytime drama Web site (1997–98).

Sheldon Goldfarb. Archivist, Alma Mater Society of the University of British Columbia. Ph.D., English, University of British

Columbia. Author, *William Makepeace Thackeray: An Annotated Bibliography, 1976–1987* (1989). Editor, *Catherine,* by William Makepeace Thackeray (1999).

Jill Gregg Clever, A.A., B.A., M.L.I.S. Graduate of Michigan State University, Thomas Edison State College, and Wayne State University. Business-technology specialist, Toledo–Lucas County Public Library.

Justin Gustainis. Professor of communication, State University of New York at Plattsburgh. Author, *American Rhetoric and the Vietnam War* (1993).

Audrey Kupferberg. Film consultant and archivist. Instructor, State University of New York at Albany. Co-author, *Matthau: A Life* (2002); *Meet the Mertzes* (1999); and *Angela Lansbury: A Life on Stage and Screen* (1996). Contributing editor, *Leonard Maltin's Family Viewing Guide.* Contributing writer, *St. James Encyclopedia of Popular Culture* (2000); *Women Filmmakers & Their Films* (1998); and *The American Film Institute Catalog of Feature Films.*

Edward Moran. Writer of American culture, music, and literature. Associate editor, *World Musicians* (1999); *World Authors* (1996); and *Random House Dictionary of the English Language* (1987; 1991). Contributing writer, *St. James Encyclopedia of Popular Culture* (2000). Editor, *Rhythm,* a magazine of world music and global culture (2001).

Sara Pendergast. President, Full Circle Editorial. Vice president, Group 3 Editorial. Co-editor, *St. James Encyclopedia of Popular Culture* (2000). Co-author, *World War I Reference Library* (2001), among other publications.

Tom Pendergast. Editorial director, Full Circle Editorial. Ph.D., American studies, Purdue University. Author, *Creating the Modern Man: American Magazines and Consumer Culture* (2000). Co-editor, *St. James Encyclopedia of Popular Culture* (2000).

Karl Rahder. M.A., University of Chicago Committee on International Relations. Author, several articles on international history and politics.

Chris Routledge. Freelance writer and editor. Ph.D., American literature, University of Newcastle upon Tyne (UK). Author, "The Chevalier and the Priest: Deductive Method in Poe, Chesterton, and Borges," in *Clues: A Journal of Detection*

(2001). Editor, *Mystery in Children's Literature: From the Rational to the Supernatural* (2001).

Robert E. Schnakenberg. Senior writer, History Book Club. Author, *The Encyclopedia Shatnerica* (1998).

Steven Schneider. Ph.D. candidate, philosophy, Harvard University; Ph.D. candidate, cinema studies, New York University. Author, *An Auteur on Elm Street: The Cinema of Wes Craven* (forthcoming). Co-editor, *Horror International* (forthcoming) and *Dark Thoughts: Philosophic Reflections on Cinematic Horror* (forthcoming). Contributing writer, *British Horror Cinema* (2002); *Car Crash Culture* (2001); and numerous film journals.

Robert C. Sickels. Assistant professor of American film and popular culture, Whitman College. Ph.D., English, University of Nevada. Author, "A Politically Correct Ethan Edwards: Clint Eastwood's The Outlaw Josey Wales" in *Journal of Popular Film & Television* (forthcoming); "'70s Disco Daze: Paul Thomas Anderson's Boogie Nights and the Last Golden Age of Irresponsibility" in *Journal of Popular Culture* (forthcoming). Contributor, *St. James Encyclopedia of Popular Culture* (2000).

Popular culture—as we know it—was born in America, though historians disagree as to exactly when. Was it in 1893, when magazine publishers used new technologies to cut the costs of their magazines to a dime and sell hundreds of thousands of copies? Or was it in 1905, when the invention of the nickelodeon brought low-cost films to people all across the nation? Or was it back in 1886, when Richard Sears and Alvah Roebuck sent out their first catalog, which allowed people from all over to choose from among hundreds and then thousands of the same goods?

No matter the exact date, by the turn of the twentieth century, American magazine publishers, retailers, moviemakers, and other entertainers were bringing their goods before larger numbers of Americans than ever before. These magazines, movies, advertisements, shopping experiences, sports teams, and more were what we know as "popular culture," because they could be enjoyed firsthand by masses of Americans.

The story of America as revealed by its popular culture is complex and fascinating. Readers of *Bowling, Beatniks, and Bell-Bottoms: Pop Culture of 20th-Century America* will discover, for example, that the comedic forms first developed by vaudeville comedians at the turn of the century lived on in film, radio, and finally television. They will learn that black musicians created the musical forms that are most distinctly American: blues and jazz. And they will realize that popular culture reacted to things like war and economic depressions in ways that were surprising and unexpected. The study of popular culture has a great deal to teach the student who is interested in how people use entertainment and consumption to make sense of their lives and shape their experience.

Bowling, Beatniks, and Bell-Bottoms gathers together essays that reflect the variety, diversity, and excitement of American popular culture of the twentieth century. This collection focuses more on events, fads, programs, performances, and products than on biographies of people, which are well documented in other sources. Even so, brief biographies of notables are sprinkled throughout. With approximately 750 essays on individual topics and dozens of overviews of pop culture trends, *Bowling, Beatniks, and Bell-Bottoms* covers a great deal of American popular culture, though not nearly enough. There are hundreds more people, bands, TV programs, films, and products that were worthy of mention but were left out due to space consideration. Our advisory board of media specialists, however, helped assure that the most prominent and studied subjects were included.

Have you ever wondered how the Slinky was invented, what Velveeta cheese is made of, or what people danced to before rock and roll? Those answers are in *Bowling, Beatniks, and Bell-Bottoms,* along with many others. It is our hope that this collection will bring both information and pleasure to all students of American culture.

Organization

Bowling, Beatniks, and Bell-Bottoms is arranged chronologically by decade over five volumes (two decades per volume). The approximately 750 entries are grouped into nine topic sections: Commerce, Fashion, Film and Theater, Food and Drink, Music, Print Culture, Sports and Games, TV and Radio, and The Way We Lived (though not all topics appear in every decade). Many subjects can easily appear in several different decades, so those essays are placed in either the decade in which the product was invented or the fad initiated, or in the decade in which the subject was most prominent or popular. In addition, several of the essays could have appeared under different topics (such as a book that was made into a movie), so those essays appear under the topic where it was best known. Users should make frequent use of the index or the two additional tables of contents (arranged alphabetically by entry name and by topic category) to locate an entry.

Essays range in length from 150 to 1000 words, with the majority averaging less than 500 words. Every essay aims to describe the topic and analyze the topic's contribution to popular culture. Each essay lists additional sources on the topic, including books, magazine or journal articles, and Web sites. Whenever possible, references to books are geared to younger readers. The editors have personally visited every Web site mentioned and believe that these sites contain content that will assist the reader in understanding the subject. Due to the nature of the World Wide Web, it is possible that not all Web links will still function at the time of publication.

Bowling, Beatniks, and Bell-Bottoms also provides these features:

- A timeline that highlights key historic and pop culture events of the twentieth century

- A general overview of each decade

- A multipaged "At a Glance" box that breaks down "What We Said," "What We Read," "What We Watched," "What We Listened To," and "Who We Knew"

- An overview of each topic section in each decade

- More than 300 photos and illustrations

- Extensive use of cross references (pointing to decade, topic, and volume)

Acknowledgments

This collection simply could not have been created without the diligent efforts and true professionalism of some of the best writers we know: Timothy Berg, Charles Coletta, Rob Edelman, Tina Gianoulis, Justin Gustainis, Audrey Kupferberg, Edward Moran, Chris Routledge, and Bob Schnakenberg. Also worthy of mention are the contributions of Jill Gregg Clever, Sheldon Goldfarb, Karl Rahder, Steven Schneider, and Robert Sickels.

At U•X•L, we would like to thank Julia Furtaw for suggesting that we revisit the subject of American popular culture for younger readers, and Larry Baker for his good humor and skilled handling of the various stages of book production. Much appreciation goes to Theresa Murray, who thoroughly copyedited all five volumes and compiled the detailed subject index, as well as to Jim Buchanan and Bookcomp Inc./Nighthawk Design for their typesetting work. We'd like also to thank the staff of the Snohomish, Washington, branch of the Sno-Isle Regional Library for processing our innumerable book requests with such efficiency and good cheer. Rebecca, Mike, Penny, Vina, Eileen, and everyone else: Thank you. We truly appreciate the work you do.

This book is dedicated to our children, Conrad and Louisa, who provided valuable insights into the entries on Pokémon and Beanie Babies, and who will soon be old enough to find this book in their school libraries. Happy reading, kids!

Comments and Suggestions

We welcome your comments on *Bowling, Beatniks, and Bell-Bottoms*. Please send correspondence to: Editors, *Bowling, Beatniks, and Bell-Bottoms*, U•X•L, 27500 Drake Rd., Farmington Hills, MI 48331-3535; call toll-free: 800-877-4253; fax to 248-414-5043; or send e-mail via www.gale.com.

—Sara Pendergast and Tom Pendergast, Editors

TIMELINE

1900   On January 29, Ban Johnson forms the American League to compete against baseball's National League.

1900   In February, Eastman Kodak introduces the Brownie Camera.

1900   In March, the Good Roads Campaign tries to build support for better roads. At the time, there are only ten miles of paved roads in the nation.

1900   On March 31, the first ad for an automobile appears in *The Saturday Evening Post.*

1900   On April 23, Buffalo Bill Cody's *Wild West Show* opens at Madison Square Garden in New York City.

1900   On November 6, Republican William McKinley is reelected U.S. president, with New York governor Theodore Roosevelt as his vice president.

1900   On November 12, *Floradora,* one of the most popular theatrical musicals of the decade, premieres in New York. It runs for more than five hundred performances.

1901   On February 25, U.S. Steel is formed out of ten companies and becomes the world's largest industrial corporation.

1901 On March 13, steel tycoon Andrew Carnegie donates $2.2 million to fund a New York public library system.

1901 On September 6, President William McKinley is shot by an assassin in Buffalo, New York, and dies eight days later from complications from gangrene due to improperly dressed wounds. Theodore Roosevelt becomes president.

1901 On October 16, President Theodore Roosevelt starts a national controversy when he dines with black leader Booker T. Washington in the White House.

1902 The Teddy Bear is introduced, named after President Theodore Roosevelt.

1902 On January 1, in the first Rose Bowl football game, the University of Michigan defeats Stanford 49-0.

1902 On March 18, Italian opera singer Enrico Caruso produces his first phonographic recording.

1902 On April 16, Tally's Electric Theater, the first theater solely devoted to presenting motion pictures, opens in Los Angeles, California.

1902 On December 21, Guglielmo Marconi transmits the first wireless signals across the Atlantic Ocean.

1903 *Redbook* magazine is founded.

1903 The Portage Lakers of Houghton, Michigan—the first professional hockey team from the United States—win the International Hockey League championship.

1903 On January 22, the United States signs a 99-year lease on what will become the Panama Canal Zone, where they will build a canal that connects the Caribbean Sea to the Pacific Ocean.

1903 In February, the *Ladies' Home Journal* becomes the first American magazine to reach one million paid subscriptions.

1903 On May 23, two men make the first transcontinental automobile trip from San Francisco to New York in sixty-four days. Upon returning home, one driver is ticketed for exceeding the speed limit of six miles per hour.

1903 On August 14, Jim Jeffries defeats James J. "Gentleman Jim" Corbett to retain the world heavyweight boxing title.

1903 On September 12, Scott Joplin's ragtime opera *A Guest of Honor* begins a midwest tour.

1903 In October, the Boston Pilgrims defeat the Pittsburgh Pirates in the first World Series to pit an American League team against a National League team.

1903 On December 1, Edwin S. Porter's film *The Great Train Robbery* is considered the first Western and the first American film with a plot.

1903 On December 17, Wilbur and Orville Wright make the first sustained flight at Kitty Hawk, North Carolina.

1904 The Ford Motor Company sells fourteen hundred of its Model A cars.

1904 On April 20, the World's Fair opens in St. Louis, Missouri.

1904 On May 5, Cy Young pitches baseball's first perfect game.

1904 On November 8, Theodore Roosevelt is reelected president.

1905 The German navy launches the first submarine.

1905 African American leader W. E. B. Du Bois helps found the Niagara Movement, an organization to advance African American issues.

1905 On May 5, the *Chicago Defender,* the first major black newspaper, begins publication.

1905 In June, the era of the nickelodeon begins when Harry Davis's Pittsburgh, Pennsylvania, movie theater offers continuous movie showings. By the end of the decade, more than eight thousand nickel-admission movie theaters are in operation.

1905 On June 18, the Twentieth Century Limited begins train service between Chicago, Illinois, and New York City and boasts a travel time of only eighteen hours.

1906 Kellogg's Corn Flakes breakfast cereal is introduced.

1906 In February, Upton Sinclair publishes *The Jungle,* a novel depicting the horrible conditions in the meat-packing industry. The work prompts the passage of the Meat Inspection Act.

1906 On April 14, President Theodore Roosevelt coins the term "muckraking" when he criticizes journalists who expose abuses and corruption and miss the larger social picture.

1906 On April 18, a major earthquake and fire destroy much of San Francisco, California.

1906 On May 3, the First Annual Advertising Show in New York City heralds the beginning of an important American industry.

1906 On November 21, the first voice radio transmission travels eleven miles from Plymouth to Brant Rock, Massachusetts.

1907 Work begins on the Panama Canal.

1907 On January 23, in what newspapers call the "trial of the century," millionaire Harry K. Thaw is tried for the murder of world-famous architect Stanford White over the honor of Thaw's wife, showgirl Evelyn Nesbit.

1907 On June 10, French motion picture pioneers Auguste and Louis Lumière announce they have developed a method for producing color film.

1907 On July 8, Florenz Ziegfeld's musical revue, the *Ziegfeld Follies,* opens in New York.

1907 On December 3, actress Mary Pickford makes her stage debut in *The Warrens of Virginia.*

1908 The world's first skyscraper, the forty-seven-story Singer Building, is completed in New York City.

1908 The General Motors Corporation is formed and soon becomes the biggest competitor of the Ford Motor Company.

1908 In March, the Original Independent Show, organized in New York, includes works by American painters Edward Hopper, George Bellows, and Rockwell Kent.

1908   On September 6, Isreal Zangwill's play *The Melting Pot* opens in New York City; the title becomes an internationally recognized description of the United States.

1908   On October 1, the Ford Motor Company unveils its Model T with a price tag of $825. It soon becomes the best-selling automobile of its time.

1908   On November 3, former U.S. secretary of war William Howard Taft is elected president.

1908   On December 26, Jack Johnson defeats Tommy Burns to become the first black world heavyweight boxing champion. His victory is considered an outrage by white racists.

1909   The fifty-story Metropolitan Life Insurance Tower in New York City becomes the world's tallest building.

1909   The Ford Motor Company manufactures nineteen thousand Model T cars.

1909   On March 16, the Federal Bureau of Investigation is created as a federal law enforcement agency.

1909   On March 23, former president Theodore Roosevelt leaves for a safari in Africa. He is paid $50,000 by *Scribner's* for his account of the trip.

1909   On April 6, U.S. Navy commander Robert Peary reaches the North Pole.

1909   On May 3, the first wireless press message is sent from New York City to Chicago, Illinois.

1909   On July 12, the U.S. Congress asks the states to authorize a national income tax.

1910   Western novelist Zane Grey's book *Heritage of the Desert* becomes a huge commercial success, starting his career of bringing the American West to the reading world.

1910   Levis Strauss and Company begins making casual play clothes for children.

1910   The Boy Scouts of America are founded in Chicago, Illinois.

1910   On February 28, Russian ballerina Anna Pavlova makes her American debut at the Metropolitan Opera House in New York City.

1910   On March 28, the first one-man show by artist Pablo Picasso opens at photographer and editor Alfred Stieglitz's 291 Gallery in New York City.

1910   In November, the National Association for the Advancement of Colored People (NAACP) publishes the first issue of *The Crisis* magazine, edited by W. E. B. Du Bois.

1910   On November 3, the Chicago Grand Opera opens with a production of *Aida,* by Giuseppe Verdi.

1911   Irving Berlin composes "Alexander's Ragtime Band," the song that popularized ragtime music.

1911   Air conditioning is invented.

1911   *Photoplay,* the first movie fan magazine, is published.

1911   On March 25, in New York City, 146 female workers are killed in the Triangle Shirtwaist Factory fire, alerting Americans to the dangers women face in industrial labor.

1911   On May 23, President William Howard Taft dedicates the New York Public Library.

1911   On May 30, the first Indianapolis 500 auto race is won by Ray Harroun with an average speed of 74.59 mph.

1911   On August 8, *Pathe's Weekly,* the first regular newsreel to be produced in the United States, is released to motion picture theaters.

1911   On December 19, the Association of American Painters and Sculptors is founded.

1912   New Mexico and Arizona become the forty-seventh and forty-eighth states.

1912   The Little Theater in Chicago, Illinois, and the Toy Theater in Boston, Massachusetts, the first influential little theaters in the United States, are founded.

1912   Dancers Irene and Vernon Castle start a craze for ballroom dancing.

1912 On April 15, the *Titanic* sinks on its maiden voyage from Ireland to the United States, killing 1,517.

1912 In August, photographer and editor Alfred Stieglitz devotes an entire issue of his periodical *Camera Work* to the modern art movement.

1912 On August 5, former president Theodore Roosevelt is nominated as the presidential candidate of the newly formed Progressive Party.

1912 On October 31, *The Musketeers of Pig Alley,* a film by D. W. Griffith that points out the social evils of poverty and crime on the streets of New York, is released.

1912 On November 5, New Jersey governor Woodrow Wilson is elected president.

1912 On December 10, the Famous Players Film Company registers for copyright of the five-reel feature film *The Count of Monte Cristo,* directed by Edwin S. Porter.

1913 The 792-foot-high Woolworth Building in New York City becomes the world's tallest building, a record it holds until 1930.

1913 The first crossword puzzle is published.

1913 The Jesse Lasky Feature Play Co., which later would become Paramount Pictures, is established in Hollywood, California.

1913 The Panama Canal is completed, and officially opens on August 15, 1914.

1913 On February 17, the International Exhibition of Modern Art, known as the Armory Show, opens in New York City. It is the first opportunity for many Americans to view modern art.

1913 On February 25, the Sixteenth Amendment to the Constitution is approved, authorizing a federal income tax.

1913 On March 24, the million dollar, eighteen-hundred-seat Palace Theatre opens in New York City.

1913 On May 31, the Seventeenth Amendment to the Constitution is approved, providing for the direct election of U.S. senators.

1914 On February 13, the American Society of Composers, Authors, and Publishers (ASCAP), an organization that seeks royalty payments for public performances of music, is founded in New York City.

1914 In March, comedian Charles Chaplin begins to evolve the legendary character of the Little Tramp in the film *Mabel's Strange Predicament.*

1914 On July 3, the first telephone line connects New York City and San Francisco, California.

1914 On August 3, World War I starts in Europe when Germany invades Belgium. Soon all of Europe is drawn into the conflict, though the United States remains neutral.

1914 On September 5, a German submarine scores its first kill, sinking the British cruiser *Pathfinder,* as World War I intensifies.

1914 In September, in the World War I Battle of the Marne, Germany's advance into France is halted.

1914 On November 3, the first American exhibition of African sculpture opens at the 291 Gallery in New York City.

1914 On December 3, the Isadorables, six European dancers trained by American dancer Isadora Duncan, perform at Carnegie Hall in New York City after escaping with Duncan from her war-torn Europe.

1915 The first taxicab appears on the streets of New York City.

1915 The first professional football league is formed in Ohio and is called simply the Ohio League.

1915 Modern dancers Ruth St. Denis and Ted Shawn found the Denishawn School of Dancing in Los Angeles, California.

1915 Five hundred U.S. correspondents cover World War I in Europe.

1915 On March 10, the Russian Symphony Orchestra plays the American debut performance of the symphony *Prometheus* by Aleksandr Scriabin at Carnegie Hall in

New York City. Color images are projected onto a screen as part of the show.

1915   On December 10, the Ford Motor Company completes its one millionth Model T automobile.

1916   The Boeing Aircraft Company produces its first biplane.

1916   Newspaper publisher William Randolph Hearst inaugurates the *City Life* arts section as a supplement to his Sunday newspapers.

1916   In November, inventor and radio pioneer Lee De Forest begins to transmit daily music broadcasts from his home in New York City.

1916   On November 7, Woodrow Wilson is reelected president after campaigning on the pledge to keep the United States out of the war in Europe.

1917   The Russian Revolution brings communism to Russia, setting the stage for nearly a century of intermittent conflict with the United States.

1917   Showman George M. Cohan composes the song that was a musical call-to-arms during World War I: "Over There."

1917   Motion picture pioneer Cecil B. DeMille directs *The Little American,* a patriotic melodrama starring Mary Pickford.

1917   On April 6, the United States declares war on Germany after German submarines continue to attack U.S. merchant ships.

1917   On May 28, Benny Leonard wins the lightweight boxing championship, which he holds until his retirement in 1924 while building a record of 209-5; he makes a comeback in 1931.

1917   On August 19, the managers of the New York Giants and Cincinnati Reds are arrested for playing baseball on Sunday.

1917   On October 27, sixteen-year-old Russian-born violinist Jascha Heifetz makes his debut American performance at Carnegie Hall in New York City.

1918   The annual O. Henry Awards for short fiction are inaugurated in honor of short story writer O. Henry (a pseudonym for William Sydney Porter).

1918   On January 8, President Woodrow Wilson delivers his "Fourteen Points" address before Congress, outlining his plans for the shape of the postwar world.

1918   In March, *The Little Review* begins to serialize the novel *Ulysses,* by James Joyce, which features stream of consciousness techniques and a kind of private language.

1918   On November 11, Germany signs an armistice with the Allies, ending the fighting in World War I.

1918   In December, the Theatre Guild is founded in New York City.

1919   *Maid of Harlem,* an all-black-cast musical starring "Fats" Waller, Mamie Smith, Johnny Dunn, and Perry Bradford, draws enthusiastic crowds at the Lincoln Theatre in New York City.

1919   On January 29, Prohibition begins with the adoption of the Eighteenth Amendment to the Constitution, which bans the manufacture, sale, and transportation of intoxicating liquors.

1919   On February 5, United Artists, an independent film distribution company, is founded by Charles Chaplin, Douglas Fairbanks, D. W. Griffith, and Mary Pickford.

1919   On June 28, the Treaty of Versailles is signed by the Allied powers, officially ending World War I. Germany is forced to pay costly reparations for the damage it caused during the war.

1919   On July 4, Jack Dempsey defeats Jess Willard to win the world heavyweight boxing championship.

1919   On October 31, the Provincetown Players stage *The Dreamy Kid,* by Eugene O'Neill, with an all-black cast.

1919   On December 22, Attorney General A. Mitchell Palmer authorizes government raids on communists, anarchists, and other political radicals. These "Palmer raids" are part of a nationwide "red scare."

1920   Sinclair Lewis publishes the novel *Main Street.*

1920   Douglas Fairbanks stars in the film *The Mark of Zorro.*

1920   On January 5, the Radio Corporation of America (RCA) is founded and becomes a leading radio broadcaster.

1920   On February 12, the National Negro Baseball League is founded.

1920   On August 20, the first radio news bulletins are broadcast by station 8MK in Detroit, Michigan.

1920   On August 26, the Nineteenth Amendment to the Constitution gives women the right to vote.

1920   On September 28, eight Chicago White Sox players are charged with throwing the 1919 World Series in what becomes known as the "Black Sox Scandal." They are eventually banned from the game for life.

1920   On September 29, New York Yankee Babe Ruth breaks his own single-season home run record with 54 home runs.

1920   On November 1, Eugene O'Neill's play *The Emperor Jones* opens in New York City.

1920   On November 6, U.S. senator Warren G. Harding of Ohio is elected president.

1921   The Ford Motor Company announces a plan to produce one million automobiles a year.

1921   The Phillips Gallery in Washington, D.C., becomes the first American museum of modern art.

1921   In this year, 13 percent of Americans own telephones.

1921   On March 10, the first White Castle hamburger chain opens in Wichita, Kansas.

1921   On April 11, radio station KDKA in Pittsburgh, Pennsylvania, broadcasts the first sports event on radio, a boxing match between Johnny Ray and Johnny Dundee. Later that year, the World Series is broadcast.

1921   On May 23, *Shuffle Along* is the first black Broadway musical written and directed by African Americans.

1921 On July 29, Adolf Hitler is elected dictator of the Nazi Party in Munich, Germany.

1921 On September 8, the first Miss America pageant is held in Washington, D.C.

1921 On November 2, Margaret Sanger founds the American Birth Control League in New York City, raising the anger of many religious groups, especially Catholic groups.

1922 Robert Flaherty releases the documentary film *Nanook of the North.*

1922 Irish author James Joyce publishes *Ulysses,* which is banned in some countries for its alleged obscenity.

1922 F. Scott Fitzgerald publishes *Tales of the Jazz Age.*

1922 The American Professional Football Association changes its name to the National Football League (NFL).

1922 *Reader's Digest* magazine is founded.

1922 Al Jolson pens the popular song "Toot Toot Tootsie."

1922 On May 5, Coco Chanel introduces Chanel No. 5, which becomes the world's best-known perfume.

1922 On August 28, the first advertisement is aired on radio station WEAF in New York City.

1922 On December 30, the Union of Soviet Socialist Republics (USSR) is established with Russia at its head.

1923 Cecil B. DeMille directs the epic film *The Ten Commandments.*

1923 Charles Kettering develops a method for bringing colored paint to mass-produced cars.

1923 Bessie Smith's "Down Hearted Blues" is one of the first blues songs to be recorded.

1923 *Time* magazine begins publication.

1923 On April 6, trumpet player Louis Armstrong records his first solo on "Chimes Blues" with King Oliver's Creole Jazz Band.

1923 On August 3, President Warren G. Harding dies and Vice President Calvin Coolidge takes office.

1924 John Ford directs the Western film *The Iron Horse*.

1924 The Metro-Goldwyn-Mayer (MGM) film studio is formed in Hollywood, California.

1924 Evangelist Aimee Semple McPherson begins broadcasting from the first religious radio station, KFSG in Los Angeles, California.

1924 The stock market begins a boom that will last until 1929.

1924 On January 1, there are 2.5 million radios in American homes, up from 2,000 in 1920.

1924 On February 12, the tomb of King Tutankhamen, or King Tut, is opened in Egypt after having been sealed for four thousand years.

1924 On February 24, George Gershwin's *Rhapsody in Blue* is performed by an orchestra in New York City.

1924 On March 10, J. Edgar Hoover is appointed director of the Federal Bureau of Investigation.

1924 In June, the Chrysler Corporation is founded, and competes with General Motors and Ford.

1924 On November 4, incumbent Calvin Coolidge is elected president.

1925 In one of the most famous years in American literature, F. Scott Fitzgerald publishes *The Great Gatsby*, Ernest Hemingway publishes *In Our Time*, and Theodore Dreiser publishes *An American Tragedy*.

1925 Lon Chaney stars in the film *The Phantom of the Opera*.

1925 *EWSM Barn Dance* radio program begins broadcasting from Nashville, Tennessee; the name is later changed to *Grand Ole Opry* and it becomes the leading country music program.

1925 The magazine *The New Yorker* begins publication and features the prices paid for bootleg liquor.

1925 In February, the Boeing aircraft company builds a

plane capable of flying over the Rocky Mountains with a full load of mail.

1925 On May 8, the Brotherhood of Sleeping Car Porters, founded by A. Philip Randolph, is one of the first black labor unions.

1925 In July, in the Scopes "Monkey" trial, a Tennessee teacher is tried and found guilty of teaching evolution in a trial that attracts national attention.

1925 On August 8, forty thousand Ku Klux Klan members march in Washington, D.C., to broaden support for their racist organization.

1926 Latin idol Rudolph Valentino stars in the film *The Son of the Sheik.*

1926 Ernest Hemingway publishes *The Sun Also Rises.*

1926 The Book-of-the-Month Club is launched to offer quality books to subscribers.

1926 On March 7, the first transatlantic radiotelephone conversation links New York City and London, England.

1926 On March 17, *The Girl Friend,* a musical with songs by Richard Rodgers and Lorenz Hart, opens on Broadway.

1926 On April 18, dancer Martha Graham makes her first professional appearance in New York City.

1927 Al Jolson stars in the film *The Jazz Singer,* the first film to have sound. Clara Bow—the "It" girl—stars in *It.*

1927 On January 1, the Rose Bowl football game is broadcast coast-to-coast on the radio.

1927 On April 7, television is first introduced in America, but investors are skeptical.

1927 On May 21, Charles Lindbergh completes his nonstop flight from New York City to Paris, France, and is given a hero's welcome.

1927 On May 25, the Ford Motor Company announces that production of the Model T will be stopped in favor of the modern Model A.

1927   On September 22, the Jack Dempsey–Gene Tunney heavyweight championship fight becomes the first sports gate to top $2 million.

1927   On December 4, Duke Ellington's orchestra beings a long run at the Cotton Club nightclub in Harlem, New York.

1927   On December 27, the Oscar and Hammerstein musical *Show Boat* opens on Broadway in New York City.

1928   On April 15, the New York Rangers become the first American team to win the National Hockey League Stanley Cup.

1928   On May 11, WGY in Schenectady, New York, offers the first scheduled television service, though the high price of televisions keeps most people from owning them.

1928   On July 30, the Eastman Kodak company introduces color motion pictures.

1928   On November 6, former U.S. secretary of commerce Herbert Hoover is elected president.

1928   On December 13, George Gershwin's *An American in Paris* opens at Carnegie Hall in New York City.

1928   On December 26, swimmer Johnny Weissmuller retires from competition after setting sixty-seven world records.

1929   Mickey Mouse makes his first appearance in *Steamboat Willie,* an animated film made by Walt Disney.

1929   Commercial airlines carry 180,000 passengers in the year.

1929   Ernest Hemingway publishes *A Farewell to Arms,* a novel set during World War I.

1929   Nick Lucas's "Tiptoe through the Tulips with Me" and Louis Armstrong's "Ain't Misbehavin'" are two of the year's most popular songs.

1929   On February 14, in the Saint Valentine's Day Massacre, gunmen working for Chicago, Illinois, mobster Al Capone gun down seven members of a rival gang.

1929 On October 29, the stock market collapses on a day known as "Black Tuesday," marking the start of what will become the Great Depression.

1930 Grant Wood paints *American Gothic*.

1930 The Continental Baking company introduces Wonder Bread, the first commercially produced sliced bread.

1930 Unemployment reaches four million as the economy worsens.

1930 On January 14, jazz greats Benny Goodman, Glenn Miller, Jimmy Dorsey, and Jack Teagarden play George and Ira Gershwin's songs, including "I've Got a Crush on You," in the musical *Strike Up the Band* at the Mansfield Theater in New York City.

1930 On March 6, General Foods introduces the nation's first frozen foods.

1930 On May 3, Ogden Nash, a poet who will become famous for his funny, light verse, publishes "Spring Comes to Murray Hill" in the *New Yorker* magazine and soon begins work at the magazine.

1930 On September 8, the comic strip *Blondie* begins.

1930 On October 14, *Girl Crazy*, starring Ethel Merman, opens at New York's Guild Theater. The musical features songs by George Gershwin, Walter Donaldson, and Ira Gershwin, including "I Got Rhythm" and "Embraceable You."

1931 The horror films *Dracula* and *Frankenstein* are both released.

1931 Nevada legalizes gambling in order to bring revenue to the state.

1931 On March 3, "The Star Spangled Banner" becomes the national anthem by congressional vote.

1931 On April 30, the Empire State Building, the tallest building in the world, opens in New York City.

1931 On June 3, Fred and Adele Astaire perform for the last time together on the first revolving stage.

1931 On July 27, *Earl Carroll's Vanities,* featuring naked chorus girls, opens at the three-thousand-seat Earl Carroll Theater in New York City.

1931 On October 12, the comic strip *Dick Tracy* begins.

1932 Edwin Herbert Land, a Harvard College dropout, invents Polaroid film.

1932 On May 2, *The Jack Benny Show* premieres as a variety show on radio and runs for twenty-three years and then another ten years on television.

1932 On July 30, the Summer Olympic Games open in Los Angeles, California, and feature record-breaking performances by Americans Babe Didrikson and Eddie Tolan.

1932 On July 31, in German parliamentary elections, the Nazi Party receives the most seats but is unable to form a government.

1932 On November 7, the radio adventure *Buck Rogers in the Twenty-Fifth Century* premieres on CBS, and runs until 1947.

1932 On November 8, New York governor Franklin D. Roosevelt is elected president, promising to take steps to improve the economy. In his first one hundred days in office, Roosevelt introduces much legislation to use the government to aid those harmed by the Great Depression.

1932 On December 27, Radio City Music Hall opens at the Rockefeller Center in New York City.

1933 President Franklin D. Roosevelt presents the nation with his first radio address, known as a "fireside chat."

1933 Walt Disney releases the feature film *The Three Little Pigs.*

1933 On January 3, *The Lone Ranger* radio drama premieres on WXYZ radio in Detroit, Michigan.

1933 On January 30, Nazi leader Adolf Hitler becomes chancellor of Germany. Hitler soon seizes all power and sets out to attack his party's political enemies.

1933 On May 27, fan dancer Sally Rand attracts thousands with her performance at the Chicago World's Fair that celebrated the Century of Progress.

1933 On September 30, *Ah, Wilderness,* acclaimed American playwright Eugene O'Neill's only comedy, opens at the Guild Theater in New York City.

1933 On December 5, the Twenty-first Amendment to the Constitution puts an end to Prohibition.

1934 The first pipeless organ is patented by Laurens Hammond. The Hammond organ starts a trend toward more electrically amplified instruments.

1934 Dashiell Hammett publishes *The Thin Man,* one of the first hard-boiled detective novels.

1934 The Apollo Theater opens in Harlem, New York, as a showcase for black performers.

1934 German director Fritz Lang flees Nazi Germany to make movies in the United States.

1934 On May 5, bank robbers and murderers Bonnie Parker and Clyde Barrow are killed by lawmen in Louisiana.

1934 On July 1, the Motion Picture Producers and Distributors of America (MPPDA) association creates the Hay's Office to enforce codes that limit the amount and types of sexuality and other immoral behavior in films.

1934 On July 22, "Public Enemy No. 1" John Dillinger is shot and killed outside a Chicago, Illinois, theater by FBI agents and local police.

1934 On August 13, Al Capp's *Li'l Abner* comic strip debuts in eight newspapers.

1934 On August 19, Adolf Hitler is declared president of Germany, though he prefers the title Führer (leader).

1935 One out of four American households receives government relief as the Depression deepens.

1935 Twenty million Monopoly board games are sold in one week.

1935 The first Howard Johnson roadside restaurant opens in Boston, Massachusetts.

1935 The Works Progress Administration Federal Arts Projects, some of President Franklin D. Roosevelt's many New Deal programs, give work to artists painting post offices and other federal buildings.

1935 In April, *Your Hit Parade* is first heard on radio and offers a selection of hit songs.

1935 On April 16, the radio comedy-drama *Fibber McGee and Molly* debuts on NBC and runs until 1952.

1935 On May 24, the first nighttime major league baseball game is played in Cincinnati, Ohio.

1935 On October 10, *Porgy and Bess,* known as the "most American opera of the decade," opens in New York City at the Alvin Theater. The music George Gershwin wrote for the opera combined blues, jazz, and southern folk.

1936 American Airlines introduces transcontinental airline service.

1936 Ten African American athletes including Jesse Owens win gold medals in the Summer Olympics held in Berlin, Germany, embarrassing Nazi leader Adolf Hitler, who had declared the inferiority of black athletes.

1936 Dust storms in the Plains states force thousands to flee the region, many to California.

1936 Popular public-speaking teacher Dale Carnegie publishes his book *How to Win Friends and Influence People.*

1936 To increase feelings of nationalism, the Department of the Interior hires folksinger Woody Guthrie to travel throughout the U.S. Southwest performing his patriotic songs such as "Those Oklahoma Hills."

1936 In the Soviet Union, the Communist Party begins its Great Purge, executing anyone who resists the party's social and economic policies. By 1938, it is estimated that ten million people have been killed.

1936 Throughout Europe, countries scramble to form alliances with other countries for what seems to be a likely war. Germany and Italy join together to support the military government of Francisco Franco in Spain, while Great Britain and France sign nonaggression pacts with the Soviet Union.

1936 On July 18, the Spanish Civil War begins when Spanish military officers rise up against the Republican government of Spain.

1936 In October, the New York Yankees win the first of four World Series in a row.

1936 On November 3, Franklin D. Roosevelt is reelected as president of the United States.

1936 On November 23, the first issue of *Life* magazine is published.

1937 Dr. Seuss becomes a popular children's book author with the publication of *And to Think That I Saw It on Mulberry Street.*

1937 The Hormel company introduces Spam, a canned meat.

1937 A poll shows that the average American listens to the radio for 4.5 hours a day.

1937 *Porky's Hare Hunt,* a short animated cartoon by Warner Bros., introduces audiences to the Bugs Bunny character and the talents of Mel Blanc, the voice of both Bugs Bunny and Porky Pig.

1937 The first soap opera, *Guiding Light,* is broadcast. It continues as a radio program until 1956 and moves to television.

1937 British writer J. R. R. Tolkien publishes *The Hobbit.*

1937 On June 22, black boxer Joe Louis knocks out Jim Braddock to win the world heavyweight boxing championship.

1937 On December 21, *Snow White and the Seven Dwarfs,* the first feature-length animated film, is presented by Walt Disney.

1938 Glenn Miller forms his own big band and begins to tour extensively.

1938 On January 17, the first jazz performance at Carnegie Hall in New York City is performed by Benny Goodman and His Orchestra, with Duke Ellington, Count Basie, and others.

1938 In June, the character Superman is introduced in *Action Comics #1*. By 1939, he appears in his own comic book series.

1938 On August 17, Henry Armstrong becomes the first boxer to hold three boxing titles at one time when he defeats Lou Ambers at New York City's Madison Square Garden.

1938 On October 31, Orson Welles's radio broadcast of H. G. Wells's science fiction novel *The War of the Worlds* is believed to be a serious announcement of Martian invasion by listeners and panic spreads throughout the country.

1938 On November 11, singer Kate Smith's performance of "God Bless America" is broadcast over the radio on Armistice Day.

1939 Singer Frank Sinatra joins the Tommy Dorsey band, where he will soon find great success.

1939 Federal spending on the military begins to revive the economy.

1939 Pocket Books, the nation's first modern paperback book company, is founded.

1939 The National Collegiate Athletic Association (NCAA) holds it first Final Four championship basketball series, which is won by the University of Oregon.

1939 *Gone with the Wind,* David O. Selznick's epic film about the Civil War, stars Vivien Leigh and Clark Gable.

1939 *The Wizard of Oz* whisks movie audiences into a fantasyland of magic and wonder. The film stars Judy Garland and includes such popular songs as "Somewhere Over the Rainbow," "Follow the Yellow Brick Road," and "We're Off to See the Wizard."

1939 On May 2, baseball great Lou "The Iron Man" Gehrig ends his consecutive game streak at 2,130 when he removes himself from the lineup.

1939 On September 1, German troops invade Poland, causing Great Britain and France to declare war on Germany and starting World War II. Days later, the Soviet Union invades Poland as well, and soon Germany and the Soviet Union divide Poland.

1940 The radio program *Superman* debuts, introducing the phrases "Up, up, and away!" and "This looks like a job for Superman!"

1940 On February 22, German troops begin construction of a concentration camp in Auschwitz, Poland.

1940 The first issue of the comic book *Batman* is published.

1940 On May 10, German forces invade Belgium and Holland, and later march into France.

1940 On June 10, Italy declares war on Britain and France.

1940 On June 14, the German army enters Paris, France.

1940 On August 24, Germany begins bombing London, England.

1940 On November 5, President Franklin D. Roosevelt is reelected for his third term.

1940 On November 13, the Disney film *Fantasia* opens in New York City.

1941 "Rosie the Riveter" becomes the symbol for the many women who are employed in various defense industries.

1941 *Citizen Kane,* which many consider the greatest movie of all time, is released, directed by and starring Orson Welles.

1941 On January 15, A. Philip Randolph leads the March on Washington to call for an end to racial discrimination in defense-industry employment. President Franklin D. Roosevelt eventually signs an executive order barring such discrimination.

1941 On March 17, the National Gallery of Art is opened in Washington, D.C.

1941 On July 1, CBS and NBC begin offering about fifteen hours of commercial television programming each week—but few consumers have enough money to purchase television sets.

1941 On October 19, German troops lay siege to the Russian city of Moscow.

1941 On December 7, Japanese planes launch a surprise attack on the U.S. naval and air bases in Pearl Harbor, Hawaii, and declare war against the United States.

1941 On December 11, the United States declares war on Germany and Italy in response to those countries' declarations of war.

1941 On December 15, the annual Rose Bowl football game is moved from Pasadena, California, to Durham, North Carolina, to avoid the chance of a Japanese bombing attack.

1942 Humphrey Bogart and Ingrid Bergman star in *Casablanca,* set it war-torn Europe.

1942 On February 19, President Franklin D. Roosevelt signs an executive order placing all Japanese Americans on the West Coast in internment camps for the rest of the war.

1942 On May 5, sugar rationing starts in the United States, followed by the rationing of other products.

1942 In June, American troops defeat the Japanese at the Battle of Midway.

1942 On December 25, the comedy team of Abbott and Costello is voted the leading box-office attraction of 1942.

1943 Gary Cooper and Ingrid Bergman star in *For Whom the Bell Tolls,* the film version of the novel by Ernest Hemingway.

1943 On January 25, the Pentagon, the world's largest office complex and the home to the U.S. military, is completed in Arlington, Virginia.

1943 On March 14, composer Aaron Copland's *Fanfare for the Common Man* premieres in Cincinnati, Ohio.

1943 On March 30, the musical *Oklahoma!* opens on Broadway in New York City.

1943 During the summer, race riots break out in Detroit, Michigan, and Harlem, New York.

1943 On September 8, Italy surrenders to the Allies.

1943 On November 9, artist Jackson Pollock has his first solo show in New York City.

1943 On December 30, *Esquire* magazine loses its second-class mailing privileges after it is charged with being "lewd" and "lascivious" by the U.S. Post Office.

1944 *Seventeen* magazine debuts.

1944 *Double Indemnity,* directed by Billy Wilder, becomes one of the first of a new genre of movies known as *film noir.*

1944 On March 4, American planes bomb Berlin, Germany.

1944 On June 6, on "D-Day," Allied forces land in Normandy, France, and begin the liberation of western Europe.

1944 On June 22, the Serviceman's Readjustment Act, signed by President Franklin D. Roosevelt, provides funding for a variety of programs for returning soldiers, including education programs under the G.I. Bill.

1944 On August 25, Allied troops liberate Paris, France.

1944 On November 7, Franklin D. Roosevelt is reelected for an unprecedented fourth term as president.

1945 Chicago publisher John H. Johnson launches *Ebony* magazine.

1945 The radio program *The Adventures of Ozzie and Harriet* debuts.

1945 On January 27, the Soviet Red Army liberates Auschwitz, Poland, revealing the seriousness of German efforts to exterminate Jews.

1945 On April 12, President Franklin D. Roosevelt dies of a cerebral hemorrhage and Vice President Harry S. Truman takes over as president.

1945 On April 21, Soviet troops reach the outskirts of Berlin, the capital of Germany.

1945 On April 30, German leader Adolf Hitler commits suicide in Berlin, Germany, as Allied troops approach the city.

1945 On May 5, American poet Ezra Pound is arrested in Italy on charges of treason.

1945 On May 8, Germany surrenders to the Allies, bringing an end to World War II in Europe.

1945 On August 6, the United States drops the first atomic bomb on the Japanese city of Hiroshima, killing more than fifty thousand people.

1945 On August 9, the United States drops a second atomic bomb on Nagasaki, Japan.

1945 On September 2, Japan offers its unconditional surrender onboard the U.S.S. *Missouri* in Tokyo Bay, bringing an end to World War II.

1946 The Baby Boom begins as the birthrate rises 20 percent over the previous year.

1946 *It's a Wonderful Life,* starring Jimmy Stewart and directed by Frank Capra, becomes one of the most popular Christmas movies of all time.

1946 On January 10, the first General Assembly of the United Nations meets in London, England.

1946 On June 19, Joe Louis knocks out Billy Conn in the first heavyweight boxing match ever shown on television, retaining his title.

1946 On December 11, country singer Hank Williams cuts his first single, "Calling You."

1947 On January 29, Arthur Miller's play *All My Sons* opens in New York City.

1947 On March 12, President Harry S. Truman announces his "containment" policy aimed at stopping the spread of communism. It will later become known as the Truman Doctrine.

1947 On March 21, Congress approves the Twenty-second

Amendment which limits the president to two four-year terms in office. The amendment is ratified in 1951.

1947 On April 10, Jackie Robinson breaks the "color barrier" when he signs a contract to play for professional baseball's Brooklyn Dodgers. He is later named "Rookie of the Year" by *The Sporting News*.

1947 Beginning September 30, the World Series is televised for the first time as fans watch the New York Yankees defeat the Brooklyn Dodgers in seven games.

1947 On October 13, the Hollywood Ten, a group of film directors and writers, appears before the House Un-American Activities Committee (HUAC).

1947 On December 3, Tennessee Williams's *A Streetcar Named Desire* opens on Broadway in New York City.

1948 The Baskin-Robbins ice cream chain opens.

1948 On April 3, Congress approves $6 billion in Marshall Plan aid for rebuilding European countries.

1948 On May 14, the state of Israel is established.

1948 On May 29, the play *Oklahoma!* closes after a record 2,246 performances.

1948 On June 25, heavyweight boxing champion Joe Louis knocks out Joe Walcott for his twenty-fifth title defense and announces his retirement from boxing following the fight.

1948 On September 13, Margaret Chase Smith of Maine becomes the first woman elected to the U.S. Senate.

1948 On November 2, incumbent Harry S. Truman is elected president.

1949 Builder Abraham Levitt and his sons begin construction on a Long Island, New York, suburb called Levittown which will become a symbol for the postwar housing boom.

1949 On February 10, Arthur Miller's *Death of a Salesman* opens on Broadway in New York City.

1949 On April 4, the North Atlantic Treaty Organization (NATO) is formed by the United States and twelve

other mainly European countries to provide for mutual defense.

1949 On September 23, American, British, and Canadian officials reveal that the Soviet Union has successfully detonated an atomic bomb.

1949 On October 1, the Communist People's Republic of China is proclaimed.

1950 The first Xerox copy machine is produced.

1950 Miss Clairol hair coloring is introduced, making it easy for women to dye their hair at home.

1950 Desegregation continues when Charles Cooper becomes the first black player in the National Basketball Association and Althea Gibson becomes the first black woman to compete in a national tennis tournament.

1950 In March, the Boston Institute of Contemporary Art and New York's Metropolitan Museum and Whitney Museum release a joint statement on modern art opposing "any attempt to make art or opinion about art conform to a single point of view."

1950 On May 8, President Harry S. Truman sends the first U.S. military mission to Vietnam.

1950 On June 30, U.S. combat troops enter the Korean War.

1950 On October 2, *Peanuts,* the comic strip written and drawn by Charles Schulz, debuts in seven U.S. newspapers.

1951 *The Caine Mutiny,* a war novel by Herman Wouk, is published and soon becomes one of the longest lasting best-sellers of all time, holding its place on the *New York Times* list for 48 weeks.

1951 On April 5, Julius and Ethel Rosenberg receive death sentences for allegedly giving secret information to the Soviet Union.

1951 On June 25, CBS offers the first color television broadcast.

1951 On August 5, the soap operas *Search for Tomorrow* and *Love of Life* premiere on CBS.

1951 On October 15, the sitcom *I Love Lucy* premieres on CBS.

1951 On November 18, the news program *See It Now,* hosted by Edward R. Murrow, premieres on CBS.

1952 *Gunsmoke* debuts as a radio drama. In 1955, the Western drama moves to TV where it lasts until 1975. The show, which starred James Arness as Marshal Matt Dillon, becomes the longest running prime-time TV show with continuing characters.

1952 In January, *American Bandstand,* a popular teen-oriented music program, debuts as a local show in Philadelphia, Pennsylvania. Dick Clark, its most famous host, joins the show in 1956.

1952 On January 14, *The Today Show* debuts on NBC.

1952 In September, *The Old Man and the Sea,* a short novel by Ernest Hemingway, is printed in *Life* magazine, and is the Book-of-the-Month Club's co-main selection.

1953 On October 5, the New York Yankees become the first team in history to win five consecutive World Series when they defeat the Brooklyn Dodgers.

1952 In November, *Bwana Devil,* the first 3-D movie, is released.

1952 On November 4, World War II general Dwight D. Eisenhower is elected president.

1953 *Playboy* becomes the first mass-market men's magazine and rockets to popularity when it publishes nude pictures of rising movie star Marilyn Monroe.

1953 IBM introduces its first computer, the 701.

1953 On January 1, Hank Williams, the father of contemporary country music, dies at age 29 from a heart disease resulting from excessive drinking.

1953 On April 3, the first national edition of *TV Guide* is published.

1953 On July 27, the Korean War ends.

1953 On September 13, Nikita Khrushchev is named first secretary of the Soviet Union's Communist Party.

1953 In November, an eleven-day photoengravers strike leaves New York City without a daily newspaper for the first time since 1778.

1954 Senator Joseph McCarthy leads hearings into the presence of communists in the U.S. Army; his actions are later condemned by the Senate.

1954 *Sports Illustrated* becomes the first glossy weekly magazine about sports.

1954 Swanson Foods introduces the first TV dinners.

1954 On April 4, legendary conductor Arturo Toscanini makes his final appearance conducting the NBC Symphony Orchestra. The concert is broadcast on the radio live from New York City's Carnegie Hall.

1954 On April 4, Walt Disney signs a contract with ABC to produce twenty-six television films each year.

1954 On May 14, the Soviet Union joins with seven Eastern European countries to form the Warsaw Pact, a union of nations pledged to mutual defense.

1954 On May 17, with its *Brown v. Board of Education* decision, the U.S. Supreme Court ends segregation in public schools.

1954 In July, the Newport Jazz Festival debuts in Newport, Rhode Island.

1954 On July 19, "That's All Right, Mama" and "Blue Moon of Kentucky," the first professional records made by Elvis Presley, are released on Sun Records.

1954 On September 27, *The Tonight Show* debuts on NBC.

1954 In October and November, Hungary tries to leave the Warsaw Pact but is attacked and reclaimed by the Soviet Union.

1955 Velcro is invented.

1955 *The $64,000 Question* debuts and soon becomes the most popular game show of the 1950s.

1955 In January, Marian Anderson becomes the first black singer to appear at the Metropolitan Opera.

1955   On January 19, President Dwight D. Eisenhower holds the first televised presidential news conference.

1955   In March, *The Blackboard Jungle,* the first feature film to include a rock and roll song on its soundtrack— "Rock Around the Clock," by Bill Haley and The Comets—opens. The song becomes the country's number-one single in July.

1955   On April 12, large-scale vaccinations for polio are administered throughout the United States.

1955   On July 17, the Disneyland amusement park opens in Anaheim, California.

1955   On September 30, actor James Dean dies after his Porsche roadster slams into another car on a California highway.

1955   On October 13, poet Allen Ginsberg gives the first public reading of *Howl,* his controversial poem-in-progress.

1955   On December 5, Rosa Parks refuses to give up her seat to a white man on a bus in Montgomery, Alabama, sparking a bus boycott that will become a key moment in the Civil Rights Movement.

1956   On June 20, Loew's Inc. releases MGM's pre-1949 film library—excluding *Gone with the Wind* (1939)—for television broadcast.

1956   On November 6, President Dwight D. Eisenhower is reelected.

1956   On November 30, videotape is first used commercially on television, during the broadcast of CBS's *Douglas Edwards with the News.*

1957   On September 26, the landmark musical *West Side Story,* a modern-day adaptation of *Romeo and Juliet* by William Shakespeare, opens on Broadway at the Winter Garden Theatre in New York City.

1957   On October 5, the Soviet Union launches the satellite *Sputnik,* the first man-made satellite in space.

1958   On August 26, Alaska becomes the forty-ninth state.

1958 On October 2, Leonard Bernstein begins his first season as director of the New York Philharmonic.

1958 On October 16, sponsors drop the NBC quiz show *Twenty-One* after a grand jury investigation determines that contestants were provided with pre-show answers.

1959 On January 2, revolutionary leader Fidel Castro assumes power in Cuba.

1959 On February 3, rock and roll legends Buddy Holly, Ritchie Valens, and J. P. Richardson (known as "The Big Bopper") die in a plane crash outside Clear Lake, Iowa.

1959 On August 21, Hawaii becomes the fiftieth state.

1959 On October 21, the Solomon R. Guggenheim Museum, designed by architect Frank Lloyd Wright, opens in New York City.

1960 Designer Pierre Cardin introduces his first fashion designs for men.

1960 On January 3, the Moscow State Symphony begins a seven-week tour at New York City's Carnegie Hall, becoming the first Soviet orchestra to perform in the United States.

1960 On February 11, Jack Paar, host of *The Tonight Show,* walks off the show when an NBC censor deletes a joke from his performance.

1960 On February 20, black students in Greensboro, North Carolina, stage sit-ins at local lunch counters to protest discrimination.

1960 In April, the New York state legislature authorizes the City of New York to purchase Carnegie Hall, which was scheduled for demolition.

1960 On April 1, Lucille Ball and Desi Arnaz appear for the last time as Lucy and Ricky Ricardo on *The Lucy-Desi Comedy Hour.*

1960 On May 5, the Soviet Union announces the capture of American pilot Francis Gary Powers, whose U-2 spy plane was shot down over the Soviet Union.

1960   On September 26, U.S. senator John F. Kennedy of Massachusetts and Vice President Richard M. Nixon appear in the first televised presidential debate.

1960   On October 13, jazz trumpeter Louis Armstrong begins a goodwill tour of Africa, partially sponsored by the U.S. State Department.

1960   On November 8, U.S. senator John F. Kennedy of Massachusetts is elected president.

1961   On January 20, Robert Frost reads his poem "The Gift Outright" at the inauguration of President John F. Kennedy.

1961   On January 27, soprano Leontyne Price first performs at New York's Metropolitan Opera.

1961   In April, folk singer Bob Dylan makes his debut at Gerde's Folk City in New York City's Greenwich Village.

1961   On April 12, Soviet cosmonaut Yuri Gagarin becomes the first man to orbit the Earth.

1961   During the summer, Freedom Rides across the South are aimed at desegregating interstate bus travel.

1961   On August 15–17, East Germany constructs the Berlin Wall, separating communist East Berlin from democratic West Berlin.

1961   On October 1, Roger Maris sets the single-season home run record with 61 homers.

1962   On February 10, Jim Beatty become the first person to run a mile in less than four minutes with a time of 3:58.9.

1962   On May 30, jazz clarinetist Benny Goodman begins a six-week, U.S. State Department–arranged tour of Russia.

1962   On July 10, the *Telstar* satellite is launched and soon brings live television pictures to American television viewers.

1962   On August 5, actress Marilyn Monroe dies from an overdose of barbiturates.

1962   On September 25, Philharmonic Hall, the first completed building of New York's Lincoln Center for the Performing Arts, is inaugurated by Leonard Bernstein and the New York Philharmonic.

1962   On September 29, *My Fair Lady* closes on Broadway after 2,717 performances, making it the longest-running show in history.

1962   In October, the United States and the Soviet Union clash over the presence of Soviet missiles in Cuba.

1962   On October 1, James Meredith becomes the first black person to enroll at the University of Mississippi as federal troops battle thousands of protestors.

1963   On January 8, *Mona Lisa,* by Leonardo da Vinci, is shown at Washington's National Gallery, the first time the painting ever has appeared outside the Louvre in Paris, France.

1963   On May 7, the Guthrie Theatre in Minneapolis, Minnesota, the first major regional theater in the Midwest, opens.

1963   On November 22, President John F. Kennedy is assassinated in Dallas, Texas, and Vice President Lyndon B. Johnson assumes the presidency.

1963   On November 24, the murder of alleged presidential assassin Lee Harvey Oswald is broadcast live on television.

1964   Ford introduces its Mustang, a smaller sporty car.

1964   On February 9, the Beatles make their first appearance on American television, on *The Ed Sullivan Show.*

1964   On February 25, Cassius Clay (who later changes his name to Muhammad Ali) beats Sonny Liston to become the heavyweight boxing champion of the world.

1964   In May, the just-remodeled Museum of Modern Art in New York City reopens with a new gallery, the Steichen Photography Center, named for photographer Edward Steichen.

1964   On July 2, President Lyndon B. Johnson signs the

Civil Rights Act of 1964, which bans racial discrimination in public places and in employment.

1964   On August 7, in the Gulf of Tonkin Resolution, Congress gives President Lyndon B. Johnson the power to use military force to protect U.S. interests in Vietnam.

1964   On November 3, incumbent Lyndon B. Johnson is elected president.

1965   In January, Bob Dylan plays an electric guitar on his new single, "Subterranean Homesick Blues."

1965   On February 21, black leader Malcolm X is murdered in Harlem, New York.

1965   On March 8, the first U.S. combat troops are sent to Vietnam.

1965   On April 26, *Symphony No. 4* by Charles Ives is performed in its entirety for the first time by the American Symphony Orchestra, conducted by Leopold Stokowski.

1965   On May 9, piano virtuoso Vladimir Horowitz returns to the Carnegie Hall stage after a twelve-year "retirement."

1965   On June 2, in a letter to President Lyndon B. Johnson, Pulitzer Prize–winning poet Robert Lowell declines an invitation to attend a White House arts festival, citing his "dismay and distrust" of American foreign policy.

1965   In July, Bob Dylan and his electric guitar are booed off the Newport Folk Festival stage.

1965   On September 29, President Lyndon B. Johnson signs into law the Federal Aid to the Arts Bill.

1965   On October 15, demonstrations against the Vietnam War occur in forty U.S. cities.

1965   On December 9, *A Charlie Brown Christmas* becomes the first *Peanuts* special to air on TV.

1966   The National Organization for Women (NOW) is established.

1966   On June 8, the National Football League and the American Football League merge.

1966 On July 12, rioting by blacks breaks out in twenty U.S. cities over racial discrimination.

1966 On August 29, the Beatles play their last live concert.

1966 On December 8, philanthropist, horse breeder, and art collector Paul Mellon donates his collection of British rare books, paintings, drawings, and prints, valued at over $35 million, to Yale University.

1967 On January 15, in the first Super Bowl, the Green Bay Packers defeat the Kansas City Chiefs, 35-10.

1967 On February 18, the National Gallery of Art arranges to purchase Leonardo da Vinci's *Ginevra dei Benci* for between five and six million dollars, the highest price paid to date for a single painting.

1967 In June, the Monterey International Pop Festival, an important early rock music event, is held in California.

1967 On June 20, Muhammad Ali is stripped of his boxing titles after being found guilty of tax evasion.

1967 On July 23, federal troops are called in to put a stop to rioting in Detroit, Michigan. Forty-three people are killed in the rioting, which lasts a week.

1967 On November 9, the first issue of *Rolling Stone* magazine is published. On the cover is a portrait of the Beatles's John Lennon.

1967 In December, Universal News, the last of the movie newsreel companies, closes because it is unable to compete with television news.

1968 On January 30, North Vietnam launches the Tet Offensive, escalating the war in Vietnam.

1968 On April 4, civil rights leader Martin Luther King Jr. is murdered in Memphis, Tennessee.

1968 On April 19, *Hair* opens on Broadway, at New York City's Biltmore Theatre.

1968 On June 5, presidential candidate Robert F. Kennedy is murdered in Los Angeles, California.

1968 On September 16, presidential candidate Richard Nixon appears as a guest on TV's *Rowan and Martin's*

Laugh-In and delivers one of the show's signature lines: "Sock it to me."

1968 On November 1, the Motion Picture Association of America inaugurates its film ratings system.

1968 On November 5, former vice president Richard Nixon is elected president.

1969 Hot pants make their first appearance.

1969 On July 20, U.S. astronaut Neil Armstrong becomes the first man to walk on the moon when the *Apollo XI* mission succeeds.

1969 On August 15–17, the Woodstock Music and Art Fair is held on a six-hundred-acre hog farm in upstate New York.

1969 On November 15, a quarter million Vietnam War protestors march in Washington, D.C.

1969 On December 6, a festivalgoer is murdered during the Altamont Rock Festival in California.

1970 Soviet cosmonauts spend seventeen days in space, setting a new record for space longevity.

1970 Across the nation, protests continue over the ongoing Vietnam War.

1970 Rock stars Jimi Hendrix and Janis Joplin die within three weeks of each other, both as a result of drug overdoses.

1970 In March, three women—Elizabeth Bishop, Lillian Hellman, and Joyce Carol Oates—win National Book Awards.

1970 On May 4, National Guard members shoot antiwar protesters at Kent State University in Ohio.

1970 On April 10, the Beatles disband.

1970 On April 30, U.S. and South Vietnamese troops invade Cambodia, which has been sheltering North Vietnamese troops.

1970 On September 6, four airliners bound for New York

are hijacked by Palestinian terrorists, but no passengers are harmed.

1970 On September 19, *The Mary Tyler Moore Show* debuts on CBS.

1970 On September 21, *Monday Night Football* debuts on ABC.

1970 On October 2, the Environmental Protection Agency (EPA) is created to regulate environmental issues.

1971 Disney World opens in Orlando, Florida.

1971 Hot pants become a fashion sensation.

1971 On January 2, cigarette advertising is banned from television and radio.

1971 On February 6, British troops are sent to patrol Northern Ireland.

1971 On February 9, the European Economic Community, a precursor to the European Union, is established.

1971 On March 8, Joe Frazier defeats Muhammad Ali to retain the world heavyweight boxing title.

1971 On April 20, the U.S. Supreme Court rules that students can be bused to end racial segregation in schools.

1971 In June, the Twenty-sixth Amendment to the Constitution lowers the legal voting age to eighteen.

1971 On June 13, the *New York Times* publishes the "Pentagon Papers" which reveal Defense Department plans for the Vietnam War.

1971 In September, a prison uprising in Attica, New York, ends with forty-three people killed, including ten hostages.

1971 On October 12, the rock musical *Jesus Christ Superstar* opens on Broadway in New York City.

1971 On October 13, baseball teams play in the first night World Series game.

1971 On December 25, "Christmas bombing" occurs in North Vietnam.

1972 In a sign of the cooling of Cold War tensions, East and West Germany and North and South Korea each enter into negotiations to normalize relations.

1972 *Ms.* magazine begins publication.

1972 Pong, the first video game available to play at home, becomes popular, as does the first video game machine, Odyssey, introduced by Magnavox.

1972 On February 14, the musical *Grease* opens on Broadway in New York City.

1972 On February, 21, President Richard Nixon begins a seven-day visit to Communist China.

1972 On May 22, President Richard Nixon begins a nine-day visit to the Soviet Union.

1972 On June 17, the Watergate scandal begins with the arrest of five men caught trying to bug the Democratic National Committee headquarters at the Watergate building in Washington, D.C. The investigation soon reveals deep corruption in the Nixon administration.

1972 On July 24, the United Nations asks the United States to end its bombing of North Vietnam.

1972 On August 12, the last American combat troops leave Vietnam.

1972 On November 8, cable TV channel HBO premieres in Pennsylvania with 365 subscribers.

1973 Three major American cities—Los Angeles, California; Atlanta, Georgia; and Detroit, Michigan—elect a black mayor for the first time.

1973 Investigations into the Watergate affair capture the public attention and shatter the Nixon administration.

1973 The Sears Tower, the world's tallest building, is completed in Chicago, Illinois.

1973 Ralph Lauren designs the costumes for the film *The Great Gatsby,* helping build his reputation.

1973 Fantasy-adventure game Dungeons and Dragons is created by Dave Arneson and Gary Gygax.

1973   The first Internet is set up by the U.S. Department of Defense as a way of connecting all the department's computers.

1973   On January 14, the Miami Dolphins win the Super Bowl and become the first professional football team to finish a season undefeated.

1973   On October 16, the Organization of Petroleum Exporting Countries (OPEC) declares an embargo (ban) on the export of oil to the United States and other Western countries.

1973   On October 23, the House of Representatives begins impeachment proceedings against President Richard Nixon.

1974   The Ramones launch the American punk movement with their performances at the New York City club CBGB.

1974   The streaking fad sweeps the country.

1974   President Richard Nixon tours the Middle East and the Soviet Union.

1974   On January 18, Israel and Egypt sign a peace accord that ends their long armed conflict.

1974   On April 8, Hank Aaron of the Atlanta Braves breaks Babe Ruth's lifetime home run record when he hits his 715th career homer.

1974   In May, screenwriter Dalton Trumbo, who had been blacklisted in the 1950s during Senator Joseph McCarthy's anticommunist crusades, receives an Oscar award for the 1957 film *The Brave One*.

1974   On August 8, Richard Nixon becomes the first U.S. president to resign from office amid evidence of a cover-up of the Watergate affair.

1974   On August 9, Vice President Gerald Ford is sworn in as president. Less than a month later, he officially pardons former president Richard Nixon.

1974   On September 8, motorcycle stunt rider Evel Knievel tries to jump a rocket over the Snake River Canyon in Idaho but falls short.

1974 On October 3, Frank Robinson joins the Cleveland Indians as major league baseball's first black manager.

1974 On October 30, boxer Muhammnad Ali regains his world heavyweight boxing title by defeating George Foreman.

1974 In December, unemployment hits 6.5 percent amid a prolonged economic slump, and rises to 8.9 percent by May 1975.

1975 The video cassette recorder (VCR) is invented by Sony Corporation in Japan.

1975 The first personal computer, the Altair 8800, is sold in a kit form.

1975 The cult film *The Rocky Horror Picture Show* is released.

1975 Skateboarding becomes popular, and mood rings and pet rocks are popular fads.

1975 Rock star Bruce Springsteen appears on the cover of both *Time* and *Newsweek* thanks to his popular album *Born to Run*.

1975 The Soviet Union and the United States cooperate in the manned *Apollo-Soyuz* space mission.

1975 On January 5, the all-black musical *The Wiz* opens on Broadway in New York City. It eventually tallies 1,672 performances.

1975 On April 30, Saigon, the capital of South Vietnam, is invaded by the communist North Vietnamese, ending the Vietnam War.

1975 On October 1, the Organization of Petroleum Exporting Countries (OPEC) raises crude oil prices by 10 percent.

1975 On October 11, *Saturday Night Live* debuts on NBC.

1976 The first personal computer, the Apple, is developed by Steve Jobs and Steve Wozniak. The Apple II, introduced a year later, offers color graphics.

1976 Model and actress Farrah Fawcett-Majors sets a trend with her feathered haircut and appears on millions of posters in her tiny red bathing suit.

1976   On July 4, the United States celebrates its bicentennial.

1976   On November 2, former Georgia governor Jimmy Carter is elected president.

1976   On November 6, *Gone with the Wind* is broadcast on TV for the first time.

1977   The film *Saturday Night Fever* helps make disco music popular.

1977   Studio 54 becomes New York City's hottest nightclub featuring disco music.

1977   Egyptian artifacts from the tomb of King Tutankhamen, or King Tut, draw huge audiences across the nation.

1977   Alex Haley's book *Roots* becomes a best-seller after the airing of the TV miniseries based on the book.

1977   On January 21, President Jimmy Carter signs an unconditional pardon for most Vietnam-era draft evaders.

1977   On February 8, *Hustler* magazine publisher Larry Flynt is convicted of obscenity.

1977   In April, the Christian Broadcasting Network (CBN) makes its debut.

1977   On August 16, Elvis Presley, the king of rock and roll, dies at Graceland, his Memphis, Tennessee, mansion.

1978   The Walkman personal cassette player is introduced by Sony.

1978   On July 25, the first human test-tube baby is born in England.

1978   On September 17, U.S. president Jimmy Carter hosts negotiations between Israeli prime minister Menachem Begin and Egyptian president Anwar Sadat at Camp David, Maryland.

1978   On October 13, punk rock musician Sid Vicious of the Sex Pistols is arrested for the stabbing death of his girlfriend.

1978 On November 18, Jim Jones and over nine hundred followers of his People's Temple cult are found dead after a mass suicide in Jonestown, Guyana.

1978 On December 5, the Soviet Union and Afghanistan sign a treaty of friendship, and within a year U.S. support for the Afghan government disappears.

1979 Eleven people are trampled to death at a Who concert in Cincinnati, Ohio.

1979 Jerry Falwell organizes the Moral Majority to lobby politicians regarding the concerns of Christian fundamentalists.

1979 On January 1, the United States and the People's Republic of China establish formal diplomatic relations.

1979 On March 28, a major accident in the nuclear reactor at the Three Mile Island power plant near Harrisburg, Pennsylvania, raises concerns about nuclear power.

1979 On November 4, Iranian militants seize the U.S. embassy in Tehran, Iran, and take fifty-two hostages, whom they will hold for nearly a year.

1979 On December 27, the Soviet Union invades Afghanistan, beginning more than two decades of war and disruption in that country.

1980 Post-it notes are created by 3M chemist Arthur Fry.

1980 On February 22, the U.S. Olympic ice hockey team wins the gold medal, sparking national celebration.

1980 On April 12, the United States votes to boycott the Summer Olympics in Moscow to protest the Soviet presence in Afghanistan.

1980 On April 21, the Mariel boatlift begins, bringing 125,000 refugees from Cuba to Florida before being halted in September.

1980 In June, the CNN cable TV network debuts.

1980 On August 19, a report issued by the *Los Angeles Times* indicates that 40 to 75 percent of NBA players use cocaine.

1980 On November 4, former California governor Ronald Reagan is elected president.

1980 On November 21, the "Who Shot J.R.?" episode of *Dallas* draws the largest television audience of all time.

1980 On September 4, Iraq begins an eight-year war with Iran.

1980 On October 2, in his last fight, heavyweight boxer Muhammad Ali is defeated by World Boxing Council champion Larry Holmes.

1980 On December 8, former Beatles musician John Lennon is shot and killed in New York City.

1981 Nintendo's "Donkey Kong" is the most popular coin-operated video game.

1981 NASA launches and lands the first reusable spacecraft, the space shuttle.

1981 On January 13, the National Collegiate Athletic Association (NCAA) votes to sponsor women's championships in twelve sports after the 1981–82 season.

1981 On January 20, American hostages held at the U.S. embassy in Tehran, Iran, are released on the day of President Ronald Reagan's inauguration.

1981 On January 23, the United States withdraws support for the Marxist government of Nicaragua and begins to support antigovernment rebels known as Contras.

1981 On March 26, comedian Carol Burnett wins a $1.6 million libel lawsuit against the tabloid *National Enquirer*.

1981 On July 29, Great Britain's Prince Charles marries Lady Diana Spencer in an event televised around the world.

1981 On August 1, the Music Television Network (MTV) starts offering music videos that soon become as important as the actual music.

1981 On September 21, Sandra Day O'Connor is confirmed as the first woman to serve on the U.S. Supreme Court.

1982	The compact disc is introduced.
1982	The popular movie *E.T.: The Extra–Terrestrial* sets box office records.
1982	Michael Jackson's album *Thriller* is the year's most popular recording.
1982	Americans frustrate themselves trying to solve Rubik's Cube, a popular puzzle.
1982	On April 2, Argentina invades the Falkland Islands off its coast, sparking a short war with Great Britain, which claims the islands.
1982	On June 7, Graceland, the late Elvis Presley's Memphis, Tennessee, home, is opened as a tourist attraction.
1982	On July 27, AIDS is officially named.
1982	On September 15, *USA Today* becomes the first national newspaper.
1982	On October 7, *Cats* opens on Broadway in New York City and will become the decade's most popular musical.
1983	First lady Nancy Reagan announces a "War on Drugs."
1983	Sally Ride becomes the first woman astronaut in space when she joins the crew of the space shuttle *Challenger*.
1983	Actor Paul Newman introduces his own line of spaghetti sauces to be sold in grocery stores; he uses the proceeds to benefit charities.
1983	On February 28, the farewell episode of the sitcom *M*A*S*H* is seen by 125 million viewers.
1983	On March 23, President Ronald Reagan proposes a space–based antimissile defense system that is popularly known as "Star Wars."
1983	On April 18, terrorists bomb the U.S. embassy in Beirut, Lebanon, killing sixty-three.
1983	On September 1, the Soviet Union shoots down a

Korean Air Lines flight that has strayed into its airspace, killing 269.

1983   On October 25, three thousand U.S. soldiers invade the Caribbean island nation of Grenada to crush a Marxist uprising.

1983   In November, Cabbage Patch Kids dolls, with their soft faces and adoption certificates, become the most popular new doll of the Christmas season.

1984   Trivial Pursuit becomes the nation's most popular board game.

1984   *The Cosby Show* debuts on NBC.

1984   Rap group Run–DMC is the first rap group to have a gold album.

1984   Apple introduces a new personal computer, the Macintosh, with a dramatic advertising campaign.

1984   On November 6, Ronald Reagan is reelected president.

1984   On December 3, a Union Carbide plant in Bhopal, India, leaks poison gas that kills two thousand and injures two hundred thousand.

1985   Nintendo Entertainment System, a home video game system that has brilliant colors, realistic sound effects, and quick action, is introduced to the United States.

1985   On March 16, U.S. journalist Terry Anderson is kidnapped in Lebanon; he will be held until December 4, 1991.

1985   In April, Coca–Cola changes the formula of its popular soft drink and the public reacts with anger and dismay, prompting the company to reissue the old formula as Classic Coke.

1985   On July 13, British rock star Bob Geldof organizes Live Aid, a charity concert and album to aid the victims of African famine.

1985   On October 2, the death of handsome movie star Rock Hudson from AIDS raises awareness about the disease.

1986   Country singer Dolly Parton opens a theme park in Tennessee called Dollywood.

1986   On January 28, the space shuttle *Challenger* explodes upon liftoff, killing all astronauts and one teacher who were aboard.

1986   On February 26, Robert Penn Warren is named the first poet laureate of the United States.

1986   On April 26, a serious meltdown at the Chernobyl nuclear power plant near Kiev, Ukraine, releases a radioactive cloud into the atmosphere and is considered a major disaster.

1986   On May 1, in South Africa, 1.5 million blacks protest apartheid (the policy of racial segregation). Around the world, foreign governments place sanctions on South Africa.

1986   On June 10, Nancy Lieberman becomes the first woman to play in a men's professional basketball league when she joins the United States Basketball League.

1986   On July 15, the United States sends troops to Bolivia to fight against drug traffickers.

1986   On July 27, Greg LeMond becomes the first American to win France's prestigious Tour de France bicycle race.

1986   In October, it is discovered that members of the Reagan administration have been trading arms for hostages in Iran and illegally channeling funds to Contras in Nicaragua. This Iran–Contra scandal will eventually be investigated by Congress.

1986   On November 22, twenty-one-year-old Mike Tyson becomes the youngest heavyweight boxing champion when he defeats World Boxing Council champ Trevor Berbick.

1987   On March 19, televangelist Jim Bakker resigns after it is revealed that he has been having an adulterous affair with church secretary Jessica Hahn.

1987   On June 25, Soviet leader Mikhail Gorbachev announces *perestroika,* a program of sweeping economic reforms aimed at improving the Soviet economy.

1987 On October 3, Canada and the United States sign a free-trade agreement.

1987 On October 17, the stock market experiences its worst crash in history when it drops 508 points.

1987 On November 11, Vincent van Gogh's painting *Irises* is sold for $53.9 million.

1988 McDonald's opens twenty restaurants in Moscow, Russia.

1988 Singer Sonny Bono is elected mayor of Palm Springs, California.

1988 On February 5, former Panamanian dictator General Manuel Noriega is charged in a U.S. court with accepting bribes from drug traffickers.

1988 On February 14, Ayatollah Khomeini of Iran calls author Salman Rushdie's book *The Satanic Verses* offensive and issues a death sentence on him. The author goes into hiding.

1988 On April 14, Soviet forces withdraw from Afghanistan after ten years of fighting in that country.

1988 On July 3, believing it is under attack, a U.S. warship shoots down an Iran Air passenger liner, killing 290 passengers.

1988 On November 8, Vice President George Herbert Walker Bush is elected president.

1988 On December 21, Pan Am Flight 747 explodes over Lockerbie, Scotland, killing 259 on the flight and 11 on the ground. Middle Eastern terrorists are eventually charged with the crime.

1989 On March 24, the Exxon *Valdez* oil tanker runs aground in Alaska, spilling 240,000 barrels of oil and creating an environmental disaster.

1989 In May, more than one million Chinese demonstrate for democracy in Beijing.

1989 In June, Chinese troops crack down on demonstrators in Tiananmen Square, drawing attention to the repressive government.

1989 On August 9, Colin R. Powell becomes the United States's first black chairman of the Joint Chiefs of Staff.

1989 On August 23, the Soviet states of Lithuania, Latvia, and Estonia demand autonomy from the Soviet Union. Later, across the former Soviet dominated region, Soviet republics and satellite countries throw off communist control and pursue independence.

1989 On August 24, former baseball star Pete Rose is banned from baseball for life because it is believed that he bet on games in which he was involved.

1989 On October 15, Wayne Gretzky of the Los Angeles Kings becomes the National Hockey League's all-time leading scorer with his 1,850th point.

1989 On October 17, a major earthquake hits the San Francisco, California, area.

1989 On December 16, American troops invade Panama and seize dictator General Manuel Noriega. Noriega will later be convicted in U.S. courts.

1989 On December 22, the Brandenburg Gate in Berlin is officially opened, allowing people from East and West Berlin to mix freely and signaling the end of the Cold War and the reunification of Germany.

1990 The animated sitcom *The Simpsons* debuts on the FOX network.

1990 Ken Burns's documentary *The Civil War* airs on PBS.

1990 British scientist Tim Berners-Lee invents the World Wide Web.

1990 On April 25, the Hubble Space Telescope is deployed in space from the space shuttle *Discovery*.

1990 On July 26, President George Herbert Walker Bush signs the Americans with Disabilities Act, which provides broad protections for those with disabilities.

1990 On August 2, Iraq invades Kuwait, prompting the United States to wage war on Iraq from bases in Saudi Arabia. Much of this conflict, called the Persian Gulf War, is aired live on television and makes CNN famous for its coverage.

1990   On October 3, East and West Germany are reunited.

1991   Mass murderer Jeffrey Dahmer is charged with killing fifteen young men and boys near Milwaukee, Wisconsin.

1991   On March 3, U.S. general Norman Schwarzkopf announces the end of the Persian Gulf War.

1991   In October, confirmation hearings for U.S. Supreme Court justice nominee Clarence Thomas are carried live on television, and feature Anita Hill's dramatic accusations of sexual harassment. Despite the charges, Thomas is confirmed.

1991   On November 7, Los Angeles Lakers basketball star Earvin "Magic" Johnson announces that he has contracted the HIV virus.

1991   On December 8, leaders of Russia and several other former Soviet states announce the formation of the Commonwealth of Independent States.

1992   On April 29, riots erupt in Los Angeles, California, following the acquittal of four white police officers in the beating of black motorist Rodney King. The brutal beating had been filmed and shown widely on television.

1992   On May 21, Vice President Dan Quayle criticizes the CBS sitcom *Murphy Brown* for not promoting family values after the main character has a child out of wedlock.

1992   In August, the Mall of America, the nation's largest shopping mall, opens in Bloomington, Minnesota.

1992   On August 24, Hurricane Andrew hits Florida and the Gulf Coast, causing a total of over $15 billion in damage.

1992   On October 24, the Toronto Blue Jays become the first non–U.S. team to win baseball's World Series.

1992   On November 3, Arkansas governor Bill Clinton is elected president, defeating incumbent George Herbert Walker Bush and strong third party candidate H. Ross Perot.

1992 On December 17, the United States, Canada, and Mexico sign the North American Free Trade Agreement (NAFTA).

1993 Jack "Dr. Death" Kevorkian is arrested in Michigan for assisting in the suicide of a terminally ill patient, his nineteenth such action.

1993 On February 26, six people are killed when terrorists plant a bomb in New York City's World Trade Center.

1993 On April 19, more than eighty members of a religious cult called the Branch Davidians are killed in a mass suicide as leaders set fire to their compound following a fifty-one-day siege by federal forces.

1993 In July and August, the Flood of the Century devastates the American Midwest, killing 48.

1994 Tiger Woods becomes the youngest person and the first black to win the U.S. Amateur Golf Championship.

1994 Special prosecutor Ken Starr is appointed to investigate President Bill Clinton's involvement in a financial scandal known as Whitewater. The investigation will ultimately cover several scandals and lead to impeachment proceedings against the president.

1994 In January, ice skater Nancy Kerrigan is attacked by associates of her rival, Tonya Harding, at the U.S. Olympic Trials in Detroit, Michigan.

1994 On May 2, Nelson Mandela is elected president of South Africa. The black activist had been jailed for decades under the old apartheid regime and became the country's first black president.

1994 On August 11, major league baseball players go on strike, forcing the cancellation of the playoffs and World Series.

1994 On November 5, forty-five-year-old boxer George Foreman becomes the oldest heavyweight champion when he defeats Michael Moorer.

1995 On April 19, a car bomb explodes outside the Alfred P. Murrah Federal Office Building in Oklahoma City, Oklahoma, killing 168 people. Following a manhunt, antigovernment zealot Timothy McVeigh is captured, and later is convicted and executed for the crime.

1995   On September 1, the Rock and Roll Hall of Fame opens in Cleveland, Ohio.

1995   On September 6, Cal Ripken Jr. of the Baltimore Orioles breaks the long-standing record for most consecutive baseball games played with 2,131. The total reaches 2,632 games before Ripken removes himself from the lineup in 1998.

1995   On October 3, former football star O. J. Simpson is found not guilty of the murder of his ex-wife and her friend in what many called the "trial of the century."

1996   Three years after the introduction of H. Ty Warners's Beanie Babies, the first eleven toy styles are retired and quickly become collector's items.

1996   On September 26, American astronaut Shannon Lucid returns to Earth after spending 188 days in space—a record for any astronaut.

1996   On November 5, Bill Clinton is reelected to the presidency.

1997   Researchers in Scotland successfully clone an adult sheep, named Dolly.

1997   The Hale-Bopp comet provides a nightly show as it passes by the Earth.

1997   Actress Ellen DeGeneres becomes the first openly gay lead character in her ABC sitcom *Ellen*.

1997   On January 23, Madeleine Albright becomes the first woman sworn in as U.S. secretary of state.

1997   On March 27, thirty-nine members of the Heavens Gate religious cult are found dead in their California compound.

1997   On April 13, Tiger Woods becomes the youngest person and the first black to win a major golf tournament when he wins the Masters with the lowest score ever.

1997   On June 19, the play *Cats* sets a record for the longest-running Broadway play with its 6,138th performance.

Timeline

1997 On June 20, four major tobacco companies settle a lawsuit with states that will cost companies nearly $400 billion.

1997 On June 28, boxer Mike Tyson is disqualified when he bites the ear of opponent Evander Holyfield during a heavyweight title fight.

1997 On July 5, the *Pathfinder* spacecraft lands on Mars and sends back images and rock analyses.

1997 On August 31, Britain's Princess Diana is killed in an auto accident in Paris, France.

1998 Mark McGwire of the St. Louis Cardinals sets a single-season home run record with 70 home runs.

1998 The final episode of the popular sitcom *Seinfeld* is watched by an estimated audience of seventy-six million.

1998 On January 22, Unabomber Ted Kaczynski is convicted for a series of mail bombings and sentenced to life in prison.

1998 On March 24, the movie *Titanic* wins eleven Academy Awards, tying the record set by *Ben-Hur* in 1959.

1998 On April 10, a new drug for male impotence known as Viagra hits the market and is a popular sensation.

1998 On August 7, terrorists explode bombs outside the U.S. embassies in Nairobi, Kenya, and Dar es Salaam, Tanzania.

1998 In November, Jesse "The Body" Ventura—a former professional wrestler—is elected governor of Minnesota.

1998 On December 19, the House of Representatives initiates impeachment proceedings against President Bill Clinton, but the U.S. Senate acquits Clinton on two charges in early 1999.

1999 The U.S. women's soccer team wins the World Cup by defeating China.

1999 On March 24, NATO launches a bombing campaign against Serbia to stop its actions in Kosovo.

1999 On March 29, the Dow Jones Industrial Average closes above 10,000 for the first time in history thanks to a booming stock market dominated by high-tech companies.

1999 On April 20, in Littleton, Colorado, two students go on a vicious shooting spree, killing themselves and twelve other students.

1999 On September 24, *IKONOS*, the world's first commercial, high-resolution imaging satellite, is launched into space; it can detect an object on Earth as small as a card table.

Bowling, Beatniks, and Bell-Bottoms

Pop Culture of 20th-Century America

1960s
An Era of Pessimism and Activism

While the 1950s are stereotyped—sometimes unfairly—as a decade of quiet optimism, prosperity, and social conformity, the 1960s are often stereotyped—rather accurately—as a decade of turbulence, political activism, and growing discontent. During the course of the decade, the American military became increasingly involved in the war in Vietnam (1954–75), sparking massive protests at home. The assassination of four important American leaders, including President John F. Kennedy (1917–1963), raised fears that the United States was no longer a peaceful nation. Organized protests by women, African Americans, homosexuals, and antiwar activists challenged the American social structure.

The 1960s began with a wave of optimism as Americans elected U.S. senator John F. Kennedy of Massachusetts to the presidency. Kennedy was the youngest person and the first Catholic elected to the nation's highest office. He encouraged Americans to "Ask not what your country can do for you—ask what you can do for your country." It was a good time to inspire Americans to greatness, for the country was increasingly seen as the leading example of peace and democracy in the world. The United States was also the most prosperous nation in the world. Its gross national product (the value of all goods produced in the nation) grew 36 percent from 1960 to 1965.

1960s At a Glance

What We Said:

"And that's the way it is . . .": The famous words of *CBS Evening News* anchor man Walter Cronkite as he closed each nightly newscast.

Brodie: A tight turn in a car, known later as a "donut." Youths in hot cars pulled brodies to make their tires smoke and squeal; girls were very impressed.

Charlie: One of many terms used by soldiers fighting in the Vietnam War to refer to the enemy. The term "Charlie" comes from the second word in the abbreviation of Viet Cong, V. C. In Morse code, the C stands for Charlie. Other terms for the enemy were far harsher.

Counterculture: A catch-all term used to describe anyone who diverged from the values of the majority.

Dropping out: Though one could drop out of anything, and "drop out" is often used to refer to someone who leaves school, in the 1960s "dropping out" meant leaving "normal" society for the bohemian life of a hippie.

Establishment: A term used by hippies or members of the counterculture to refer to those in power, whether they be parents, corporate bosses, or the government.

"Far Out!": A hippie expression for something that was especially interesting or exciting.

Fox: An attractive woman. Boxer Muhammad Ali made the term popular in an interview with *Time* magazine in 1963.

Groovy: Anything that was cool or exhilarating. The word originated in the jazz culture of the 1930s, but became a favorite word in the 1960s.

Hippies: People who rejected mainstream values and enjoyed a free and even decadent lifestyle. Descendants of the 1950s' Beatniks, stereotypical hippies wore long hair (whether man or woman), smoked marijuana, and experimented with drugs like marijuana and LSD.

Pig: A derisive term for a police officer.

"Right on": A response to something that indicated that you agreed with it completely.

"Sock it to me!": This silly phrase was one of many popularized on the TV comedy *Rowan and Martin's Laugh-In.*

What We Read:

***To Kill a Mockingbird* (1960):** Harper Lee's first novel made publishing history by being chosen by three book clubs in its first year of publication, winning a Pulitzer Prize in 1961, and going into fourteen printings. In 1961, the book spent one hundred weeks on the best-seller lists.

***The Rise and Fall of the Third Reich* (1960):** This surprise non-fiction best-seller about Adolf Hitler's Germany by journalist William Shirer remained atop the best-seller list for thirty-nine weeks.

***Catch-22* (1961):** Joseph Heller's first novel is based on his experiences during World War II. The book was a favorite with young readers; by mid-decade *Newsweek* reported that some readers were so enthralled with the book that they had become members of what it called the "Heller cult." Some

•••••►

This spirit of youthful energy, optimism, and prosperity fueled the American government in the 1960s. The government began to address lingering social injustices in the nation. Under both Kennedy and his successor, Lyndon B. Johnson (1908–1973), the government extended new protections to minorities and women and created important programs to lessen the impact of poverty. The government also sponsored young men who did not want to go to Vietnam wore army field jackets with Yossarian, the main character in *Catch-22,* nametags.

Silent Spring (1962): This work by Rachel Carson is widely credited for recharging the environmental movement. This best-seller detailed the damage done to the environment by the usage of chemicals in agriculture.

Seven Days in May (1962): Fletcher Knebel's gripping tale of an attempt to execute a military takeover of the U.S. government.

A Moveable Feast (1964): Not long before ending his life, one of the century's most famous novelists and short story writers, Ernest Hemingway, published this memoir of his early life in Paris, France.

The Spy Who Came in from the Cold (1964): The first best-seller by British novelist John Le Carré, who would go on to make a career writing best-selling spy novels set amid Cold War tensions. They were the perfect novels for the age.

Herzog (1964): This important novel by Saul Bellow, who later won the Nobel Prize for literature, tells the story of a man trying to reconcile his ideals with the life he has led.

Dune (1965): This sci-fi novel written by Frank Herbert won the first-ever Nebula award for science fiction and eventually became the best-selling science fiction book in history, selling over twelve million copies.

In Cold Blood (1966): Truman Capote's harrowing true tale of the mass murder of a Kansas family combined journalism with fictional techniques in a new form of writing that became part of the "new journalism" associated with Tom Wolfe.

Valley of the Dolls (1966): Jacqueline Susann's novel about the lurid lives of those in show business was labeled trash by the critics, but sold in the millions and was later made into a popular movie of the same name.

Rolling Stone (1967–): The first rock 'n' roll magazine, this venture launched by editor and publisher Jann Wenner covered all areas of the 1960s youth movement and remains popular to this day.

Airport (1968): Arthur Hailey's novel about an airplane disaster in a snowstorm remained a best-seller for half the year and spawned a string of disaster movies in the 1970s.

Whole Earth Catalogue (1968): This guide to environmentally-sensitive products and hippie lifestyles, compiled by Stewart Brand, became the unofficial handbook of the counterculture.

I'm OK, You're OK (1969): This book by psychiatrist Thomas Harris became a bible to members of the "me generation," as evidenced by the one million copies of the book that sold in the 1970s.

What We Watched:

Wagon Train (1957–65): Set in the late 1800s, this show told a story each week about different people traveling along the wagon trail from St. Joseph, Missouri, to California.

Bonanza (1959–73): This Western set itself apart from the many others by being filmed especially

●●●●●➤

scientific research that enabled the nation to send astronauts to the moon. Yet this same spirit also drove the government to gradually step up American involvement in what amounted to a civil war in the distant nation of Vietnam. American forces were sent to aid the South Vietnamese, who were fighting against communist forces in North Vietnam. The Vietnam War was promoted as a righteous crusade against the spread of for color viewing. The program encouraged many to buy the new hot product—color televisions. Unlike other Westerns, the storylines were centered on the loving, loyal Cartwright family.

***The Andy Griffith Show* (1960–68):** This show brought to life a fictional small rural Southern town named Mayberry. The characters were ordinary and likeable. The story centered around the characters played by Andy Griffith, who played the calm, reasonable sheriff, and Don Knotts, who played his bumbling deputy.

***Psycho* (1960):** Alfred Hitchcock's horror film offered audiences a stabbing scene that has been called one of the scariest moments in film history.

***The Beverly Hillbillies* (1962–71):** This sitcom about simple country folk who struck it rich and moved to Beverly Hills, California, poked fun at the differences between rural and city life.

***The Sound of Music* (1965):** This popular musical about the singing Von Trapp Family starred Julie Andrews. The score was the last collaboration of the famous songwriter team of Richard Rodgers and Oscar Hammerstein.

***Doctor Zhivago* (1965):** This epic drama was the last great film by director David Lean and popularized the song "Lara's Theme."

***The Graduate* (1967):** This movie, starring Dustin Hoffman, was viewed by some as a light comedy, by others as a statement about the generation

gap, and still others as a keen illustration of the alienation felt by many in their late twenties.

***Jungle Book* (1967):** Walt Disney's animation of Rudyard Kipling's story about a boy who grows up in the jungle.

***Rowan and Martin's Laugh-In* (1968–73):** This comedy series was the top rated prime-time show in 1968 and 1969 and revolutionized the presentation of comic variety programs. It presented flashes and zooms of celebrities delivering rapid-fire one-liners, bikini-clad dancers, and slapstick routines. The show's editing style was unique to television at the time.

***2001: A Space Odyssey* (1968):** This science fiction film astounded viewers with its stunning visual effects.

What We Listened To:

Elvis Presley: The King still topped the charts in 1960 with "Are You Lonesome Tonight?" "It's Now or Never," and "Stuck on You."

Soundtrack albums: Two of the most successful of the 1960s were from *The Sound of Music,* featuring such favorites as "My Favorite Things" and "Do-Re-Mi," and *West Side Story,* with "America" and "Tonight."

"Blowin' in the Wind" (1962): Bob Dylan's protest song cemented his position as the leading singer/songwriter performing folk music that protested the established rules of society during the decade.

The Beatles: The Fab Four burst onto the American music scene following their appearance on *The Ed*

●●●●●➤

communism, but the bungled war effort soon led many to question why Americans were fighting in Vietnam.

Lurking beneath the prosperity and official optimism of the decade were powerful forces of discontent. Not everyone in the United States was content with the way things were going. African Americans, especially those living in the South, were angry about their continuing mistreatment and about racism in

1960s
At a Glance (continued)

Sullivan Show in late 1963 with such hits as "I Want to Hold Your Hand," "Can't Buy Me Love," "I Feel Fine," "She Loves You," and "A Hard Day's Night"; the British Invasion had begun.

"Surfin'" (1961): The Beach Boys' sunshine pop song started their rise to pop stardom. Brian Wilson and the gang introduced the world to the California lifestyle and briefly challenged the popularity of the Beatles.

Sgt. Pepper's Lonely Hearts Club Band (1967): The Beatles' landmark album marked a distinctive shift in the band's style and showed the influences of drug use.

"I'm a Believer" (1966) and **"Daydream Believer"** (1967): These singles by the Monkees cemented the popularity of this band made up of actors who were chosen more for their looks than their ability to play music.

"Respect" (1967): This soul song became a hit for Aretha Franklin, who continued to top the soul charts for the remainder of the decade.

Are You Experienced? (1968): This psychedelic rock album by the Jimi Hendrix Experience topped the album charts.

Motown Records: This Detroit-based record company sold more 45s than any other in the country with the talents of singers Marvin Gaye, Gladys Knight and the Pips, the Supremes, Smokey Robinson, and Stevie Wonder.

Drug-induced music: Such musicians as Jim Morrison and the The Doors, Jimi Hendrix, Janis Joplin, and the Grateful Dead experimented with music under the influence of a variety of drugs. Many of them would not outlive the decade.

Who We Knew:

Muhammad Ali (1942–): The most eloquent and powerful boxing champion of the decade. Born Cassius Clay, he used his popularity to spread the word about his Islam faith and to speak out against racism. He also uttered the lines: "Float like a butterfly, sting like a bee" and "I'm the greatest!"

First astronauts on the moon: Neil Armstrong (1930–) and Edwin "Buzz" Aldrin (1930–) landed on the moon on July 20, 1969, with Armstrong announcing, "The *Eagle* has landed." Within hours, more than a third of America watched Armstrong on television as he stepped onto the moon's surface and said, "That's one small step for man, one giant leap for mankind."

Johnny Carson (1925–): When he took over *The Tonight Show* from Jack Paar in 1962, Johnny Carson established himself as one of the most prominent comedians and television hosts in America. For thirty years, he was known as the "king of late night."

John F. Kennedy (1917–1963): The young, popular president was assassinated on November 22, 1963. His death and funeral were broadcast on television to millions of viewers around the world.

Timothy Leary (1920–1996): A Harvard researcher whose research and personal experimentation with psychedelic drugs led him to be fired from Harvard in 1963 and to become a leader of the

•••••➤

schools, in the workplace, and throughout American culture. Their movement for civil rights, begun in the 1950s, was ably led by the Reverend Martin Luther King Jr. (1929–1968), but also by radical black activist Malcolm X (Malcolm Little, 1925–1965). Civil rights groups staged protests throughout the decade to bring about change. These protests sometimes grew quite violent, and racists responded with violence in turn. Still, drug counterculture in the 1960s. He encouraged people to experience an alternative reality by taking drugs. He coined the phrase "Tune in, turn on, drop out."

Reverend Martin Luther King Jr. (1929–1968): This leader of the civil rights movement attracted national attention to blacks' growing resentment of segregation laws. He led thousands in several marches and protests including the Montgomery bus boycott (1955–56) and the March on Washington, where he gave his famous "I Have a Dream" speech in 1963. He was assassinated in 1968.

Charles Manson (1934–): This cult figure—leader of the so-called Manson Family—masterminded the slaughtering of numerous high-profile people, including director Roman Polanski's pregnant wife Sharon Tate, in hopes of encouraging a race war. The murders and the following trial attracted massive media attention and horrified the nation.

Thurgood Marshall (1908–1993): The first African-American Supreme Court justice (1967). This lawyer-turned-judge made a national name for himself in 1954 while presenting the oral arguments for the *Brown v. Board of Education of Topeka* case in front of the Supreme Court to win the end of segregated schools.

Ralph Nader (1934–): The nation's biggest consumer advocate since the mid–1960s. He formed consumer protection groups, including the Center for the Study of Responsive Law, to investigate industry and product safety and to lobby for protective legislation.

Elizabeth Taylor (1932–): By the 1960s, this former child actor had become the most popular film star of the decade. Her many marriages, her extravagant lifestyle, her precarious health, and her glamorous roles kept her firmly in the public eye.

Twiggy (1949–): The Mod Look that became popular at the end of the decade was inspired by English model Leslie Hornsby, known as Twiggy for her stick-like appearance. Her thin physique and fashion sense were copied by American women and even the toy maker Mattel made a Twiggy doll in 1967.

by the late 1960s, the civil rights movement had gained many of its goals.

The women's rights movement was largely inspired by the gains won by the civil rights movement. Feminists had long complained about their secondary role in American society. In the 1960s, they too organized marches and other forms of protest to draw attention to the lack of equality in wages between men and women and to women's right to control over reproductive decisions. By the end of the 1960s, the size of the female workforce had grown by 50 percent and women enjoyed greater sexual freedoms.

Another of the many movements of the 1960s was the anti-war movement. As more and more American troops were sent to Vietnam in the mid-1960s, many Americans—but especially American youths—began to question why America was involved in the war. They claimed that America was using its vast power to crush a legitimate movement for freedom, that the American military unfairly drew upon blacks and poor people to man its armies, and that the nation itself had grown greedy and power-hungry. By the late 1960s, the antiwar movement had become increasingly active and visible—and had attracted the sympathy of many Americans.

A common factor in all of these social movements was the participation of youths. American youths were growing increasingly alienated from the values of their parents. They felt that Americans were not practicing their own values when they segregated blacks, kept women in positions of inferiority, and waged war against a poor and distant nation. Across America—but primarily on college campuses and in bigger cities—American youths rejected their parents' values, questioned authority of all sorts, and created a vibrant youth culture of their own. The most extreme expression of this growing youth culture was the hippie movement, whose members grew their hair long, rejected many social conventions, experimented with drugs, and sometimes lived in communal groups known as communes.

The discontent and tumult that came to characterize the 1960s was made most evident in the high-profile assassinations that shook the decade. First came the killing of John F. Kennedy in Dallas, Texas, in 1963, an event that sent the entire nation into mourning. Malcolm X, the leader of a radical Black Muslim group, was gunned down in Harlem, New York, while giving a speech in 1965. In 1968, civil rights leader Martin Luther King Jr. and Democratic presidential candidate Robert F. Kennedy (1925–1968) were gunned down in separate killings. In their own way, each of these leaders had expressed hopes and dreams that were appealing to the youth movement. Young Americans were especially alarmed by their untimely deaths.

American popular culture was also affected by the youth and other social movements of the decade. Rock and roll, the music of youth, continued to grow and thrive as a musical form, helped along by the immense popularity of the Beatles, a British group. American movies took on bolder, more controversial subjects and echoed the turbulence of their times in ways that movies had not before. Even sports figures reflected the spirit of the times, with boxer Cassius Clay supporting the Black Muslim cause and changing his name to Muhammad Ali (1942–)

and pro football player Joe Namath (1943–) projecting the image of the youthful playboy. With the exception of television news, which brought the graphic violence of the Vietnam War into American homes, television programming remained a stronghold of family values, thanks to programs like *Bonanza* (1959–73) and *Sesame Street* (1969–).

1960s
Commerce

Until the 1990s, the 1960s marked the longest uninterrupted period of American economic expansion. The American economy was the largest in the world. Its giant corporations, such as General Motors, IBM, Procter & Gamble, and Coca-Cola extended their influence and dominance to every corner of the globe. American companies grew ever larger during the decade. In 1962, the five largest industrial companies accounted for 12 percent of American manufacturing assets. The largest five hundred companies controlled 66 percent of such assets. Big business dominated the American economic landscape.

Individual Americans did very well during the decade, too. By the end of the decade, the average American's real income had increased 50 percent since 1950, giving Americans a standard of living that was envied throughout the world. Median family income rose from $8,540 in 1963 to $10,770 by 1969. Americans used their growing discretionary income (income not needed for basic necessities) on a growing number of consumer goods.

Retailing continued to change to suit Americans' tastes for consumer goods. Wal-Mart and Kmart emerged as the leading examples of a new kind of variety store. Both stores carried a range of merchandise, from clothes to hardware to toys, that was offered at a discount price. Critics of the stores accused them of contributing to the death of the small-town storekeeper, who could not compete with the chain's low prices.

Two companies tapped into the growing power of American advertising to make themselves household names. Budweiser became the country's—and soon the world's—most popular beer, thanks largely to advertisements on sports programs and a growing distribution network. A new company, Nike, popularized the athletic shoe by associating its products with famous athletes. Many other products influenced popular culture in the decade.

Budweiser

The Anheuser-Busch brewing company traces its history to St. Louis, Missouri, in 1857. It first made the popular Budweiser Lager Beer there in 1876. By 2002, one in every five alcoholic drinks sold in the United States was a "Bud." It is sold in over sixty countries worldwide and brewed in such countries as Japan, Canada, and the United Kingdom. Not only is Budweiser America's favorite, it is also the world's best-selling beer. Like Coca-Cola, the "King of Beers" has become an international symbol for the American way of life.

By 1901, the Anheuser-Busch company was producing over one million barrels of beer every year. During **Prohibition** (see entry under 1920s–The Way We Lived in volume 2), Anheuser-Busch made a Budweiser "near-beer" (with lower amounts of alcohol) to protect its market share. When Prohibition ended in 1933, the famous Budweiser Clydesdale horses reminded Americans that Bud was a traditional American drink. Since then, Budweiser advertising has become almost as popular as the drink itself. In 1969, "Bud Man" pushed the idea that Bud was a man's drink with the slogan "This Bud's for you." Anheuser-Busch also prides itself on encouraging "responsible" drinking. That claim has helped make Budweiser popular with a wide range of drinkers. As the twentieth century closed, advertising campaigns involved talking frogs and lizards, and gimmicks such as theme parks and the Bud Bowl, in which beer bottles play a game of football. Into the new century, the "True" advertising campaign, including the "Whassup?" catchphrase, aimed to make Budweiser the first choice for sports fans everywhere.

In 1997, almost half the beer sold worldwide was Budweiser. Never mind that the drink itself has little to distinguish it over other mass-produced beers. Using one of the most efficient brewing processes in the world, Anheuser-Busch has been blamed for squeezing out more interesting beers and driving local microbreweries out of business. Through clever marketing, Budweiser has become far more than just a beer. When beer drinkers around the world buy Bud, they are also buying into the biggest "brand" of them all, the American Dream itself.

—*Chris Routledge*

For More Information

Anheuser-Busch Companies. http://www.anheuser-busch.com (accessed March 15, 2002).

Hernon, Peter, and Terry Ganey. *Under the Influence: The Unauthorized Story of the Anheuser-Busch Dynasty.* New York: Simon & Schuster, 1991.

Rhodes, Christine P., ed. *The Encyclopedia of Beer.* New York: Henry Holt, 1997.

Gap

With more than 3,800 stories in the United States, Europe, and Japan, Gap is a specialty retailer that sells clothing, accessories, and personal-care products for men, women, and children. Gap, Inc. sells products using three brand names and stores: Gap, Banana Republic, and Old Navy. Based in San Francisco, Gap, Inc. was founded in 1969 by Dan and Doris Fisher. Gap went public in 1976, offering 1.2 million shares of stock to investors. In 1983, the firm purchased Banana Republic and hired Millard Drexler (1944–) as president of its Gap division. He became president of Gap, Inc. in 1987 and CEO in 1995. By 2001, the firm employed more than 166,000 people worldwide and had revenues in excess of $13 billion.

During the 1980s and 1990s, Gap, Inc. underwent expansion that established it as a significant brand name in U.S. retailing. GapKids opened its first store in 1983, and Gap Outlet (originally called Gap Warehouse) opened in 1993. Its Old Navy Brand debuted in 1994 and achieved $1 billion in annual sales within four years. The firm made a commitment to online retailing when it opened its online store in 1997, followed by Web sites for GapKids and babyGap in 1998, Banana Republic in 1999, and Old Navy in 2000.

In general, the Banana Republic stores try to convey a more sophisticated image for an upscale customer, whereas Gap stores appeal to a broader midrange of customers. The Old Navy chain is designed to appeal to younger customers by emphasizing "fun, fashion, and value" through a store experience that delivers "energy and excitement." Although Gap, along with other retail-store chains, has been criticized for blandness and uniformity in its selling environments, the firm maintains that it tailors its stores "to appeal to unique markets" by developing multiple formats and designs.

In the 1990s, Gap was one of several large retailers that came under fire by labor and human-rights organizations for selling apparel made abroad under sweatshop conditions (long hours for low wages in uncomfortable surroundings). It responded by developing a Code of Vendor Conduct that required its vendors (sellers of goods; in this case, the clothing manufacturers that sell to Gap) to abide by higher standards when dealing with its labor force. While acknowledging that some of its suppliers have factories in emerging nations that are just being to industrialize, Gap maintains that some of these jobs can offer a "coveted alternative to subsistence farming, or no work at all." The firm claims that it monitors working conditions with its network of Vendor Compliance Officers working with labor and religious organizations, and that it tries to make a positive impact "one vendor at a time, one worker at a time, one day at a time."

—Edward Moran

For More Information

Gap Inc. http://www.gap.com (accessed March 13, 2002).
Nevaer, Louis E. V. *Into—and Out of—the Gap: A Cautionary Account of an American Retailer.* Westport, CT: Quorum Books, 2001.

G.I. Joe

Since its introduction in 1964, G.I. Joe has been one of the most popular toys for boys. The Hasbro Company created G.I. Joe as the first action figure doll for boys. A real G.I. is an enlisted person in the U.S. armed forces. This G.I. stood a foot tall, had moveable joints so that he could be posed in many different ways, and he wore military fatigues, dog tags, and boots. As a war toy, G.I. Joe joined a long tradition of military toys for boys.

Hasbro hoped to repeat the popularity of the **Barbie doll** (see entry under 1950s—Commerce in volume 3), the beautiful and popular doll for girls that was introduced in 1959. But getting boys to accept the idea of playing with a doll took some work. Hasbro overcame boys' dislike of dolls by making its doll a military figure. G.I. Joe was everything Barbie was not: rugged, bearded, and with a scar on his face to let everyone know that G.I. Joe was a man of action. Like Barbie, Hasbro offered countless accessories for the G.I. Joe dolls. G.I. Joe drove a military jeep, carried guns and grenades, and wore combat boots. In this way, Hasbro made the G.I. Joe attractive to boys and overcame the stigma of playing with dolls. G.I. Joe was not a doll, Hasbro said, but rather an "action figure." Hasbro kept interest in the action figure by introducing ever more elaborate accessories, including other military vehicles, space capsules, a talking version of the doll, and a "kung-fu grip" that let the figure hold things in its hands more easily.

G.I. Joe was at times a controversial toy. In the late 1960s, as protests against American involvement in the Vietnam War (1954–75) reached their peak, G.I. Joe became a symbol for some people of how children were taught to love war from a young age. In the years since its introduction, the G.I. Joe doll has been marketed in various sizes and with various missions, and he has appeared in **comic books** (see entry under 1930s–Print Culture in volume 2) and **television** (see entry under 1940s–TV and Radio in volume 3) shows. By 1993, over 250 million G.I. Joe dolls had been sold. The toy remained popular among young boys (and toy collectors) into the twenty-first century.

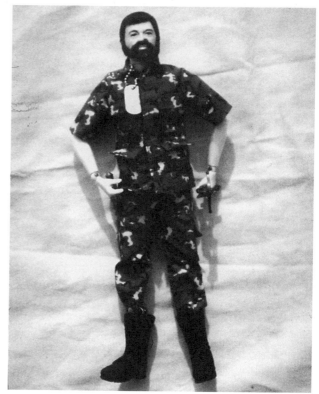

G.I. Joe was the first action figure targeted especially for boys. *Photograph by Michael Reed. Corbis-Bettmann. Reproduced by permission.*

—*Timothy Berg*

For More Information

Cross, Gary. *Kids' Stuff: Toys and the Changing World of American Childhood.* Cambridge, MA: Harvard University Press, 1997.

G.I. Joe Interactive. http://www.gijoe.com (accessed March 13, 2002).

Miller, G. Wayne. *Toy Wars: The Epic Struggle Between G.I. Joe, Barbie, and the Companies That Make Them.* New York: Times Books, 1998.

Santelmo, Vincent. *The Complete Encyclopedia to G.I. Joe.* Iola, WI: Krause Publications, 1997.

Kmart

Kmart is an all-purpose, all-American chain store. In the last decades of the twentieth century, it came to represent the typical shopping experience for millions of blue collar and middle-class Americans. Kmarts generally are single-story, parking lot-size structures, where customers can find and purchase an astonishing array of items at a reasonable price. Everything from bookcases to baby clothes, clocks to CDs, earrings to edibles, paint supplies to perfume to picture frames can be found at Kmart.

In the early years of the twentieth century, Americans made most of their purchases in small, specialized stores known as "mom-and-pop" stores. Meat was available through butchers; dairy products were procured directly from dairy farms; and a range of edibles lined the shelves of grocery stores. Tools, nails, and screws were found in hardware stores. Dresses and suits could be purchased in men's or women's clothing stores. Then, throughout the twentieth century, larger emporiums began replacing specialized stores as primary shopping outlets. Department stores like Macy's and Gimbels offered a wider range of merchandise all under one roof. Supermarket chains replaced grocery stores. Because such stores had the purchasing power to acquire merchandise from suppliers in bulk, prices could be lower than those offered by the smaller, individually owned competition.

The 1960s was the advent of the Kmart-style discount retailer. These large discount stores offered the product variety found in department stores, but at even lower prices. Kmart is a spin-off of S. S. Kresge, a **dime store** (see entry under 1900s–Commerce in volume 1) chain. The initial Kmart appeared in Garden City, Michigan, a suburb of Detroit, in 1962. Eight years later, more than four hundred Kmarts were in business across the country, bringing in billions in sales. In the ensuing decades, the chain kept expanding, opening over two thousand stores, some of which were just miles apart. In 1989, Kmart became America's top-grossing retailer. However, Kmart is not the lone store of its type. **Wal-Mart** (see entry under 1960s–Commerce in volume 4) and Target, for example, also commenced operations in 1962. Often, competing stores, essentially offering the same merchandise, are found opposite each other along the same roadways.

If one individual came to represent the discount merchandising phenomenon, it was the dynamic Sam Walton (1918–1992), founder of Wal-Mart. In fact, during the 1990s, Wal-Mart—Kmart's arch-rival, whose stores generally were newer and larger—surpassed Kmart as the nation's leading discount retailer. In an effort to modernize its image—and to keep up with Wal-Mart and Target—Kmart began renovating its stores, adding brighter lights, wider aisles, and more sophisticated displays. Model Kathy Ireland (1963–), actress Jaclyn Smith (1947–), and homemaking queen Martha Stewart (1941–) became celebrity-sponsors of lines of inexpensive "designer" merchandise. Kmart even opened a four-level store in midtown Manhattan.

But economic problems began to plague Kmart more seriously in the twenty-first century. In January 2002, Kmart filed for bankruptcy; less than two months later, it announced plans to close 284 stores and lay off 22,000 employees in 40 states in an attempt to reorganize itself. The future of Kmart—the first store of its type to open branches across the country, and the first to challenge the large department stores for retail supremacy—is uncertain.

–Rob Edelman

For More Information

Blackwell, Roger. *From Mind to Market: Reinventing the Retail Supply Chain.* New York: HarperCollins, 1997.

"Kmart Corporation News." *Bluelight.com.* http://www.kmartcorp.com/corp/story/index.stm (accessed March 13, 2002).

Peterson, Roger. *The Future of U.S. Retailing.* Westport, CT: Quorum Books, 1992.

Nike

Founded in 1962, Nike, Inc. was one of the first designers of special shoes for athletes. The corporation has been at the forefront of **advertising** (see entry under 1920s–Commerce in volume 2) and marketing techniques since the 1980s. Although Nike has continued to identify itself with athletes and athletic achievement, Nike sneakers are just as likely to be worn by nonathletes who simply want a stylish designer casual shoe.

Nike got its start in Eugene, Oregon, and was the creation of two men, Bill Bowerman (1911–1999) and Philip Knight (1938–). Bowerman was a track-and-field coach at the University of Oregon who was constantly searching for an athletic shoe that would help his teams run faster and jump higher. Knight was a businessman who had been a runner on one of Bowerman's teams when he was in college. Knight and Bowerman teamed up in 1962, first to import Japanese running shoes,

Nike's line of Air-Force basketball shoes in 1982. *Bettmann/Corbis. Reproduced by permission.*

then to experiment with their own designs. They called their company Blue Ribbon Sports.

Though Knight and Bowerman were successful in creating shoes that improved athletes' performance on the field, they had to figure out how to sell their shoes to a wider market. In 1972, they adopted the name Nike, after the winged Greek goddess of victory, and their trademark "swoosh." The trademark was designed by Carolyn Davidson, a Portland State University graphic design student. Knight and Bowerman also designed an advertising campaign that featured ads, not for specific shoes, but for victory itself, employing through the years famous winning athletes like basketball's **Michael Jordan** (1963–; see entry under 1990s–Sports and Games in volume 5) and tennis champions John McEnroe (1959–) and Monica Seles (1973–). Nike ads often feature sweating athletes in dramatic motion with the company slogan, "Just Do It."

Beginning in the 1980s, some people began to criticize Nike's employment practices. They pointed out that Nikes are not manufactured in the United States but in countries like China, Indonesia, and Vietnam, where labor is much cheaper and workers are treated badly. These critics have organized many demonstrations and boycotts of the company's products.

The quality of Nike's shoe design and its creative approach to advertising has made the company a continuing success. Millions of people have bought Nike shoes, both as athletic wear and as a fashion statement. By 2000, Nike was selling 40 percent of all sneakers sold worldwide, earning billions of dollars in sales, and employing thousands of workers in its factories around the world. Nike sponsors hundreds of athletic teams and events, and the Nike "swoosh" has become one of the most recognized symbols in the world.

—Tina Gianoulis

For More Information

Clifford, Mark L. "'On the Inside, It's Hell': Despite Improvements, Nike Workers Face Tough Conditions." *Business Week* (July 29, 1996): pp. 46–48.

Collins, David R. *Philip Knight: Running with Nike.* Ada, OK: Garrett Educational Corp., 1992.

Hays, Scott. *The Story of Nike.* Mankato, MN: Smart Apple Media, 2000.

Miller, Annetta. "Just Doing It." *Newsweek* (October 2, 1995): pp. 64–66.

Nike. http://www.nike.com (accessed March 13, 2002).

Strasser, J. B, and Laurie Becklund. *Swoosh: The Unauthorized Story of Nike and the Men Who Played There.* New York: HarperInformation, 1993.

Valium

The first of the so-called "blockbuster" drugs, the tranquilizer Valium, first available to the public in the early 1960s, was the top selling prescription drug during the 1970s. It was called a blockbuster because it was marketed and sold to a wide variety of people to help them control anxiety, nervousness, and tension. Over the next two decades, both the doctors who prescribed the drug and their patients who took it began to realize that Valium had several negative effects, and its popularity has decreased. However, Valium's fame as an aid to relaxation is still widespread. Most people will understand that the suggestion "Take a Valium!" means "Calm down!"

Valium is the brand name for a drug called diazepam, which is a tranquilizer (calming medication). Diazepam was invented in the late 1950s by a Swiss drug company called Hoffmann-La Roche, who began to market it in the early 1960s. It was the perfect drug for a society coping with rapid changes brought about by the **civil rights movement** (see entry under 1960s—The

Way We Lived in volume 4), the women's liberation movement, and the **sexual revolution** (see entry under 1960s–The Way We Lived in volume 4), social movements that left many Americans feeling anxious. The new drug Valium seemed to be a kind of miracle cure for anxiety. Doctors prescribed it widely, for everyone from overworked executives to young housewives who were stressed by the many demands of their families. The 1966 novel by Jacqueline Susann (1918–1974), *Valley of the Dolls,* and the 1966 hit song "Mother's Little Helper" by the **Rolling Stones** (see entry under 1960s–Music in volume 4) reflect the effects of Valium pills on women during that time.

The popularity of brand-name Valium suffered somewhat in the mid-1980s, when Hoffmann-La Roche's patent on the drug expired. This allowed other companies to make their own less expensive brands of diazepam to compete with Valium. By the late 1980s, both doctors and patients were beginning to discover that the drug had some unpleasant effects, called "side effects" by the drug industry. Valium often made those who took it sleepy and uncoordinated; some experienced difficulty remembering and an increased anxiety after they stopped taking the drug. Worst of all, many who took Valium became addicted to its calming effects and had problems trying to quit using the drug. As the seriousness of these effects became more obvious, Valium became less popular, both with doctors and patients. Drug companies continue to experiment, seeking a drug that will offer the tranquilizing effects of Valium without the negative effects.

—Tina Gianoulis

For More Information

Colburn, Don. "Valium in an Age of Anxiety: The Drug Remains the Tranquilizer of Choice for Millions." *The Washington Post* (February 17, 1987): p. WH9.

Dyson, Cindy. *Valium and Other Downers*. Philadelphia: Chelsea House, 2000.

Tavris, Carol. "Valium, Cigarettes, and Memory." *Vogue* (December 1987): pp. 40–41.

Winger, Gail. *Valium, the Tranquil Trap*. New York: Chelsea House, 1986.

Wal-Mart

Both loved and hated by shoppers worldwide, the Wal-Mart family of discount stores has grown in less than forty years from a single business in a small Arkansas town in 1962 to one

of the world's largest corporations. Wal-Mart operated eleven hundred stores around the world in the year 2000. The Wal-Mart strategy of combining low prices with a huge inventory and attentive customer service has changed retail sales practices across the United States. Many complain that large Wal-Mart stores change the nature of the towns where they open by taking business away from small, locally owned shops and forcing them to close. Others, however, cheer the coming of Wal-Mart to their town, because the stores make available a wide variety of goods at prices that working families can afford.

Wal-Mart was founded by Sam Walton (1918–1992), an Oklahoma native who had operated **dime stores** (see entry on under 1900s—Commerce in volume 1)—also called "five-and-ten stores"—first in Newport, Arkansas, then in Bentonville, Arkansas. Walton believed that the small towns of America offered great opportunity for the knowledgeable retailer. He opened his first Wal-Mart Discount City in 1962 in Rogers, Arkansas. Soon Wal-Marts were opening across the South and Midwest. Walton's philosophy of drawing customers in with deep price cuts and keeping them with friendly customer service proved successful.

From a small beginning in 1962, Wal-Mart grew into a billion-dollar empire by the end of the twentieth century. *AP/Wide World Photos. Reproduced by permission.*

However, Wal-Mart employees have not always been happy, nor have the citizens of the communities where the store opens. The store has been involved in dozens of legal disputes about discrimination against employees on the basis of sex and disability. Wal-Mart has also been accused of unfair business practices and selling goods made with sweatshop labor (employees who suffer poor working conditions, low pay, and long hours). Many activists have tried to prevent the store coming into their community, claiming that the presence of Wal-Mart takes business away from downtown areas and therefore weakens the entire town.

But Wal-Mart continues to grow, in small towns and in larger cities. By the early 1980s, sales had risen to $3.4 billion, and two new stores were opening each week. In 2002, Wal-Mart reached the number one position in the Fortune 500 list of largest companies in the United States. Walton was an enthusiastic manager, leading his employees in cheers and in "Sam's Pledge," which was recited with right hands raised: "From this day forward, every customer that comes within ten feet of me, I'm going to look him in the eye, I'm going to smile, I'm going to greet him with a 'Good morning,' or a 'Good afternoon,' or a 'What can I do for you?'—so help me Sam!"

—Tina Gianoulis

For More Information

Anderson, Sarah. "Wal-Mart's War on Main Street." *The Progressive* (November 1994): pp. 19–22.

Bowermaster, Jon. "When Wal-Mart Comes to Town: Independence, Iowa." *New York Times Magazine* (April 2, 1989): pp. S28–30.

"A Life of Fines and Beating." *Business Week* (October 2, 2000): pp. 122–25.

Quinn, Bill. *How Wal-Mart Is Destroying America (and the World) and What You Can Do About It.* Berkeley, CA: Ten Speed Press, 2000.

Sidey, Hugh, "The Two Sides of the Sam Walton Legacy." *Time* (April 20, 1992): pp. 50–54.

"Small-town Hit." *Time* (May 23, 1983): pp. 43–45.

Wal-Mart: Welcome to Wal-Mart Stores! http://www.walmartstores.com/wmstore/wmstores/HomePage.jsp (accessed March 13, 2002).

Walton, Sam. *Sam Walton and Wal-Mart.* New York: Doubleday, 1992.

Xerox Copiers

Xerox copiers offered the world the ability to make clean, easy, quick copies on paper. Using photoelectric technology, the

Xerox copier could copy a page with the press of a button. The copier quickly replaced the messy mimeograph machine and the time-consuming offset printing processes.

Chester F. Carlson (1906–1968) invented the photocopy machine in his spare time in the late 1930s. His first machines were not immediately appealing to the business community. By 1944, he had failed to sell his patented process and joined with the Battelle Memorial Institute to further perfect the process. Within three years, Battelle had joined with the Haloid Xerox company to sell the machines, but the first ones were difficult to operate. More research resulted in the Xerox copier, Model 914, marketed in 1961 to great success. Profits of the company reached $500 million within three years. The Xerox copier literally changed the way people worked with paper. Xerox Model 914 was honored by inclusion in the Smithsonian Institution's National Museum of American History in 1985.

Newer models continue to populate offices around the world. Like **Kleenex** brand tissues and **Band-Aid** brand bandages (see these two entries under 1920s–Commerce in volume 2), in many people's minds, the Xerox brand has become the generic brand for its product: when one wants to photocopy a paper, one xeroxes it.

—Sara Pendergast

For More Information

Flatow, Ira. *They All Laughed*. New York: HarperCollins, 1992.

Silverman, Steve. "Xerography." *About.com*. http://inventors.about.com/gi/dynamic/offsite.htm?site=http://home.nycap.rr.com/useless/xerox/xerox.html (accessed March 13, 2002).

"There Isn't Any Profit Squeeze at Xerox." *Fortune* (Vol. 66, July 1962): pp. 151–55.

"Xerox." *Jones Telecommunications and Multimedia Encyclopedia*. http://www.digitalcentury.com/encyclo/update/xerox.html (accessed March 13, 2002).

1960s
Fashion

As with other areas of American popular culture, fashion underwent a real transition in the 1960s, from conservatism to excess, from social conformity (doing what society expects) to individuality ("doing your own thing"). The fashion icon (symbol of fashion) of the first years of the decade was first lady Jacqueline Kennedy (1929–1994), wife of the popular young president John F. Kennedy (1917–1963). Jacqueline Kennedy, with her simple yet tasteful clothes, was featured in most of the popular fashion magazines of the day. However, the refined conservatism of the first lady soon gave way to much bolder styles.

Around 1964, British designer Mary Quant (1934–) designed the "mod look," which became especially popular among young women. Miniskirts, brightly colored dresses, dark eye makeup, and wild blouses, stockings, and accessories became the rage. Styles shifted rapidly from year to year. A thin, mod British model named Twiggy (1949–) soon replaced Jackie Kennedy as the dominant fashion trendsetter. As the women's rights movement gained influence, women also grew more independent in their fashion choices. Some women went braless, and many began to wear pants for the first time.

Men, too, were affected by the new freedom in fashion. The buzz cut went out of style as the dominant haircut for men, and men increasingly went to stylists instead of barbers to keep their hair in fashion. By the end of the decade, male hippies could be seen wearing their extremely long hair in ponytails. The gray flannel suit also went out of style as men sought new options, even in business wear. Ties grew wider and colors bolder. Among young men, jeans and a T-shirt remained the most popular clothing choice.

Bell-Bottoms

Bell-bottoms–pants that flare out at the cuffs–have had many different associations during the last half of the twentieth

A man models a pair of bell-bottoms. *Barnabas Bosshart/Corbis Corporation. Reproduced by permission.*

century. First part of a military uniform, later the symbol of those who opposed war, bell-bottoms have tended to arouse strong emotions. Some have condemned them as a fashion mistake, whereas others have worn them as a bold fashion statement.

Bell-bottomed pants were designed as part of a sailor's traditional clothing. They have long been part of various naval uniforms. Wide legs made it easy to pull wet pants off over heavy boots, helping those who fell overboard to discard heavy clothing. The flared legs could then be filled with air to provide a flotation device. Onboard ship, sailors sometimes washed decks in bare feet, and bell-bottoms could be rolled up easily to keep dry.

During the 1960s, as American youth became involved in various radical political and artistic movements, a nonconformist (outside of what society expects) culture began to develop. Called "bohemians" and **"hippies"** (see entry under 1960s—The Way We Lived in volume 4), these young people rejected commercial fashions and often shopped for cheap, practical clothes at Army-Navy Surplus stores—where they found the Navy's denim bell-bottoms. Embellished with embroidery and patches, these bell-bottoms became a symbol of the flamboyant hippie counterculture. Some made bell-bottoms out of straight leg jeans by inserting a triangle of fabric into the side seam of the pants. Eventually, fashion caught up with the counterculture. Clothing manufacturers began to design stylish bell-bottoms, some with legs so wide they were nicknamed "elephant bells."

By the mid-1970s, bell-bottoms were no longer a political statement. They were universally popular and available in a variety of fabrics. Along with other showy fashions of the 1970s, they soon went out of style, however. Bell-bottoms soon became a synonym for being hopelessly out of date. Bell-bottoms returned to fashion with the name "flares" in the 1990s, as part of a 1970s retro style and as a version of the baggy fashions associated with **rave** (see entry under 1990s–Music in volume 5) culture. (Raves are night-long parties at which large numbers of people dance, listen to a disc jockey play "techno" music that uses the beat of the music as a hypnotic tool to alter the listeners' consciousnesses, and sometimes use drugs.)

—Tina Gianoulis

For More Information

"Bellbottoms." *Bad Fads Museum.* http://www.badfads.com/pages/fashion/bellbottom.html (accessed March 14, 2002).

"Bellbottoms." *Yesterdayland.* http://www.yesterdayland.com/popopedia/shows/fashion/fa1073.php (accessed March 14, 2002).

"Break Out Your Bell-Bottoms: From Madonna to Main Street, Groovy '60s Fashions Are Back—with a Twist." *People Weekly* (January 28, 1991).

Doc Martens

Bavarian physician Klaus Maertens designed his famous "air cushion sole" boots in 1945 to protect his feet after a skiing accident. The first pair of boots was actually made from old tires. In the late 1960s, the "1460" boot became part of the battle dress of British fascist (right-wing) skinheads, a group of radical youths. The police who arrested them soon came to favor the comfortable Dr. Maertens shoe. Along with tartan trousers, the boot became an icon of the **punk** (see entry under 1970s—Music in volume 4) subculture in the late 1970s.

Since the 1970s, Doc Martens, or "DMs" as they are known in the United Kingdom, have been the world's number one cult footwear. Within a decade, Doc Martens had hit the mainstream. Sold in upmarket department stores, almost 70 percent of the boots were bought by women in the 1990s. Available in the traditional oxblood (reddish brown color) or black leather, in 2001 they also came painted with colorful floral patterns. For the environmentally conscious, Doc Martens are also available in a leather-free "vegetarian" version.

—Chris Routledge

For More Information

Dr. Martens. http://www.drmartens.com/Homepage.asp (accessed March 14, 2002).

Mary Kay Cosmetics

Without a storefront or an advertising budget, Mary Kay Cosmetics has managed to become one of the largest sellers of beauty aids in the world, employing over four hundred thousand sales people and selling more than $800,000 worth of cosmetics each year. The secret to the company's huge success is the combination of direct (door-to-door) sales techniques, a program of rewards that motivates its sales people to excel, and the unfailing energy of the company founder, Mary Kay Ash (1918–2001). Even in an era when door-to-door sales have fallen dramatically, the name Mary Kay is one of the most recognized product names in the United States.

Mary Kay Ash was born in Houston, Texas, in 1918. Because her father was ill and her mother worked full time to support the family, young Mary Kay learned to take care of herself while still a child. She married at seventeen, soon divorced, and by the late 1930s was a single mother of three, needing once again to take care of herself. She found a job selling household products door-to-door and discovered she had a gift for sales. Her skill at selling products led to advancement at work, but she soon reached the limit of success available to women in most businesses at that time. In 1963, after her employers promoted a man she had trained to be her supervisor, Mary Kay had had enough. She quit that job and decided to form her own company. She created a company in which women would not be limited by the prejudice of male bosses. At her company, women would be rewarded and made to feel like valuable members of a team.

Since its beginning in 1964, Mary Kay Cosmetics has continued to fulfill its founder's dream. Of its hundreds of thousands of employees, only about two thousand are men. Although most Mary Kay saleswomen once were housewives seeking extra income, the company's success now lures executives and business-school graduates away from corporate jobs. A born-again Christian, Mary Kay Ash was part preacher and part cheerleader to her employees. Her motivational speeches and the company anthem, "I've Got the Mary Kay Enthusiasm Down in My Heart," are as much a part of the organization as the cosmetics themselves. Based on a "pyramid" structure, where sales people recruit other sales people and then get a percentage of the money earned by those they recruit, Mary Kay Cosmetics also has an elaborate rewards program to inspire its sales crew. At the annual convention in Dallas, Texas, successful employees are awarded diamond rings, mink coats, free vacations, and pink Cadillacs.

—*Tina Gianoulis*

For More Information

Ash, Mary Kay. *Mary Kay—You Can Have it All: Lifetime Wisdom from America's Foremost Woman Entrepreneur.* Roseville, CA: Prima Publishing, 1998.

Coughlin, Ellen K. "Making a Business of Belief: Sociologist Examines the Direct-Selling Industry in America." *The Chronicle of Higher Education* (Vol. 35, no. 45, July 19, 1989): pp. 4–7.

Farnham, Alan. "Mary Kay's Lessons in Leadership." *Fortune* (September 20, 1993): pp. 68–75.

"Mary Kay Ash." *Current Biography* (Vol. 56, no. 5, May 1995): pp. 14–19.

Mary Kay: Enriching Women's Lives. http://www.marykay.com/start.asp (accessed March 14, 2002).

Wiley, Kim Wright. "Cold Cream and Hard Cash." *Savvy* (June 1985): pp. 36–43.

Miniskirts

First introduced to the fashion world in 1965, the miniskirt was part of a widespread wave of sexual openness and personal

A model wears a wool jacket over a miniskirt at a fashion show in 1966. *AP/Wide World Photos. Reproduced by permission.*

freedom that was sometimes called the **sexual revolution** (see entry under 1960s–The Way We Lived in volume 4). The short skirts that exposed four or more inches of a woman's thigh were not only lighthearted but sexy. The skirts also represented a movement away from society's restrictions on women's freedom.

The first miniskirts to appear on Paris fashion runways were created by French fashion designer André Courrèges (1923–), who was tired of the old-fashioned designs and prim knee-length skirts that dominated the fashion of the early 1960s. Courrèges wanted to introduce a radical new look that would bring youth, freedom, and originality to the world of fashion, so he dressed his models in simple A-line dresses (flared bottom and close-fitting top) that ended four inches above the knee. Flat-soled white boots completed the "mod" look. Though some critics were horrified by the new style, many others were charmed, and the miniskirt caught on quickly. London designer Mary Quant (1934–) shortened the skirt still further, and changed Courrèges's flared skirt to a tight, body-hugging shape. Famous models like Twiggy (1949–) popularized the new skirt, and it quickly became a commercial success. Although many women lacked the courage to wear the new minis, much less the even shorter microminis that followed, hemlines in general went up, and women's fashions became bolder and freer than before, representing a change in women's attitudes about themselves.

Miniskirts are usually identified with the mid-1960s, but they have resurfaced on the fashion scene several times since then. In the mid-1980s, pop singer **Madonna** (1958–; see entry under 1980s–Music in volume 5) introduced a popular new style of dress that included a revival of the miniskirt. The early 1990s saw another return of the revealing style.

—*Tina Gianoulis*

For More Information

Milbank, Caroline Rennolds. "A Mini Splendid Thing." *Interview* (Vol. 17, no. 9, September 1987): pp. 130–32.

"Miniskirts." *Yesterdayland.* http://www.yesterdayland.com/popopedia/shows/fashion/fa1634.php (accessed March 14, 2002)

Schneider, Karen. "Up, Up and Hooray! Designer André Courrèges Celebrates 25 Years of Miniskirt Fame." *People Weekly* (July 9, 1990): pp. 79–82.

Twiggy (1949–) ....

The original **supermodel** (see entry under 1980s–Fashion in volume 5), in the late 1960s, Twiggy (born Lesley Hornby) became an icon (a symbol) of "Swinging London" and gained international fame. Her image filled the fashion magazines, and she even had a **Barbie doll** (see entry under 1950s–Commerce in volume 3) designed in her likeness. In the 1950s, women like **Marilyn Monroe** (1926–1962; see entry under 1950s–Film and Theater in volume 3) traded on their full figures and mature sexuality. In contrast, Twiggy's big-eyed skinny boyishness was virtually sexless. Her slender figure was a major break from earlier versions of femininity. Twiggy was the essence of groovy Britishness in the 1960s, but her influence has also been blamed for the growth of eating disorders among young women. Her ninety-one-pound frame became an unrealistic dieting target for weight-conscious women the world over.

Twiggy appeared in several films in the 1970s and also had several hit records in the United Kingdom. The look she began remains an influence on the fashion industry in the twenty-first century. In 2001, Twiggy herself made occasional appearances on British television and promoted her own line of skin-care products.

—Chris Routledge

For More Information

Twiggy. *Twiggy: How I Probably Just Came Along on a White Rabbit at the Right Time, and Met the Smile on the Face of the Tiger.* New York: Hawthorn Books, 1968.

Twiggy Lawson's Official Site. http://www.twiggylawson.co.uk (accessed March 14, 2002).

1960s
Film and Theater

Moviemaking remained in a slump at the start of the 1960s. Moviemakers struggled to come up with successful strategies to combat the rising popularity of television, which kept former movie viewers at home. One strategy was to make big-budget spectacles that TV producers simply could not make. *Cleopatra*, released in 1963, starring Elizabeth Taylor (1932–) and Richard Burton (1925–1984), was just such a film. It cost $37 million to make and included lavish sets and exotic filming locations. Filmgoers loved such movies, but there were only so many that could be made each year.

Moviemakers also attracted audiences by making another kind of movie that could not air on TV—movies that contained sex, violence, or unconventional behavior. Comedies like *The Apartment* (1960) and *Kiss Me, Stupid* (1964), dramas like *The Graduate* (1967) or *Bonnie and Clyde* (1967), and adventure pictures like the James Bond films *Dr. No* and *Goldfinger* (1964)— all had content that was deemed too "mature" for TV.

Mature content soon became one of the film industry's biggest problems, as groups like the Catholic Legion of Decency publicized their ratings of movies that were deemed unacceptable. In 1968, the Motion Picture Association of America started a voluntary rating system that is still in use. The system included the ratings G (general audiences), M (mature; later changed to GP, then PG), R (restricted), and X (no one under 18 admitted). (PG-13 was added in 1984.) In 1969, the film *Midnight Cowboy* won the Academy Award for best picture despite an X rating that was given to the film for its homosexual content. (Years later, *Midnight Cowboy* was reclassified with an R rating.)

Despite these limitations, filmmakers produced some of history's best known films in the decade, including the science-fiction films *Planet of the Apes* (1968) and *2001: A Space Odyssey* (1968) and the horror film *Psycho* (1960). Another popular film was *West Side Story* (1961), adapted from the popular Broadway play of the same name. A thriving American-theater culture provided several other plays that made it to the big screen, including *Who's Afraid of Virginia Woolf?* (1962; filmed in 1966) by Edward Albee (1928–) and *The Odd Couple* (1965; filmed in 1968 and made into a television series in 1970) by Neil Simon (1927–). *Hair* (1968; filmed in 1978) became the first rock-and-roll musical.

Beach Movies

During the mid-1960s, one of cinema's most successful kind of film was the beach-movie genre. These low-budget, hastily produced features celebrated California's beaches, surfing, and teen culture. One series of films starred Frankie Avalon (1940–) and Annette Funicello (1942–) as "Frankie" and "Dee Dee"—two wholesome teens who descended upon the beach with dozens of their friends every summer. The group lived free from the interference of parents and without financial worries. They spent their days surfing, partying, dancing, skydiving, and enjoying other innocent entertainments. In Andrew Edelstein's *The Pop Sixties,* William Asher (1921–), the director of several of the beach movies, described the premise of the series: "It's all good clean fun. No hearts are broken, and virginity prevails."

American International Pictures (AIP), which had profited during the 1950s with low-budget horror and juvenile delinquent films like *Reform School Girls* (1957) and *I Was a Teenage Werewolf* (1957), produced the beach movies. Sam Arkoff (1918–2001) and James Nicholson (1916–1972), AIP executives, noted that the audience for their delinquent teen films was shrinking while movies featuring clean-cut, wholesome teenagers, like *Gidget* (1959) and *Where the Boys Are* (1960), were playing to large crowds. They decided to capitalize on the trend by producing *Beach Party* (1963). The plot for this film (and all those in the series) revolves around the romance between excitable Frankie and curvaceous Dee Dee. Funicello's character wants to marry Avalon's, but he is afraid of settling down. Numerous musical numbers, melodramatic subplots, slapstick comedy, and chases balanced the romantic aspects of the beach movies. The core beach movies produced by AIP between 1963 and 1966 include *Beach Party* (1963), *Muscle Beach Party* (1964), *Bikini Beach* (1964), *Beach Blanket Bingo* (1965; generally considered the best of the series), *How to Stuff a Wild Bikini* (1965), and *Ghost in the Invisible Bikini* (1966).

A movie poster from *Beach Blanket Bingo*. *CinemaPhoto/ Corbis Corporation. Reproduced by permission.*

Ironically, Funicello never wore a bikini in any of the films. Walt Disney (1901–1966), her mentor, requested she wear only modest one-piece bathing suits to protect her innocent image.

The beach movies were complete fantasy, as the turbulent social issues of the 1960s never invaded Frankie and Annette's domain. The gang never worried about being drafted to Vietnam, they were racially segregated, and they never had sex. The adults who appeared in the series were comic villains who did not understand the teens and constantly attempted to ruin their parties. Among the established adult celebrities who appeared in the beach movies were Vincent Price (1911–1993), Don Rickles (1926–), Paul Lynde (1926–1982), Boris Karloff (1887–1969), Linda Evans (1942–), Buddy Hackett (1924–), Morey Amsterdam (1908–1996), Elsa Lanchester (1902–1986), and silent-film legend Buster Keaton (1895–1966). The adult actor most associated with the films is Harvey Lembeck (1923–1982), who played "Erich Von Zipper," a Brando-inspired yet comically played motorcycle-gang leader.

American International Pictures attempted to repeat the beach movies' success by presenting their stars in similar films away from an ocean setting. These films include *Ski Party* (1965), *Fireball 500* (1966), and *Dr. Goldfoot and the Bikini Machine* (1965). By the late 1960s, however, the novelty of the films had worn off and their stars had grown too old to convincingly portray teens. Furthermore, audiences were demanding more realistic cinematic depictions of the young adult experience. In 1987, Avalon and Funicello starred in *Back to the Beach,* in which they mocked their wholesome images.

—*Charles Coletta*

For More Information

Arkoff, Sam. *Flying Through Hollywood By the Seat of My Pants*. New York: Birch Lane, 1992.

Edelstein, Andrew. *The Pop Sixties*. New York: Ballantine Books, 1985.

McGee, Mark Thomas. *Fast and Furious: The Story of American International Pictures*. Jefferson NC: McFarland, 1984.

Staehling, Richard. "The Truth About Teen Movies." In *Kings of the Bs*. New York: Dutton, 1975.

Dr. Strangelove

Dr. Strangelove, Or: How I Learned to Stop Worrying and Love the Bomb, directed by Stanley Kubrick (1928–1999), is widely regarded as a masterpiece of "black comedy" (a work that derives humor from a subject not usually considered humorous). For most people, nuclear war would probably top the list of unfunny subjects, but Kubrick demonstrated otherwise, earning the film three Oscar nominations in the process.

The 1964 film was based on a novel by Peter George (1924–1996) called *Red Alert* (1958). It is interesting to note that George's novel in turn inspired the 1962 novel *Fail-Safe* by Eugene Burdick (1918–1965) and Harvey Wheeler (1914–). *Fail-Safe* was a grimly realistic story about a computer failure that nearly causes a nuclear war. The film version of *Fail-Safe* was released in 1964, the same year as *Dr. Strangelove*.

In *Dr. Strangelove,* psychotic Air Force general Jack D. Ripper (Sterling Hayden, 1916–1986) orders the thirty-four nuclear bombers under his command to attack the Soviet Union. The air crews, thinking war has broken out, obey their orders without question. One of the bombers is commanded by Major T. J. "King" Kong (Slim Pickens, 1919–1983), who talks like an Oklahoma cowboy.

At the Pentagon's War Room, President Merkin Muffley (Peter Sellers, 1925–1980) is briefed on the emergency by the head of the Strategic Air Command, General Buck Turgidson (George C. Scott, 1927–1999). The Soviet ambassador is also present, and he warns the Americans that the Soviet Union has built a secret "Doomsday Machine." If the U.S.S.R. comes under nuclear attack, the machine will automatically trigger a set of explosions that will destroy the whole planet.

President Muffley frantically tries to recall the bombers, although he is advised against it by his nuclear strategy expert, Dr. Strangelove (also played by Peter Sellers). A wheelchair-bound ex-Nazi, Strangelove cold-bloodedly suggests that nuclear war might not be so bad, after all, with proper management.

The president is unable either to recall the bombers or to persuade the Soviets to stop their "Doomsday Machine." The American planes bomb their targets (one of the last scenes shows Major "King" Kong astride one of the bombs, riding it like a bronco all the way to eternity). The world thus ends, not with a whimper, but with a very big and darkly humorous bang.

—*Justin Gustainis*

For More Information

Carnes, Mark C., ed. *Past Imperfect.* New York: Henry Holt, 1995.

Dirks, Tim. "Dr. Strangelove, Or: How I Learned to Stop Worrying and Love the Bomb." *Greatest Films.* http://www.filmsite.org/drst.html (accessed March 14, 2002).

Larkin, Patrick J. "Dr. Strangelove, Or: How I Learned to Stop Worrying and Love the Bomb." *Kubrick Multimedia Film Guide.* http://www.indelibleinc.com/kubrick/films/strangelove/ (accessed March 14, 2002).

Seed, David. *American Science Fiction and the Cold War: Literature and Film.* Chicago: Fitzroy Dearborn, 1999.

Easy Rider

In the late 1960s, a good number of young Americans were becoming unhappy with American society. These **baby boomers** (see entry under 1940s—The Way We Lived in volume 3), whose parents had survived the **Great Depression** (1929–41; see entry under 1930s—The Way We Lived in volume 2) during the 1930s and World War II (1939–45) a decade later, viewed with disdain what they regarded as their parents' lack of concern with the way the world was shaping up. They were questioning their country's military presence in Vietnam (1954–75). They were experimenting with sex and drugs and had embraced the liberating sounds of **rock and roll** (see entry under 1950s—Music in volume 3) music. In this regard, America was in the middle of a cultural revolution, with the result being the creation of a youth-oriented "counterculture." Up until that time, moviemakers mostly had ignored that revolution—that is, until the release of *Easy Rider* (1969), a low-budget film that mirrored a generation's changing lifestyle and became an instant counterculture classic. However, *Easy Rider* was more than just a declaration of youthful alienation. Produced on a $400,000 budget, it earned $19 million in domestic box office and $40 million worldwide, hefty figures for the era.

Easy Rider is the saga of Wyatt (or "Captain America"), played by Dennis Hopper (1936–), and Billy, played by Peter Fonda (1939–), two motorcycle-riding, drug-taking dropouts who sell a load of **cocaine** (see entry under 1980s—The Way We Lived in volume 5) and set off on a journey from the California-Mexico border to New Orleans, Louisiana. They are accompanied by a soundtrack filled with rock classics of the era. The song most associated with the film is "Born to be Wild" by Steppenwolf. As they cycle cross-country, they find a nation that views them with hostility because of their long hair, nonconformist dress, and mode of transportation. Eventually, they are shot and killed by a pair of rednecks (short-haired, traditionalist Southern white males) riding in a pick-up truck.

Three talents emerged from the success of *Easy Rider*. Dennis Hopper, who also directed the film and coauthored its screenplay, had been acting on-screen since the mid-1950s. Always a rebel, his attitude toward traditional **Hollywood** (see entry under 1930s—Film and Theater in volume 2) filmmaking and filmmakers resulted in his being shunned by the moviemaking

establishment. Peter Fonda, who cowrote the script, is the son of Henry Fonda (1905–1982), a Hollywood legend whose career lasted from the 1930s through the 1980s. He is also the brother of actress Jane Fonda (1937–), who then was receiving attention as a high-profile activist against the Vietnam War. Before *Easy Rider*, Peter Fonda had acted with little impact in several films. He had begun establishing a rebel hero image in *The Wild Angels* (1966), playing a Hell's Angels motorcycle gang leader. Finally, Jack Nicholson (1937–), then a ten-year veteran of low-budget films, offered a star-making performance as a civil rights lawyer who joins Wyatt and Billy on their journey.

Nicholson's character, George Hanson (who also is killed by rednecks during the course of the story) expressed the film's counterculture-versus-mainstream point of view—and spoke to the youth of America—when he declared, "What you represent to them is freedom. . . . It's real hard to be free when you're bought and sold in the marketplace. . . . They're not free. . . . Then they're gonna get real busy killin' and maimin' to prove to you that they are."

—Rob Edelman

For More Information

Dalton, Stephen. "Endless Highway." *Uncut* (September 1998): pp. 30–35.

Dirks, Tim. "Easy Rider." *Greatest Films.* http://www.filmsite.org/easy. html (accessed March 14, 2002).

Easy Rider (film). Columbia Pictures, 1969.

Hardin, Nancy, and Marilyn Schlossberg. *Easy Rider: Original Screenplay by Peter Fonda, Dennis Hopper, and Terry Southern, Plus Stills, Interviews, and Articles.* New York: Signet, 1969.

The Graduate

The late 1960s were a time of radical change in the United States. Young people—and, in particular, **baby boomers** (see entry under 1940s–The Way We Lived in volume 3), who were the middle-class offspring of the veterans of World War II (1939–45), and who had grown up amid the prosperity and conformity of the 1950s—were questioning the preordained paths their lives were supposed to take. It was assumed that males would complete college, find high-paying jobs, marry, and live in the **suburbs** (see entry under 1950s–The Way We Lived in volume 3) while commuting to work and supporting their wives and children. The very nature of their manhood depended on their being "good providers" for their families. Meanwhile, their wives would remain at home raising their offspring. For a woman, a career—and financial independence—would be out of the question. In order to fit into the American mainstream, young people had to accept these expected roles: the very same roles played by their parents. In this regard, these coming-of-age baby boomers had no options.

The Graduate (1967), directed by Mike Nichols (1931–), is the perfect cultural artifact of its time in that it is a movie about options and is one of the milestones of late-1960s American cinema. It also mirrors the feelings of alienation (separation from society) that characterized the era. Many baby boomers felt dissatisfied as a result of the Vietnam War (1954–75) and the real and perceived insincerities of American society. Finally, the fate of its title character remains refreshingly unclear, a fact that reflects the reality that life is complex and happy endings are never guaranteed.

The Graduate is the story of Benjamin Braddock, a young man who is lacking direction and self-esteem. Benjamin, played by Dustin Hoffman (1937–) in a star-making performance, has

just completed college and has returned to his suburban California roots. His future already seems ordained by his elders. It is assumed that Ben will marry the perfect girl and become yet another faceless, soulless suburbanite and corporate paper-pusher. The hypocrisy of his elders is symbolized by the character of Mrs. Robinson (Anne Bancroft, 1931–), the middle-aged mother of Elaine (Katharine Ross, 1942–), a pretty college student in whom Benjamin eventually becomes romantically interested. However, instead of encouraging this otherwise healthy relationship, Mrs. Robinson seduces young Benjamin.

At his core, Benjamin Braddock is no stereotypical 1960s radical. His hair is short, and he is no rabble-rousing drug abuser or draft dodger or war protester. The soundtrack music accompanying his story is the gentle sounds of **Simon and Garfunkel** (see entry under 1960s–Music in volume 4), rather than the harsher, more aggressive sounds of the **Rolling Stones** (see entry under 1960s–Music in volume 4) or the Doors. All Benjamin wants is the space to determine the future course of his life. Yet the pretensions of his elders will not allow him this opportunity.

Dustin Hoffman and Anne Bancroft, in a famous scene from *The Graduate*. *The Kobal Collection. Reproduced by permission.*

As his story concludes, and he evolves to the point where he chooses to ignore his elders and rescue Elaine as she is about to marry a man she does not love, Ben Braddock is striking a blow for independence, individuality, and self-determination.

Back in 1967, his actions had baby boomers cheering and nodding in recognition. Yet while the ending of *The Graduate* may be triumphant, it is in no way happy. How well do Benjamin and Elaine really know one another? Altogether appropriately, the smiles fade from their faces—and it is clear that their future together is in no way assured.

—*Rob Edelman*

For More Information

Macklin, F. Anthony. "'Benjamin Will Survive . . . ': Interview with Charles Webb." *Film Heritage* (Vol. 4, 1968): pp. 1–6.
Webb, Charles. *The Graduate.* New York: New American Library, 1963.

Hair

Hair was a landmark **Broadway** (see entry under 1900s—Film and Theater in volume 1) musical in the late 1960s. It was groundbreaking on several accounts. *Hair* not only portrayed the era's youth culture but also gloriously celebrated it. Its characters were way outside the mainstream of American society: They were **hippies** (see entry under 1960s—The Way We Lived in volume 4) who used drugs and shocking language. *Hair* relied on experimental theater techniques that focused on the themes of the musical and the portrayal of a lifestyle, rather than on character and plot development. *Hair* earned the distinction of being the first-ever rock musical. The cast members ignored the "fourth wall" of the theater—the invisible wall that separates actors and audience—by coming on stage from the audience, rather than from backstage. Finally, at the finale of the first act, during the celebrated "Be-In" sequence, the actors removed their clothes.

Hair was the creation of Broadway performers Gerome Ragni (1935–1991) and James Rado (1932–), who in the mid-1960s believed that the music, styles, and viewpoints of the then-developing youth culture might be translated to the stage. To research the project, they conducted interviews with young people who had embraced the **civil rights movement** (see entry

A 1968 stage production of *Hair*.
AP/Wide World Photos.
Reproduced by permission.

under 1960s—The Way We Lived in volume 4) and the anti-Vietnam War (1954–75) sentiments and who were experimenting with drugs and sex. Next, they collaborated with composer Galt MacDermot (1928–), resulting in the creation of an agreeably bouncy score that highlighted the antics of the show's characters. Among them: Claude, who has just been drafted into the military; his drop-out pal Berger; and Sheila, a college student and antiwar activist.

Joseph Papp (1921–1991), the legendary organizer of the New York Shakespeare Festival, produced the show, which opened off-Broadway at the Public Theatre on October 29, 1967. The full title was *Hair: An American Tribal Rock Musical*. It eventually moved to Cheetah, a popular Greenwich Village discotheque. At this point, its director was Gerald Freedman (1927–). After being completely revamped and redesigned by a new director, Tom O'Horgan (1926–), and others—additional songs were added and the concept (idea of the play itself) almost completely replaced the narrative (story to be told). This version of *Hair* opened on Broadway at the Biltmore Theatre on April 19, 1968.

Many establishment critics neither liked nor understood *Hair* and dismissed the show as vulgar trash. Other, more open-minded reviewers hailed it for its freshness and honesty. *Hair* may have lost the Best Musical Tony Award to *1776,* a more traditionally structured musical, but it was wildly popular and remained on Broadway until 1972. Productions were mounted across the country and, soon, throughout the world. At its height, fourteen national companies performed the musical. Eleven cast albums were recorded, in different languages. During its first two years alone, approximately four million people saw *Hair* on stage.

By the time *Hair* was revived on Broadway (in 1978), and made into a film (in 1979), American society had drastically changed, and the show seemed dated. Today *Hair* is a period piece, a product of the time in which it emerged. It nonetheless remains a show that altered the look and sound—and expanded the possibilities—of the Broadway musical.

—*Rob Edelman*

For More Information

Davis, Lorrie, and Rachel Gallagher. *Letting Down My Hair.* New York: Arthur Fields, 1973.

Hair (film). United Artists, 1979.

Horn, Barbara Lee. *The Age of Hair: Evolution and Impact of Broadway's First Rock Musical.* New York: Greenwood Press, 1991.

A Hard Day's Night

In 1963, "Beatlemania" was sweeping the world. The **Beatles** (see entry under 1960s—Music in volume 4), a Liverpool, England, rock-pop group whose members were John Lennon (1940–1980), Paul McCartney (1942–), George Harrison (1943–2001), and Ringo Starr (1940–), were capturing the souls and hearts of young people worldwide. *A Hard Day's Night* (1964) is a comic film depicting a representative day in the lives of the early Beatles.

Unlike dozens of other films built around popular rock performers, *A Hard Day's Night* was a highly entertaining musical comedy that deftly used the personalities of each Beatle while incorporating dazzling, free-flowing visuals. Director Richard Lester (1932–) employed fast-motion and slow-motion and other cinematic trickery to keep the film moving and to present the "Fab Four" as likable, loony, and "hip."

Before breaking up in 1970, the Beatles collaborated on several other films: *Help!* (1965), a follow-up to *A Hard Day's Night*; *Yellow Submarine* (1968), an animated feature; and *Let It Be* (1970), a documentary. While each is entertaining, none captures the Beatles in their early-career freshness as memorably as *A Hard Day's Night*.

—Rob Edelman

For More Information

Ebert, Roger. "A Hard Day's Night" *Chicago Sun Times*. http://www.suntimes.com/ebert/greatmovies/hard_day_night.html (accessed March 15, 2002)

A Hard Day's Night (film). United Artists, 1964.

Zacharek, Stephanie. "A Hard Day's Night." *Salon.com*. http://www.salon.com/ent/movies/review/2000/12/01/hard_days_night/ (accessed March 15, 2002).

Horror Movies

The subjects and settings for horror movies are as limitless as one's nightmares. Some films use the classic horror settings of ruined castles, graveyards, and haunted houses. Others find terror in quiet suburban streets. Sometimes innocent children can be as frightening as zombies, and everyday objects can be possessed by evil spirits. To scare people, horror films can use graphic violence, screaming, and bucketloads of blood and gore, or they can hint at what lurks in the shadows. From the early days of cinema, horror movies have terrified, shocked, and entertained. Their changing styles have matched the worries and fears of successive generations of moviegoers.

Horror movies began by adapting popular novels by writers such as Mary Shelley (1797–1851), Bram Stoker (1847–1912), and others. It was only natural for the new film industry to cash in on the success of novels like **Frankenstein** (1819) and **Dracula** (1897; see entries on these two entries under 1930s–Film and Theater in volume 2). Early silent horror movies came from a tradition of German "expressionist" cinema, a style that aimed to capture human emotion "in the raw." Films such as *The Cabinet of Dr. Caligari* (1919) by Robert Wiene (1880–1938) and

Jason, the hockey-mask-wearing killer from the *Friday the 13th* horror film series. *Archive Photos. Reproduced by permission.*

Nosferatu (1922) by F. W. Murnau (1888–1931) certainly succeeded in speaking directly to their audiences' sense of the monstrous and grotesque. In one famous scene in *Nosferatu,* Dracula enters the bedroom of a defenseless sleeping woman. We see only the shadow of his bony hand creep across the bed. When it reaches the spot over her heart, the shadow-hand clenches into a fist, taking her to join the undead. The twisted Count Dracula in *Nosferatu* as portrayed by Max Schreck (1879–1936) remains one of the most haunting vampire performances ever.

In the years that followed, Universal Pictures began making horror movies after the German style. From the mid-1920s, Universal made a series of films that have become classics of the horror genre (type). *Dracula* and *Frankenstein,* both released in 1931, made stars of their leading actors Bela Lugosi (1882–1956) and Boris Karloff (1887–1969), respectively. The face of Karloff as Frankenstein's monster has become so famous that it often represents the face of the actual monster in newspapers and magazines. These films inspired many imitators and sequels, including those made by Hammer Films in the United Kingdom. Beginning with *The Curse of Frankenstein* in 1957, the Hammer horror movies were far more sexy and violent than their predecessors. They helped trigger a revival of the genre in the late 1950s.

Psycho (see entry under 1960s—Film and Theater in volume 4), by Alfred Hitchcock (1899–1980), began a new trend toward psychological thrills in 1960. With its "haunted house" standing in the background of the Bates Motel, this masterpiece of horror by the celebrated Hitchcock highlights the point that real horror lies not in spooks and ghouls but in disturbed minds, such as that of the film's leading male character, Norman Bates. Many horror movies of the following twenty years made a similar point. During the 1970s, however, the focus of mainstream films shifted away from well-drawn mental turmoil and more towards slashing violence. The suggestive titles of *Texas Chainsaw Massacre* (1974) and *Driller Killer* (1979) are typical of so-called splatter movies. Many such films have been blamed for inspiring copycat real-life killings and have been banned or heavily censored. Of course these restrictions have made the films even more popular.

The 1970s also saw "demonic child" films become popular, notably **The Exorcist** (1973; see entry under 1970s–Film and Theater in volume 4) and *The Omen* (1976). These films responded to real parental fears about sick or difficult children, though, certainly, few parents faced such extreme examples. By the end of the 1980s, popular series such as *Halloween* and *Friday the 13th* had run to several sequels and there was little appetite at the time for further episodes. By making Hannibal Lecter a representative of the battle between good and evil, *The Silence of the Lambs* (1990) merged the suspense thriller with the horror movie. Its sequel, *Hannibal* (2001), failed to capture the imagination in quite the same way, but movies like *Seven* (1995) and *Kiss the Girls* (1997) are part of a trend that dominated the 1990s.

Since the 1930s, horror movies have changed and developed with public tastes. By the 1980s and 1990s, they ranged from traditional supernatural horror movies, such as *A Nightmare on Elm Street* (1984), directed by Wes Craven (1939–), to films that seem to parody the horror movie while being scary at the same time. In 2000, *Scary Movie* took this even further by parodying **Scream** (1996; see entry under 1990s–Film and Theater in volume 5), a film that was itself a parody of sorts.

Horror movies speak to one's darkest fears. At their best, in films like *Frankenstein* and *Psycho,* horror movies help define their age. The twentieth century closed amid fears of computer failures and meteorite storms, eclipsing the domestic terrors of the horror movie. But like any good monster, the horror movie is certain to return just when we least expect it.

—Chris Routledge

For More Information

Aylesworth, Thomas G. *Movie Monsters.* Philadelphia: Lippincott, 1975.

Cohen, Daniel. *Masters of Horror.* New York: Clarion Books, 1984.

Hardy, Phil, Tom Milne, and Paul Willemen, eds. *The Encyclopedia of Horror Movies.* London: Harper Collins, 1995.

Jancovich, Mark. *Horror.* London: B. T. Batsford, 1992.

Manchel, Frank. *An Album of Modern Horror Films.* New York: F. Watts, 1983.

McCarty, John. *Movie Psychos and Madmen: Ninety Years of Mad Movies, Maniacs and Murderous Deeds.* Minneapolis: Carol Publishing Group, 1993.

Powers, Tom. *Movie Monsters.* Minneapolis: Lerner Publications, 1989.

James Bond Films

Ian Fleming's creation, secret agent James Bond, was not an overnight success. Although the novels made money for author Fleming (1908–1964) and his publisher, they were not **best-sellers** (see entry under 1940s–Commerce in volume 3) at first. Nine years elapsed between the first Bond novel, *Casino Royale* (1953), and the first movie in the series, *Dr. No* (1962). The film did well enough so that its producers, Harry Saltzman (1915–1994) and Albert Broccoli (1909–1996), decided on a sequel. The release of *From Russia with Love* in 1963 was given a big boost in the United States by the news that Fleming's novel was one of the favorite books of President John F. Kennedy (1917–1963). The third film, *Goldfinger* (1964), was a financial blockbuster. The "James Bond craze" was under way.

James Bond—Agent 007—was played in the first five films by little-known Scottish actor Sean Connery (1930–), who followed *Goldfinger* with *Thunderball* (1965) and *You Only Live Twice* (1967). By then, the conventions of the Bond film had been well established: exotic locations, eye-popping special effects, incredible spy gadgets supplied by "Q" Branch, ironic one-liners delivered by the hero, and beautiful "Bond girls," wearing just enough clothing to avoid an "R" rating. During the 1960s, Bond's popularity led to a host of imitators, both in film (superspies Derek Flint and Matt Helm) and on television, with shows like *I Spy, Secret Agent,* and *The Man From U.N.C.L.E.* The Bond movies also inspired a big-budget spoof, *Casino Royale,* in 1967.

Connery left the role and was replaced in *On Her Majesty's Secret Service* (1969) by George Lazenby (1939–), an Australian-born model with no acting experience, who only lasted for one year. After Connery's one-film return in *Diamonds Are Forever* (1971), Roger Moore (1927–) took over the role with *Live and Let Die* (1973). He brought a lighter touch to the Bond role in this film as well as in *The Man with the Golden Gun*

Sean Connery and Honor Blackman in a scene from the 1964 James Bond movie *Goldfinger*. *John Springer Collection/Corbis Corporation. Reproduced by permission.*

(1974), *The Spy Who Loved Me* (1977), *Moonraker* (1979), *For Your Eyes Only* (1981), and *Octopussy* (1983). In *The Living Daylights* (1987) and *License To Kill* (1989), Timothy Dalton (1946–) played Bond as the deadly serious professional assassin that Fleming had originally created. Dalton's approach did not appeal to fans, and he was soon replaced by Pierce Brosnan (1953–). Brosnan combined Moore's charm with Connery's ruthlessness in *Goldeneye* (1995), *Tomorrow Never Dies* (1997), and *The World Is Not Enough* (1999). The most successful series in motion-picture history, the James Bond films continue to find new approaches to the same formula that first drew audiences in the 1960s.

—*Justin Gustainis*

For More Information

Barnes, Alan. *Kiss Kiss Bang! Bang!: The Unofficial James Bond Film Companion.* Woodstock, NY: Overlook Press, 1998.

Krofchok, Bryan. *Bondian.com: A Field Guide to the Phenomenon Created by British Author Ian Fleming.* http://www.bondian.com (accessed March 14, 2002).

Dick Van Dyke and Julie Andrews (top) and Karen Dotrice and Matthew Garber (bottom) in a scene from *Mary Poppins*. *The Kobal Collection. Reproduced by permission.*

Pfeiffer, Lee, and Dave Worrall. *The Essential Bond: The Authorized Guide to the World of 007*. New York: Harper Entertainment, 1999.

Rubin, Steven Jay. *The Complete James Bond Movie Encyclopedia*. Chicago: Contemporary Books, 1990.

Rubin, Steven Jay. *The James Bond Films: A Behind the Scenes History*. Westport, CT: Arlington House, 1981.

Mary Poppins

Mary Poppins is a magical governess who, in her original incarnation, has an incalculable effect on the four Banks children—Jane, Michael, and twins John and Barbara—in early twentieth-century London. She started out as the central character in a series of books penned by Australian-born writer P. L. (Pamela Lyndon) Travers (1899–1996). The first was titled *Mary Poppins* (1934). Travers's Mary may be strict and egotistical, but she is no ordinary nanny. Among her talents are sliding *up* banisters and communicating with animals—and herein lies her charm.

Travers's character gained her most everlasting popularity in a delightful feature film, co-produced by Walt Disney (1901–1966) and released by his studio. The film deftly blends music and comedy, live action and animation. This *Mary Poppins* (1964) features only two children, Jane and Michael, who are the offspring of London banker Banks and his suffragette wife. The film earned Academy Awards for its score, the song "Chim-Chim-Cheree," its visual effects and editing, and Best Actress for Julie Andrews (1935–), making her screen debut. The screen Mary, as played by Andrews, is unlike the original. While no less magical, she is endlessly cheery, as sweet as cotton candy, and "practically perfect," as the title character would say.

—*Rob Edelman*

For More Information

Demers, Patricia. *P. L. Travers*. Boston: Twayne Publishers, 1991.

Draper, Ellen Dooling, and Jenny Koralek, ed. *A Lively Oracle: A Centennial Celebration of P. L. Travers, Creator of Mary Poppins*. Burdett, NY: Larson Publishers, 1999.

Lawson, Valerie. *Out of the Sky She Came: The Life of P. L. Travers, Creator of Mary Poppins.* Sydney: Belladonna Books, 1999.
Mary Poppins (film). Walt Disney Productions, 1964.

The Odd Couple

Since the 1960s, Neil Simon (1927–) has been, at least from a commercial point of view, the undisputed king of American playwrights. Of all the hits he has penned, *The Odd Couple* is arguably his most celebrated and most often performed. At its core, it is a comedy about a pair of divorced roommates who are complete opposites in their habits and lifestyles. Oscar Madison is a New York sportswriter who revels in his slobbishness. He adores gulping down junk food. To him, a ketchup stain on a white shirt is a mark of distinction. Oscar resides in an eight-room Riverside Drive apartment, where the entire play is set, and his life is in upheaval because his friend Felix Unger has entered his realm. Felix is a neat-freak photographer who is obsessed with cooking gourmet meals, purifying the air, and removing every speck of dust from Oscar's domain. To Felix, "ring around the collar" (dirt on the inside of a shirt collar) is a catastrophe. Even though in personality Oscar and Felix are like oil and water, and even though they drive each other crazy, they do care about each other. Their friendship persists despite their differences.

The Odd Couple opened on **Broadway** (see entry under 1900s–Film and Theater in volume 1) on March 10, 1965, and quickly became a smash hit. Walter Matthau (1920–2000), long a respected Broadway actor and supporting player on screen, won major stardom and a Tony Award playing Oscar. No less impressive was Art Carney (1918–) as Felix. Until then, Carney was best known for playing thick-brained sewer worker Ed Norton on television's **The Honeymooners** (1955–56, 1971; see entry under 1950s–TV and Radio in volume 3).

Since its Broadway debut, *The Odd Couple* has been endlessly recycled. First it became a hit movie (released in 1968), with Matthau replaying Oscar and Jack Lemmon (1925–2001) cast as Felix. Then *The Odd Couple* was a TV **sitcom** (see entry under 1950s–TV and Radio in volume 3), with Tony Randall (1920–) and Jack Klugman (1922–) playing Felix and Oscar from 1970 to 1975. The two recreated the roles in *The Odd Couple: Together Again* (1993), a made-for-TV movie. *The Oddball Couple*

(1975–77), an ABC-TV cartoon, centered on Fleabag, a slobbish dog, and Spiffy, a clean cat. *The New Odd Couple* (1982–83), a brief TV sitcom, featured an African American Oscar and Felix. Also in the 1980s, Simon revised the play by rewriting the characters as women and renaming them Olive Madison and Florence Unger. Three decades after playing them onscreen, Matthau and Lemmon revived Oscar and Felix on screen in *The Odd Couple II* (1998), written by Simon.

Most impressive of all, however, is the durability of *The Odd Couple* as a stage play. For decades, it has been revived on stages across the world, from community theaters in small towns across America to high-profile productions in the world's largest cities.

Finally, the term "odd couple" has entered the English language to describe any unlikely pair of total opposites who have become linked in one way or another.

—*Rob Edelman*

For More Information

The Odd Couple (film). Paramount Pictures, 1968.
Simon, Neil. *The Comedy of Neil Simon.* New York: Random House, 1971.
Simon, Neil. *Rewrites.* New York: Simon & Schuster, 1996.

Planet of the Apes

The 1968 science fiction film *Planet of the Apes* portrayed a world turned upside down, in which apes are the masters and humans are treated like animals. The movie's exceptional make-up effects and memorable performances made it a box-office smash that inspired numerous sequels and spin-offs, including a 2001 remake.

Based on a novel by French author Pierre Boulle (1912–1994), *Planet of the Apes* starred Charlton Heston (1924–) as George Taylor, the leader of a crew of futuristic astronauts. When their ship crash-lands on a planet in the distant future, Taylor is captured by talking apes, imprisoned, and threatened with medical experimentation. With the help of some sympathetic chimps, he escapes the clutches of the evil Dr. Zaius and takes off into the desert "Forbidden Zone," where he learns that he is not on an alien world at all, but merely on the Earth of the future!

Charlton Heston as astronaut George Taylor in 1968's *Planet of the Apes*. *The Kobal Collection. Reproduced by permission.*

Directed by Franklin Schaffner (1920–1989), *Planet of the Apes* was one of the first big-budget science-fiction epics of the 1960s. The film made over $25 million and earned mostly favorable reviews. Its lifelike ape makeup and shocking ending helped it win the hearts of moviegoers looking for escapist sci-fi fare. But the movie also had deeper messages about the dangers of nuclear war, racial intolerance, and even the humane treatment of animals. As Taylor, Heston gave one of his most unforgettable performances, grunting and scowling his way through a series of indignities put upon him by his ape captors.

Roddy McDowall (1928–1998), as the chimp scientist Cornelius, and Kim Hunter (c. 1922–) as Dr. Zira, were also quite effective.

Planet of the Apes spawned four feature-film sequels over the next five years. In 1974, it was adapted for **television** (see entry under 1940s—TV and Radio in volume 3), as a live-action series starring McDowall, and again that same year as a **Saturday-morning cartoon** (see entry under 1960s—TV and Radio in volume 4) series. The 1970s saw an explosion of *Apes* merchandise, everything from lunch boxes to action figures. The *Apes* movies remained so popular when they were re-run on TV that 20th Century Fox announced plans for a big-screen remake, directed by Tim Burton (1958–) and released in the summer of 2001. The remake, most critics agreed, did not compare with the original except in the excellence of the special effects.

—*Robert E. Schnakenberg*

For More Information

Ape City. http://www.ape-city.com/index.html (accessed March 15, 2002).

Boulle, Pierre. *Planet of the Apes.* New York: Random House, 1963; Ballantine, 2001.

Greene, Eric. *Planet of the Apes as American Myth: Race and Politics in the Films and Television Series.* Jefferson, NC: McFarland & Company, 1996.

Heston, Charlton. *In the Arena.* New York: Boulevard Books, 1997.

Hofstede, David. *Planet of the Apes: An Unofficial Companion.* Toronto: ECW Press, 2001.

Psycho

Psycho (1960) is one of the most famous films of all time and quite possibly the most influential **horror movie** (see entry under 1960s—Film and Theater in volume 4) in history. Directed by Alfred Hitchcock (1899–1980), *Psycho* (1960) made "Norman Bates" a household name. The movie traded the vampires, zombies, and mummies of the horror film's past for an all-too-human monster. *Psycho* also secured for its director the flattering title of "The Master of Suspense."

The screenplay for *Psycho* was adapted by Joseph Stefano (1922–) from a novel by Robert Bloch (1917–1994), who had based the character of Norman on real-life Wisconsin serial killer Ed Gein (1906–1984). *Psycho* tells the story of Marion

Crane, an attractive woman who steals some money from her job and leaves town. She stops at a roadside motel, where the manager is a nice but awkward young man named Norman. In a shocking twist that had audiences literally screaming in the aisles, Marion is brutally murdered while taking a shower that evening by what looks like an old woman with a foot-long carving knife. Never before had the central character of a commercial film been killed off less than halfway through the picture! After a private investigator assigned to the case gets killed as well, Marion's sister and boyfriend track her to the Bates Motel. They discover to their horror that the killer is actually Norman, a textbook sufferer of multiple-personality disorder who dresses up just like his dead mother whenever sexual or threatening feelings arise in him. Although a police-employed psychologist "explains" the cause of Norman's illness at film's end, there is little doubt that whatever motivates him lies outside the bounds of anything rational minds can understand.

The character of Marion Crane was played by Janet Leigh (1927–), the mother of Jamie Lee Curtis (1958–), who followed in her mother's footsteps and starred in the 1987 horror film *Halloween*. Leigh's shrieking shower scene went down in history as one of the scariest—and most memorable—moments on film. Anthony Perkins (1932–1992) portrayed the demented Norman Bates.

When *Psycho* first opened, it received mostly lukewarm reviews from critics. Public reaction to the film was staggering, however, with people lining up around the block for tickets. Clearly, Hitchcock had found a way to tap into America's collective psyche: by making the monster so very normal, and by joining together sex, madness, and murder, he effectively predicted the headlines of many of the coming decades' top news stories.

—Steven Schneider

For More Information

"Alfred Hitchcock's *Psycho*." *House of Horrors*. http://www.houseofhorrors.com/psycho.htm (accessed March 15, 2002).

Arginteanu, Judy. *The Movies of Alfred Hitchcock*. Minneapolis: Lerner Publications, 1994.

Leigh, Janet, with Christopher Nickens. *Psycho: Behind the Scenes of the Classic Thriller*. New York: Harmony Books, 1995.

Rebello, Stephen. *Alfred Hitchcock and the Making of Psycho*. New York: Dembner Books, 1990.

2001: A Space Odyssey

Directed by Stanley Kubrick (1928–2000), the film *2001: A Space Odyssey* was hailed as an artistic masterpiece when it opened in 1968. Based on a 1951 short story by British science-fiction writer Arthur C. Clarke (1917–), the beautifully photographed film took audiences on a wondrous journey through outer space. It also introduced one of Hollywood's most coldly menacing screen villains, the murderous supercomputer HAL 9000.

In a way, *2001* is the complete story of mankind. It begins in prehistoric times, among our ape ancestors, and ends with explorations into outer space. Tying the various parts of the story together is a strange object, a large black slab, which keeps appearing throughout space and time. Some have suggested that this object represents God, or some kind of alien civilization. The filmmakers deliberately left its true meaning unclear. The mystery of this object generated much discussion among moviegoers when *2001* first appeared, and continues to do so many years later.

The bulk of *2001* takes place onboard a spaceship, *Discovery,* carrying astronauts Dave Bowman and Frank Poole (played by Keir Dullea, 1936–, and Gary Lockwood, 1937–, respectively). Sent to investigate the appearance of the mysterious black slab on the moon, the spacemen are initially opposed in their efforts by their onboard computer, HAL. Possessed of artificial intelligence and also, apparently, feelings, HAL attempts to destroy the ship and its crew before it can complete its mission. In the end, one of the astronauts defeats HAL and reaches the moon. There he finds a strange life force awaiting him and undergoes a bizarre transformation.

One of the first big-budget special-effects movies, *2001* is filled with moments of great beauty and technical wizardry. Director Kubrick used the classical music of Richard (REE-kart) Strauss (1864–1949), for example, in one memorable scene that depicts the astronauts "dancing" in space. Also, the notion of man-made machines with artificial intelligence was years ahead of its time in 1968. Although mankind in the *real* 2001 may not have achieved the scientific leaps portrayed in the film, *2001: A Space Odyssey*'s lessons about the dangers of technology and the search for meaning in the universe remain timely today.

—Robert E. Schnakenberg

Scene from the Stanley Kubrick
classic *2001: A Space Odyssey.*
The Kobal Collection.
Reproduced by permission.

For More Information

Bizony, Piers, and Arthur C. Clarke. *Filming the Future.* London: Aurem
Press, 2000.

Pringle, David, ed. *The Ultimate Encyclopedia of Science Fiction.* London:
Carlton, 1996.

Staskowski, Andrea. *Science Fiction Movies.* Minneapolis: Lerner Publications, 1992.

Schwam, Stephanie, and Martin Scorcese, eds. *The Making of 2001: A
Space Odyssey.* New York: Modern Library, 2000.

2001: A Space Odyssey Internet Resource Archive. http://www.palantir.
net/2001 (accessed on March 15, 2002).

1960s

Music

The 1960s saw a real flowering of popular music styles. Unlike the 1950s, in which the birth of rock and roll dominated the decade, jazz, pop, and folk music all gathered devoted listeners in the 1960s. Rock and roll continued to grow as a musical form, with a clear split between "hard," rebellious rock and lighter, "soft" rock—which sounded a lot like pop music.

Folk music was reborn in the 1960s thanks to several young performers who wanted to rescue the musical form from what they saw as its sad decline. Bob Dylan (1941–), Joan Baez (1941–), and the group Peter, Paul, and Mary adopted folk styles—simple musical arrangements played on acoustic instruments—but filled them with political commentary on contemporary issues. Their songs addressed the problems of the civil rights movement of the 1950s and 1960s and the Vietnam War (1954–75) and helped them gain huge audiences. As the decade wore on, folk merged into folk-rock as performers increasingly used electrified instruments and more sophisticated songwriting. Dylan and the group Simon and Garfunkel led the way in folk rock.

Rock and roll music in the 1960s was dominated by one group: the Beatles. Launched in Liverpool, England, this four-man group first appeared in the United States in 1964 on *The Ed Sullivan Show*. The popularity of the Beatles remained strong throughout the decade. Other British groups followed the Beatles, creating what became known as the British Invasion. The Rolling Stones, the Animals, and the Who all soon had hits in the United States. In a strange twist, an American TV production company known as Screen Gems decided to copy the success of the Beatles by inventing a band of its own modeled on the boys from Liverpool. The Monkees consisted of four handsome actors, three of whom did not even know how to play their instruments. This did not keep them from having several number-one singles—with the music played by others.

Rock music soon split into several streams. Some bands produced lighter music with pleasing lyrics to sell to pop radio stations. Other bands pursued rock music as a form of protest or a form of artistic exploration. This more mature rock music used sophisticated recording techniques and exotic instruments. Two former soft rock bands led the way: the Beach Boys with *Pet Sounds* (1966) and the Beatles with *Sgt. Pepper's Lonely Hearts Club Band* (1967). Other bands—notably those from San Francisco, California—pushed rock to have an even harder edge. The Grateful Dead, Jefferson Airplane, and Janis Joplin (1943–1970) helped create a form known as psychedelic rock. Jimi Hendrix (1942–1970) and others experimented with sounds known as acid rock. In addition, two music festivals revealed the highs and lows of the rock and roll subculture: Woodstock (1969) and Altamont (1969).

Some of the most popular music of the decade originated from Motown Records in Detroit, Michigan. Merging gospel, jazz, rhythm and blues (R&B), and rock and roll, Motown founder Berry Gordy Jr. (1929–) and his team of songwriters created the bands that had some of the biggest hits of the decade. Diana Ross (1944–) and the Supremes, Smokey Robinson (1940–) and the Miracles, the Temptations, the Four Tops, Marvin Gaye (1939–1984), and Stevie Wonder (1950–) all got their start at Motown.

Altamont

Altamont was a large outdoor concert held on December 6, 1969, at the Altamont Speedway near Livermore, California. There were numerous large concerts in the latter years of the 1960s, including the famous **Woodstock** (see entry under 1960s—Music in volume 4) concert (1969) in New York state, but Altamont was different. The show was organized by English rock group the **Rolling Stones** (see entry under 1960s—Music in volume 4) as the final concert of their 1969 concert tour. Although it was meant as a thank-you gift to their fans, the concert was a disaster, resulting in violence and murder. To many people, Altamont represents the symbolic end of the 1960s.

Problems began almost as soon as the concert was announced. Changes in the concert site and the problems of providing food, water, and restrooms for more than three hundred thousand people left the organizers ill-prepared for the large crowd. The organizers also tried to save money by employing the Hell's Angels Motorcycle Club to act as security guards.

Members of the Hell's Angels Motorcycle Club worked security at Altamont, but ended up provoking violence by beating concert-goers. *William L. Rukeyser/Archive Photos. Reproduced by permission.*

They were to be paid with $500 worth of beer. This club was known for loud motorcycles, a distinctive dress style of leather boots and jackets, facial hair, and rebellious and often illegal behavior. As the show began with groups such as Santana, Jefferson Airplane, and Crosby, Stills, Nash, and Young, the Hell's Angels began to beat people in the crowd who wandered too close to the stage. These fights got seriously out of hand when the Rolling Stones were on stage. The Hell's Angels stabbed and kicked to death a young African American man named Meredith Hunter (1951–1969) not far from the stage. Although the Rolling Stones were unaware of the murder when it happened, the escalating violence forced them to end their show abruptly.

To many people, the show demonstrated that the counter-culture of **hippies** (see entry under 1960s–The Way We Lived in volume 4) and other freedom-loving young people, with their interest in spreading love and peace during the 1960s, also had its dark side. Altamont signaled to many that the era of peace and love associated with the 1960s was over.

—*Timothy Berg*

For More Information

Booth, Stanley. *The True Adventures of the Rolling Stones*. New York: Vintage Books, 1985.

Eisner, Jonathan. *Altamont*. New York: Avon Books, 1970.

Hotchner, A. E. *Blown Away: The Rolling Stones and the Death of the 1960s*. New York: Simon & Schuster, 1990.

Maysles, David, and Albert Maysles. *Gimme Shelter*. New York: ABCO Pictures, 1970.

Smith, R. J. "Altamont at 20." *The Village Voice* (November 28, 1989): p. 73.

Beach Boys

No other musical group has ever captured the sound of fun in the sun, good times, and growing up like the Beach Boys did. They helped define the California beach music sound. They provided a soundtrack for the 1960s because their music spoke to teenagers going through the difficult transition to adulthood. Throughout the 1960s and beyond, the Beach Boys expressed the desires, dreams, and hopes of many young people in the United States.

The Beach Boys began with the Wilson brothers forming the nucleus of the group: Brian (1942–) writing songs and playing bass, Carl (1946–1998) on guitar, and Dennis (1944–1983) on drums. They were joined by friend Al Jardine (1942–) on guitar and cousin Mike Love (1941–) on vocals in 1961. As the band got going, instrumental surf music was emerging as a popular musical style in southern California. The Beach Boys took that guitar sound and added lush vocal harmonies and lyrics about teenage life to make their own unique style. Capitol Records signed them to a contract in 1962. They produced hit after hit for the next four years. Such songs as "Surfin' U.S.A.," "Little Surfer Girl," and "Catch a Wave" captured the fun of being at the beach. Songs like "Little Deuce Coupe" and "409" celebrated teenagers' love of cars. "Good Vibrations" and "California Girls" defined the good times and warmth of Southern California in the 1960s.

As their sound matured, the Beach Boys also captured the pain of growing up. "In My Room" and "Don't Worry Baby" expressed the uncertainty of young love. In 1966, the Beach Boys released *Pet Sounds,* considered by many to be a pop masterpiece. Largely the work of group leader Brian Wilson, *Pet Sounds* was a lush and complex album with a distinct musical

The Beach Boys: (clockwise, from upper left) Mike Love, Brian Wilson, Carl Wilson, Dennis Wilson, and Al Jardine. *AP/Wide World Photos. Reproduced by permission.*

sound that expressed the longing to both become an adult but also to hang on to the innocence of youth. Although it did not sell as well as their earlier records, it was an innovative and influential record. The Beach Boys would have only a few other hits after 1966, but the Wilson-less band (Brian suffered through health problems and Dennis and Carl died) continue on as a touring group, playing their surfing hits for new generations of fans well into the 1990s. Although their music defined a time and a place (southern California in the early 1960s), their sound remains timeless, an important part of American musical history.

—*Timothy Berg*

For More Information

The Beach Boys: Good Vibrations: Thirty Years of The Beach Boys. Capitol Records, 1993.

Brian Wilson Official Web Site. http://www.brianwilson.com/ (accessed March 15, 2002).

Gaines, Steven S. *Heroes and Villains: The True Story of the Beach Boys.* New York: New American Library, 1986.

Sanford, William R., and Carl Green. *The Beach Boys.* Mankato, MN: Crestwood House, 1986.

White, Timothy. *The Nearest Faraway Place: Brian Wilson, the Beach Boys, and the Southern California Experience.* New York: Henry Holt, 1994.

Beatles

In the history of **rock and roll** (see entry under 1950s—Music in volume 3), no group has had quite the impact on music and culture as did the Beatles, a quartet from Liverpool, England, consisting of John Lennon (1940–1980), Paul McCartney (1942–), George Harrison (1943–2001), and Ringo Starr (1940–). When they hit the world music stage in 1963, they reinvigorated rock and roll, moved the music in new directions, and set fashion and cultural trends, something they continued to do until their breakup in 1970. More than any other band, the Beatles set a standard for songwriting, musicianship, and cultural impact that has never been surpassed.

The group formed in the late 1950s when Lennon formed a group called the Quarrymen. McCartney joined him, and Harrison followed soon after. After changing their name to the Beatles, they began to win fans both in Liverpool, then in Hamburg, Germany, and later around England. In 1962, Starr joined the group, replacing Pete Best (1941–) on drums. By 1963, they had developed an original sound, grounded in the 1950s rock-and-roll style of Chuck Berry (1926–), Buddy Holly (1936–1959), and **Elvis Presley** (1935–1977; see entry under 1950s—Music in volume 3) and black **rhythm and blues** (R&B; see entry under 1940s—Music in volume 3) music. What also set the Beatles apart from other groups in 1963 was that they wrote their own music. By the time they hit the United States in early 1964, Lennon and McCartney had forged a unique songwriting style, one they showcased in such early hits as "I Want to Hold Your Hand," "Love Me Do," and "She Loves You." Their look also set them apart: long hair (for 1964 standards), identical suits, and short boots (later called "Beatle boots"). The band's early hits exploded across Great Britain and the United States in 1964, setting off a wave of fan frenzy called "Beatlemania." Fans went wild, screaming and yelling, during the Beatles' concerts or personal appearances. Beatlemania was captured in the Beatles' first feature film, *A Hard Day's Night* (see entry under 1960s—Film and Theater in volume 4) which showcased a day in the lives of the Beatles.

After this early success, the Beatles continued to grow as musicians and songwriters. They stopped touring in 1966, preferring to devote their time to recording. Moving away from their early song style, which focused on romantic love, the Beatles began to experiment with new themes and sounds. Their

albums *Rubber Soul* (1965) and *Revolver* (1966) redefined what **pop music** (see entry under 1940s—Music in volume 3) could be about, with more obscure lyrics and a wider variety of sounds (distortion, Indian instruments called sitars, tape loops, and other sound effects). This experimentation went even further on their 1967 album *Sgt. Pepper's Lonely Hearts Club Band*. This was the first "concept album" in rock, meaning that all the songs were organized around one idea. In this case, the concept was the Beatles posing (sort of) as a fictional band. That album, and the following one, *Magical Mystery Tour*, established the psychedelic sound and represented the height of the Beatles' experimentation with sound. Those records featured some of the Beatles' best songs as well, including Lennon's complex songs "A Day in the Life," "Strawberry Fields Forever," and "I Am the Walrus," and McCartney's softer songs "When I'm Sixty-Four," "The Fool on the Hill," and "Penny Lane."

In the later 1960s, the Beatles released an important double album called *The Beatles,* more popularly called the *White Album* by fans because of its blank white cover. The *White Album* moved away from the psychedelic sound and produced some

The Beatles: (left to right) Paul McCartney, George Harrison, Ringo Starr, and John Lennon. *The Kobal Collection. Reproduced by permission.*

great singles ("Lady Madonna" and "Revolution," for example). By this time, tensions within the group were beginning to show. The *White Album* was essentially a series of solo projects, lacking the group's former closeness. They sought to recover that togetherness by getting back to their roots in early rock and roll in the "Get Back" sessions that later became the *Let It Be* album, released in 1970. Those sessions were tense, but after taking a break, the Beatles got together for one last album, 1969's *Abbey Road,* considered by many to be their most mature and finest album. It featured a stunning collection of songs, including Harrison's beautiful "Something" and "Here Comes the Sun," Starr's "Octopus's Garden," Lennon's "Come Together" and "Because," and McCartney's "Golden Slumbers" and "You Never Give Me Your Money." The album closed with a long medley of tunes, ending in an explosive jam called, appropriately, "The End."

Abbey Road was to be the last great musical statement from what many consider to be the greatest band in the history of popular music. Although they were only on the international stage for a mere seven years, their influence on other musicians is incalculable, and rock music has never been the same since.

—Timothy Berg

For More Information

The Beatles. *The Beatles Anthology.* San Francisco: Chronicle Books, 2000.

Hertsgaard, Mark. *A Day in the Life: The Music and Artistry of the Beatles.* New York: Delacorte Press, 1995.

Martin, Marvin. *The Beatles: The Music Was Never the Same.* New York: Franklin Watts, 1996.

Woog, Adam. *The Beatles.* San Diego: Lucent Books, 1998.

Bob Dylan (1941–)

Folk singer Bob Dylan was born Robert Allen Zimmerman in Duluth, Minnesota, and released his first album, *Bob Dylan,* in 1961. Although it featured only two of his own songs, Dylan soon emerged as one of the most important singer-songwriters in the American **folk music** (see entry under 1960s—Music in volume 4) and **rock and roll** (see entry under 1950s—Music in volume 3) traditions. Despite having one of the most unusual singing voices of any major performer, as a lyricist Dylan has been compared with poet John Keats (1785–1821). Songs like "Blowin' in the Wind" and "The Times They Are A-Changin'" are among the most powerful protest songs of the 1960s.

Criticized by fans for his move to electric instruments in 1965, Dylan has produced over forty official albums, including such critically acclaimed releases as *Highway 61 Revisited* (1965), *Blonde on Blonde, Blood on the Tracks* (1975), and *Time Out of Mind* (1997). In the late 1980s, Dylan formed The Traveling Wilburys along with George Harrison (1943–2001), Jeff Lynne (1947–), Roy Orbison (1936–1988), and Tom Petty (1952–); the band recorded two albums. With few exceptions, the quality of his work has remained high, most recently exemplified by the 2001 Grammy Award–winning album *Love & Theft*. In 2001, he continued to play live to sell-out crowds.

—Chris Routledge

For More Information

Aaseng, Nathan. *Bob Dylan, Spellbinding Songwriter*. Minneapolis: Lerner Publications, 1987.

Bob Dylan.com. http://www.bobdylan.com (accessed March 18, 2002).

Pennebaker, D. A., director. *Don't Look Back* (video). Hollywood, CA: Paramount, 1986.

Richardson, Susan. *Bob Dylan*. New York: Chelsea House, 1995.

Shelton, Robert. *No Direction Home: The Life and Music of Bob Dylan*. New York: Da Capo Press, 1997.

Eight-Track Tapes

When the eight-track tape and tape player were introduced in 1965, it seemed that a high point had been reached in luxurious modern technology. No longer limited to the random choices of a radio station, teenagers and hip adults could carry tapes of their favorite recording artists with them to the park or beach. Better yet, they could choose which tunes to listen to while driving in their car. It is perhaps one of the most common ironies of popular culture that one decade's most modern triumph can, like the eight-track tape, become the next decade's old news.

The eight-track tape was invented by William Powell Lear (1902–1978), famous for developing the Learjet, a small aircraft prized by corporations and business travelers. Lear developed a process for dividing magnetic recording tape into eight

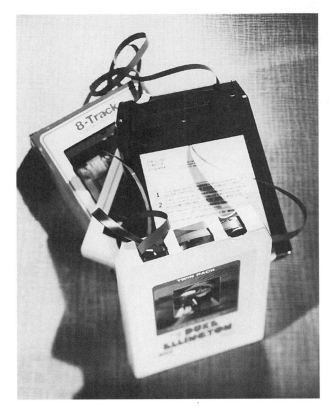

Eight-track tapes. *David Arky/Corbis Corporation. Reproduced by permission.*

channels, or tracks. This increased the recording time, without damaging the sound quality, and allowed one continuous loop of tape to be wound into a portable cartridge.

Lear was not only a good engineer, he was also a creative marketer. He worked out a deal with the Ford Motor Company. In 1966, a factory-installed eight-track tape player became an option on new Ford cars. Everyone seemed to want the new technology. In 1966, sixty-five thousand eight-track players were sold. By 1967, Chrysler and **General Motors** (see entry under 1900s—The Way We Lived in volume 1) were also offering their customers eight-track players. Taking music along became a part of American driving culture.

The peak years of the eight-track were 1967 through 1975. Then, improvements in the tape quality of smaller cassettes and decreasing quality in eight-tracks led consumers away from the eight-track tape. By the mid-1980s, eight-track tapes were no longer being manufactured or sold and were quickly on their way to becoming a joke about out-of-date 1970s culture, along with **bell-bottomed pants** (see entry under 1960s—Fashion in volume 4) and giant Afro hairdos. There are a few exceptions to this attitude, however. Some **country music** (see entry under 1940s—Music in volume 3) labels still release albums on eight-track to appeal to truckers who still have eight-track players in their trucks. Some new **alternative-rock** (see entry under 1990s—Music in volume 5) bands release albums of their music on homemade eight-track tapes.

—*Tina Gianoulis*

For More Information

Greenberg, Corey. "Melancholy and the Infinite Loop: Eight-Track Tape and Music Enjoyment." *Audio* (Vol. 81, no. 5, May 1997): pp. 40–42.

Kirkeby, Marc. "Eight-track Tapes Going but Not Quite Gone." *Rolling Stone* (October 16, 1980): p. 36.

8-Track Heaven. http://www.8trackheaven.com (accessed March 15, 2002).

Folk Music

For a long time, the term "folk music" meant music made by ordinary people rather than by professional musicians. In many cultures around the world, and over many generations, songs were handed down from one person to the next. Good folk songs survived over time because they spoke to basic human emotions and told stories that everyone could relate to. In the twentieth century, with the rise of commercial popular music, folk music was no longer just music made by ordinary folks; it became a style of music that had commercial appeal as well.

During the twentieth century in the United States, folk music went through a number of transformations. In the 1930s, during the **Great Depression** (see entry under 1930s–The Way We Lived in volume 2), folk singers sang songs about the hard times people were going through. One of the most important artists was Woody Guthrie (1912–1967), who sang topical songs (songs about current issues in society) and protest songs about outlaws, politics, and class relations. His most famous song is probably "This Land Is Your Land," which celebrated the United States as a place for everyone, not just for the rich. It continues to be sung today. In the 1940s and 1950s, other folk singers rose to prominence. Pete Seeger (1919–) played the banjo on his own and in the Weavers, one of the most important folk groups of the 1950s. Among other topics, The Weavers sang about political life from a radical perspective, something that got them into trouble during the anticommunist hysteria of the early 1950s. Seeger went on to a long career bringing folk music to crowds large and small.

Although ordinary folks continued to sing folk music, in the 1960s there was something of a folk music revival, when dozens of new bands and artists rediscovered folk songs and made them into successful hit songs. Groups such as the Kingston Trio and Peter, Paul, and Mary were among the more commercially successful. But the folk revival also produced artists such as **Bob Dylan** (1941–; see entry under 1960s–Music in volume 4), who began his career singing his own topical folk songs, such as "Blowin' in the Wind." This folk revival also led **rock and roll** (see entry under 1950s–Music in volume 3) musicians to experiment with softer, folk sounds, resulting in a style called "folk-rock," perhaps best represented by the group the Byrds.

Although the folk-rock revival faded by the 1970s, the popularity of folk music has continued since then as an important style of music that continues to draw new fans. By the end of the twentieth century, folk music could still mean the old songs that ordinary people sang to themselves and their friends, but it could also refer to a category of popular music that featured acoustic instruments and singing. Either way, folk music remains an important musical style and an important link to the American past.

—*Timothy Berg*

For More Information

Cantwell, Robert. *When We Were Good: The Folk Revival.* Cambridge, MA: Harvard University Press, 1996.

Marcus, Greil. *Invisible Republic: Bob Dylan's Basement Tapes.* New York: Henry Holt, 1997.

Neff, Maryl. *Folk Music.* http://www.coe.ufl.edu/courses/EdTech/Vault/Folk/Definition.htm#Basic (accessed March 15, 2002).

Nettl, Bruno. *Folk Music in the United States.* 3rd ed. Detroit: Wayne State University Press, 1976.

Smith, Harry, ed. *Anthology of American Folk Music.* Washington, DC: Smithsonian Folkways Recordings, 1997.

Uncle Tom's Folk Music History Page. http://www.jsfmusic.com/Uncle_Tom (accessed March 15, 2002).

Grateful Dead

The Grateful Dead was one of the most popular and enduring of all musical groups. The Dead came of age during the mid-to-late 1960s, an era in which the lyrics and sounds of **rock and roll** (see entry under 1950s—Music in volume 3) music were coming under the influence of the drug-related experiences of musicians and fans alike.

Indeed, much of the Grateful Dead's image is related to the hallucinatory drugs (which produce strange sounds and visions) and psychedelia (the music, art, and writing influenced by the use of such drugs) that characterized pop culture in the late 1960s. The group's musical roots are in traditional **blues** (see entry under 1920s—Music in volume 2), **folk** (see entry under 1960s—Music in volume 4), and **bluegrass** (see entry under 1940s—Music in volume 3). The group's sum and substance may be directly linked to the free-spiritedness and nonconformity of the **Beat Movement** (see entry under 1950s—Print Culture in volume 3) of the 1950s. Additionally, the success enjoyed by the Dead has been nonconventional by music industry standards. Most musical acts win their initial fame by topping the record charts with a Top Ten hit. But not the Dead: They earned their popularity first by performing in the San Francisco Bay area and then by constant touring. The group did not release a Top Ten record until 1987, with "Touch of Grey." Through the years, the group produced studio-recorded albums, but fans insisted that the spirit of the Dead could only be fully appreciated by experiencing them in concert.

The band was formed in San Francisco, California, in 1965. The original Grateful Dead included Jerry Garcia (1942–1995), the group's most famous and charismatic member, who even inspired a Ben & Jerry's ice cream flavor (Cherry Garcia); Bob Weir (1947–); Ron "Pigpen" McKernan (1945–1973); Bill Kreutzmann (1946–); and Phil Lesh (1940–). Most rock groups from any era disappear after several years; their popularity wanes, or their members disperse and go solo or form other bands. Although members and music of the Dead changed through the years, with other musicians and songwriters having a major influence on the group, the Dead essentially remained the Dead. A key to their popularity and longevity has been the obsessive loyalty of their fans, who are known as Deadheads. These followers, to whom the Dead is nothing short of a religion, are eager consumers of anything Dead related, from magazines, Web sites, and **cable TV** (see entry under 1970s—TV and Radio in volume 4) and **radio** (see entry under 1920s—TV and Radio in volume 2) programs to recordings and bootlegs (unauthorized recordings, usually of live concerts) that are issued and reissued. The cult surrounding the Dead emerged after a call to fans, titled "Dead Freaks Unite—Who Are You? Where Are You?," was printed in their 1971 album *The Grateful Dead* (also known as *Skulls and Roses*).

Over two decades later, the Dead remained the highest-grossing concert band in the United States. Following Garcia's death in 1995, the band stopped recording and touring, though surviving members occasionally reunite. But into the twenty-first century, the band remains an industry unto itself—as well as a living link to the counterculture of the 1950s and 1960s.

—*Rob Edelman*

For More Information

Brandelius, Jerilyn Lee. *The Grateful Dead Family Album*. New York: Warner Books, 1989.

Dodd, David G., and Diana Spaulding, eds. *The Grateful Dead Reader*. New York: Oxford University Press, 2000.

Gans, David. *Conversations with the Dead: The Grateful Dead Interview Book*. New York: Citadel Press, 1991.

Gans, David, and Peter Simon. *Playing in the Band: An Oral and Visual Portrait of The Grateful Dead*. New York: St. Martin's Press, 1985.

Greenfield, Robert. *Dark Star: An Oral Biography of Jerry Garcia*. New York: William Morrow, 1996.

Harrison, Hank. *The Dead*. Millbrae, CA: Celestial Arts, 1980.

Jackson, Blair. *Garcia: An American Life*. New York: Viking Press, 1999.

Jackson, Blair. *Goin' Down the Road: A Grateful Dead Traveling Companion*. New York: Harmony, 1992.

Rocco, John, and Brian Rocco, eds. *Dead Reckonings: The Life and Times of The Grateful Dead*. New York: Schirmer Books, 1999.

Ruhlman, William. *The History of The Grateful Dead*. New York: Gallery, 1990.

Trager, Oliver. *The American Book of The Dead: The Definitive Grateful Dead Encyclopedia*. New York: Fireside Books, 1997.

Monkees

The huge success of the first two **Beatles** (see entry under 1960s–Music in volume 4) films, *A Hard Day's Night* (1964; see entry under 1960s–Film and Theater in volume 4) and *Help* (1965), prompted producers Bob Rafelson (1933–) and Bert Schneider (c. 1933–) to try duplicating the form on **television** (see entry under 1940s–TV and Radio in volume 3). They envisioned a show built around a real **rock and roll** (see entry under 1950s–Music in volume 3) band whose members would play themselves. Like the Beatles films, each show would feature minimal plot, a great deal of dashing around (called "romp" by the producers) by the characters, and the group's songs as part of the soundtrack. The result was *The Monkees*.

The band consisted of Englishman Davy Jones (1945–) and Americans Peter Tork (1942–), Micky Dolenz (1945–), and Mike Nesmith (1942–). At first, none of the boys except Nesmith could play any musical instrument. Instead, they were chosen for their cute looks, adequate acting skills, and above-average pop-singing ability.

The Monkees succeeded both as a band and as a TV show. Their initial albums were recorded using studio musicians, although the four stars picked up instrumental skills quickly. "Last Train to Clarksville," their first single, was a top-ten hit. It was followed by five others, including "Daydream Believer," "Valerie," "Girl," and "I'm a Believer." Their albums sold in the millions.

The TV show was extremely successful in its first season (1966–67), winning both high ratings and an Emmy Award for Best Comedy Series. As intended from the start, the show fed album and concert sales, and vice versa. However, the show's ratings declined in its second season, and it was canceled in 1968. The same year, a bizarre Monkees movie, *Head*, was released, produced by Rafelson. The film was cowritten by him and by actor Jack Nicholson (1937–). The film flopped at the box office, and the Monkees broke up shortly thereafter.

The band (without Nesmith) reassembled for a successful tour in 1986, sparking a mini Monkees revival. The next year, an attempt was made to revive the Monkees concept with new band members, but the resulting TV show and album both failed miserably.

All four original members came together to tour in 1996 and 1997, but the reunion was temporary. Jones and Dolenz formed a Monkees-themed duet and began touring in 2001.

—Justin Gustainis

The Monkees: (left to right) Mike Nesmith, Peter Tork, Davy Jones, and Micky Dolenz. *Frank Driggs Collection/Archive Photos. Reproduced by permission.*

For More Information

Baker, Glenn A. *Monkeemania: The True Story of the Monkees.* New York: St. Martin's Press, 1986.

Bronson, Harold. *Hey, Hey, We're the Monkees.* Santa Monica, CA: General Publishing Group, 1996.

Dolenz, Micky, and Mark Bego. *I'm a Believer: My Life of Monkees, Music, and Madness.* New York: Hyperion, 1993.

Hey, Hey . . . It's the Monkees Home Page. http://www.monkees.net (accessed March 18, 2002).

Wincentsen, Edward. *The Monkees: Memories and the Magic.* Pickens, SC: Wynn, 2000.

Motown

Motown Records helped define soul music during the 1960s. Motown was one of the most important, and popular, sounds in all of American **pop music** (see entry under 1940s–Music in volume 3). Founded by Berry Gordy Jr. (1929–) in 1959 in Detroit, Michigan, the label's name came from a popular nickname for Detroit. "Motown" was short for "motor town," because of Detroit's importance as the most important automobile manufacturing center in the world. Gordy's passion for music came with a unique ability to nurture great songwriting and musical talent. That ability would make Motown one of the most successful recording companies in pop-music history.

Gordy created a distinct sound for Motown's records by modeling the company after the automobile industry's assembly-line production method. He developed a stable of songwriters and musicians to provide a uniform sound for all of the company's records, including the songwriting team of Eddie Holland (1939–), Lamont Dozier (1941–), and Brian Holland (1941–), and musicians such as bassist James Jamerson (1938–1983). The songwriters and musicians provided the assembly-line structure. As products for this assembly line, Gordy scouted Detroit and other areas for local vocal talent, hiring promising singers as either solo stars or as vocal groups. His efforts produced such talents as Marvin Gaye (1939–1984), Stevie Wonder (1950–), Diana Ross (1944–) and the Supremes, the Temptations, the Four Tops, Martha and the Vandellas, and Smokey Robinson (1940–) and the Miracles, among many others. In the 1960s, Motown produced fifty-six number-one pop and **rhythm and blues** (R&B; see entry under 1940s–Music in volume 3) hits, including "My Girl" by the Temptations, "Baby

Love" by the Supremes, "The Tracks of My Tears" by Smokey Robinson and the Miracles, and "Reach Out, I'll Be There" by the Four Tops. These songs only hint at the enormous number of hits the company had in the 1960s. It was difficult to turn on a **radio** (see entry under 1920s–TV and Radio in volume 2) in the 1960s for long without hearing a Motown record.

By the early 1970s, Motown was moving in new directions. The assembly-line sound broke down as some of Motown's biggest talents moved in their own creative directions (most notably Wonder and Gaye). The company moved to Los Angeles, California, in 1973, ending the label's official connection to Detroit. Despite these changes, the Motown sound lives on, as the hit records from the 1960s continue to be played on radio stations. The many great songs Motown produced have earned themselves a treasured place in American popular culture.

—*Timothy Berg*

The Temptations: Eddie Kendricks is surrounded by (clockwise from upper left) Melvin Franklin, Paul Williams, Otis Williams, and David Ruffin. *Archive Photos. Reproduced by permission.*

For More Information

Classic Motown. http://www.motown.com/classicmotown (accessed March 18, 2002).

Folsom, Burton W. "Berry Gordy and Motown Records: Lessons for Black History Month." *Mackinac Center for Public Policy.* http://www.mackinac.org/print.asp?ID=344 (accessed March 18, 2002).

George, Nelson. *Where Did Our Love Go? The Rise and Fall of the Motown Sound.* New York: St. Martin's Press, 1985.

Miller, Jim, ed. *The Rolling Stone Illustrated History of Rock and Roll.* New York: Rolling Stone Press, 1980.

Smith, Suzanne E. *Dancing in the Street: Motown and the Cultural Politics of Detroit.* Cambridge, MA: Harvard University Press, 1999.

Waller, Don. *The Motown Story.* New York: Charles Scribner's Sons, 1985.

Rolling Stones
• •

The Rolling Stones arrived in the United States with the British Invasion of **rock and roll** (see entry under 1950s–Music

The original Rolling Stones lineup, in January 1967: (left to right) Charlie Watts, Bill Wyman, Mick Jagger, Keith Richards, and Brian Jones. *Corbis Corporation. Reproduced by permission.*

in volume 3) in the mid-1960s. They quickly emerged as one of the most important musical groups in rock history, bringing a new, harder edge to rock while keeping it grounded in the **blues** (see entry under 1920s–Music in volume 2). Formed in the early 1960s in England, the original lineup consisted of Mick Jagger (1943–) on vocals, Keith Richards (1943–) and Brian Jones (1942–1969) on guitars, Charlie Watts (1941–) on drums, and Bill Wyman (1936–) on bass. The group took its name from a song by bluesman Muddy Waters (1915–1983), "Rolling Stone," and they began by covering blues and early rock tunes.

The Stones soon began writing their own songs. In May 1965, their first big hit, "(I Can't Get No) Satisfaction" hit the British and American airwaves. The Stones developed a bad-boy image that was in stark contrast to the wholesome demeanor of the **Beatles** (see entry under 1960s–Music in volume 4) and other British Invasion groups. Some of this image came from their wild hairstyles, clothing, and behavior, but it was in their songs that the Stones pushed the limits of rock music in new directions. "Satisfaction" played on youthful impatience with the world, "Paint It Black" commented on depression, and "Let's Spend the Night Together" put sexuality front and center. Their 1966 album *Aftermath* was their most important work from this period.

The period from 1968 to 1974 was the Stones' most creative period. The Stones took on an even more original blues sound with the replacement of Brian Jones (who died in 1969) with guitarist Mick Taylor (1948–). This new creativity resulted in a number of landmark rock albums, including *Beggar's Banquet* (1968), *Let It Bleed* (1969), *Sticky Fingers* (1971), and the double album *Exile on Mainstreet* (1972). They also released a number of hit singles, including "Jumpin' Jack Flash," "Brown Sugar," "Sympathy for the Devil," and "Honky Tonk Women" among many others. This period also saw their disastrous concert at **Altamont** (see entry under 1960s–Music in volume 4), chronicled in the film *Gimme Shelter*. After Taylor left the group in 1975 (replaced by Ron Wood, 1947–), the Stones continued to produce hit albums, most notably *Some Girls* (1978) and *Tattoo You* (1981). By the end of the 1990s, the Rolling Stones were still making good music and touring the world, drawing enthusiastic fans with their original mix of rock and blues.

—*Timothy Berg*

For More Information

Christgau, Robert. "The Rolling Stones." In *The Rolling Stone Illustrated History of Rock and Roll*. Edited by Jim Miller. New York: Rolling Stone Press, 1980.

Hotchner, A. E. *Blown Away: The Rolling Stones and the Death of the Sixties*. New York: Simon & Schuster, 1990.

The Rolling Stones. http://www.the-rolling-stones.com (accessed March 15, 2002).

Simon and Garfunkel

Pioneers in the musical style that became known as "folk-rock," Simon and Garfunkel were one of the most popular musical acts of the golden age of **rock and roll** (see entry under 1950s–Music in volume 3): the mid-1960s to the mid-1970s.

Paul Simon and Art Garfunkel, both born in 1941, became friends in junior high school. As "Tom and Jerry," they recorded their first song, "Hey, Schoolgirl," on a small record label in 1957. They performed solo in the early 1960s—Simon recording as Jerry Landis, Garfunkel as part of Tico and the Triumphs.

The two came together again in 1964 and recorded their first album as Simon and Garfunkel, *Wednesday Morning, 3 AM.* The album sold poorly, but a producer friend took one of its tracks, the folk-style "Sounds of Silence," layered electric guitar and drums over it, and got it released as a single. The new record proved extremely popular, and Simon and Garfunkel were suddenly stars. They hastily reworked some songs Simon had recorded solo on a British label, and the result was their second album, *Sounds of Silence,* released in 1965 to both critical acclaim and financial success.

The next album, *Parsley, Sage, Rosemary and Thyme* (1966), produced the hit singles "Scarborough Fair/Canticle," "A Hazy Shade of Winter," and "At the Zoo." *Bookends* (1968) produced the hits "America" and "Old Friends" and the huge hit "Mrs. Robinson," which was specially written for the soundtrack of the 1967 Mike Nichols (1931–) movie **The Graduate** (see entry under 1960s–Film and Theater in volume 4), starring Dustin Hoffman (1937–) in his first major film role.

The last Simon and Garfunkel album was 1970's *Bridge Over Troubled Water,* their most popular of all their albums. It produced hits with "Cecelia," "Baby Driver," "El Condor Pasa," and the extremely successful title song, which, atypically, featured Garfunkel on lead vocal. The duo then split up, driven apart by creative differences and personal conflict. They appeared together only twice thereafter: at a George McGovern (1922–) benefit in 1972 and at a 1981 concert in New York's Central Park. They also collaborated on two recorded singles: "My Little Town" (1975) and "What a Wonderful World" (1978), with James Taylor (1948–). Simon and Garfunkel each continued with solo careers—and also some acting—with Simon's career being more successful, highlighted by two Grammy Award–winning albums, *Still Crazy After All These Years* (1975) and *Graceland* (1986).

—*Justin Gustainis*

For More Information

Art Garfunkel.com. http://www.artgarfunkel.com (accessed March 18, 2002).

Cohen, Mitchell S. *Simon and Garfunkel: A Biography in Words and Pictures.* New York: Sire Books, 1977.

Humphries, Patrick. *Bookends: The Simon and Garfunkel Story.* New York: Proteus, 1982.

Kingston, Victoria. *Simon and Garfunkel: The Biography.* New York: Fromm International, 1996.

Morella, Joe, and Patricia Barey. *Simon and Garfunkel: Old Friends.* New York: Carol Publishing Group, 1991.

Simon and Garfunkel Online Resource. http://home.att.net/~sandg/index.htm (accessed March 18, 2002).

Warner Brothers Records. *Paul Simon.com.* http://www.paulsimon.com (accessed March 18, 2002).

Barbra Streisand (1942–)

Singer-actress-producer-director Barbra Streisand has won fame as a recording artist, a **television** (see entry under 1940s–TV and Radio in volume 3) performer, and a stage and screen star. Her greatest asset has been her voice. At once powerful and tender, it oozes raw emotion and allows Streisand to be equally at home singing show tunes, pop ballads, and Christmas carols. Without argument, hers is one of the great voices of her generation.

Streisand's early career was one of accomplishment and honor. She earned her initial celebrity on **Broadway** (see entry under 1900s–Film and Theater in volume 1) in a show-stopping supporting role as Miss Marmelstein in the musical *I Can Get It for You Wholesale* (1962). The Grammy Award–winning *The Barbra Streisand Album* (1963) became the first of her countless, top-selling record albums; since its release, her records have sold more than sixty million copies. However, Streisand really became a star when she played the legendary comedienne Fanny Brice (1891–1951) in the Broadway musical *Funny Girl* (1964).

Streisand also conquered television. *My Name is Barbra* (1965), her initial TV special, was an Emmy Award winner. She also appeared as a guest star opposite the legendary singer Judy Garland (1922–1969) on Garland's television series, *The Judy Garland Show* (1963–64). The showcasing of Streisand signaled that Streisand's voice was—and would be—on a level with that of Garland's.

Streisand became a movie star with her first feature, the screen version of *Funny Girl* (1968), which earned her a Best Actress Academy Award. Some of her subsequent films have been hits, but more than a few have not been as successful. She also began directing films. With *Yentl* (1983), she became the first woman to coauthor, star in, produce, and direct a feature film.

Streisand has been a controversial entertainment-industry figure. Some who have worked with her have described her as difficult and an egomaniac; meanwhile, Streisand has defended herself by alleging that her detractors are unable to deal with a woman in power. What remains unchallenged, however, is her cult popularity among her countless die-hard fans and her greatness as a singer.

—*Rob Edelman*

For More Information

Edwards, Anne. *Streisand: A Biography*. Boston: Little Brown, 1997.
Nickens, Christopher. *The Films of Barbra Streisand*. Secaucus, NJ: Carol Publishing Group, 1998.
Riese, Randall. *Her Name Is Barbra*. Secaucus, NJ: Carol Publishing Group, 1993.
Spada, James. *Streisand: Her Life*. New York: Crown Publishers, 1995.

Woodstock

The Woodstock Music and Arts Fair, which took place near Bethel, New York, over three days in August 1969, was both a massive concert and a symbol for the youth culture of the 1960s. In the late 1960s, rock festivals, most notably the Monterey Pop Festival in 1967, were gaining in popularity. Woodstock at first seemed as if it would be simply another **rock and roll** (see entry under 1950s—Music in volume 3) music festival, but because of its size and the number and stature of the artists who performed there, the name Woodstock stands out as the most famous of all rock festivals.

Hoping for three days of peace and music (and profits), a group of four young businessmen decided to hold a music festival in the town of Woodstock, New York, known for its arts community. As they began planning, and as they hired more and more famous musical acts to perform, the festival grew too big and was eventually moved to a dairy farm, owned by Max Yasgur (1920–1973), near the town of Bethel, not far from Woodstock. The size of the festival would prove to be a big problem. As the festival day approached, more than five hundred thousand young people descended on the small farming community of Bethel, creating significant problems. The festival organizers were not prepared for traffic jams; insufficient food, toilets, and medical care; and security and drug problems, among many others. Adding to these problems, two rain storms drenched the audience and created a mud bath out of the farm.

Despite these problems, and the disaster they created, the festival was a significant musical event, featuring such important rock acts as The Who; Jimi Hendrix (1942–1970); Janis Joplin (1943–1970); Jefferson Airplane; Crosby, Stills, Nash, and Young; Joe Cocker (1944–); and Santana. More than a musical event, Woodstock became a symbol for the idealism of the **hippie** (see entry under 1960s–The Way We Lived in volume 4) youth and for young people in general in the late 1960s. Despite the many problems, the crowd was largely peaceful, and they kept their spirits up, many feeling that they were part of history in the making; they were not wrong. When a music festival at **Altamont** (see entry under 1960s–Music in volume 4), California, erupted into violence and murder a few months later, many looked back at the peaceful Woodstock festival as the last gasp of 1960s youthful idealism. Woodstock was, in many ways, a symbolic high point for the 1960s generation, proving that peace and love were possible in the world, if only for a moment.

—Timothy Berg

Former Lovin' Spoonful lead singer John Sebastian performs to the hundreds of thousands of people who attended the Woodstock Music and Arts Fair in August 1969. *Photograph by Henry Diltz. Corbis Corporation. Reproduced by permission.*

For More Information

Makower, Joel. *Woodstock: The Oral History.* New York: Doubleday, 1989.

Morthland, John. "Rock Festivals." In *The Rolling Stone Illustrated History of Rock and Roll.* Edited by Jim Miller. New York: Rolling Stone Press, 1980.

1969 Woodstock Festival & Concert. http://www.woodstock69.com/ (accessed March 18, 2002).

Spitz, Bob. *Barefoot in Babylon: The Creation of the Woodstock Music Festival.* New York: Norton, 1989.

Woodstock.com. http://www.woodstock.com (accessed March 18, 2002).

1960s
Print Culture

American literature thrived in the 1960s, helped along by a culture that valued thinking—especially the thinking of young people who questioned the values of adults. A number of individuals who are now considered among America's best writers placed novels on the bestseller lists, including William Faulkner (1897–1962) with *The Reivers* (1962), Saul Bellow (1915–) with *Herzog* (1964), Truman Capote (1924–1984) with *In Cold Blood* (1966), and Kurt Vonnegut Jr. (1922–) with *Slaughterhouse Five* (1969). Not all Americans were fond of such serious literature, however, and many turned to lighter fare. Other best-sellers in the decade included the James Bond novels by Ian Fleming (1908–1964), *Hotel* (1965) and *Airport* (1968) by Arthur Hailey (1920–), and *Valley of the Dolls* (1966) by Jacqueline Susann (1921–1974). These "trashier" novels were often made into popular films, a trend that grew increasingly prevalent in the 1960s. Among the surprise hits of the decade were *To Kill a Mockingbird* (1960), a powerful story of racism set in a small town in Alabama by first-time author Harper Lee (1926–), and *Stranger in a Strange Land* (1961), the first science-fiction novel to make the *New York Times* best-seller list, by Robert Heinlein (1907–1988). Another science-fiction novel, *Dune* (1965) by Frank Herbert (1920–1986), soon attained classic status among science-fiction fans.

Young adult and children's literature grew in popularity during the decade, helped along by increased funding for libraries. *The Catcher in the Rye* (1951) by J. D. Salinger (1919–) remained the book that marked the passage into adolescence in America, and it was widely taught in schools. Other books modeled on Salinger's classic, including *The Outsider* (1967) by S. E. Hinton (1950–) and *From the Mixed-Up Files of Mrs. Basil E. Frankweiler* (1967) by E. L. Konigsburg (1930–), gave serious literary attention to the trials of growing up and became favorites with young readers. Younger children enjoyed *Where the Wild Things Are* (1963) by Maurice Sendak (1928–) and a continuing stream of books from America's best-known children's author, Dr. Seuss (Theodor Seuss Geisel; 1904–1991).

The magazine market continued to go through a process of transition that began in the 1950s when more Americans looked to the TV for news and entertainment. The *Saturday Evening Post,* once considered the essential American magazine, closed its doors in 1969, signaling the end of the era of the general magazine. But new magazines did thrive—if they catered to a specialized audience. *Rolling Stone,* launched in 1967, became the magazine for lovers of rock and roll. The *Advocate* was launched the same year to serve a growing homosexual market. Comic-book lovers continued to make up a significant market. They enjoyed the stories told by the leading comic-book company of the decade, Marvel Comics, and its newest creation, the Spider-Man, created in 1962.

Advocate

Billing itself as "the national gay & lesbian newsmagazine," the *Advocate* is a bimonthly magazine that has established a reputation as the "magazine of record" for the homosexual community in the United States. The first issue, called the *Los Angeles Advocate,* appeared in 1967—a full two years before the June 1969, Stonewall riots in New York City that brought **gay liberation** (see entry under 1960s—The Way We Lived in volume 4) to the nation's attention. It was published as an outgrowth of a local gay newsletter entitled *PRIDE* (for Personal Rights in Defense and Education). The newsletter had been created by Richard Mitch, Bill Rand, and Sam Winston as a response to Mitch's 1966 arrest in a police raid at a Los Angeles gay bar. The aim of *PRIDE* was to inform the local community of events that were having an influence on their lives and to help political activists find a voice.

The first issue (five hundred copies) of the *Los Angeles Advocate*—secretly printed in the basement of ABC Television's studios—appeared on September 12, 1967; it was twelve pages long and sold for twenty-five cents at gay bars and shops. In 1968, Rand and Winston purchased rights to the publication. Joined by gay activist Jim Kepner (c. 1923–1997), they vowed to make it a national publication. They changed its name to the *Advocate* in April 1970. In 1975, David B. Goodstein (1932–1985) purchased the magazine and managed it until his death. in 1985. During his tenure, the magazine lost its radical political edge and became more of a commercial tabloid. Editor John Preston (1945–1994) and publisher Niles Merton deepened the magazine's political and cultural coverage. In 1984, the *Advocate* was redesigned in a glossy newsmagazine format. It became even more mainstream in 1992, when publisher Sam Watters spun off the sexually explicit classified advertising into a separate publication.

Although it has been criticized for neglecting coverage of women and people of color and for its slow response to the **AIDS** (see entry under 1980s–The Way We Lived in volume 5) crisis, the *Advocate* is recognized as the most influential alternative-sexuality magazine of its era.

—Edward Moran

For More Information

The Advocate. http://www.advocate.com (accessed March 18, 2002).

Bull, Chris. *Witness to Revolution: The Advocate Reports on Gay and Lesbian Politics, 1967–1999*. Los Angeles: Alyson Books, 1999.

Califia, Pat. *The Advocate Adviser: America's Most Popular Gay Columnist Tackles the Questions That the Others Ignore*. Boston: Alyson Publications, 1991.

Oliver, Marilyn Tower. *Gay and Lesbian Rights: A Struggle*. Springfield, NJ: Enslow, 1998.

Silver, Diane. *The New Civil War: The Lesbian and Gay Struggle for Civil Rights*. New York: Franklin Watts, 1997.

Thompson, Mark, ed. *Long Road to Freedom: The Advocate History of the Gay and Lesbian Movement*. New York: St. Martin's Press, 1994.

Cosmopolitan

Though it was originally founded in 1883 as a general interest periodical, *Cosmopolitan* magazine was revamped in 1965 as a journal devoted to the interests of the modern young career woman. Since that time, it has become one of the nation's most successful magazines. The "*Cosmo* girl," as the magazine refers to its readership, is confident, independent, glamorous, and sexual. Though many feminists have criticized the magazine for projecting an image of modern womanhood that is shallow and stereotyped, *Cosmopolitan*'s sassy style still attracts readers in the twenty-first century.

Cosmopolitan was the creation of Helen Gurley Brown (1922–), who in 1962 wrote a controversial bestseller called *Sex and the Single Girl.* Daring for its time, the book openly discussed women as sexual beings and asserted that women could choose to remain single and still be happy and sexually active. Based on the success of the book, Brown and her husband, David Brown, approached the Hearst Corporation in 1965 and were allowed to take over an aging magazine known as *Cosmopolitan.* The Browns changed everything but the name of the magazine.

Cosmopolitan soon came to represent the changing role of women in the new, sexually permissive society of the 1970s. With its focus on relationships, career, sex, and beauty, *Cosmo* became notorious for its racy covers, featuring articles with titles like "How to Please Your Man in Bed," "Land That Man, Ace Your Job, and Look Your Sexiest Ever!," and "The Bedside Astrologer." Circulation rose rapidly, helped along by such outrageous "firsts" as a nude pinup of actor Burt Reynolds (1936–), which appeared in a 1972 issue. By 2000, circulation had reached almost three million in the United States, and versions of *Cosmo* were being published in thirty-one countries around the world, including Japan, Poland, and Chile.

—*Tina Gianoulis*

For More Information

Brown, Helen Gurley. "HGB Remembers the Cosmo Years." *Cosmopolitan.* (February 1997): pp. 344–47.

Brown, Helen Gurley. *I'm Wild Again: Snippets from My Life and a Few Brazen Thoughts.* New York: St. Martin's Press, 2000.

"Cosmopolitan." *iVillage.* http://cosmo.women.com/cos (accessed March 18, 2002).

Dune

● ●

The 1965 epic novel by Frank Herbert (1920–1986) about a desert planet has become one of the most successful science-fiction series ever. The original novel, *Dune,* led to five sequels and two films as well as a variety of nonfiction books, games, and **Internet** (see entry under 1990s—The Way We Lived in volume 5) sites. In addition, after the death of Herbert, his son, Brian Herbert (1947–), began publishing a series of "prequels" to the original story. The prequels focused on events set prior to the story told in *Dune.*

Set in a distant galaxy, *Dune* is the story of Paul Atriedes, son of Duke Leto, whose family is ordered by the Emperor to take charge of Arrakis, a desert planet that is the sole source for an addictive spice that produces mystical powers in some people. Before long, Duke Leto is betrayed and killed by agents of his mortal enemy, Baron Vladimir Harkonnen. Most of the Duke's subjects are either killed or enslaved, but a few escape, along with Paul and his mother, Jessica. The pair are taken in by the Fremen, the warlike native people of Arrakis. In time, Paul leads the Fremen in a war to reclaim their planet from the Harkonnens. *Dune* explores important questions concerning ecology, religious fanaticism, and national self-determination.

The saga, which explores the interconnected fates of the planet Arrakis, the Fremen, and the Atriedes family, was continued by Herbert in *Dune Messiah* (1970), *Children of Dune* (1976), *God Emperor of Dune* (1981), *Heretics of Dune* (1984), and *Chapterhouse Dune* (1985).

The original novel was filmed in 1984 by David Lynch (1946–), who would later create the TV series *Twin Peaks*. The film starred Kyle MacLachlan (1959–) as Paul Atriedes. It did poorly at the box office but has gained a cult following. The book was filmed again by director John Harrison as *Frank Herbert's Dune*. It was shown as a three-part miniseries on the cable channel Sci-Fi in January 2001 and was well received by *Dune* fans. The fans felt the miniseries was much closer to the original novels.

Brian Herbert's prequels began in 2000 with *House Atreides*, and was followed by *House Harkonnen* in 2001; *The Butlerian Jihad* was scheduled to follow.

—*Justin Gustainis*

For More Information

Herbert, Brian, ed. *The Notebooks of Frank Herbert's Dune*. New York: Perigee Books, 1988.

Herbert, Frank. *Dune*. New York: Chilton, 1965; Ace Books, 1990.

McNelly, Willis E., compiler. *The Dune Encyclopedia*. New York: Berkley Books, 1984.

Vinge, Joan D. *The Dune Storybook*. New York: Putnam Publishing, 1984.

Marvel Comics

Marvel Comics is one of the leading publishers of **comic books** (see entry under 1930s—Print Culture in volume 2) and boasts some of the most popular characters in the superhero genre (category). Such figures as **Spider-Man** (see entry under 1960s–Print Culture in volume 4), **Captain America** (see entry under 1940s–Print Culture in volume 3), the Incredible Hulk, Daredevil, the Fantastic Four, the Silver Surfer, and the X-Men have filled the pages of Marvel comic books. Publisher Martin Goodman (1908–1992) founded the company as Timely Comics in 1939. In the 1960s, the company, renamed Marvel Comics, revolutionized the comic-book industry and set the standard for superhero storytelling for decades.

During the 1940s, Timely Comics was a second-string comic-book publisher that lagged far behind DC Comics. DC Comics covered the exploits of many popular superheroes like **Superman, Batman** (see these two entries under 1930s–Print Culture in volume 2), and **Wonder Woman** (see entry under 1940s–Print Culture in volume 3). Timely's leading heroes of that era were the Human Torch, the Sub-Mariner, and Captain America, the living embodiment of national patriotism. Timely's comics were especially popular during World War II (1939–45) because its heroes were frequently depicted crusading against the Axis powers (nations including Germany, Italy, and Japan, who opposed the United States and its allies during the war). When the war ended, however, sales of Timely's superhero comics plummeted and the line was eventually discontinued. The 1950s saw the company distribute comics from the crime, **Western** (see entry under 1930s–Film and Theater in volume 3), romance, humor, and horror genres, but by the end of the 1950s, Marvel had become a marginal player in the comics industry.

In the 1960s, Marvel resurrected its superhero line and infused it with edgy, contemporary storylines. Writer-editor Stan Lee (1922–), along with other Marvel artists and writers, including Wally Wood (1927–1981), Jack Kirby (1917–1994), Steve Ditko (1927–), John Romita (1917–1994), Vince Colletta (1923–1991), and Neal Adams (1941–), introduced a new breed of superhero who overcame flaws to triumph over evil. In 1961, the Fantastic Four were the first such characters to reach the public. Readers were drawn to these heroes, who seemed to spend as much time bickering with one another as they did battling villains. The character who best demonstrated the "Marvel Style" was Spider-Man, who was neurotic, impulsive, unsure of himself, and still a superhero. Marvel remained the comic-industry leader into the 1980s. In 1996, however, the company filed for bankruptcy after suffering financial difficulties.

Marvel recovered from its economic woes by 2000 and saw the production of several film and **television** (see entry under 1940s—TV and Radio in volume 3) treatments based on its characters, notably *X-Men* (2000) and *Spider-Man* (2002). In recent years, the comic-book industry has struggled to maintain an audience in an era in which potential readers spend more time in front of their TVs and computers. Still, Marvel continues to produce exciting stories of its anxiety-ridden heroes for a core audience of fans.

—Charles Coletta

For More Information

Daniels, Les. *Marvel: Five Fabulous Decades of the World's Greatest Comics*. New York: Harry N. Abrams, 1991.

Duin, Steve, and Mike Richardson. *Comics Between the Panels*. Milwaukie, OR: Dark Horse Comics, 1998.

Jones, Gerard, and Will Jacobs. *The Comic Book Heroes*. Rocklin, CA: Prima Publishing, 1998.

Pustz, Matthew. *Comic Book Culture: Fanboys and True Believers*. Jackson: University Press of Mississippi, 1999.

Marvel. http://www.marvel.com (accessed March 18, 2002).

Wright, Bradford. *Comic Book Nation: The Transformation of Youth Culture in America*. Baltimore: The Johns Hopkins University Press, 2001.

Rolling Stone

From its beginnings in 1967 as a countercultural publication appealing to **hippies** (see entry under 1960s—The Way We Lived in volume 4) and other cultural radicals, *Rolling Stone* magazine has come to symbolize the triumph of 1960s antiestablishment values as embodied in **rock and roll** (see entry under 1950s—Music in volume 3) music and relaxed attitudes about drugs and sexuality. In this sense, *Rolling Stone* can be considered the exact opposite of such mainstream publications as the **Saturday Evening Post** (see entry under 1900s—Print Culture in volume 1) or **Reader's Digest** (see entry under 1920s—Print Culture in volume 2).

Rolling Stone was founded by Jann Wenner (1946–), a twenty-one-year-old dropout with $7,500 in borrowed capital. In the first issue—which featured John Lennon on the cover—Wenner editorialized that "*Rolling Stone* is not just about music, but also about the things and attitudes that the music embraces." The magazine's title was inspired by a song by bluesman Muddy Waters (1915–1983). The song itself had borrowed its title from

Rolling Stone founder Jann Wenner in 1970, three years after he started the popular rock music magazine. *Corbis Corporation. Reproduced by permission.*

the old proverb, "A rolling stone gathers no moss." Initially, the magazine was designed to look like an underground newspaper: it was printed on newsprint in a quarterfold format, even though Wenner wanted to make it look professional and well-edited. Still, *Rolling Stone*'s image as a hippie publication continued well into the 1970s. Its first issue sold only about 6,000 copies. By 1974, it had a circulation of 325,000, a figure that rose to 1.25 million by 1998. In the early 1970s, more than eight out of ten of its readers were under twenty-five years old. In its early days, to increase sales, the magazine offered new subscribers a free roach clip (a holder for marijuana cigarettes.)

Rolling Stone's motto, "All the News That Fits" was chosen as an irreverent commentary on the **New York Times** (see entry under 1900s—Print Culture in volume 1), with its slogan "All the News That's Fit to Print." *Rolling Stone* devoted much of its early editorial space to long and comprehensive articles and interviews about the rock-music scene, something no other publication attempted in such depth. It won a 1970 National Magazine Award for articles on the **Altamont** (see entry under 1960s—Music in volume 4) rock concert and on serial killer Charles Manson (1934–). One of its most prominent writers during this period was Hunter Thompson (1937–), known as the "gonzo journalist" for his aggressive and subjective writing style. In 1975, it scooped other publications by publishing firsthand reporting of the Patty Hearst (1954–) kidnapping. By the mid-1970s, *Rolling Stone* was including more political and cultural commentary in its pages. In 1977, the publication moved to New York and changed its "underground" format to a standard, four-color tabloid. As the years went on, mainstream writers like Truman Capote (1924–1984) and Tom Wolfe (1931–) contributed articles to the magazine. By the 1990s, faced with competition from such publications as *Spin* and *Vibe*, *Rolling Stone* continued to de-emphasize its coverage of music in favor of articles on politics, technology, and fashion.

—*Edward Moran*

For More Information

Anson, Robert Sam. *The Rise and Fall of the Rolling Stone Generation.* Garden City, NY: Doubleday, 1981.

Draper, Robert. *Rolling Stone Magazine: The Uncensored History.* Garden City, NY: Doubleday, 1990.

Rolling Stone. http://www.rollingstone.com (accessed March 18, 2002).

Seymour, Corey, "On the Cover of *Rolling Stone:* A Twenty-Fifth Anniversary Special." *Rolling Stone* (December 10, 1992): pp. 147–54.

Spider-Man

Since 1962, a mild-mannered newspaper photographer has been battling crime as the Amazing Spider-Man in a monthly **comic-book** (see entry under 1930s–Print Culture in volume 2) series published by **Marvel Comics** (see entry under 1960s–Print Culture in volume 4). Many years after his debut, Spider-Man remains Marvel's most popular character and a pop-culture icon (symbol) on par with **Superman** and **Batman** (see these two entries under 1930s–Print Culture in volume 2). A feature-film version of the superhero's adventures, released in 2002, starring actor Tobey Maguire (1975–), seemed sure to introduce "Spidey" to an even wider audience.

Created by Marvel Comics' editor-in-chief Stan Lee (1922–), Spider-Man made his first appearance in issue #15 of *Amazing Fantasy* in August 1962. There the character's origin and powers were explained. Teenager Peter Parker was bitten by a radioactive spider while attending a science lecture. The bite gave him the proportional strength of a spider, as well as the ability to stick to walls and a special "spider sense" that tingles whenever there is danger. The resourceful Parker then constructs a red and blue costume, attaches a set of "web shooters" to his wrists, and assumes the identity of Spider-Man. At first, he hopes to cash in on his superpowers. When his beloved Uncle Ben is killed because of his own carelessness, Parker realizes that "with great power comes great responsibility" and dedicates his life to fighting crime.

As drawn by original artist Steve Ditko (1927–), Spider-Man is a dynamic character who swings through the streets of New York on a ropelike web and catches criminals in his elaborate sticky nets. Ditko also created many of the comic book's signature supervillains, from the frightening Green Goblin to the

An unidentified actor in a Spider-Man outfit scales a building in Jerusalem in 1995. *Photograph by Brian Hendler. AP/Wide World Photos. Reproduced by permission.*

bizarre, eight-armed Dr. Octopus. Lee's writing truly made Spider-Man unique. In Lee's vision, Peter Parker was a character the ordinary teenage reader could relate to, not an alien like Clark Kent (Superman) or *Batman*'s stiffly proper Bruce Wayne. With his wisecracks and his all-too-human flaws, Spider-Man was, in Lee's famous phrase, "the superhero who could be you." This approach proved so popular that Marvel adopted it for virtually all its titles and became the number-one comic-book publisher in the world. Spider-Man himself branched out, over the decades, into several other monthly titles, numerous live-action and cartoon TV series, and, in 2002, a big-budget Hollywood blockbuster.

—*Robert E. Schnakenberg*

For More Information

Lee, Stan. *Origins of Marvel Comics.* New York: Simon & Schuster, 1974.
Lee, Stan, and Steve Ditko. *Marvel Masterworks Presents the Amazing Spider-Man.* New York: Marvel Books, 1999.
Simon, Joe, with Jim Simon. *The Comic Book Makers.* New York: Crestwood/II Publications, 1990.

Whole Earth Catalog

The *Whole Earth Catalog* was the brainchild of Stewart Brand (1938–), who first published it in 1968. It was essentially a catalog of ideas, books, new technologies, and other ideas Brand thought were worthy of wider notice. It was an alternative, offbeat publication that in many ways symbolized the spirit of searching that characterized the late 1960s.

Like any other catalog, the *Whole Earth Catalog* offered a wide variety of items, accompanied by short descriptions and pictures. Unlike other catalogs, nothing was for sale. Believing that "information wants to be free," Brand wrote the catalog as a way to get lots of good information to as many people as possible. The catalog accepted no advertising and only reviewed those items that the editors thought would be a positive force for change. In the first edition of the catalog, Brand focused on a few key areas of knowledge, including the environment, shelter and land use, communications, community, and learning. The section on shelter and land use, for example, had ideas for better, more energy-efficient housing design, solar and wind power, and other alternative technologies.

Part of Brand's mission with the *Whole Earth Catalog* was to put power back in the hands of the people, an attitude that was very much a part of the late 1960s youth counterculture. Brand said the catalog's purpose was to empower "the individual to conduct his own education, find his own inspiration, shape his own environment, and share his adventure with whoever is interested." In the late 1960s, because young people were fed up with government, their parents, and the powerful in society, they sought to take their lives and futures into their own hands, on their own terms, and live by their own values, not those given to them by society. The *Whole Earth Catalog,* and its later updates and additions, helped people find the tools to live by their own values. Brand later won the National Book Award for his work with the *Whole Earth Catalog.* He published numerous updates and a magazine, *Whole Earth.*

—*Timothy Berg*

For More Information

Brand, Stewart, ed. *The Whole Earth Catalog.* Self-published, 1968; San Rafael, CA: Point Foundation, 1998.

Gitlin, Todd. *The Sixties.* New York: Bantam, 1987.

Rheingold, Howard, ed. *The Millennium Whole Earth Catalog: Access to Tools and Ideas for the Twenty-First Century.* San Francisco: Harper-SanFrancisco, 1994.

Whole Earth. http://www.wholeearthmag.com (accessed March 18, 2002).

1960s

Sports and Games

The 1960s saw professional sports finally attain dominance in the hearts of American sports fans. The overlapping seasons of professional baseball, football, hockey, and basketball offered sports fans year-round entertainment, and television broadcasting increased in sophistication to make sports coverage more exciting. It also helped that the 1960s were filled with dramatic moments and glamorous sports stars.

No one team dominated major league baseball, as seven different teams won the World Series. Perhaps the most astonishing World Series win went to the 1969 New York Mets, who had finished next-to-last in 1968. The "Amazin' Mets," as they were known, provided thrills for every fan who roots for the underdog. The 1960s were the decade of stars, as players like Roger Maris (1934–1985), Mickey Mantle (1931–1995), Maury Wills (1932–), Sandy Koufax (1935–), Frank Robinson (1935–), Carl Yastrzemski (1939–), and others set records and thrilled fans.

Professional football became the most popular American sport in the 1960s, surpassing baseball in attendance and in television viewership. Men, mostly, across the nation gave up their Sunday afternoons to watch the games, and for most of the decade they could choose between the National Football League (NFL) and the American Football League (AFL). The two leagues played their first championship game—called the Super Bowl—against each other in 1967, with the NFL's Green Bay Packers easily defeating the AFL's Kansas City Chiefs, 35-10. The most dominant team of the decade, the Packers won the next Super Bowl, too, beating the Oakland Raiders, 33-14. But Super Bowl III was a different story: The New York Jets of the upstart AFL proved the league's worth—and silenced AFL naysayers—by beating the Baltimore Colts, 16-7, behind the heroics of quarterback Joe Namath (1943–).

The National Basketball Association (NBA) grew in popularity and size throughout the decade. Beginning the decade with just eight teams, it grew to seventeen teams by the end of the decade and in 1965 drew over five million fans to its games.

The Boston Celtics were the era's dominant team, winning nine of ten NBA championships. The Celtics were led by their dominating center, Bill Russell (1934–), who had a great rivalry with fellow big man Wilt Chamberlain (1936–1999), who played for the Philadelphia Warriors, San Francisco Warriors, Philadelphia 76ers, and Los Angeles Lakers. In an era known for the gains made by African Americans, black players came to dominate the game of professional basketball. College basketball also remained very popular, and was dominated in the decade by the UCLA team coached by John Wooden (1910–) and, after 1967, by a seven-foot player named Lew Alcindor (1947–), who later changed his name to Kareem Abdul-Jabbar.

Other sports also drew fan's attention. The single most celebrated athlete of the decade was boxer Cassius Clay, who took the name Muhammad Ali (1942–) after winning the heavyweight crown in 1964. Ali dominated the heavyweight class for years, and he entertained the world with his witty boasts, such as "I float like a butterfly and sting like a bee." The Olympics continued to raise its profile as a sporting event, thanks to substantial television coverage and to growing corporate sponsorship of the games. Inspired by Americans' growing love of sports, in 1961 ABC-TV introduced a new style of sports show called *Wide World of Sports* which, in its famous opening lines, promised that it was "spanning the world to give you the constant variety of sports—the thrill of victory and the agony of defeat, the human drama of athletic competition."

Muhammad Ali (1942–)

On three separate occasions, Muhammad Ali won the title of heavyweight boxing champ. He was more than a fighter, however; he was one of the most beloved *and* one of the most despised public figures of his time. Ali earned his first fame in 1960 (when he was still known by his birth name, Cassius Clay), winning a gold medal at the Rome **Olympics** (see entry under 1900s—Sports and Games in volume 1), and secured his initial title by beating Sonny Liston (1932–1970) in 1964.

Ali was not the first African American boxing champ, but like **Jack Johnson** (1878–1946; see entry under 1900s—Sports and Games in volume 1) before him, Ali courted controversy on several fronts. He was a spirited soul who said and did as he

Muhammad Ali stands over opponent Sonny Liston during a 1965 bout. *AP/Wide World Photos. Reproduced by permission.*

pleased. He was a master of self-promotion, declaring "I am the greatest" for all to hear. This attitude rankled those white people who felt that the young champ did not "know his place" as a Negro (the accepted term for African Americans in the 1960s). They were bothered further when the boxer announced that he had become a Black Muslim and changed his name from Clay to Ali. Then he refused to submit to the military draft and was convicted of draft evasion. For this final offense, he was stripped of his title by the World Boxing Association in 1967. He was condemned on editorial pages and over dinner tables across America.

Ali's conviction was overturned, however, and he returned to the ring in 1971. Before retiring a decade later, he participated in several classic ring battles with Joe Frazier (1944–) and George Foreman (1949–). Back in the late 1960s, Ali—despite his controversy—arguably was the most famous human on earth, a hero in Africa, in third-world nations, and in the ghettos of America. In dramatic fashion, the Parkinson's Disease–afflicted Ali lit the Olympic torch at the 1996 Summer Olympics in Atlanta, Georgia. As he aged, and his old enemies died out, Ali became one of the world's most respected and beloved sports legends.

—Rob Edelman

For More Information

Bockris, Victor. *Muhammad Ali*. New York: Cooper Square Press, 2000.

Early, Gerald, ed. *The Muhammad Ali Reader*. New York: R. Weisbach Books, 1999.

Hook, Jason. *Muhammad Ali: The Greatest*. Austin, TX: Raintree/Steck Vaughn, 2001.

Sanford, William R., and Carl R. Green. *Muhammad Ali*. New York: Crestwood House, 1993.

Tessitore, John. *Muhammad Ali: The World's Champion*. New York: F. Watts, 1998.

Dallas Cowboys

Started in 1960, the Dallas Cowboys of the **National Football League** (see entry under 1920s—Sports and Games in volume 2) soon became one of the most prominent teams in the history of all professional football, and they endure as "America's Team." Few teams in league history can boast a higher national profile or a more consistent record of success.

Dozens of football legends were Cowboys, including Tom Landry (1924–2000), the team's longtime head coach; quarterbacks "Dandy" Don Meredith (1938–), Roger Staubach (1942–), and Troy Aikman (1966–); running backs Tony Dorsett (1954–) and Emmitt Smith (1969–); and defensive standouts including Bob Lilly (1939–), Lee Roy Jordan (1941–), Ed "Too Tall" Jones (1951–), and Randy White (1953–). In 1980, Lilly became the first Cowboy to enter the Professional Football Hall of Fame.

The team is also known for its cheerleaders. The Dallas Cowboy Cheerleaders combined sports with entertainment and set the standard for professional cheerleaders.

—Rob Edelman

For More Information

Donovan, Jim, Ken Sins, and Frank Coffey. *The Dallas Cowboys Encyclopedia: The Ultimate Guide to America's Team*. Secaucus, NJ: Carol Publishing Group, 1999.

Golenbock, Peter. *Cowboys Have Always Been My Heroes: The Definitive Oral History of America's Team*. New York: Warner Books, 1997.

Landry, Tom, and Greg Lewis. *Tom Landry: An Autobiography.* Grand Rapids, MI: Zondervan Publishing House, 1990.

St. John, Bob. *Tex! The Man Who Built the Dallas Cowboys.* Englewood Hills, NJ: Prentice-Hall, 1988.

Stowers, Carlton. *Dallas Cowboys: The First Twenty-Five Years.* Dallas: Taylor Publishing, 1984.

Sugar, Bert Randolph. *I Hate the Dallas Cowboys: And Who Elected Them America's Team Anyway?* New York: St. Martin's Griffin, 1997.

Frisbee

Along with the balloon tire bicycle and the **skateboard** (see entry under 1950s–Sports and Games in volume 3), the Frisbee is a key accessory of late twentieth-century American childhood. Plastic flying discs were marketed as the "Flyin' Saucer" by the Pipco company in the late 1940s, but the first "Frisbee" was made by the Wham-O Toy Company in 1957. The flying disc that began life as a pie tin became popular on California beaches and never really went away.

By the late 1960s, laid-back Frisbee fans worked on throwing the Frisbee as straight and as far as possible. They also played Frisbee Golf, Ultimate Frisbee, and Freestyle Frisbee. With its trick throws, juggling, behind-the-back catches, and other flashy moves, Freestyle caught the public imagination in the 1970s. In the 1990s, Ultimate Frisbee was a growing worldwide sport. Despite the high-tech distractions of the twenty-first century, Frisbee remains very popular with humans. Dogs have always been the best Frisbee catchers, though.

—Chris Routledge

For More Information

Johnson, Stancil E. D. *Frisbee: A Practitioner's Manual and Definitive Treatise.* New York: Workman Publishing Company, 1975.

The Ultimate Handbook. http://www.ultimatehandbook.com/index.html (accessed on March 19, 2002).

Evel Knievel (1938–)

Daredevil motorcycle stuntmen are a rarity, far outnumbered by auto racers, skiers, or track-and-field athletes, let alone players from all sports. For years, Evel Knievel has had this field

virtually all to himself. His successes—and his spectacular failures—have earned him a fame saved for mainstream athletes and movie stars.

Knievel—who was born Robert Craig Knievel—has an unusually varied background. He has been a ski-jump champion, a professional hockey player, a car salesman, a hunting guide, a con man, and a safecracker. He entered the profession that would earn him international fame in 1965 when he created an outfit called Evel Knievel's Motorcycle Daredevils. He won headlines on New Year's Day in 1968 when he successfully jumped his motorcycle over the fountains in front of the Caesar's Palace hotel in Las Vegas, Nevada. Even though he crash-landed and spent a month in a coma, his reputation was made. He followed up with additional jumps, on locations ranging from the Los Angeles Coliseum to Idaho's Snake River Canyon to Ohio's Kings Island, where he piloted his motorcycle over fourteen Greyhound busses.

Knievel's many crashes left his body mangled. He broke his pelvis while attempting to leap over thirteen double-decker buses at London's Wembley Stadium in 1975. The following year, he received major injuries while leaping over a tank filled with live sharks in the Chicago Amphitheater.

Miniature reproductions of Knievel's Stuntcycle became a popular toy in the 1970s. He was the subject of a Hollywood film biography, *Evel Knievel* (1971), and starred as himself on screen in *Viva Knievel!* (1977). Indeed, his death-defying exploits have won him near-folk hero status.

—*Rob Edelman*

For More Information

An American Legend: Evel Knievel Merchandise and Memorabilia. http://www.evel1.com/ (accessed March 19, 2002).

Collins, Ace. *Evel Knievel: An American Hero.* New York: St. Martin's Press, 1999.

Evel Knievel: Motorcycle Daredevil. http://www.who2.com/evelknievel.html (accessed March 19, 2002).

Scalzo, Joe. *Evel Knievel and Other Daredevils.* New York: Grosset and Dunlap, 1974.

Joe Namath (1943–)

In an era when star athletes were supposed to be idealized, clean-living role models for fans young and old, Joseph William Namath was a startling exception. After starring at the University of Alabama, Namath (often nicknamed Joe Willie) became quarterback of the New York Jets, of the upstart American Football League (AFL), signing a then-record $427,000 contract in 1964.

It was for good reason that Namath was nicknamed "Broadway Joe": he earned as many headlines for his bachelor-pad, party-boy lifestyle as for his exploits on the field. He gained everlasting fame, however, when he boldly—and accurately—predicted that his AFL-champion Jets would beat the highly favored Baltimore Colts, of the more established **National Football League** (NFL; see entry under 1920s–Sports and Games in volume 2), in **Super Bowl** (see entry under 1960s–Sports and Games in volume 4) III in 1969. The Jets' 16-7 victory not only proved to the NFL that its AFL baby brothers were fast maturing—the two leagues ended up merging soon afterwards—but affirmed that Namath could back up his boasting with on-field heroics.

Namath had a stellar career with the Jets from 1965 to 1976, and retired after he spent the 1977 season with the Los

Angeles Rams. He was elected to the Pro Football Hall of Fame in 1985.

—Rob Edelman

For More Information

"Broadway Joe." *SportsLine.com.* http://www.cbs.sportsline.com/u/fans/celebrity/namath (accessed March 19, 2002).

Namath, Joe. *Football for Young Players and Parents.* New York: Simon & Schuster, 1986.

Sanford, William R. *Joe Namath.* New York: Crestwood House, 1993.

Super Bowl

Since 1967, professional football's annual championship game, dubbed the Super Bowl, has been played on a Sunday in January. At first just a novelty, the game has grown in popularity so that it stands as something of an unofficial national holiday. There are Super Bowl parties from coast to coast, and the game is televised around the world to enthusiastic audiences.

The first Super Bowl pitted the Green Bay Packers of the **National Football League** (see entry under 1920s—Sports and Games in volume 2) against the Kansas City Chiefs of the American Football League. The game was designed to settle the score between the rival leagues, each vying for national supremacy. The Packers won that game, and the following one, but in 1969 the AFL's New York Jets created the first Super Bowl sensation (in the first of the games to be officially called the "Super Bowl") with a shocking upset of the NFL's Baltimore Colts. The surprising outcome forced the NFL to reconsider its opposition to merging with the AFL. A year later, the two leagues became one.

With no rival league to challenge it, the NFL grew in popularity, and so did the Super Bowl. Now crafted to match the playoff winner in each of two conferences, the game is played in a different city each year and attracts huge crowds and high TV ratings. The football contests themselves have often been unimpressive, but the "scene" surrounding the game, including celebrities, elaborate halftime shows, and widespread betting on the outcome, have turned the Super Bowl into a national extravaganza. **Television** (see entry under 1940s—TV and Radio in volume 3) advertisers, attracted by the lure of enormous TV audiences, began paying top dollars for commercial time on the network broadcast. As a result, the Super Bowl became a kind of showcase for the best and most expensive TV ads. The annual "Bud Bowl" contests, Apple Computer's memorable futuristic "1984" ad, and the Pets.com sock puppet were just a few of the famous commercials to debut during Super Bowl telecasts.

Among the Super Bowl's most notable performers have been Joe Montana (1956–), the San Francisco 49ers quarterback who led his team to three Super Bowl victories; **Joe Namath** (1943–; see entry under 1960s–Sports and Games in volume 4), the Jets quarterback who guaranteed victory in Super Bowl III; and John Elway (1960–), who led the Denver Broncos to back-to-back wins in the 1990s. With the advent of **satellite** (see entry under 1950s–The Way We Lived in volume 3) TV, the Super Bowl continues to grow in popularity and attracts ever-increasing worldwide audiences.

–Robert E. Schnakenberg

For More Information

Brenner, Richard J. *The Complete Super Bowl Story: Games I–XXIII.* Minneapolis: Lerner Publications, 1990.

Buckley, James, Jr. *Super Bowl Heroes.* New York: Dorling Kindersley, 2000.

Didinger, Ray. *The Super Bowl: Celebrating a Quarter-Century of America's Greatest Game.* New York: Simon & Schuster, 1990.

Resciniti, Angelo. *Super Bowl Excitement.* St. Petersburg, FL: Willowisp Press, 1994.

Superbowlhistory.com. http://www.superbowlhistory.com/ (accessed March 19, 2002).

Twister

The ultimate way to make guests relax and start laughing at a party, Twister is a game in which players turn a spinner that tells them which hand or foot to place on which colored circle on the large game board (a thin floor mat). Players' arms and legs become tangled, leading to falls and laughs. The object of the game is to be the last player to lose his or her balance.

Twister was released by the **Milton Bradley Company** (see entry under 1900s–Sports and Games in volume 1) in 1966 and was introduced to the American public on *The Tonight Show* (see entry under 1950s–TV and Radio in volume 3) on NBC. When viewers watched the show's host, **Johnny Carson** (1925–; see entry under 1960s–TV and Radio in volume 4), play the

Teens enjoy playing the game **Twister.** *Corbis Corporation. Reproduced by permission.*

game with glamorous movie star Eva Gabor (1919–1995), it prompted three million people to go buy their own Twister game.

A fun game for children, Twister also appeals to adults, who have invented variations such as combat Twister which involves actively trying to push other players off balance, and nude Twister, popular during the **sexual revolution** (see entry under 1960s–The Way We Lived in volume 4) of the 1960s and 1970s.

Twister has appeared in many films and **television** (see entry under 1940s–TV and Radio in volume 3) shows, notably the

1991 film *Bill and Ted's Bogus Journey*, where the heroes play a hilarious game of Twister with Death.

—*Tina Gianoulis*

For More Information

Asakawa, Gil, and Leland Rucker. *The Toy Book*. New York: Alfred A. Knopf, 1992.

Hoffman, David. *Kid Stuff: Great Toys from Our Childhood*. San Francisco: Chronicle Books, 1996.

Polizzi, Rick, and Fred Schaefer. *Spin Again: Board Games from the Fifties and Sixties*. San Francisco: Chronicle Books, 1991.

Wide World of Sports

As TV sets were becoming staples in American households during the 1950s, individual sporting events made for popular, low-cost programming. Then, at the dawn of the 1960s, *Wide World of Sports,* also known as *ABC's Wide World of Sports,* debuted. The show was a new type of sports program. Rather than focus on one sport, it presented a variety of athletic events in one show. Each week, *Wide World of Sports* transported the viewer across the United States and around the world. The show featured many athletes who otherwise would not be seen on **television** (see entry under 1940s–TV and Radio in volume 3): bobsled racers, bodybuilders, gymnasts, figure skaters, ski jumpers, surfers, swimmers, divers, auto racers, stunt motorcyclists, rodeo performers, and track-and-field athletes. All the while, the show spotlighted the human side of sports. In addition to presenting races, bouts, and meets (often live via satellite), *Wide World of Sports* revolutionized sports coverage by including "up close and personal" features on athletes. The show's rallying cry, "The thrill of victory and the agony of defeat," not only became one of the most familiar catchphrases on TV but captured the essence of athletic competition.

Over the years, many high-profile sportscasters were associated with *Wide World of Sports,* including Frank Gifford (1930–), Chris Schenkel (1923–), Howard Cosell (1918–1995), Bud Palmer (1920–), and Keith Jackson (1928–). The one sports commentator most closely associated with the show, however, is Jim McKay (1921–). He was on hand for the very first broadcast, which aired on April 29, 1961, and featured the Drake Relays, from Des Moines, Iowa, and the Penn Relays, from

Philadelphia, Pennsylvania. (Relays are track-and-field events.) Across the decades, McKay traveled over 4.5 million miles to cover events for the program, reporting on over one hundred different sports in forty-plus countries and across the United States. McKay earned further fame as a longtime host of the **Olympics** (see entry under 1900s–Sports and Games in volume 1). In 1968, he became the first sportscaster ever to win an Emmy Award, for his work on *Wide World of Sports.*

The show's format was the brainchild of Roone Arledge (1931–), the future ABC Sports and News president. The show ran for ninety minutes on Saturdays, and occasionally appeared on Sundays. Sporting events that later merited their own separate coverage—the Wimbledon tennis tournament, World Cup soccer, the British Open golf tournament—first aired on *Wide World of Sports.*

The success of *Wide World of Sports,* and other groundbreaking endeavors such as ***Monday Night Football*** (see entry under 1970s–Sports and Games in volume 4), helped solidify the status of ABC as the major network dominating sports coverage. With the rise of **ESPN** (see entry under 1970s–TV and Radio in volume 4) as an all-day sports network, *Wide World of Sports* began losing its shine in the late 1980s. On January 3, 1998, it was announced that the show had been canceled. On April 29, 2001, ABC aired a two-hour-long fortieth anniversary retrospective.

—*Rob Edelman*

For More Information

McKay, Jim, with Jim McPhee. *The Real McKay: My Wide World of Sports.* New York: Dutton, 1998.

Sugar, Bert Randolph. *Thrill of Victory: The Inside Story of ABC Sports.* New York: Hawthorn Books, 1978.

1960s

TV and Radio

Television cemented its grip on American attention spans during the 1960s. The industry added channels and improved the quality of its color pictures. However, some Americans became increasingly critical of television programming in the decade. They worried that TV would, in the words of many a concerned parent, "rot their children's minds."

Federal Communications Commission chairman Newton Minow (1926–) summed up the concerns about television in his address to the National Association of Broadcasters in 1961. "When television is good," said Minow, "nothing—not the theater, not the magazines or newspapers—nothing is better. But when television is bad, nothing is worse." He challenged broadcasters to watch their TV shows for an entire day. Minow assured them, in words that became his most famous, that they would observe "a vast wasteland."

Minow was right—TV in the 1960s was both good and bad. Sports programming improved dramatically during the decade, as broadcasters and camera crews learned how to make the games dramatic. Television news proved its merits with five days of nearly continuous coverage of the 1963 assassination of President John F. Kennedy (1917–1963). Later in the decade, coverage of the Vietnam War (1954–75) and the *Apollo* moon landings helped make TV the primary way that Americans got their news. A new format of news program called *60 Minutes* premiered in 1968.

Americans enjoyed watching the Westerns, situation comedies (sitcoms), and action-adventure shows that made up the majority of network programming, but few could claim that these shows were of great quality. The decade was characterized by silly shows like *Gilligan's Island* (1964–67), *Bewitched* (1964–72), *The Beverly Hillbillies* (1962–71), and *Hawaii Five-O* (1968–80). The most innovative programs—*The Smothers Brothers Comedy Hour* (1967–70) and *Rowan & Martin's Laugh-In* (1968–73)—were variety shows with political and satirical content. In fact, *The Smothers Brothers* show was so controversial that it was canceled.

Those concerned about the quality of television, especially of the quality of programming for children, were cheered by the creation of the Corporation for Public Broadcasting in 1967. This led to the founding of the Public Broadcasting System (PBS) in 1969 and to the airing of such quality children's TV shows as *Sesame Street* (1969–) and *Mister Rogers' Neighborhood* (1966–2001).

With TV as Americans' first choice for news, as well as drama, comedy, and adventure stories, radio was forced to take on a different role in American entertainment. The spread of portable transistor radios and of car radios made radio a portable form of entertainment, and radios provided music and news for those on the go. By 1967, it was estimated that 90 percent of all radio programming was music. Stations diversified to carry different types of music, from rock to classical, folk to country. One of the most popular radio formats was the Top 40 station, which played only the most popular hits in America.

Whether Americans got their entertainment from radio or TV, they had to submit to the ever-increasing tide of advertising that interrupted broadcasts—but also made them possible. People complained about all the ads, but the truth was that most of the costs of airing programs were carried by advertisers, who were willing to pay top dollar to be able to tell huge audiences about the latest and greatest new product.

The Andy Griffith Show

In the 1960s, a series of popular television comedies—among them **The Beverly Hillbillies** (1962–71; see entry under 1960s—TV and Radio in volume 4), *Petticoat Junction* (1963–70), and *Green Acres* (1965–71)—spotlighted rural southern Americans. Many critics and viewers believed the best was *The Andy Griffith Show* (1960–68).

The Andy Griffith Show is set in the sleepy southern town of Mayberry, North Carolina. Its primary character is Andy Taylor (Andy Griffith, 1926–), Mayberry's likable, level-headed sheriff. Taylor, a widower, is surrounded by an appealing cast of supporting characters: Opie (Ron Howard, 1954–), his son; Aunt Bee (Frances Bavier, 1902–1989), his sympathetic aunt, who lives with Andy and helps raise Opie; and Barney Fife (Don Knotts, 1924–), his comically incompetent deputy.

When Griffith left the show in 1968, it continued for three more seasons as *Mayberry, R.F.D.* (1968–71), with the new lead character, Sam Jones (Ken Berry, 1933–), surrounded with some new and some old characters. *The Andy Griffith Show* can still be seen in reruns and remains a charming and entertaining view of life in idyllic small-town America.

—*Rob Edelman*

For More Information

The Andy Griffith Show Rerun Watchers Club. http://www.mayberry.com (accessed March 20, 2002).

BarneyFife.com. http://www.barneyfife.com (accessed March 20, 2002).

Beck, Ken. *The Andy Griffith Show Book.* New York: St. Martin's Press, 1995.

Brower, Neal. *Mayberry 101: Behind the Scenes of a TV Classic.* Winston-Salem, NC: John Blair, 1998.

Harrison, Dan. *Inside Mayberry.* New York: HarperPerennial, 1994.

Kelly, Richard Michael. *The Andy Griffith Show.* Winston-Salem, NC: John Blair, 1981.

Lindsay, George, with Ken Beck and Jim Clark. *Goober in a Nutshell.* New York: Avon Books, 1995.

The Beverly Hillbillies

The Beverly Hillbillies, which aired on CBS from 1962 until 1971, was one of the most popular **sitcoms** (see entry under 1950s–TV and Radio in volume 3) in **television** (see entry under 1940s–TV and Radio in volume 3) history. Although the series was criticized for its backwoods humor, audiences embraced the misadventures of the mountaineer family who discovered oil on their rural property and subsequently moved to the land of swimming pools and movie stars—Beverly Hills, California. The series' great success led CBS to air a number of rural-based comedies for the next decade.

Its memorable theme song was performed by **bluegrass** (see entry under 1940s–Music in volume 3) stars Lester Flatt (1914–1979) and Earl Scruggs (1924–). In the song, the audience learns how Jed Clampett (Buddy Ebsen; 1908–) discovered "bubbling crude" on his land and became an instant millionaire. He is soon convinced to transplant his clan to California. Making the journey with Jed are his gorgeous tomboy daughter Elly May (Donna Douglas, 1933–), his dim-witted nephew Jethro Bodine (Max Baer Jr., 1937–), and his mother-in-law Daisy Moses, known as "Granny" (Irene Ryan, 1902–1973). The Clampett fortune is housed in the Commerce Bank and administered by greedy bank president Milburn Drysdale (Raymond

The Clampett family of *The Beverly Hillbillies:* (clockwise from upper left) Donna Douglas, Irene Ryan, Max Baer Jr., and Buddy Ebsen. *Archive Photos. Reproduced by permission.*

Bailey, 1904–1980) and his plain, sensible assistant Miss Jane Hathaway (Nancy Kulp, 1921–1991). Most of the series' humor derives from the culture clash between the simple mountain people and the sophisticated city slickers. The Clampetts are thoroughly unfamiliar with modern conveniences and attitudes. They refer to their mansion's swimming pool as a "cee-ment pond" and mistake a billiards table for a formal dining set. Both the country and city characters are broad stereotypes, but hardly offensive. Many episodes focus on Elly May's collection of animals, Jethro's idiotic schemes, and Granny's unhappiness with city life.

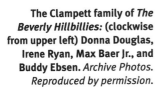

Critics scorned series creator Paul Henning (1911–) and dismissed *The Beverly Hillbillies* as juvenile, foolish, and overly broad. Audiences, however, loved the program and made it TV's highest rated series by its third episode. The series also holds the distinction of having one of its episodes (concerning the Clampetts confusing a kangaroo for a giant jackrabbit) rank as one of TV's all-time highest rated episodes. Those who condemn the show as overly simplistic ignore that it was both very well written and very well acted. The series generated a wealth of merchandise and two popular spin-offs—*Petticoat Junction* (which aired on CBS from 1963 to 1970) and *Green Acres* (which aired on CBS from 1965 to 1971). In 1971, CBS grew tired of its image as the "hillbilly network" and canceled all its rural comedies.

The Beverly Hillbillies continued to thrive into the 1980s and 1990s in syndication (the reshowing of a series as reruns on independent TV stations). In 1993, a film version of the series featuring Jim Varney (1949–2000), Lily Tomlin (1939–), and Cloris Leachman (1926–) was unsuccessful. That film's failure did little to dim the American public's affection for the original series and its homespun humor.

—*Charles Coletta*

For More Information

The Beverly Hillbillies. http://www.pcperspectives.com/hillbillies (accessed March 20, 2002).

Clark, Jim. *Granny's Beverly Hillbillies Cookbook*. Nashville: Rutledge Hill Press, 1994.

Cox, Stephen. *The Beverly Hillbillies*. New York: HarperPerennial, 1993.

Herb, Sam. "The Beverly Hillbillies." *TVparty*. http://www.tvparty.com/recbev.html (accessed March 20, 2002).

Mitz, Rick. *The Great TV Sitcom Book*. New York: R. Marek Publishers, 1983.

Strasser, Todd. *The Beverly Hillbillies: A Novelization*. New York: Harper Paperbacks, 1993.

Bewitched

The situation comedy *Bewitched,* which aired from 1964 until 1972 on ABC, was one of television's most popular programs during an era dominated by a number of fantasy- or supernatural-based comedy shows. The series centered on the marriage of a beautiful young witch named Samantha (Elizabeth

Montgomery, 1933–1995) to Darrin Stephens (Dick York, 1928–1992; also played later by Dick Sargent, 1930–1994), an advertising executive who demanded that his wife give up her powers of sorcery in order that they might live a normal middle-class suburban life together. Samantha's mother Endora (Agnes Moorehead, 1900–1974) often disrupted the couple's happiness, as she disliked her son-in-law and his prohibition against witchcraft. She was further frustrated by Samantha's willingness to live without magic.

Bewitched and the other fantasy **sitcoms** (see entry under 1950s—TV and Radio in volume 3) of the 1960s provided much needed escapist entertainment from the decade's social and political upheavals. The series was a critical and popular hit as it injected the supernatural into sitcom suburbia. Elizabeth Montgomery, the daughter of actor Robert Montgomery (1904–1981), became an international celebrity as she enchanted audiences with both her beauty and comedic skills. Her trademark was the "magical" nose twitch by which Samantha cast her spells. Most of the episodes revolved around the comedic mishaps stemming from Samantha using her powers despite her husband's prohibition. It was not uncommon to meet famous figures from history, have people transformed into animals, or see furniture floating around the Stevens' household. Much of the show's comedy derived from Samantha's attempting to hide her abilities from nosy neighbor Gladys Kravitz (Alice Pearce, 1917–1966; later, Sandra Gould, 1916–1999). Among the most popular episodes of the series were those devoted to Tabitha, Darrin and Samantha's baby daughter, who had inherited her mother's magic skills. A son, Adam, was born to the TV couple late in the series.

Although Montgomery was the program's star, the series boasted one of the strongest ensemble casts on **television** (see entry under 1940s—TV and Radio in volume 3). Among the witches and warlocks who regularly caused mischief at the Stevens' were the bumbling Aunt Clara (Marion Lorne, 1888–1968), Uncle Arthur (Paul Lynde, 1926–1982), and Samantha's father Maurice (who was played by the great Shakespearean actor Maurice Evans, 1901–1989). David White (1916–1990) played Larry Tate, Darrin's excitable boss. Montgomery often appeared in a dual role as Serena, Samantha's kooky cousin. The series ended its run in 1972, as more cutting edge sitcoms like *All in the Family* (see entry under 1970s—TV and Radio in volume 4) gained popularity. *Tabitha*, a short-lived sitcom sequel following the adventures of the Stevens' grown daughter, aired in the 1977–78 season.

Bewitched has remained popular in syndication (the re-release of programs to independent TV stations) for over thirty years as new generations of viewers become enchanted by Montgomery's Samantha. Some consider the Stephenses as TV's first "mixed marriage." Others view Samantha as an early feminist icon (symbol of feminism) who attempted to balance her own abilities with her husband's expectations of a wife's duties.

—Charles Coletta

For More Information

The Bewitched and Elizabeth Montgomery Web Site. http://www.bewitched.net (accessed March 20, 2002).

Mascaro, Victor. *Vic's Bewitched Page.* http://members.tripod.com/~bewitchvic/main.html (accessed March 20, 2002).

Mitz, Rick. *The Great TV Sitcom Book.* New York: R. Marek Publishers, 1983.

Pilato, Herbie. *The Bewitched Book: The Cosmic Companion to TV's Most Magical Supernatural Situation Comedy.* New York: Delta, 1992.

Rogers, Kasey. *The Bewitched Cookbook.* New York: Kensington Books, 1996.

Bonanza

American popular culture has long been fascinated with stories of pioneer life on the frontier and tales of the Old West. This phenomenon was especially true in the 1950s and 1960s when Western-themed programs dominated the **television** (see entry under 1940s–TV and Radio in volume 3) networks. *Bonanza,* which ran from 1959 to 1973, was one of the most popular and long-lasting of these programs. The series was one of TV's highest-rated shows of the 1960s. Audiences tuned in each week to see the adventures of the all-male Cartwright clan as they tended to their 1,000-square-mile Ponderosa Ranch outside of Virginia City, Nevada, in the years following the Civil War (1861–65).

Adults of the 1960s had grown up on **Western** (see entry under 1930s–Film and Theater in volume 2) movies featuring cowboy heroes like **John Wayne** (1907–1979; see entry under 1930s–Film and Theater in volume 2) and Roy Rogers (1911–1998). They made up the bulk of the television audience and enjoyed what were known as "adult Westerns." These programs, like **Gunsmoke** (1955–75; see entry under 1950s–TV and Radio in volume 3), *Maverick* (1957–62), and *Bonanza* avoided the common Western cliches (stagecoach holdups, bank robberies, head-'em-off-at-the-pass chases) in favor of character development and a low-key tone. On *Bonanza,* Ben Cartwright (Lorne Greene, 1915–1987) had three grown sons: the serious and introspective Adam (Parnell Roberts, 1928–); Hoss (Dan Blocker, 1928–1972), an innocent and gentle giant; and Little Joe (Michael Landon, 1936–1991), the handsome and impulsive youngest son. Scholar Michael Barson, in *TV Genres,* credits the program's appeal to the contrast it provided to real life in the turbulent 1960s. He states, "This was a show about family. . . . The Cartwrights were able to survive more than a decade's worth of divisiveness and struggle, just as America itself did [during the Vietnam era (1954–75)]."

Bonanza holds the distinction of being the first Western to be televised in color. The popular Western is recalled as helping to dramatically increase sales of the new color TV sets. *Bonanza* is further remembered for its enlightened treatment of Native Americans and African Americans in many of its episodes. Pa Cartwright and his sons provided morality lessons each week within the Western format. The series ended in 1973. In the 1990s, following the deaths of most of the original cast members, several *Bonanza* TV movies aired starring the real children of Greene, Blocker, and Landon as the next generation of Cartwrights.

—Charles Coletta

For More Information

Bonanza . . . The WebSite! http://bonanza1.com/ (accessed March 19, 2002).

Marschall, Rick. *History of Television.* New York: Gallery Books, 1986.

Ross, Brian, ed. *TV Genres.* Westport, CT: Greenwood Press, 1985.

Shapiro, Melaney. *Bonanza: The Unauthorized Story of the Ponderosa.* Las Vegas: Pioneer Books, 1993.

Johnny Carson (1925–)

Johnny Carson, who hosted **The Tonight Show** (see entry under 1950s–TV and Radio in volume 3) on NBC from 1962 until 1992, was the undisputed king of late-night **television** (see entry under 1940s–TV and Radio in volume 3) and one of the medium's most successful personalities. Carson combined Mid-western charm, a slightly naughty wit, and expert interviewing skills as he welcomed the nation's top celebrities, funniest comedians, and interesting ordinary citizens onto his program.

Each installment of *The Tonight Show* began with Carson's introduction by his longtime sidekick Ed McMahon (1923–): "Heeeeere's Johnny!" The show began with a comic mono-logue—a comic routine presented by Carson, by himself on stage—that allowed Carson to poke fun at the day's events. The monologue always ended with Carson's trademark gesture: He would pretend he was swinging a golf club. Carson then sat at his desk and performed comic bits or character sketches. Finally, he interviewed celebrities or hosted performing acts. One of the most noteworthy shows occurred on December 17, 1969, when thirty-seven-year-old singer Tiny Tim (Herbert Khaury, 1932–1996) married seventeen-year-old Miss Vicky (Victoria May Budinger; 1952–) live on TV.

Many late-night programs challenged Carson over the years, but none proved successful. When Carson retired in 1992, comedian Jay Leno (1950–) became host of *The Tonight Show*. **David Letterman** (see entry under 1980s—TV and Radio in volume 5), who had hoped to succeed Carson, took his show (which had followed Carson's in the late-night lineup) over to CBS to compete against Leno. Johnny Carson set the standard for late-night network programming and influenced Leno, Letterman, and all the hosts who have followed him into the genre (category) of late-night TV.

—Charles Coletta

For More Information

Cox, Stephen. *Here's Johnny: Thirty Years of America's Favorite Late Night Entertainment.* New York: Harmony Books, 1992.

Here's Johnny! The Official Tonight Show Website. http://www.johnnycarson.com/carson/ (accessed March 11, 2002).

The King of Late Night! (video). Buena Vista Home Video, 1994.

Leamer, Laurence. *King of the Night: The Life of Johnny Carson.* New York: Morrow, 1989.

Daytime Talk Shows

The daytime talk show is one of the most popular and prof-itable of all TV programming formats. Audiences enjoy them

One of the more successful afternoon talk show hosts was Mike Douglas (far left), here with entertainer Tiny Tim and his wife and daughter in 1972. *AP/Wide World Photos. Reproduced by permission.*

because they present celebrities candidly, not as actors playing roles. The more issue-oriented shows cover a range of relevant topics, everything from personal tragedy and triumph to self-improvement. Daytime talk shows range in tone from responsible and uplifting to racy and melodramatic. Finally, producers and networks favor talk shows because they are inexpensive to make.

On the more celebrity-oriented shows, a host first entertains the audience with a comic monologue (a speech given by only one person) or a song. Then, one by one, the guests appear and chat with the host. Usually, the celebrity has been booked because he or she has a new film, **television** (see entry under 1940s—TV and Radio in volume 3) show, or record to promote, so the conversation eventually spotlights that product. In this regard, a celebrity appearance on a talk show is little more than a publicity stunt, a convenient way to maximize the hype surrounding that product.

The format of the celebrity-focused daytime talk show was originated by Sylvester "Pat" Weaver (1908–2002), an NBC TV executive who created *Today* (1952–) and **The Tonight Show** (1954–; see these two entries under 1950s—TV and Radio in volume 3). The more successful hosts of such shows are entertainers in their own right; for example, singers Mike Douglas (1925–), of *The Mike Douglas Show* (1961–82); Dinah Shore (1916–1994), of the shows *Dinah's Place* (1970–74) and *Dinah!* (1974–80); and comedienne Rosie O'Donnell (1962–), of *The Rosie O'Donnell Show* (1996–2002).

On the issue-oriented programs, the host usually leads a discussion on the subject of the day. Guests range from individuals who have been victimized by everything from sexual abuse to fad diets, corporate or government bureaucracy to racism or sexism, along with experts in the field. Phil Donahue (1935–), host of *The Phil Donahue Show* (1970–77) and *Donahue* (1977–96), became the first talk-show host to earn national recognition with this format. In the 1990s, his popularity was eclipsed by Oprah Winfrey (1954–) and *The Oprah Winfrey Show* (1986–). While confessional in nature, the Donahue and Winfrey shows nonetheless set out to educate and uplift the viewer.

During the 1990s, many issue-oriented shows became more confrontational and exploitative: they encouraged guests to confront each other about problem relationships and often exploited people's sad situations. Shows hosted by Maury Povich (1939–), Jenny Jones (1946–), Sally Jessy Raphael (c. 1943–), Montel Williams (1956–), Geraldo Rivera (1943–), Ricki Lake (1968–), and, most notoriously, Jerry Springer (1944–) fit into this category. Particularly on *The Jerry Springer Show* (1991–), guests might be adulterers or individuals with unconventional religious or political views. What they share is a willingness to come on television and reveal all in exchange for their fifteen minutes in the spotlight. On occasion, such shows have led to tragedy. In March 1996, a heterosexual male appeared on *The Jenny Jones Show* (1991–) knowing that he would meet a secret admirer. He felt humiliated after learning on-camera that the wooer was a gay male. Later, he went to the admirer's home and shot him to death. In a civil suit, the show was found negligent, and the victim's family was awarded $25 million.

Most daytime talk shows are named for their hosts, who become celebrities in their own right. Occasionally, a show is hosted by a duo. Among the most popular twosomes were Regis Philbin (1933–) and Kathie Lee Gifford (1953–), whose personalities and teasing made *Live with Regis and Kathie Lee* (1989–2000) a ratings hit. Gifford left in 2000, but her replacement, soap opera star Kelly Ripa (1970–), kept the newly titled *Live with Regis and Kelly* just as popular.

—*Rob Edelman*

For More Information

Day, Nancy. *Sensational TV: Trash or Journalism?* Springfield, NJ: Enslow, 1996.

Lowe, Janet C. *Oprah Winfrey Speaks: Insights from the World's Most Influential Voice.* New York: John Wiley & Sons, 1998.

Munson, Wayne. *All Talk: The Talk Show in Media Culture.* Philadelphia: Temple University Press, 1993.

Postman, Neil. *Amusing Ourselves to Death: Public Discourse in the Age of Show Business.* New York: Viking Press, 1985.

Scott, Gini Graham. *Can We Talk?: The Power and Influence of Talk Shows.* New York: Insight Books, 1996.

Dr. Kildare

Dreamily handsome Richard Chamberlain (1935–) was a heartthrob of young teenage girls in the 1960s when he starred on the hit medical drama, *Dr. Kildare* (1961–66). Chamberlain's character, James Kildare, was a young intern learning his profession at Blair General Hospital, a large urban medical facility. Young Kildare, whose specialty was internal medicine, stood in contrast to older Dr. Leonard Gillespie, played by Raymond Massey (1896–1983). Dr. Gillespie was Kildare's tough, seasoned mentor and the hospital's senior staff physician. Kildare was constantly attempting to win the fatherly Gillespie's respect while mastering the basics of good doctoring and grappling with the problems of his patients and the responsibilities of his profession. Although tame by the standards of contemporary TV medical shows, *Dr. Kildare* did offer a realistic view of life inside a hospital and the everyday stresses and dilemmas faced by doctors and patients.

The show was based on a series of stories written by Frederick Schiller Faust (1893–1944), a productive writer who published over 260 books using several pen names, including"Max Brand" for his Kildare fiction. Faust based the character on his best friend, George Winthrop "Dixie" Fish (1895–1977), an eminent urologist. Faust was serving as a war correspondent for *Harper's* magazine when he was killed during World War II (1939–45).

The *Dr. Kildare* TV series was preceded by sixteen Kildare-related feature films (released between 1938 and 1947). The series was also followed by a brief, unsuccessful TV reworking, *Young Dr. Kildare* (1972). Another doctor drama aired during the original *Kildare* run: the rugged Vincent Edwards (1928–1996) had the title role in *Ben Casey* (1961–66).

—*Rob Edelman*

For More Information

Brand, Max. *Calling Dr. Kildare*. New York: Dodd, Mead, 1940.
Brand, Max. *Dr. Kildare Takes Charge*. New York: Dodd, Mead, 1940.
Brand, Max. *The Secret of Dr. Kildare*. New York: Dodd, Mead, 1940.

Flipper

The trusty dolphin character Flipper dazzled youthful audiences with its debut in the 1963 feature film of the same name. Later, the popular bottle-nosed mammal made a return appearance in the film sequel *Flipper's New Adventure* (1964), and then starred in a **television** (see entry under 1940s–TV and Radio in volume 3) series, *Flipper* (1964–68). Three decades later, the dolphin reappeared in another TV series called *Flipper* (1995). Finally, amid a nostalgic wave of motion pictures based on hit 1960s TV series, the mammal again appeared in a new film, once again titled *Flipper* (1996).

What makes this character so appealing is its seeming ability to communicate and interact with humans. Flipper is a playful and mischievous character, but in times of danger, Flipper acts with death-defying courage.

In the first film, which takes place in the Florida Keys, Flipper is an injured dolphin who befriends a twelve-year-old fisherman's son named Sandy Ricks. Sandy and his mother nurse Flipper back to good health. However, because Sandy prefers to play with Flipper rather than do his chores, his dad insists that Sandy stop spending time with the dolphin. Eventually, Flipper shows his mettle by locating a new fishing ground and even rescuing Sandy from life-threatening sharks. The subsequent Flipper stories, all of which also feature Sandy, combine moments of Flipper being happy and playful with climactic sequences of danger wherein the dolphin battles enemies and rescues people in distress.

Flipper is presented as a male, but "he" was played by female dolphins. The first one cast in the role was named Mitzi. At a time when it was rare for dolphins to perform tricks involving interaction with people, Mitzi learned to fetch a boy from the water and carry him on her back. Later, for the first TV series, a dolphin named Suzy was chosen to play the lead role.

The Flipper character was the invention of movie and TV underwater stuntman Ricou Browning (1930–). Browning trained Mitzi to do all the stunts for the screen and employed his son Ricky to act as the subject of many of Flipper's stunts. Later, Suzy learned almost forty maneuvers to make Flipper's actions on TV exciting and believable.

—*Audrey Kupferberg*

For More Information

Edelson, Edward. *Great Animals of the Movies.* Garden City, NY: Doubleday, 1980.

Flipper (film). Metro-Goldwyn-Mayer, 1963.

Flipper (film). Universal, 1996.

Flipper's New Adventure (film). Metro-Goldwyn-Mayer, 1964.

Rothel, David. *Great Show Business Animals.* San Diego: A. S. Barnes and Company, 1980.

The Fugitive

Of the many **television** (see entry under 1940s–TV and Radio in volume 3) series that debuted in the 1960s and then became classics, one of the most popular was *The Fugitive.* This story of an innocent man on the run from the law while trying to find his wife's real killer fascinated the American people. In fact, the last episode of the series, "The Judgement," in which fugitive Richard Kimble finally catches up to the real killer, was the highest rated single episode of a TV series at the time and remained so until the final episode of *M*A*S*H* (see entry under 1970s–TV and Radio in volume 5) in 1983. When "The Judgement" aired in 1967, 72 percent of Americans watching TV that night were tuned to the show.

Legend has it that the show was based on the case of Dr. Sam Sheppard (1923–1970), convicted and then acquitted of his wife's still unsolved murder. According to the show's creator, Roy Huggins (1914–2002), however, the idea actually was based more on the classic tale, *Les Miserables,* by Victor Hugo

(1802–1885). When the show first aired in 1963, it became an almost instant hit. It inspired several other series based on its idea, but none were as successful as the original. The slicked-back hair of star David Janssen (1931–1980) even became a popular hairstyle for men for a time. For several years after the show left the air, *The Fugitive* still had a hold on Americans. In fact, several Supreme Court justices were such fans of the show, it has been said that the story of an innocent man sentenced to death helped sway them into abolishing the death penalty in 1972.

The Fugitive faded from memory for many years until the Arts & Entertainment Network began showing reruns, which proved extremely popular. So popular were the reruns that the show was made into a very successful motion picture starring Harrison Ford (1942–) in 1993. An updated version of the show, starring Tim Daly (1956–), ran from 2000 to 2001. This show was updated to include extensive use of computers and the **Internet** (see entry under 1990s–The Way We Lived in volume 5), technology that was not available to the public during the original series.

–*Jill Gregg Clever*

David Janssen as Richard Kimble in *The Fugitive.* *AP/Wide World Photos. Reproduced by permission.*

For More Information

Deane, Bill. *Following the Fugitive: An Episode Guide and Handbook to the 1960s Television Series.* Jefferson, NC: McFarland & Company, 1996.

"The Fugitive." *Classic U.S. Television Collective.* http://web.ukonline.co.uk/craig.pierce2/fugitive.html (accessed March 20, 2002).

Robertson, Ed. *The Fugitive Recaptured: The 30th Anniversary Companion to the Television Classic.* Universal City, CA: Pomegranate Press, 1993.

Gilligan's Island

Gilligan's Island, which originally aired from 1964 to 1967, is both one of the most loved and hated programs in **television**

(see entry under 1940s—TV and Radio in volume 3) history. Critics claimed that the show was absurd and juvenile, calling it TV at its worst. Audiences, however, responded positively to the wacky characters and the slapstick physical humor. Although the series was in production for only three seasons, the popularity of *Gilligan's Island* has allowed it to remain in constant syndication (the rebroadcasting of programs on independent television channels). It also inspired several highly rated reunion TV movies, as well as animated programs and countless items of merchandise.

Series creator Sherwood Schwartz (c. 1917–) endured a long struggle to bring his program to television. He tried to create a **sitcom** (see entry under 1950s—TV and Radio in volume 3) whose characters represented all the various social, financial, and educational levels of modern

Alan Hale as Skipper (left) and Bob Denver as Gilligan in *Gilligan's Island*. *Bettmann/ Corbis. Reproduced by permission.*

America. The program's familiar theme song introduced the audience to the crew and passengers of the shipwrecked pleasure boat, the *S. S. Minnow*: Skipper Jonas Grumby (Alan Hale Jr., 1918–1990), First Mate Gilligan (Bob Denver, 1935–), millionaire Thurston Howell III (Jim Backus, 1913–1989) and his wife Lovey (Natalie Schafer, 1900–1991), movie star Ginger Grant (Tina Louise, c. 1935–), Professor Roy Hinkley (Russell Johnson, 1924–), and farm girl Mary Ann Summers (Dawn Wells, 1938–). Although the characters were more like cartoon characters than like fully rounded individuals, the actors played their parts with a lovable humanity that endeared them to generations of TV viewers.

Every episode of *Gilligan's Island* involved the castaways attempting to both adjust to their new surroundings and discover a way off the island. The series had its own unique oddball logic. Fans have long wondered why the passengers took so many changes of clothes on their originally scheduled three-hour tour; how the castaways could create so many "luxury" items (like huts, cars, and record players) and yet fail to fix the hole in their boat; and why did they never kill Gilligan when he constantly ruined their attempts at rescue? Furthermore, although the series was set on an uncharted island, many guest stars appeared unexpectedly to raise the possibility of a trip home, only to leave the main characters still stranded.

Gilligan's Island lived on after its cancellation by CBS in 1967. In 1978, the TV movie *Rescue from Gilligan's Island* became one of the highest rated programs in broadcast history. Its success led to several other reunion specials including *The Harlem Globetrotters on Gilligan's Island* (1981). While the series may be considered "lowbrow" entertainment by many, it has won fans for over thirty years, making it an American pop-culture institution.

—*Charles Coletta*

For More Information

Denver, Bob. *Bob Denver's Gilligan's Island Fan Club.* http://www.bobdenver.com/ (accessed March 20, 2002).

Denver, Bob. *Gilligan, Maynard, & Me.* Secaucus, NJ: Carol Publishing Group, 1993.

Johnson, Russell. *Here on Gilligan's Isle.* New York: HarperPerennial, 1993.

Schwartz, Sherwood. *Inside Gilligan's Island: From Creation to Syndication.* New York: St. Martin's Press, 1994.

Surviving Gilligan's Island: The Incredible True Story of the Longest Three-Hour Tour in History (video). CBS-TV, 2001.

Wells, Dawn. *The Official Gilligan's Island's Mary Ann Web Site.* http://www.dawn-wells.com/ (accessed March 20, 2002).

Hawaii Five-O

From 1968 until 1980, *Hawaii Five-O* earned high ratings as a solid **television** (see entry under 1940s—TV and Radio in volume 3) drama that showcased heroic detectives of the Hawaiian State Police confronting evildoers amidst Hawaii's lush, tropical scenery. Filmed on location, the series is credited with drawing millions of tourists to the Islands. In addition, the series' distinctive musical score, with its pounding theme, became quite popular.

The series, created by producer Leonard Freeman (1920–1974), was an immediate success. Jack Lord (1920–1998) starred as Steve McGarrett, the tough and hard-driving chief detective of Five-O. He projected a no-nonsense attitude as he battled corruption and, occasionally, communism in America's fiftieth state. Lord was known for his craggy features and black pompadour (hair brushed high off the forehead) hairstyle.

Viewers enjoyed watching McGarrett and his team fight the Hawaiian underworld. Their most significant enemy was the red Chinese spy Wo Fat, played by Khigh Dhiegh (1910–1991). McGarrett's primary assistant was the young Danny "Danno" Williams, played by James MacArthur (1937–), the adopted son of actress Helen Hayes (1900–1993) and playwright Charles MacArthur (1895–1956). Each week, millions tuned in to hear McGarrett repeat the line "Book 'em, Danno," as the various members of Hawaii's criminal element were hauled off to jail.

Although Lord and MacArthur were Caucasians from the mainland, Hawaiian-born actors portrayed many other members of the Five-O unit. Kam Fong (1918–), who appeared as Detective Chin Ho Kelly, had actually served on the Honolulu Police Department for eighteen years prior to joining the program. After ten seasons, Fong tired of the role and asked to be released from the series. In 1978, his character was killed in the line of duty. The following season concluded with the departure of MacArthur.

Without McGarrett's two most trusted aides, the series seemed to lose much of its dramatic spark. Lord remained with the program for an additional year. The series concluded in April 1980 with McGarrett finally defeating his greatest nemesis, Wo Fat. When it left the air, *Hawaii Five-O* was the longest continually running police drama in TV history.

—*Charles Coletta*

For More Information

Hawaii Five-O Home Page. http://www.mjq.net/fiveo/ (accessed March 20, 2002).

Rhodes, Karen. *Booking Hawaii Five-O: An Episode Guide and Critical History of the 1968–1980 Television Detective Series.* Jefferson, NC: McFarland and Company, 1997.

Mister Ed
● ●

Mister Ed (1961–66), a CBS **sitcom** (situation comedy; see entry under 1950s–TV and Radio in volume 3), featured a mischievous horse who "talked" only to its owner, an architect named Wilbur Post, played by Alan Young (1919–). Mister Ed, played by a Golden Palomino named Bamboo Harvester, "spoke" with a voice supplied by Allan "Rocky" Lane (1904–1973), an actor who had earlier appeared as a cowboy in many **Western** (see entry under 1930s–Film and Theater in volume 2) films. Lane refused to allow his name to be used in the show's credits; he was embarrassed at supplying the voice of a horse. For five seasons, the horse and his architect-owner appeared in episodes of the popular award-winning series, introduced by a lively theme song that began "A horse is a horse, of course, of course" and declared "But Mister Ed will never speak unless he has something to say."

The character of Mister Ed was created by Walter Brooks (1886–1958), who wrote several stories about Mister Ed in the *Saturday Evening Post* (see entry under 1900s–Print Culture in volume 1) and *Liberty* magazine. A pilot episode using another horse and a different set of actors was created in 1957 by director Arthur Lubin (1898–1995), who had directed six films for Universal Pictures featuring another vocal animal, **Francis the Talking Mule** (see entry under 1950s–Film and Theater in volume 3). For the **television** (see entry under 1940s–TV and Radio in volume 3) series that premiered in January 1961, Mister Ed's trainer, Lester Hilton, taught the horse to perform tricks such as unlatching his stable door, opening file cabinets, and dialing a telephone, much to the amusement of audiences and the bafflement of his owner. Mister Ed learned to "talk" using the same techniques Hilton had used with Francis. By tugging on a **nylon** (see entry under 1930s–Fashion in volume 2) fishing line attached to the horse's bridle, he made Mister Ed open his lips at the appropriate moment. Lane's voice was dubbed in to match the horse's mouth movements. Part of the show's appeal was in the comedic depiction of an animal having more "horse sense" than his befuddled human, who was frequently victimized by Mister Ed's pranks.

Mister Ed was canceled during the 1966 season, and the show went into immediate syndication (resale of the shows to independent TV stations). Bamboo Harvester–Mr. Ed–died in 1968 on Lester Hilton's ranch.

—*Edward Moran*

For More Information

Edelson, Edward. *Great Animals of the Movies*. Garden City, NY: Doubleday, 1980.

Nalven, Nancy. *The Famous Mister Ed: The Unbridled Truth about America's Favorite Talking Horse*. New York: Warner Books, 1991.

Newman, Mark. *Mister Ed Online.* http://members.aol.com/mwn3/ (accessed March 20, 2002).

Terrace, Vincent. *Encyclopedia of Television Series, Pilots, and Specials, 1937–1973.* New York: Zoetrope, 1986.

Mister Rogers' Neighborhood

For more than thirty years, television-host Fred Rogers (1928–) was the friendly "neighbor" to millions of American children. Every day, the easy-going Pennsylvanian entered the lives of youthful audiences, dispensing advice, singing songs, and introducing them to the magical Land of Make Believe.

Parents came to trust the soft-spoken host. Rogers (1928–) was an ordained minister with a background in childhood education when he developed his own program for Pittsburgh, Pennsylvania, PBS station WQED in 1966. The show, at first titled *MisteRogers Neighborhood,* combined live-action scenes of Rogers in his "television house" with puppet sequences set in the Land of Make Believe. A dinging trolley ferried viewers back and forth between the two settings. Each show began with Rogers painstakingly changing out of his suit and loafers and into a cardigan sweater and sneakers—all the while singing "Won't You Be My Neighbor." This action was designed to make small children feel at home and at ease in his presence.

Many of Rogers' "neighbors" made appearances on the show, including a perky deliveryman, Mr. McFeeley (Rogers' middle name), and a hulking baker, Chef Don Brockett. Some of these actors also appeared in the Land of Make Believe sequences, which featured a puppet king named Friday XIII and his eccentric subjects. Along the way, young viewers were taught lessons about overcoming fears, solving problems, or getting along with others. In one famous show, Mr. Rogers had to deal with the death of his pet fish. Occasionally there were songs, sung by Rogers or one of the other regulars.

This basic formula remained virtually unchanged throughout *Mister Rogers' Neighborhood*'s thirty-four-year run. While loud, colorful children's shows had come into fashion, Rogers believed that children would respond to a kinder, gentler approach. Sometimes this made the show the object of ridicule. Eddie Murphy (1961–), for example, famously spoofed Mr. Rogers as the abrasive "Mr. Robinson" on *Saturday Night Live.*

But parents felt safe leaving their kids in the care of the comforting host, and the program won numerous awards for excellence.

Fred Rogers continued making new episodes of his unique show well into his 70s. In 1998, he was honored with a Lifetime Achievement Emmy Award. Two years later, the genial host hung up his sweater for good to enjoy his retirement. The more than seven hundred episodes of *Mister Rogers' Neighborhood* continued to air in reruns, proof that the show truly was timeless.

—*Robert E. Schnakenberg*

For More Information

Collins, Mark. *Mister Rogers' Neighborhood: Children, Television, and Fred Rogers.* Pittsburgh: University of Pittsburgh Press, 1997.

DiFranco, JoAnn. *Mister Rogers: Good Neighbor to America's Children.* Minneapolis: Dillon Press, 1983

PBS. "Mister Rogers' Neighborhood." *PBS Kids.* http://pbskids.org/rogers/ (accessed March 20, 2002).

Rogers, Fred. *Mister Rogers' Playbook: Insights and Activities for Parents and Children.* New York: Berkley Books, 1986.

Fred Rogers of *Mister Rogers' Neighborhood*, putting on his sneakers as he did each day at the start of his show. *Family Communications, Inc./Archive Photos. Reproduced by permission.*

Public Broadcasting System

The Public Broadcasting System (PBS), is a nationwide network of **television** (see entry under 1940s—TV and Radio in volume 3) stations producing television programs dedicated to education, the arts, and culture. PBS accepts no advertising, receiving all its funding from the government and from the voluntary contributions of its viewers. Without having to appeal to advertisers, PBS offers a different kind of programming than the major, commercial networks do. Because of this, PBS has long been an alternative to commercial television.

As television began in the late 1930s, and as it developed in the 1940s and 1950s, there was tension between the commercial stations, owned by big corporations intent on making money, and the desire to keep some channels open for public use. Public television began with local educational broadcasts in the early 1950s. When National Education Television was formed in 1958, it broadened the programming from educational, classroom programs to focus on larger cultural programming, including arts programming, documentaries, public-affairs shows, and children's programming. Public television became a national, government-sponsored program when President Lyndon B. Johnson (1908–1973) signed the Public Broadcasting Act of 1967.

Over the years, PBS has produced a number of well-known and important television programs. Among its first and most famous shows was the children's educational program *Sesame Street* (see entry under 1970s–TV and Radio in volume 4), featuring live actors and puppets teaching children about letters, numbers, and other topics. *Sesame Street*'s puppets, called **muppets** (see entry under 1970s–TV and Radio in volume 4), included Kermit the Frog, Big Bird, Bert and Ernie, and Oscar the Grouch. The muppets became immediate favorites with kids. PBS also produced music programs like *Great Performances,* cooking shows such as *The Frugal Gourmet,* and home improvement shows like *This Old House.* PBS also aired dramatic and comedy series, including *Brideshead Revisited* and *Monty Python's Flying Circus* (see entry under 1970s–TV and Radio in volume 4). In the 1990s, PBS had great success with the series *The Civil War* and *Baseball* by acclaimed documentary filmmaker Ken Burns (1953–).

Public television has not been without its critics. Many conservatives complain that PBS is too liberal, too open to new ideas. Indeed, PBS has at times pushed the boundaries in American life by discussing controversial subjects such as homosexuality and by taking a critical stance on the Vietnam War (1954–75). Members of Congress have at times tried to withdraw funding for PBS or close it down altogether. Although never as popular as the mainstream commercial stations, PBS has provided a necessary and serious alternative to commercial television, allowing educational and cultural programs a place on the nation's airwaves.

—Timothy Berg

For More Information

Hoynes, William. *Public Television for Sale: Media, the Market, and the Public Sphere.* Boulder, CO: Westview Press, 1994.

Macy, John W., Jr. *To Irrigate a Wasteland: The Struggle to Shape a Public Television System in the United States.* Berkeley: University of California Press, 1974.

PBS. *PBS Online.* http://www.pbs.org/ (accessed March 20, 2002).

Rowan & Martin's Laugh-In

In the late 1960s, *Rowan & Martin's Laugh-In* (1968–73) was at the cutting edge of **television** (see entry under 1940s—TV and Radio in volume 3) comedy. Hosted by the popular comedy team of Dan Rowan (1922–1987) and Dick Martin (1922–), this trend-setting, fast-paced, hour-long NBC show featured zany comedy skits, corny jokes, and clever visual humor performed by a cast of regulars. Millions of viewers loved the show's suggestive humor and sense of playful, goofy chaos.

The structure of *Laugh-In* was highly unconventional. Comedy-variety shows of the time generally featured extended comic skits, but *Laugh-In* did not. Rowan and Martin themselves began each program with a comic conversation in which Martin would misinterpret and mangle the simplest statements or questions put forth by Rowan. The humor that followed centered on a series of set pieces, standard skits done every week, including "The Cocktail Party," "The Flying Fickle Finger of Fate Award," and "Laugh-In Looks at the News." The show closed with the Joke Wall, in which cast members stuck their heads out of holes in the wall and cracked one liners—and were often met with a bucket of water tossed in their direction.

The show featured a cast of comics that included Goldie Hawn (1945–), who often appeared in a skimpy bathing suit; Lily Tomlin (1939–), who appeared as Ernestine, an obnoxiously prissy, nasal-voiced telephone operator, or as Edith Ann, a cheeky little girl; Arte Johnson (1929–) and Ruth Buzzi (1936–), who played a dirty old geezer and a prudish frump with a handbag who viewed herself as the object of his unwanted advances; Alan Sues (1926–) as an idiotic sports announcer; and Henry Gibson (1935–), who often appeared with flower in hand, spouting shallow poetry. Hawn and Tomlin went on to become major stars, Hawn in movies and Tomlin in movies and on **Broadway** (see entry under 1900s—Film and Theater in volume 1).

What made *Laugh-In* such a revolutionary TV show was its fast-paced visual style. The show spawned the once wildly

popular catchphrases "Sock it to me," "You bet your bippy," "Verrry interesting," "Look that up in your Funk and Wagnalls," and "Here come de judge." Finally, the show often featured a surprise celebrity guest. Some of the era's most popular actors and TV personalities popped up on the show, usually to deliver one-liners, with their appearances often lasting only seconds. One of the oddest, and funniest, *Laugh-In* guests was Richard Nixon (1913–1994), who, in the fall of 1968, two months prior to being elected U.S. president, soberly proclaimed, in question form, "Sock it to me?"

—*Rob Edelman*

For More Information

Erickson, Hal. *From Beautiful Downtown Burbank: A Critical History of Rowan and Martin's Laugh-In, 1968–1973.* Jefferson, NC: McFarland, 2000.

"Rowan and Martin's Laugh In." *YesterdayLand.* http://www.yesterdayland.com/popopedia/shows/primetime/pt1276.php (accessed March 20, 2002).

Goldie Hawn appears in a bikini and body paint on *Rowan & Martin's Laugh-In* in November 1968. *Corbis Corporation. Reproduced by permission.*

Saturday Morning Cartoons

Since the 1960s, American children have concluded each long week of school by waking up early on Saturday mornings to view their favorite animated cartoon programs on **television** (see entry under 1940s—TV and Radio in volume 3). Saturday morning is the only period during the week in which the broadcast networks schedule entertainment programming aimed specifically at the nation's youngest TV viewers. Generations of kids have grown up watching characters like Scooby Doo, Yogi Bear, Fat Albert, Johnny Quest, the Smurfs, and the Superfriends. Through the years, many concerned parents have been alarmed by often open commercialism and violence contained in their children's favorite shows. Despite these criticisms, Saturday morning cartoons have continued to flourish and even to move beyond their traditional time period. By the 1990s,

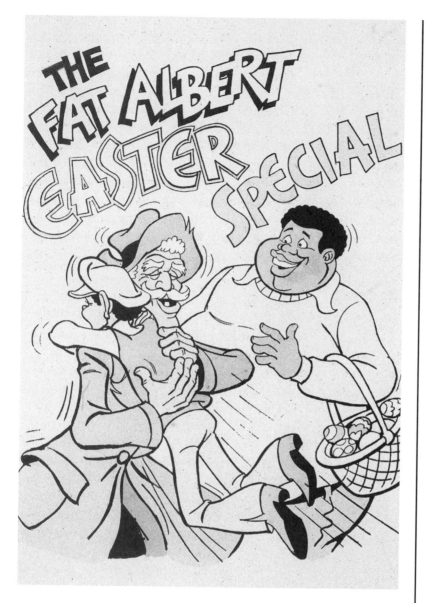

Fat Albert and the Cosby Kids, a creation of comic Bill Cosby, was a popular Saturday morning cartoon show in the 1970s. *Hulton/Archive by Getty Images. Reproduced by permission.*

entire **cable TV** (see entry under 1970s–TV and Radio in volume 4) networks were devoted to rerunning classic animated programs, and several live-action films were produced to appeal to a now-adult audience who still held an affection for their favorite cartoon personalities.

Beginning in the late 1940s, network television executives recognized the profitability in developing programming targeted to kids. Studies showed that, since the days of **radio** (see entry under 1920s–TV and Radio in volume 2), children's peak tune-in hours were between 10 A.M. and noon on Saturday mornings and 4 P.M. and 6 P.M. on weekdays. The earliest animated shows to air on TV were repackaged short features that had been created for theatrical release during the 1930s and 1940s. The first cartoon created exclusively for TV appeared in 1949 and was titled *Crusader Rabbit*. The series, developed by animator Jay Ward (1920–1989)—who later created Rocky and Bullwinkle—showcased the misadventures of a courageous bunny and his tiger sidekick. Although the series ran for several seasons, its limited success kept the networks from bringing other original animated programs to the small screen during the 1950s. A notable exception was the *Mighty Mouse Playhouse,* which aired on CBS for twelve seasons. Most of the decade's Saturday-morning fare was live-action shows featuring cowboy and astronaut hosts.

In 1957, animators William Hanna (1910–2001) and Joseph Barbera (1911–), who had previously worked in the animation department at **MGM** (see entry under 1920s—Film and Theater in volume 2), opened their own production company to create animated programs for TV. A shortage of money forced them to limit their programs to the bare essentials. They perfected a production method that, in contrast to feature-film animation, resulted in cartoons with less detail, fewer backgrounds, and less fluid movement. Characters were designed to be simple in appearance and efficient in their actions. Often, only the mouths of the characters moved. The first Hanna-Barbera program to debut on television was *The Ruff and Reddy Show* (1957), which focused on a mischievous dog and cat. The Hanna-Barbera studio soon established itself as the dominant force in Saturday-morning cartoons. They have created literally thousands of hours of TV cartoon programming for more than forty years. Among their most celebrated characters are Yogi Bear, Huckleberry Hound, Quickdraw McGraw, Augie Doggie and Doggie Daddy, Scooby-Doo, the Flintstones, the Jetsons, the Hair Bear Bunch, and the Smurfs. The great success of Hanna-Barbera's shows was not lost on the broadcast networks. By 1966, all the networks were airing extended blocks of Saturday-morning cartoon programming.

The content of most Saturday-morning cartoons has generally fallen into two basic camps: comedy programs featuring talking animals or humans in outlandish situations, and action-adventure shows starring popular superheroes. Another popular cartoon genre has been animated programs based upon live-action celebrities or programs. The first of these shows appeared in 1965 and depicted the fantasy adventures of the **Beatles** (see entry under 1960s–Music in volume 4). Others who have been transformed into animation include The Jackson Five (1971), Gary Coleman (1982), Mister T (1983), New Kids on the Block (1990), Macaulay Culkin (1991), and Jackie Chan (2000). Among the TV **sitcoms** (see entry under 1950s–TV and Radio in volume 3) transplanted to Saturday mornings were *The Brady Bunch* (see entry under 1970s–TV and Radio in volume 4), as *The Brady Kids* in 1972; *Gilligan's Island* (see entry under 1960s–TV and Radio in volume 3), as *The New Adventures of Gilligan* in 1972 and *Gilligan's Planet* in 1984; *Happy Days* (see entry under 1970s–TV and Radio in volume 4), as *Fonz and the Happy Days Gang* in 1980; *Laverne & Shirley,* as *Laverne and Shirley in the Army* in 1981; *Punky Brewster,* as *It's Punky Brewster* in 1984; and *The Dukes of Hazzard,* as *The Dukes* in 1983.

Since the late 1960s, the most persistent criticism of Saturday morning cartoons has come from parental organizations and government agencies that believe the level of violence and commercialism contained in the programs is excessive. They have argued that impressionable children might imitate the violent acts they regularly witness in animation. They also complain that many programs are little more than half-hour commercials designed to sell merchandise. In 1969, the National Association of Broadcasters announced that advertisements for toys could not air during the same show on which the products were based. Many older cartoons were re-edited to eliminate scenes of violence. The networks were further encouraged to create programs that were more educationally enriching. Among the most popular educational cartoons were the **Schoolhouse Rock** (see entry under 1970s–TV and Radio in volume 4) features that ran on ABC for more than twenty years.

In the 1980s and 1990s the networks began to limit the number of their animated programs in favor of live-action comedies like *Saved By the Bell,* which appealed to teenaged viewers. Still, cartoons continue to dominate the schedule. Saturday morning animated programming has been one of network television's most lucrative features. Today, millions of adults who were raised on these cartoons can see them repeated endlessly on cable. The sense of nostalgia produced by the Saturday morning shows is most evident in the many revivals of classic cartoon characters for the movie screen.

–*Charles Coletta*

For More Information

Barbera, Joseph. *My Life in 'Toons: From Flatbush to Bedrock in Under a Century.* Atlanta: Turner Publishing, 1994.

Burke, Timothy, and Kevin Burke. *Saturday Morning Fever.* New York: St. Martin's Griffin, 1999.

Heraldson, Donald. *Creators of Life: A History of Animation.* New York: Drake Publishers, 1985.

Kanfer, Stefan. *Serious Business: The Art and Commerce of Animation in America from Betty Boop to Toy Story.* New York: Scribner, 1997.

"Saturday Morning." *YesterdayLand.* http://www.yesterdayland.com/popopedia/shows/categories/saturday (accessed March 20, 2002).

Saturday Morning Cartoons' Greatest Hits. Universal City, CA: MCA Records, 1995. Audio Recording.

Sennett, Ted. *The Art of Hanna-Barbera.* New York: Viking Studio, 1989.

60 Minutes

From its initial broadcast in 1968, *60 Minutes* pioneered the "magazine format" of **television** (see entry under 1940s—TV and Radio in volume 3) journalism, which allowed it to run a mixture of hard news, investigative reports, personality profiles, and light feature pieces. Its prominence allowed the show to feature candid stories on the most powerful world leaders, distinguished artists, and crafty criminals of the last thirty years. After several years during which it struggled to find an audience, by the mid-1970s it became the most prestigious, most watched, and most imitated news program on television.

Don Hewitt (1922–), a producer at CBS, created *60 Minutes* as the TV equivalent of such periodicals as *Time* (see entry under 1920s—Print Culture in volume 2) and *Newsweek.* Each week, his chief correspondents would present several stories on a wide variety of topics. In 1978, writer Andy Rooney (1919–) joined the program to present his own brand of short, humorous commentary. Each portion of the program was separated by an image of a ticking stopwatch, which became the show's symbol.

60 Minutes became one of television's most popular shows with its concept of stories presented in a "Hollywood style" that emphasized attractively packaged factual events. Its great popular success and low production costs made it one of the most profitable programs in TV history. Much of the show's great appeal was based on its hard-hitting investigative reports. Presented mainly by such aggressive correspondents as Mike Wallace (1918–) and Dan Rather (1931–), the show exposed a number of real-life frauds and abuses.

The show's greatest strength came from its correspondents and their choice of stories. Harry Reasoner (1923–1991), Ed Bradley (1941–), Diane Sawyer (1945–), Morley Safer (1931–), and Lesley Stahl (1941–) were correspondents at various times and were able to deliver insightful pieces within the show's variety format. Of all the journalists associated with *60 Minutes,* none is as strongly identified with the program as is Wallace. He possesses a direct, often abrasive, style that is well suited for the show's confrontational format.

An examination of the personalities, issues, and major events covered on *60 Minutes* provides a remarkable window on America from the late 1960s onward. Hewitt created a format that has allowed for a varied presentation of ideas that have shaped the post–Vietnam War (1954–75) era. He and his correspondents revealed to the networks that factual, documentary programming could be highly successful both in terms of journalism and ratings. In 1999, CBS News introduced *60 Minutes II,* hoping to snare a large audience for the program on a different night.

—*Charles Coletta*

For More Information

Coffey, Frank. *60 Minutes: 25 Years of Television's Finest Hour.* Los Angeles: General Publishing Group, 1993.

Hewitt, Don. *Minute by Minute.* New York: Random House, 1985.

Madsen, Axel. *60 Minutes: The Power & Politics of America's Most Popular News Show.* New York: Dodd, Mead, 1984.

"60 Minutes." *CBSNews.com.* http://www.cbsnews.com/sections/60minutes/main3415.shtml (accessed March 20, 2002).

Speed Racer

Speed Racer was the first of the Japanese **anime** (see entry under 1990s–TV and Radio in volume 5) cartoons to succeed in the United States. The show became a fixture of children's **television** (see entry under 1940s–TV and Radio in volume 3) for years after its release in the United States in 1967. The half-hour show followed the adventures of a young race-car driver named Speed Racer, who drove every boy's dream car: the Mach 5. The streamlined Mach 5, the fastest car on the racing circuit,

Film and Theater in volume 2), Roddenberry patterned the weekly one-hour drama after the popular adventure series *Wagon Train*. The show debuted in September 1966. Veteran actor William Shatner (1931–) played the brash Captain Kirk. Leonard Nimoy (1931–) played his ultralogical first officer, the half-human, half-Vulcan Mr. Spock. Along with their fellow crew members, composed of different ethnic and personality types, Kirk and Spock explored the universe and encountered aliens both friendly and hostile. The warlike Klingons and the cold-blooded Romulans emerged as regular villains on the series.

The show developed a sizable cult following, but its audience was never big enough to justify its special effects budget, and NBC cancelled *Star Trek* in 1969. The show remained popular in reruns, however, and as a series of big-budget feature films, beginning with *Star Trek: The Motion Picture* in 1979. The actors from the show, particularly Shatner, became beloved pop-culture icons (symbols) and were seen in many commercials and TV guest appearances.

Twenty years passed before *Star Trek* returned to **television** (see entry under 1940s–TV and Radio in volume 3). A second series, *Star Trek: The Next Generation*, debuted in 1987 and ran for seven seasons, becoming the highest-rated syndicated show in TV history. Two other spin-off series, *Star Trek: Deep Space Nine* and *Star Trek: Voyager*, also enjoyed long runs and high ratings. A new series, *Star Trek: Enterprise*, set in the years *before* the original show aired, debuted in the fall of 2001.

The dedication of *Star Trek*'s fans, known as Trekkies, continues to make the series a truly global phenomenon. By the turn of the twenty-first century, *Star Trek* was being seen around the world in seventy-five countries. Countless *Star Trek* fan clubs exist, many of which have their own Web sites. Every year, Trekkies flock to various *Star Trek* conventions held in hotels and city centers around the globe.

—*Robert E. Schnakenberg*

Three stars of the original *Star Trek* television series: (left to right) William Shatner, as Captain James T. Kirk; DeForest Kelley, as Dr. Leonard "Bones" McCoy; and Leonard Nimoy, as Mr. Spock. *AP/Wide World Photos. Reproduced by permission.*

For More Information

Altman, Mark A., and Edward Gross. *Trek Navigator: The Ultimate Guide to the Entire Trek Saga.* New York: Little Brown, 1998.

Okuda, Michael, Denise Okuda, and Debbie Mirek. *The Star Trek Encyclopedia.* New York: Pocket Books, 1994.

Schnakenberg, Robert E. *The Encyclopedia Shatnerica.* Los Angeles: Renaissance Books, 1998.

Solow, Herbert, and Robert H. Justman. *Inside Star Trek: The Real Story.* New York: Pocket Books, 1997.

Startrek.com: The Official Star Trek Web Site. http://www.startrek.com (accessed March 20, 2002).

1960s

The Way We Lived

The political unrest and social activism of the 1960s brought dramatic changes in the way many Americans lived. The civil rights movement, the gay liberation movement, and the women's movement certainly brought changes to the lives of those who participated in these movements of the 1960s, as well as to the larger social structures these movements hoped to change. Even more powerful were the changes brought by the shapeless and leaderless "youth movement," a general trend in culture that valued the freedom and lack of responsibility enjoyed by youth.

The dominant social movement in the first half of the decade was the civil rights movement. Nonviolent protestors led by the Reverend Martin Luther King Jr. (1929–1968) participated in sit-ins and boycotts throughout the South to protest the persistent racism and segregation in the region. When southerners reacted violently, the federal government stepped in to enforce equal rights laws. One key moment in the movement was the 1963 March on Washington, D.C., which saw hundreds of thousands of Americans—including a substantial white minority—express their approval for equal rights for African Americans. The civil rights movement became more violent later in the decade, with riots in America's worst ghettos and the assassination of leaders Martin Luther King Jr. and Malcolm X (1925–1965).

Prompted by the 1963 book *The Feminine Mystique* by Betty Friedan (1921–) and by the successes of the civil rights movement, American women also joined together to press for equal rights. They formed the National Organization for Women (NOW) and sought passage of an equal rights amendment to the Constitution. Though the amendment did not pass, women did gain reforms in divorce and abortion laws and greater access to economic opportunity. The gay liberation movement of the late 1960s also began its quest for an end to discrimination against homosexuals. The women's and gay liberation movements were all part of an ongoing sexual revolution that included a new permissiveness toward all things sexual.

The most visible of the 1960s movements was the youth movement, which took many forms. College youths were especially active in the antiwar movement, which protested American involvement in the Vietnam War (1954–75). They protested on college campuses across the nation and formed an important group, the Students for a Democratic Society (SDS). Some youths rejected conventional American values altogether and became "hippies," drop outs who formed a counterculture based on free-love, drug use, and shared property. Throughout youth culture, drug use was on the rise, especially the use of marijuana and LSD. By the end of the decade, drug use had claimed the lives of many users, including rock stars Janis Joplin (1943–1970) and Jimi Hendrix (1942–1970).

Civil Rights Movement

The modern-era civil rights movement originated in the late 1940s and intensified during the subsequent two decades. African American leaders had long been lobbying for the enforcement of existing laws that prevented discrimination based on race and the passing of new laws outlawing racist practices. Meanwhile, some enlightened white Americans were realizing that African Americans were entitled to the same protections and opportunities long enjoyed by other citizens.

The necessity for the civil rights movement grew out of the reality that, prior to the 1940s—and well into the 1960s—America was a segregated society. While as much a part of the American fabric as their white brethren, African Americans were treated as second-class citizens. They remained separated from the white majority, particularly in the South, where they lived in rural poverty and their right to vote often was discounted. While the South and its "whites only" way of life seemed deeply entrenched, much of the more "progressive" North was just as segregated. African Americans across the nation lived in separate neighborhoods. They went to inferior schools. They were denied job opportunities. They could not play major league **baseball** (see entry under 1900s—Sports and Games in volume 1). They were not allowed to sit next to whites in many restaurants, drink out of the same water fountains, or socialize among whites at nightclubs. In a Hollywood movie, moviegoers would almost never find attractive African American actors playing in

love scenes or cast as heroes, nor were they portrayed as existing within their own culture. Instead, African American actors were stereotyped as dim-witted, ever-smiling servants. African American characters were always portrayed in relation to more intelligent, more educated, and more affluent white characters.

In short, African Americans were the victims of racism and separated from the American mainstream. Unlike other citizens, who came to the United States by choice, often to escape persecution or famine in their native lands, the ancestors of most blacks had arrived involuntarily, as slaves. They won their

Dr. Martin Luther King Jr. (second from left) leads a civil rights march in Washington D.C. *Courtesy of the National Archives and Records and Administration.*

freedom a century earlier, in the aftermath of the Civil War (1861–65), but the harsh reminder of their roots as slaves remained well into the twentieth century.

American society was overdue for a transformation. Commencing in the years just after the end of World War II (1939–45), event after event signaled that a segregated society was an un-American society. The American military began integrating after the war's end. Major league baseball began the process of integration with the arrival in 1947 of **Jackie Robinson** (1919–1972; see entry under 1940s–Sports and Games in volume 3) on the roster of the Brooklyn Dodgers. On movie screens, such films as *Pinky* (1949), *Intruder in the Dust* (1949), *Lost Boundaries* (1949), *Home of the Brave* (1949), and *No Way Out* (1950) all portrayed African Americans as victims of racist practices. Sidney Poitier (1924–) became Hollywood's first real African American movie star. In the 1954 case *Brown v. Board of Education,* the U.S. Supreme Court outlawed the 1896 *Plessy v. Ferguson* doctrine of "separate-but-equal." Martin Luther King Jr. (1929–1968) became a rational and eloquent spokesperson for civil rights. The 1960s saw various pro-integration and pro-voting rights boycotts, sit-ins, marches, and rallies and, finally, the passage in 1965 of the Voting Rights Act.

Nevertheless, during the 1960s, more militant African American leaders—Malcolm X (1925–1965) was the most high-profile—began earning national recognition. The nonviolence of the early civil rights movement, as personified by King, gave way to angry voices advocating an overthrowing of the system that created African American oppression. Such anger resulted in urban riots and the destruction of black communities in cities from New York to Detroit to Washington, D.C. to Los Angeles—but little actual political change. Nonetheless, this rise in political consciousness did result in a generation of perceptive African American leaders who preferred to create their own organizations and coalitions in their fight for political change, rather than link up with white liberals.

At the turn of the twenty-first century, countless individuals of color have entered the mainstream. African American doctors, lawyers, judges, police officers, business leaders, and other professionals are as respected as their white counterparts. Denzel Washington (1954–), Whoopi Goldberg (1949–), Morgan Freeman (1937–), Eddie Murphy (1961–), Chris Rock (1966–), and others have followed Poitier as bankable **Hollywood** (see entry under 1930s–Film and Theater in volume 2) stars.

Michael Jordan (1963–; see entry under 1990s–Sports and Games in volume 5) is arguably the most celebrated professional basketball player of all time, if not the most recognizable athlete in the world. In 2001, Colin Powell (1937–) became the secretary of state under newly elected president George W. Bush (1946–). Even controversial, politically conservative African Americans, such as Supreme Court justice Clarence Thomas (1948–), have taken their places in the national spotlight.

School systems and universities offer classes in black history, and African Americans have greatly influenced fashion styles and **pop music** (see entry under 1940s–Music in volume 3). Still, far too many have been left behind, victimized by poverty, hopelessness, and the ever-disturbing presence of drugs in American society. A drive-by shooting in a housing project will often go unnoticed in the media, yet a similar crime in an upscale community will be front-page news. Among the high-profile political issues of the early twenty-first century is racial profiling, or the placing under suspicion of a citizen solely because of the color of his or her skin.

Finally, in an era in which change is a constant, and yesterday's news is ancient history, it is meaningful to recall that the victories of the civil rights movement were not easily won. Paralleling civil rights progress were the assassinations of King and fellow civil rights leader Medgar Evers (1925–1963); the bombings of African American churches and the killings of innocent children and civil rights workers; and untold, unpublicized, but no less tragic events that are stark reminders of the legacy of racism.

–*Rob Edelman*

For More Information

Anderson, Terry. *The Movement and the Sixties: Protest in America from Greensboro to Wounded Knee.* Oxford: Oxford University Press, 1995.

Dickstein, Morris. *Gates of Eden: American Culture in the Sixties.* New York: Basic Books, 1977.

Dunn, John M. *The Civil Rights Movement.* San Diego: Lucent Books, 1998.

Van Deburg, William. *Black Camelot: African-American Culture Heroes in Their Times, 1960–1980.* Chicago: University of Chicago Press, 1997.

Van Deburg, William. *New Day in Babylon.* Chicago: University of Chicago Press, 1992.

Weber, Michael. *Causes and Consequences of the African American Civil Rights Movement.* Austin, TX: Raintree Steck-Vaughn, 1998.

Gay Liberation Movement

The gay liberation movement was an effort on the part of homosexual men and women to secure equal rights for themselves and to end the long history of abuse they had endured because of their sexual orientation. Gays and lesbians never fought for special rights; they simply wanted to be treated like everyone else is in the United States. When the movement gained momentum in the late 1960s, it joined a powerful chorus of voices from other groups, including women, African Americans, Native Americans, Hispanics, and others, fighting for equal rights.

For many decades, homosexual men and women had been outcasts in American society. They could reveal their sexual orientation, but they risked verbal and often physical abuse and social stigma. To avoid this, many had long remained "in the closet," hiding their true sexual identities from almost everyone, often including their parents, siblings, and coworkers. As many social movements began in the 1960s to fight for equal rights, gays and lesbians began to speak out as well. Although the problems homosexuals faced had been going on for decades, the spark that set off the gay liberation movement occurred on June 28, 1969, at the Stonewall Inn, a gay bar in New York City's Greenwich Village neighborhood. That night, police raided the bar in order to harass the gay and lesbian patrons. This occurred often, but on this night those patrons fought back, starting a small riot in the streets outside, and the gay liberation movement was born.

This event sparked a drive for a more organized and concerted effort to fight for homosexual rights. Earlier generations had made small changes in gay rights, but now many homosexuals felt empowered to speak up even more. They created new magazines such as the *Advocate* (see entry under 1960s–Print Culture in volume 4) and *Out* that served the homosexual community and brought wider awareness to their needs. They formed political organizations such as New York's Gay Liberation Front. The **AIDS** (see entry under 1980s–The Way We Lived in volume 5) health crisis that began in the early 1980s brought increased solidarity as gays and lesbians banded together to fight the disease. ACT-UP was one such group that fought for AIDS awareness.

After more than thirty years, the gay liberation movement has had a tremendous impact on American society. While gays

Gay rights activist and politician Harvey Milk (with arms raised) takes part in a gay rights parade in San Francisco, California, in the mid-1970s. *AP/Wide World Photos. Reproduced by permission.*

and lesbians still face hostility, American society has become much more accepting of gays and lesbians. **Television** (see entry under 1940s–TV and Radio in volume 3) shows such as *Will and Grace* (1998–) featured openly gay characters in positive roles. Some states have passed laws allowing for homosexual marriages. Although they still face significant resistance from some members of society, participants in the gay liberation movement have largely succeeded in bringing homosexuality "out of the closet" and bringing homosexuals closer to an equal position in American society.

—Timothy Berg

For More Information

The Advocate. http://www.advocate.com (accessed March 18, 2002).

Bull, Chris. *Witness to Revolution: The Advocate Reports on Gay and Lesbian Politics, 1967–1999.* Los Angeles: Alyson Books, 1999.

Califia, Pat. *The Advocate Adviser: America's Most Popular Gay Columnist Tackles the Questions That the Others Ignore.* Boston: Alyson Publications, 1991.

Oliver, Marilyn Tower. *Gay and Lesbian Rights: A Struggle.* Springfield, NJ: Enslow, 1998.

Silver, Diane. *The New Civil War: The Lesbian and Gay Struggle for Civil Rights.* New York: Franklin Watts, 1997.

Thompson, Mark, ed. *Long Road to Freedom: The Advocate History of the Gay and Lesbian Movement.* New York: St. Martin's Press, 1994.

Ghettos

Amid the American ideals of equal opportunity and prosperity, ghettos stand out as a glaring contradiction. Ghettos are concentrations of people in cities isolated from the rest of society by their poverty and by their racial and ethnic differences. Ghettos have existed for many centuries in many different cultures. Sometimes they are the result of deliberate government persecution, such as when Jewish people were imprisoned in ghettos in Europe at various times in its past. More often, ghettos are the result of a combination of economic and racial factors combined with government and societal indifference.

Ghettos in America began when the growth of factories in central cities made these cities less desirable because of pollution and noise. People with money left the central cities; those without the money to escape remained behind. As jobs and good incomes left, those who remained—many of whom were African Americans—had little money to keep their houses and neighborhoods in good condition. From there, neighborhoods often spiraled downward into ghettos, isolated by lack of money and by the indifference of white Americans who had left for the **suburbs** (see entry under 1950s–The Way We Lived in volume 3). The problems of ghettos became a crisis in the 1960s. A lack of job opportunities and political power, incidences of police brutality, and protests against racist policies created a dangerous mix. Eventually riots erupted in major U.S. cities, including Watts, in Los Angeles, California, in 1965, and Detroit, Michigan, and Newark, New Jersey, in 1967. These riots prompted some government action, but it was never enough to remove the root cause of the problem: poverty.

Despite these overwhelming problems, ghetto residents have managed to produce their own unique and important contributions to American culture. Ghetto conditions produced some great works of literature, including *Call It Sleep* (1934), a novel about Jewish ghetto life, by Henry Roth (1906–1995), and *A Street in Bronzeville* (1945), poetry on African American ghetto life by Gwendolyn Brooks (1917–2000). In the 1980s, **rap** (see entry under 1980s—Music in volume 5) music sprang out of the African American ghettos in such groups as Public Enemy, whose strong commentaries on police brutality, black power, and **gang** (see entry under 1980s—The Way We Lived in volume 5) life gave an important voice to oppressed ghetto residents.

Ghettos remain a pressing problem in the United States in the twenty-first century, with no easy end in sight.

—Timothy Berg

For More Information

Jargowsky, Paul A. *Poverty and Place: Ghettos, Barrios, and the American City.* New York: The Russell Sage Foundation, 1997.

Jencks, Christopher, and Paul E. Peterson, eds. *The Urban Underclass.* Washington, DC: Brookings Institution, 1991.

Kotlowitz, Alex. *There Are No Children Here: The Story of Two Boys Growing Up in the Other America.* New York: Doubleday, 1991.

Haight-Ashbury

The intersection of Haight and Ashbury streets in San Francisco, California, is both a physical place and a symbol for the hippie counterculture of the 1960s. San Francisco had long drawn people who did not fit with the mainstream of American culture. In the mid-1960s, the neighborhood around the intersection of Haight and Ashbury had begun to attract counterculture types, or **hippies** (see entry under 1960s—The Way We Lived in volume 4). Hippies were people known for their relaxed dress, long hair, and casual social attitudes. They came in part because this working-class neighborhood had cheaper rents than other parts of San Francisco did. By the mid-1960s, more than ten thousand hippies were living in the neighborhood. Shops and services sprang up to serve this group.

Left alone, Haight-Ashbury might have simply continued as a quiet hippie neighborhood. But in 1967, the neighborhood became a symbol for the emerging psychedelic music scene and the larger youth counterculture. A thriving music scene—led by the **Grateful Dead** (see entry under 1960s—Music in volume 4), the Jefferson Airplane, and Janis Joplin (1943–1970)—drew national attention. These musicians, particularly the Grateful Dead, established a large cult following that brought further attention to the neighborhood. The summer of 1967 was labeled the "Summer of Love," and its headquarters was the Haight-Ashbury neighborhood. That summer, young people from

A parade in the Haight-Ashbury district of San Francisco, California, in 1967. *AP/Wide World Photos. Reproduced by permission.*

around the country were encouraged to come visit, learn about the new counterculture that emphasized peace and love, and then return home to spread this new vision. So many people arrived, and stayed, that the neighborhood could not handle the number of people. Further complicating matters was the appeal of the neighborhood to all kinds of outsiders, many of whom had personal or social problems. More than a few teenage runaways ended up in Haight-Ashbury. Because of the music, the hippie scene, and these problems, Haight-Ashbury attracted enormous media attention in 1967, which only served to encourage more people to come to the neighborhood.

After its prime years in the late 1960s, the neighborhood declined during the 1970s. It underwent a revival in the 1980s and 1990s as a kind of tourist attraction that played up its hippie past. In addition to counterculture shops, the intersection features corporate giants such as **Gap** (see entry under 1960s— Commerce in volume 4) and Ben & Jerry's. Although far from what it was in the 1960s, Haight-Ashbury remains a symbol of youthful idealism and alternative lifestyles.

—Timothy Berg

For More Information

Hoskyns, Barney. *Beneath the Diamond Sky: Haight-Ashbury, 1965–1970*. New York: Simon & Schuster, 1997.

Perry, Charles. *The Haight-Ashbury*. New York: Rolling Stone Press, 1984.

Hippies

Though the dictionary defines a hippie as anyone who rejects the conventional customs of society, in America the hippies were the product of the countercultural movements of the 1960s and 1970s. The word "hippie" is derived from "hipster," which was once a synonym for "beatnik." The **beatniks** (see entry under 1950s–Print Culture in volume 3) of the 1950s were the spiritual ancestors of the hippies, who bloomed as the flower children of the 1960s and 1970s. Both groups shared intellectual curiosity, disdain for conventional customs and morals, affinity for recreational drugs, and tastes in music, literature, and philosophy that put them outside the mainstream.

Although the term was sometimes applied too broadly (especially by the "straights," whose world the hippies scorned), hippies tended to be gentle people who embraced colorful clothing, nonpossessive sexual relationships, the use of **marijuana** (see entry under 1960s–The Way We Lived in volume 4) and LSD, communal living, and a "live for today" philosophy. They generally rejected materialism, the Vietnam War (1954–75), the success ethic, and authority of all types. Their musical tastes favored the **Grateful Dead** (see entry under 1960s–Music in volume 4), Santana, Jefferson Airplane, Janis Joplin (1943–1970), and Indian sitar player Ravi Shankar (1920–). (A sitar is a complex, difficult-to-play classical Indian instrument.) They were the core of what became known as the "counterculture."

The "straight" world was interested in the hippies from the beginning. There were bus tours of San Francisco's Haight-Ashbury district, billed as "the only place you can visit a foreign country without leaving the United States."

Hippie images and references permeated the popular culture of the United States from the mid-1960s until the early 1970s. The most popular band in the world, the **Beatles** (see entry under 1960s–Music in volume 4), "went hippie" with their *Sgt. Pepper's Lonely Hearts Club Band* album in 1967. "Psychedelic" art and music supposedly allowed one to experience

A hippie couple. *AP/Wide World Photos. Reproduced by permission.*

the "mind-blowing" qualities of LSD without taking the drug itself. On **Broadway** (see entry under 1900s–Film and Theater in volume 1), the musical *Hair* (see entry under 1960s–Film and Theater in volume 4) opened in 1968 to celebrate the hippie lifestyle with music, dance, and a show-stopping scene in which the entire cast stood naked onstage. Hippies appeared in films ranging from *The President's Analyst* (1967) to *I Love You, Alice B. Toklas* (1968) to *Easy Rider* (1969). They also became a frequent subject for humor on the popular TV show, *Rowan and Martin's Laugh-In* (1968–73; see entry under 1960s–TV and Radio in volume 4).

The hippie culture gradually faded, as did the era that inspired it. But hippie images and references continued to appear. The characters of Cheech and Chong (Tommy Chong, 1938–; Cheech Marin, 1946–) were pothead hippie throwbacks in films like *Up in Smoke* (1978) and *Still Smokin'* (1983). The Grateful Dead (1965–95) still had a dedicated following that included many aging hippies, until the band broke up following the death of Jerry Garcia (1942–1995). In the 1990s and 2000s, the TV sit-com *Dharma and Greg* could always get an easy laugh with a reference to Dharma's "hippie parents." As the Grateful Dead used to sing, "What a long, strange trip it's been."

—Justin Gustainis

For More Information

Bisbort, Alan, and Parke Puterbaugh. *Groovy, Man: Tripping through the Psychedelic Years*. Los Angeles: General Publishing Group, 1998.

Brand, Stewart. "We Owe It All to the Hippies." *Time* (Special Issue, Spring 1995).

Hippies on the Web. http://www.rockument.com/links.html (accessed March 21, 2002).

Miller, Timothy. *The Hippies and American Values*. Knoxville: University of Tennessee Press, 1991.

Stern, Jane, and Michael Stern. *Sixties People*. New York: Alfred A. Knopf, 1990.

Lottery

In modern American culture, money is often equated with happiness. It is not surprising, then, that get-rich-quick schemes like the lottery attract millions of players looking for a big payoff. First seen in the United States in the 1800s, government lotteries were made illegal because they were so often "rigged," or designed to cheat those who bought tickets hoping to win money. In the mid-1960s, the lottery made a comeback when the states of New York and New Hampshire introduced lottery games to boost their income. Since that time state-run lotteries have grown in popularity and size. In the 1990s, thirty-eight states operated lotteries, paying out millions and earning billions of dollars each year. Huge multistate lotteries introduced in the 1990s brought potential jackpots in the hundreds of millions of dollars.

Lottery critics question whether it is right to use legalized gambling to raise money for the government. Some say that the lottery unfairly burdens poor people, because the poor are far more likely than the rich to buy lottery tickets. Others point out that there is little real benefit to the state, because most of the money raised by the lottery goes to the companies that run the lottery, leaving only about one third to be used by the states. But lottery advocates argue that lotteries pour millions of dollars into state budgets, and that much of that money is used for education. As with other forms of vice, Americans seem likely to continue their love-hate relationship with lotteries.

—Tina Gianoulis

For More Information

"Are State Lotteries Stacked Against Blacks?" *Ebony* (June 1991): pp. 126–30.

Clotfelter, Charles T., and Phillip J. Cook. *Selling Hope: State Lotteries in America.* Cambridge, MA: Harvard University Press, 1989.

Draper, Robert. "You Lose! The Sad Truth About the Texas Lottery." *Texas Monthly* (June 1993): pp. 118–35.

"Lottery History." *NASPL (National Association of State and Provincial Lotteries).* http://www.naspl.org/history.html (accessed March 21, 2002).

Weiss, Ann E. *Lotteries: Who Wins, Who Loses?* Hillside, NJ: Enslow, 1991.

Mafia

The most famous criminal organization in the United States has its origins in medieval Sicily, where wealthy landowners once hired groups of bandits to guard their estates. Eventually, the bandit **gangs** (see entry under 1980s—The Way We Lived in volume 5) grew so strong they were able to challenge the established authorities in both Sicily and Italy. Although most Mafia members are of either Sicilian or Italian descent, they represent only a small percentage of their respective cultures. Many Americans of Italian or Sicilian heritage resent the popular culture stereotypes that suggest that all those sharing their ethnic heritage are criminals.

The Mafia came to America through immigration in the 1880s and was well established in the United States by the following decade. Some experts distinguish between the Sicilian Mafia and its American counterpart by calling the latter the *Cosa Nostra* (an Italian phrase meaning, literally, "our thing").

Mafia criminal activities have always included extortion (obtaining money or information by force or threat), loansharking (lending money at high interest rates), illegal gambling, and prostitution. During **Prohibition** (the period from 1919 to 1933 when alcohol was banned in the United States; see entry under 1920s—The Way We Lived in volume 2), the Mafia (along with other criminal gangs) became wealthy as suppliers of illegal liquor. Following World War II (1939–45), Mafia "families" quickly became involved in the growing trade in illegal drugs—beginning with heroin and later adding **cocaine** (see entry under 1980s—The Way We Lived in volume 5).

For many years, little was known about the Mafia in mainstream culture. Members followed the rule of *omerta* ("silence"), with violation punishable by death. In 1963, a low-level Mafia member named Joe Valachi (1904–1971) broke the silence and spent almost a month testifying about the organization in televised Senate hearings. His story was later turned into a book, *The Valachi Papers* by Peter Maas (1929–2001), which was in turn made into a 1972 movie starring Charles Bronson (1921–).

The Mafia's greatest boost into popular culture came courtesy of author Mario Puzo (1920–1999), whose 1969 novel **The Godfather** (see entry under 1970s—Film and Theater in volume 4) was a **best-seller** (see entry under 1940s—Commerce in volume 3). The novel gave rise to three popular movies directed by Francis Ford Coppola (1939–): *The Godfather* (1972), *The Godfather: Part II* (1974), and *The Godfather: Part III* (1990). The first two films each won Best Picture Oscars, along with a host of other awards. Other important Mafia films include *Prizzi's Honor* (1985) and *Goodfellas* (1990). In 1999, pay-cable channel HBO launched *The Sopranos,* an ongoing chronicle of a New Jersey Mafia "family" that has won both high ratings and critical acclaim. Although the Mafia today plays a smaller role in American crime, thanks to years of pressure from law enforcement agencies, it continues to play a prominent role in the American imagination.

—*Justin Gustainis*

For More Information

Browne, Nick. *Francis Ford Coppola's "Godfather" Trilogy.* New York: Cambridge University Press, 1999.

Fox, Stephen R. *Blood and Power: Organized Crime in Twentieth-Century America.* New York: W. Morrow, 1989.

Hess, Henner. *Mafia & Mafiosi: Origin, Power and Myth.* London: C. Hurst, 1998.

Mafia: The History of the Mob in America (video). New York: A&E Home Video, 1993.

Messenger, Christian K. *The Godfather and American Culture: How the Corleones Became "Our Gang."* Albany: State University of New York Press, 2002.

Mobsters.TV. http://www.mobsters.tv (accessed March 21, 2002).

Porrello, Rick. *Rick Porrello's American Mafia.* http://www.americanmafia. com (accessed March 21, 2002).

Sifakis, Carl. *The Mafia Encyclopedia.* New York: Checkmark Books, 1999.

Marijuana

Marijuana (MAH-rih-WAH-nah) is an informal Mexican term for the dried leaves of the hemp plant (*Cannabis sativa*), often smoked for its mildly intoxicating effect. After alcohol and tobacco, marijuana is the most popular recreational drug in the United States, often associated with the counterculture of the 1960s. It is reportedly still smoked by an estimated three million Americans every day. Unlike alcohol and tobacco, however, its growth, possession, and use are illegal, although there is a growing interest in making it available for medical use. Marijuana has been reported to be effective in easing the discomfort of patients suffering from glaucoma (a disease of the eye that creates pressure within the eye and can result in blindness) or from terminal illnesses such as **AIDS** (see entry under 1980s—The Way We Lived in volume 5) or cancer.

The hemp plant has been widely cultivated in the United States since colonial days. There is evidence of marijuana's use in medicine in the nineteenth century. In the 1920s and 1930s, federal law-enforcement officials led a campaign to demonize marijuana (or "marihuana," as it was often spelled then) as "the devil's weed" used by Mexicans, blacks, and other minority groups. Officials spread exaggerated and unproved reports of its effects, such as violent crime, addiction, and psychosis (mental illness characterized by loss of a sense of reality). Much of this antidrug propaganda can be seen in the 1936 film *Reefer Madness,* which has become a cult classic.

From the 1980s, officials have continued to crack down on marijuana use as part of the "war on drugs." One out of six federal prisoners, or fifteen thousand inmates, has been jailed primarily for a marijuana offense, with tens of thousands more in state and local prisons. It has been estimated that one-third of the U.S. population over the age of eleven has smoked marijuana at least once. Still, it is considered politically dangerous to admit its use, as when President Bill Clinton (1946–) famously insisted that he had not inhaled the drug. Groups like the National Organization for the Reform of Marijuana Laws (NORML) campaign for its decriminalization by public "smoke-ins" and other lobbying efforts. Supporters of such reform point out that no one has ever been killed by smoking marijuana, unlike those who indulge in alcohol or tobacco.

—Edward Moran

For More Information

Grinspoon, Lester, and James B. Bakalar. *Marihuana: The Forbidden Medicine.* New Haven: Yale University Press, 1993.

Kamiya, Gary. "Reefer Madness." *Salon* (October 12, 2000); http://www.salon.com/news/feature/2000/10/12/drugs (accessed March 21, 2002).

Schleichert, Elizabeth. *Marijuana.* Springfield, NJ: Enslow, 1996.

Schlosser, Eric. "Reefer Madness." *The Atlantic* (August 1994); http://www.theatlantic.com/politics/crime/reefm.htm (accessed March 21, 2002).

Stanley, Debbie. *Marijuana and Your Lungs: The Incredible Disgusting Story.* New York: Rosen Publishing, 2000.

Martial Arts

Most commonly, the term "martial arts" refers to the systems of combat developed centuries ago in the Far East (the area of eastern and southeast Asia). A few of these disciplines involve the use of weapons such as swords, throwing stars, or short clubs, but most emphasize unarmed fighting. The best known include karate (Japan), aikido (Japan), ju-jitsu (Japan), judo (a gentler form of ju-jitsu, also from Japan), kung-fu (China), tai chi (China), and tae kwan do (Korea).

Although most of the Asian martial arts are very old, they only began to appear in American culture following World War II (1939–45). American troops encountered Japanese martial arts for the first time while fighting in the Pacific. Some soldiers were intrigued by this mode of combat, and they brought their interest home with them. As a result, martial arts schools began to open in the United States beginning in the 1950s.

American interest in martial arts accelerated with the "spy craze" of the 1960s. Several of the **James Bond films** (see entry under 1960s–Film and Theater in volume 4), such as *Goldfinger* (1964) and *You Only Live Twice* (1967), showcased martial arts, as did imitations like *Our Man Flint* (1965). On **television** (see entry under 1940s—TV and Radio in volume 3), heroes such as *The Man from U.N.C.L.E.* (1964–68) used martial arts, as did David Carradine (1936–) in the show *Kung Fu* (1972–75). *The Green Hornet* (1966–67) featured a character named Kato, played by Bruce Lee (1940–1973). Lee, a genuine kung-fu master, made a number of Hong Kong–based martial arts films. His "breakout" American film role was *Enter the Dragon* (1973), released the same year he died of a brain embolism.

Enthusiasm for martial arts films survived Lee. Several Americans, more notable for fighting skills than for acting ability, became action-movie stars in the 1970s and 1980s. These included Chuck Norris (1940–), Steven Seagal (1951–), and Cynthia Rothrock (1957–), a rare female star. In the late 1980s and 1990s, martial arts was marketed to children, with films like *3 Ninjas* (1992) and its sequels, the *Mighty Morphin Power Rangers* TV series (1993–96) and the Teenage Mutant Ninja Turtles TV show and films (1987–95). For adults, the martial arts star for the 1990s and beyond is Jackie Chan (1954–), who brings a lighter, more humorous touch to an often grim type of movie.

—*Justin Gustainis*

For More Information

Donohue, John J. *Warrior Dreams: The Martial Arts and the American Imagination.* Westport, CT: Bergin and Garvey, 1994.

The Martial Arts Network Online. http://martial-arts-network.com/ (accessed March 21, 2002).

Martialinfo.com. http://www.martialinfo.com/ (accessed March 21, 2002).

Miller, Davis. *The Tao of Bruce Lee: A Martial Arts Memoir.* New York: Harmony Books, 2000.

Skidmore, Max J. "Oriental Contributions to Western Popular Culture: The Martial Arts." *Journal of Popular Culture* (Summer 1991): pp. 129–48.

National Aeronautics and Space Administration

Since 1958, the National Aeronautics and Space Administration (NASA) has been responsible for the U.S. government's exploration of space. It also became a primary force in fueling Americans' passionate interest in space. In the years since its founding, NASA has had some spectacular successes and some dramatic failures.

The need for NASA grew out of the **Cold War** (1947-91; see entry under 1940s—The Way We Lived in volume 3), the intense rivalry between the United States and the Soviet Union. The political competition between these two superpowers moved into space in 1957 when the Soviet Union launched the first **satellite** (see entry under 1950s—The Way We Lived in volume 3), *Sputnik*. The Soviets also launched the first man into space and the first man to orbit the Earth. NASA launched Alan Shepard (1923–1998), the first American in space, in May 1961. In February 1962, John Glenn (1921–) became the first American to orbit the earth. These successes created a huge interest in space travel and made celebrities out of the first astronauts. The decision of President John F. Kennedy (1917–1963) to send a man to the moon before the 1960s ended spurred further public interest in space and an all-out effort by NASA. Although NASA suffered a huge setback when three astronauts died during a pre-liftoff fire in 1967, the agency—and the world—reached a tremendous milestone on July 20, 1969, when Neil Armstrong (1930–) and Buzz Aldrin (1930–) became the first men to walk on the moon. Broadcast on **television** (see entry under 1940s—TV and Radio in volume 3), the event held the world spellbound. More moon landings followed in the 1970s, but other than a near-disaster aboard *Apollo 13*, public interest decreased.

NASA suspended its manned flights in the early 1970s. It focused instead on its space laboratory, *Skylab*, launched in 1973, and on unmanned flights to Mars and to deep space. In 1981, NASA launched the first space shuttle, a new method of space flight that allowed astronauts to leave Earth using rockets and to land their ship like an airplane at mission's end. These reusable shuttles promised a new era in space flight. In 1986, tragedy struck the shuttle program when the space-shuttle *Challenger* blew up seconds after liftoff, killing all on board, including the first civilian in space, teacher Christa McAuliffe (1948-1986). Despite this setback, NASA continued launching the shuttles on a fairly regular basis into the twenty-first century.

NASA's efforts had a great impact on popular culture, as television shows and films came out to capitalize on the public's interest in space. In the 1960s, *Star Trek* (see entry under 1960s—TV and Radio in volume 4) and *Lost in Space* were popular TV series. The 1968 film *2001: A Space Odyssey* (see entry under 1960s—Film and Theater in volume 4) directed by Stanley Kubrick (1928–1999) was among the first serious looks at space. Some films examined the NASA programs directly, including *The Right Stuff* (1983) and *Apollo 13* (1995). NASA's main launch facility at Cape Canaveral, Florida, became a huge tourist attraction in the 1970s, giving tours and selling space souvenirs. Along with this interest, there were some who challenged the necessity of NASA's many activities that came at great financial expense. But despite this, NASA continues to direct the United States' efforts in space, keeping America's attention focused on the mysteries of space.

—Timothy Berg

For More Information

Kranz, Gene. *Failure Is Not an Option: Mission Control from Mercury to Apollo 13 and Beyond.* New York: Simon & Schuster, 2000.

Launius, Roger D., and Bertram Ulrich. *NASA and the Exploration of Space: With Works from the NASA Art Collection.* New York: Stewart, Tabori, and Chang, 1998.

McCurdy, Howard E. *Inside NASA.* Baltimore: Johns Hopkins University Press, 1993.

NASA. http://www.nasa.gov/ (accessed March 21, 2002).

Wolfe, Tom. *The Right Stuff.* New York: Bantam Books, 1983.

National Organization for Women

The National Organization for Women (NOW) was one of the major forces in the revival of the women's movement in the United States during the 1960s. Founded in 1966, NOW champions women's rights and tries to influence legislation and public policy that affects women, providing an important public voice for women in the United States.

The creation of NOW is tied to author and activist Betty Friedan (1921–), whose best-selling 1963 book, *The Feminine Mystique,* is considered the wake-up call that re-energized the women's movement. Friedan's book highlighted the problems of inequality women were encountering in American society and that these problems were shared by millions of other women. At a 1966 convention, while discussing their common concerns, Friedan and others felt the time was right for a national women's organization that would pool the efforts of many women around the country to fight for women's rights. As a result, NOW was born. Friedan became its first president and was later succeeded by activist Gloria Steinem (1934–).

In the years since its founding, NOW has fought for women's rights on many issues. One of the most important has been reproductive rights, the right of women to control when and how they have children, including their right to abortion services. They have also fought for equal pay and for equal access to promotion at work. The organization also sought to put more women into elective office, figuring that if more women were in government, these women would make laws benefiting women. Issues of domestic abuse, sexual abuse, and sexual harassment have been important concerns for NOW. Over the years, NOW was instrumental in promoting greater equality for women. That success proved challenging for the group by the 1990s. As women achieved greater equality in American life, many saw less of a need to support NOW. Nevertheless, by the end of the twentieth century, NOW had chapters in all fifty states and had more than 250,000 members. Since it began in 1966, NOW has proved to be an effective force for positive change in women's lives.

—*Timothy Berg*

For More Information

Berkeley, Kathleen C. *The Women's Liberation Movement in America*. Westport, CT: Greenwood Press, 1999.

Friedan, Betty. *The Feminine Mystique*. New York: Dell, 1963.

National Organization for Women. http://www.now.org/ (accessed March 21, 2002).

Rowbotham, Sheila. *A Century of Women*. New York: Penguin Books, 1999.

Women's rights activist Gloria Steinem (left) at a 1996 NOW rally in San Francisco, California. *AP/Wide World Photos. Reproduced by permission.*

Sexual Revolution

Once upon a time, sex was considered to be a private issue—and even a nonissue—within mainstream American society. Matters relating to sex never were discussed in public. The

accepted view was that sex was an act between a man and a woman who were married. Its primary purpose was reproductive in nature. Beginning in the mid-1960s, however, what came to be regarded as a sexual revolution took place in the United States. This revolution mostly involved younger Americans.

The sexual revolution was the outgrowth of numerous lifestyle and cultural changes that had been developing throughout the century and reached their high point in the 1960s. These changes date from the 1920s and the coming of the **Jazz** (see entry under 1900s–Music in volume 1) Age. Back then, sexual issues became a part of social interaction among the young. Sex entered literature and popular culture in the novels of F. Scott Fitzgerald (1896–1940) and in the films of Cecil B. DeMille (1881–1959). During World War II (1939–45), the increased mobility of men and women—with the latter leaving the home to join the military and work in defense plants—led to a rise in premarital sexual relations. In 1948 and 1953, Alfred Kinsey (1894–1956) published two landmark statistical studies of human sexuality, *Sexual Behavior in the Human Male* and *Sexual Behavior in the Human Female*. Kinsey's research led him to put forth a controversial viewpoint. He declared that any attempt to establish uniform rules for sexual behavior was unrealistic, not to mention unfair. This new idea would greatly influence modern conceptions of sexuality.

In 1953, Hugh Hefner (1926–) began publishing **Playboy** (see entry under 1950s–Print Culture in volume 3), a wildly successful male-oriented mass-circulation magazine that included photo layouts of nude women mixed in with feature articles and columns covering a range of subjects. A number of classic novels that previously had been censored were published in the United States. The novels, whose content was frankly sexual, included *Lady Chatterley's Lover* by D. H. Lawrence (1885–1930), and *Tropic of Cancer* and *Tropic of Capricorn* by Henry Miller (1891–1980). Beginning in the mid-1950s, young people became entranced by the liberating sounds of **rock and roll** (see entry under 1950s–Music in volume 3). All these occurrences left older, more conservative Americans asking, "What is this world coming to?"

In 1962, **Cosmopolitan** (see entry under 1960s–Print Culture in volume 1) magazine-editor Helen Gurley Brown (1922–) authored *Sex and the Single Girl*. In 1969, someone identified only as "J" published *The Sensuous Woman*. The titles of these books indicated that, first, an unmarried woman might be concerned with issues involving sex and, second, that a woman might take pleasure in sexual relations. The 1963 publication of *The Feminine Mystique,* by Betty Friedan (1921–), signaled a revival of interest in feminism. The book stimulated a discussion of sex and gender roles. In 1966, sex-issue researchers William H. Masters (1915–2001) and Virginia E. Johnson (1925–) published their initial scientific study, *Human Sexual Response*; a follow-up, *Human Sexual Inadequacy,* appeared four years later. A number of sexually explicit pulp novels (inexpensive books containing sensational material) became wildly popular; heading the list was *Valley of the Dolls* (1966), by Jacqueline Susann (1921–1974). The Hollywood Production Code fell by the wayside. The code had been in effect since the early 1930s and had decreed that on-screen sexual explicitness was forbidden in American movies. With the extinction of the code, American films began to directly deal with sex-oriented themes and relationships.

Although progressive-thinking Americans of all ages accepted this more open-minded acknowledgment of sex, viewing it as liberating to the soul, what came to be known as the sexual revolution mostly was associated with young people. Unlike their parents, who struggled economically as they came of age in the 1930s during the **Great Depression** (1929–41; see entry under 1930s–The Way We Lived in volume 2), these **baby boomers** (see entry under 1940s–The Way We Lived in volume 3) grew up with plenty of leisure time and an unrestrained intellectual curiosity. They began thirsting for new and liberating experiences, experimenting with such drugs as **marijuana** (see entry under 1960s–The Way We Lived in volume 4) and LSD. In 1960, what was to become the most popular method of birth control, the oral contraceptive pill, was made commercially available. The marketing of **The Pill** (see entry under 1950s–The Way We Lived in volume 3) and other birth control devices allowed women to experiment sexually with reduced fear of an unwanted pregnancy.

In addition, many no longer considered marriage a prerequisite for sex. In the late 1960s, a couple living together outside the sanctity of marriage was considered offbeat if not downright scandalous. By the mid-1970s, living together was a common occurrence. Furthermore, as the feminist movement took root in the late 1960s and early 1970s, women became more focused on cultivating careers and postponing marriage and motherhood, while not postponing sexual experience.

The sexual revolution also directly resulted in the beginning of the **gay liberation movement** (see entry under 1960s–The Way We Lived in volume 4). The movement began with the dramatic Stonewall rebellion in 1969. It was customary at the time for police to conduct raids on gay bars. At the Stonewall Inn in New York City's Greenwich Village, patrons fought back against police. Gay rights activists began publicly acknowledging their own sexual preference while denouncing the shame often associated with homosexuality.

Meanwhile, singles bars opened and flourished; they catered to unmarried men and women who wished to meet and perhaps finish their evening with sexual contact. Individuals seeking sexual and romantic relationships began submitting personal ads to alternative newspapers. An increasing number of sexually explicit books, films, and magazines became available to mainstream America. A small number of married couples even began "swinging," or exchanging partners for sexual purposes.

One of the unfortunate offshoots of the sexual revolution was the increase in **sexually transmitted diseases** (see entry under 1970s–The Way We Lived in volume 4), including gonorrhea, syphilis, genital warts, genital herpes, hepatitis B, and **AIDS** (see entry under 1980s–The Way We Lived in volume 5). Additionally, the sexual revolution directly led to a counter-revolution, spearheaded by conservative religious fundamentalists who were convinced that sexual openness was a sorry byproduct of the moral decay of American society. In the late 1970s, they began forming organizations and political coalitions and electing representatives to office. Their efforts—and their battles with those who believe that sexual freedom is a matter of personal freedom—continue to this day.

—Rob Edelman

For More Information

Allyn, David. *Make Love, Not War: The Sexual Revolution, an Unfettered History*. Boston: Little Brown, 2000.

Archer, Jules. *The Incredible Sixties: The Stormy Years that Changed America*. San Diego: Harcourt Brace Jovanovich, 1986.

Falk, Gerhard. *Sex, Gender, and Social Change: The Great Revolution*. Lanham, MD: University Press of America, 1998.

Friedan, Betty. *The Feminine Mystique*. New York: Dell, 1963.

Kamen, Paula. *Her Way: Young Women Remake the Sexual Revolution*. New York: New York University Press, 2000.

Masters, William H., and Virginia E. Johnson. *Human Sexual Response*. Boston: Little, Brown, 1966.

Masters, William H., and Virginia E. Johnson. *Human Sexual Inadequacy.* Boston: Little, Brown, 1970.

Students for a Democratic Society

Students for a Democratic Society (SDS) was the largest of the many organizations that opposed the Vietnam War (1954–75) from the mid-1960s to the mid-1970s. It also gave birth to the most radical and destructive of the antiwar organizations, the Weathermen.

The SDS began in the 1950s as the Student League for Industrial Democracy. The name change came in 1960, but SDS membership held little attraction for most U.S. college students until the publication of "The Port Huron Statement" in 1962. This lengthy expression of the organization's philosophy was written by Tom Hayden (1939–), who would become SDS's next president and later a major figure in the antiwar movement. The "Statement's" critique of American consumerism and racism, and its call for true participatory democracy, appealed to many students' sense of idealism. The SDS chapters began to multiply and membership rosters quickly swelled.

Early SDS activities focused on economic development projects in poverty-stricken areas and minority-voter registration. But as the Vietnam War began to escalate in the mid-1960s, SDS increasingly focused on antiwar activism. The initial demonstrations, starting in 1964, were orderly, legal, and peaceful. The failure of these activities to influence American policy, however, led to frustration and thus to more disruptive forms of protest. SDS chapters around the country became involved in unauthorized marches, student strikes, attacks on Reserve Officers' Training Corps (ROTC) programs, and occupation of campus buildings. Another form of protest included harassment of on-campus recruiters representing the military; the Central Intelligence Agency (CIA); and the Dow Chemical Company, manufacturer of napalm, a chemical used by the U.S. military in Vietnam.

In the summer of 1968, SDS participated in the demonstrations held in Chicago, Illinois, at the Democratic National Convention. Clashes between demonstrators and police became increasingly violent on both sides, resulting in a street battle the last night of the convention that government investigators later dubbed a "police riot." Hayden was one of seven protest leaders indicted on federal conspiracy charges. The "Chicago Seven," as they were known, were convicted but freed on appeal.

In 1969, the most radical elements within SDS took over the organization and purged all who did not share their extreme views. Under the new name "Weathermen"—taken from a song by **Bob Dylan** (1941–; see entry under 1960s—Music in volume 4)—they embarked on a course that included bombings, arson, and calls for the violent overthrow of the U.S. government.

—Justin Gustainis

For More Information

Collier, Peter, and David Horowitz. *Destructive Generation.* New York: Summit Books, 1989.

Gitlin, Todd. *The Sixties: Years of Hope, Days of Rage.* New York: Bantam Books, 1987.

Miller, James. *"Democracy Is in the Streets": From Port Huron to the Siege of Chicago.* New York: Simon & Schuster, 1987.

Sale, Kirkpatrick. *SDS.* New York: Random House, 1973.

Students for a Democratic Society Port Huron Statement (June 15, 1962). http://history.hanover.edu/courses/excerpts/111hur.html (accessed March 21, 2002).

1970s
The Me Decade

When journalist Tom Wolfe (1931–) surveyed the changes that had swept America in the past few years, he gave the decade a label that has stuck: "The Me Decade." Wolfe and others noticed that the dominant concerns of most people had shifted from issues of social and political justice that were so important in the 1960s to a more selfish focus on individual well-being. What was behind this sudden change in the American mood?

Economic and political shifts help to explain much of the change. From the end of the World War II (1939–45) until the end of the 1960s, the American economy had enjoyed one of its longest extended periods of growth. That growth came screeching to a halt in the 1970s, and matters got worse as the decade continued. An Arab oil embargo halted shipments of oil to the United States, forcing gas prices to raise dramatically and forcing rationing. Another oil crisis in 1979 continued the economic shock. The automobile industry was hit hard by the oil crises and by competition from carmakers in Japan. To make economic matters worse, inflation was rising, which meant that the relative prices of goods were climbing faster than wages were. Many Americans turned inward and focused their attention on their economic problems rather than on problems of politics or social justice.

Politics in the 1970s were very different from in the 1960s as well. Presidents John F. Kennedy (1917–1963) and Lyndon B.

1970s
At a Glance

What We Said:

Bogue: Disgusting or distasteful.

"Don't leave home without it": An advertising line used by American Express to remind its customers that they could use their cards nearly anywhere. Advertising-saturated Americans began using this slogan in everyday speech.

Dweeb: A loser or social outcast.

"Get a clue!": A warning that one should figure out what is going on.

Gnarly: Very cool or good.

Groupies: Fans—usually women—who followed rock stars from concert to concert, sometimes offering sexual favors.

"Like": An interjection used by teenagers to interrupt and add emphasis to their speech, as in "She was, like, so bogue." When combined with "totally," it could be used to express real approval: "Like, totally!"

Male chauvinist pig: A man who thinks women are inferior. This label was used by feminists in the women's liberation movement to blast those men who resisted their efforts to gain equal rights. Archie Bunker of TV's *All in the Family* was often called a male chauvinist pig.

Me Generation: A term used to describe people who left behind the social activism of the 1960s and focused on improving their own souls through a variety of self-help methods.

"Plop, plop, fizz, fizz, oh what a relief it is" (1977): Part of a popular advertising jingle for Alka-Seltzer, this catchy phrase was used to describe anything that brought relief.

"Yo!": Similar to "Hi" or "Hey," this greeting was popularized by Sylvester Stallone in the movie *Rocky* (1976).

What We Read:

***Bury My Heart at Wounded Knee* (1970):** This important history of the effect of white settlement on Native Americans, written by Dee Brown, was the rare historical work to become a best-seller.

***Everything You Always Wanted to Know About Sex (But Were Afraid to Ask)* (1970):** Though the sexual revolution of the late 1960s and early 1970s brought renewed sexual experimentation to the country, people still had questions about sexuality. This book, by Dr. David Reuben, answered them in a lighthearted way and stayed near the top of the nonfiction best-seller lists for nearly a year.

***Jonathan Livingston Seagull* (1970):** This parable by Richard Bach told the story of an outcast seagull who seeks perfection. Its quasi-spiritual tone appealed to readers of every religion, and it remains in print into the twenty-first century.

***Love Story* (1970):** Erich Segal's story of the love between a talented Harvard athlete and his dying girlfriend was the publishing sensation of the year, with 21 hardcover printings and an initial paperback print run of 4,350,000. It was quickly made into a movie starring Ryan O'Neal and Ali MacGraw.

***The Exorcist* (1971):** William Peter Blatty's fifth novel was the first horror story to make it to the

●●●●●➤

Johnson (1908–1972) had led popular crusades to use the government for public good. President Richard M. Nixon (1913–1994) became a symbol of the public's mistrust of politicians. He was forced from office in 1974 after the public learned of his involvement in the coverup of a break-in at the Watergate office complex. The Watergate scandal revealed the Nixon administration to be devious and corrupt. In the 1976 election, top of the *New York Times* best-seller list. The tale of a priest exorcising the demons from a young girl was made into a classic horror film in 1973.

Ms. **(1972–):** This magazine of the women's liberation movement was founded by prominent feminists Gloria Steinem and Patricia Carbine.

The Joy of Sex: A Cordon Bleu Guide to Lovemaking **(1972):** This illustrated guide to lovemaking techniques by author Alex Comfort offered help to many seeking sexual advice—and shocked others. Helpful or shocking, the book was in the top five on the best-seller list for nearly a year.

Watership Down **(1972; 1974 in the United States):** This exciting tale of a group forced to flee its home because it is being threatened by a developer had an interesting twist: the protagonists were rabbits. The publishers could not decide whether Richard Adams's story was for adults or children, but one thing was sure: everybody was reading it.

All the President's Men **(1974):** Written by *Washington Post* reporters Carl Bernstein and Bob Woodward, this exposé revealed how the authors discovered the Watergate cover-up that led to the resignation of President Richard Nixon.

People **(1974–):** The respectable version of a supermarket tabloid, *People* magazine provided insider gossip and lots of photos of celebrities, politicians, and other stars. It remains the country's leading "personality" magazine.

Roots **(1976):** Alex Haley's historical saga about his family began with Kunta Kinte, a native of Gambia who is sold into slavery in the New World. Haley's tale followed the family's difficult journey from slavery up to the present day and in 1977 was made into a television miniseries that is considered one of the best of its kind.

Your Erroneous Zones **(1977):** One of the key books of the 1970s self-help movement, this book by Wayne Dyer offered to make psychology simple enough for everybody and to help people lead happier lives. Dyer's book sold millions of copies and he remained a popular motivational speaker in the twenty-first century.

The Complete Book of Running **(1978):** James Fixx's book on running came right at the peak of the jogging craze in America, and the popularity of the book made the author a rich man before his untimely death in 1984.

What We Watched:

Marcus Welby, M.D. **(1969–76):** Robert Young played the title role of a concerned general practitioner.

All in the Family **(1971–79):** This sitcom brought realistic situations, frank language, and controversy to American television. The show centered around the blue collar lives of Archie Bunker and his wife, daughter and son-in-law.

The Flip Wilson Show **(1970–74):** This variety show hosted by African American comedian Flip Wilson featured skits, music, and appearances of the hilarious "Geraldine" (Wilson in drag).

Sanford and Son **(1972–77):** This show about a grumpy widower and his son was the first sitcom to feature a nearly all-black cast since *Amos 'n' Andy* nearly twenty years earlier. Redd Foxx, who

•••••▶

voters elected former Georgia governor Jimmy Carter (1924–) as president, largely because he had avoided Washington politics and seemed to be an honest man. In the opinion of many citizens, however, Carter's stint as president was ineffective. His unsuccessful term in office further eroded Americans' faith in what the government could accomplish.

played Sanford, would make people laugh as he threatened to join his dead wife by grabbing his chest and pretending to have a heart attack, yelling "I'm coming to join you, Elizabeth!" in nearly every episode.

M*A*S*H (1972–83): This long-running sitcom was set in a hospital camp during the Korean War and came to be one of TV's finest examples of intelligent, socially relevant programming. The final episode, aired on February 29, 1983, was seen by over 50 million viewers worldwide.

Happy Days (1974–84): Suburban life in the 1950s was romanticized in this TV comedy show, which highlighted drive-ins, leather jackets, muscle cars, and solid family life in Milwaukee, Wisconsin. The show centered around the everyday life of the Cunningham family and the character Fonzie, a single young man who epitomized coolness.

Laverne & Shirley (1976–1983): A spinoff of *Happy Days,* this sitcom, set in the 1950s, featured the misadventures of two single Milwaukee women, who shared an apartment and worked at a local brewery.

The Godfather (1972): The most influential gangster film of American cinema and the first of Francis Ford Coppola's trilogy about the Mafia.

The Exorcist (1973): The first blockbuster horror film, released after one of the most extensive preview hype campaigns. Reporting about the film's ill-effects on people even overshadowed the Watergate scandal for a short time, and its graphic violence led to new film industry regulations.

Watergate hearings (1973–74): America and the world turned on their TV sets to watch Nixon administration figures testify about the Watergate break-in and cover-up. The scandal eventually led to the first resignation of an American president, Richard Nixon.

Jaws (1975): Steven Spielberg's first major film became the first film to make more than $100 million on it initial release. With a mix of adventure, horror, and fun, the movie centered on a series of shark attacks and made audiences around the world more than a little nervous about swimming in the ocean.

Star Wars (1977): The first of George Lucas's space fantasy movies quickly established itself as a groundbreaker due to its special effects and film-related merchandise.

What We Listened To:

KISS: The flamboyant rock band was wildly popular with teenagers mostly due to members' far-out costumes and high-energy concerts that featured smoke bombs, spit blood, and breathed fire.

Elton John: The most popular pop singer/songwriter of the 1970s. Of his nineteen albums during the decade, fifteen went gold or platinum, and he continued to produce songs that ranked in the Top Forty into the 1990s.

All Things Considered: This cultural affairs and news show debuted on National Public Radio (NPR) in 1971.

•••••▶

The changing social structure of the 1970s can also be explained by the aging of the population. More and more of the baby boomers (those born in the decade after World War II) were leaving college and settling down with families of their own. They did not have time for marches against the war, and besides, the war in Vietnam was already winding down. More and more Americans turned inward, seeking comfort in

The Jackson 5: The five Jackson brothers had six top five singles by 1971. The group's littlest brother, Michael Jackson, had turned 12 in 1970 and would soon become a superstar on his own. Some of their most popular songs were "I Want You Back," "ABC," "The Love You Save," and "I'll Be There."

Rod Stewart: This British singer became popular as a solo artist with his hit song "Maggie May" in 1971.

Marvin Gaye: The successful Motown singer of the 1960s reached new heights when he released soul music that expressed both political and very personal issues. Hits included "What's Going On," "Mercy Mercy Me," and "Let's Get It On."

Kool & the Gang: This group laid the ground work for funk music with the hits "Jungle Boogie" and "Hollywood Swinging" in 1974.

Donna Summer: The queen of disco music scored big with such hits as "Love to Love you Baby" and "Last Dance."

Peter Frampton: In 1976, *Frampton Comes Alive* became the biggest selling live rock album at the time, selling more than six million copies and catapulting the former Humble Pie guitarist into brief superstardom.

The Carpenters: The brother and sister team of Richard and Karen Carpenter, sang sweet, innocent lyrics to light, pleasant melodies, hitting the Top Ten twelve times during the decade.

Rolling Stones: The rock and roll tunes of Mick Jagger and the boys remained popular throughout the 1970s; the Stones also toured the United States in 1975.

Who We Knew:

Woody Allen (1935–): Known for his quirky looks and comedic timing, Allen has become known as one of the most creative American film makers. During the 1970s, *Annie Hall* (1977), his semi-autobiographical movie about life and living in Manhattan, won him critical praise and was his most popular film.

Louise Joy Brown (1978–): The first "test-tube" baby. Born in England in 1978 by a process now known as in vitro fertilization, the little girl's birth caused many to wonder in awe and fear of the possibilities of science. The process used to create Brown is now used commonly by many couples with infertility problems.

Jane Fonda (1937–): The daughter of movie star Henry Fonda, this beautiful actress became a tremendously popular (and sometimes hated) public figure as she pursued her political agenda, led millions to better health as an ambassador for aerobic exercise, and became the wife to three powerful and wealthy men (film director Roger Vadim, 1965; politician Tom Hayden, 1973; and billionaire Ted Turner, 1991).

A. J. Foyt (1935–): The first racecar driver to win four Indianapolis (Indy) 500 races.

Jimmy Hoffa (1913–1975): The powerful Teamsters union figure led the union as vice-president in 1952 and as president in 1957 but was imprisoned

•••••➤

spiritual renewal or seeking insight by visiting therapists, reading self-help books, or exercising. Many people gave up trying to perfect the world and tried instead to perfect themselves. The exception to this trend was the growing importance of the feminist movement, which worked hard in the decade to gain equality for women in education and employment, and the environmental movement, which tried to in 1967 due to corruption charges. President Nixon agreed to commute his sentence in 1971 if Hoffa resigned as the Teamsters president. Hoffa disappeared in Bloomfield Township, Michigan, in 1975; never seen since, he is thought to have been murdered.

Billie Jean King (1943–): The winner of twenty Wimbledon titles and four Grand Slam tournaments, this women's tennis champion beat former Wimbledon champion Bobby Riggs in the "Battle of the Sexes" tennis match in 1973. Riggs had hoped to prove that men were better athletes than women, but King proved him wrong in front of fifty million TV viewers and thirty thousand live fans.

Richard M. Nixon (1913–1994): The 37th U.S. president was the first chief executive to visit China and the first to resign under threat of impeach-

ment. He was pardoned in September 1974 by his successor, Gerald Ford.

Richard Pryor (1940–): This African American comedian entertained audiences with hilarious jokes and stories about everyday black culture experiences. His performances were based on his personal and sometimes tragic social circumstances. His struggles with drug and alcohol abuse, a heart attack, a suicide attempt, and the onset of multiple sclerosis disrupted his very popular work.

Mark Spitz (1950–): This U.S. swimmer was the first Olympian to win seven gold medals at one Olympics (Munich, 1972). He had already won four Olympic medals in 1968. After his Olympic successes, he became the first athlete to earn millions of dollars by endorsing products.

Gloria Steinem (1934–): This political activist for women's rights cofounded the Women's Action Alliance in 1970 and the feminist magazine *Ms.*

step up government regulations on pollution and to protect the wilderness.

American popular culture continued to thrive in the 1970s, driven forward by the most popular form of entertainment, the television. By the 1970s, virtually every American had access to a color TV, and programming expanded to include both UHF and VHF broadcasts. By mid-decade, Americans in some cities could access cable TV, which offered even more channels. The quality of TV programming increased in the 1970s, and not just on PBS. In fact, the networks offered a number of intelligent, socially relevant shows. Still, most Americans preferred situation comedies (sitcoms) and detective shows. Sports also remained a popular preoccupation, especially for men, who could watch pro sports on TV all year long.

Music went through some exciting changes in the decade. Rock and roll continued to evolve, producing new variations such as punk rock, new wave, and heavy metal. Funk emerged as a uniquely African American musical form, and disco stole elements of funk and rock to create a popular music and dance craze.

The 1970s was in many ways a decade of fads and crazes. Whether in fashion (with bell-bottoms, hot pants, and mood rings), exercise (jogging, aerobics), play (pet rocks, video games), or dance (disco), Americans picked up new activities and products with abandon, and dropped them soon after.

The Me Decade

1970s

Fashion

Despite the bell-bottom and platform-shoe revival of the early 2000s, it is unlikely that anyone will remember the 1970s for the quality of its innovations in fashion. In fact, many of the favorite fashions of the 1970s are now remembered with humor. Hot pants, polyester leisure suits, and mood rings—what were they thinking?

The fashion excesses of the 1970s can be partially blamed on the widespread use of polyester. Clothing designers latched onto this fabric and offered Americans brightly colored knit shirts with a silky sheen, "wild" hot pants and miniskirts in an array of chemically enhanced colors, and comfortable leisure suits for wearing to the disco. The sheer novelty of the styles and colors drew people to the clothes, but it was not until the late 1970s that many realized just how ugly those clothes had become.

Novelty also explained the popularity of the mood ring. This ring, which registered the wearer's emotional state in the changing colors of the stone, became a jewelry fad in the 1970s. The 1970s did produce several important American designers, however. Both Calvin Klein (born Richard Klein, 1942–) and Ralph Lauren (born Ralph Lipschitz, 1939–) built their fashion empires in the polyester decade.

Hot Pants

Part of the flamboyant, sexually open style of fashion that produced the **miniskirt** (see entry under 1960s—Fashion in volume 4) in the 1960s, hot pants were dressy, ultra-short women's shorts made of a variety of fabrics from velvet to leather. The design of hot pants allowed them to be worn shorter than the shortest micro-miniskirt and still provide some degree of modesty.

Hot pants had been seen before, but they had been considered naughty and even a bit indecent, as they had mainly been worn by prostitutes and female nightclub performers. However, in the extravagantly flashy climate of the 1970s, many young women wore the new fashion. Allegheny Airlines even made them part of its official flight attendants' uniform. Hot pants soon went out of style and are largely considered an embarrassing reminder of 1970s excess.

—Tina Gianoulis

For More Information

"Hot Pants." *Yesterdayland.* www.yesterdayland.com/popopedia/shows/fashion/fa1459 (accessed March 22, 2002).

Ralph Lauren (1939–)

Ralph Lauren's fashion empire has sold an old-fashioned Anglo American style of clothing to an adoring public since 1967. In fact, the flagship store on Madison Avenue in New York City sells far more than just clothes. The "Polo" brand offers its devotees the dream of an upper middle-class past. The tweeds, tartans, polo shirts, and boat shoes that feature the brand name all belong to a more comfortable, leisured life than most Americans can afford. Fittingly, the peak of Lauren's fame came when he designed the wardrobe for Robert Redford (1937–) in the role of Gatsby in *The Great Gatsby* (1974).

To make his enduring American style, Lauren (born Ralph Lipschitz) combines images of "new-world" adventure with "old-world" aristocracy. He is revered and sometimes mocked for his conservative designs, but Lauren has proved adept at creating clothes that express America's fantasies about itself. He also showed he could take a joke when he appeared as himself on *Friends* (see entry under 1990s—TV and Radio in volume 5) in 1999.

—Chris Routledge

For More Information

Polo.com: Ralph Lauren. http://polo.com (accessed March 22, 2002).
Trachtenberg, Jeffrey A. *Ralph Lauren, The Man Behind the Mystique.* Boston: Little, Brown, 1988.

Leisure Suit

Fashionable during the 1970s, the leisure suit for men was a mainstream response to the casual dress style of the **hippie** (see entry under 1960s–The Way We Lived in volume 4) movement. Made of **polyester** (see entry under 1970s–Fashion in volume 4) fabric, often in bright colors and plaids, the leisure suit consisted of pants and a matching jacket, styled with an open collared. The suits helped make men's fashion less conservative. The suits also were a forerunner of modern casual Fridays, when less formal clothes may be worn to the office.

Although leisure suits represented somewhat of a breakthrough in men's fashions, they were considered ridiculous by many conservatives and radicals alike. Since the 1970s, leisure suits have often been used as an example of a fashion mistake. However, the suits have left their mark on modern culture. The white leisure suit John Travolta (1954–) wore in the 1977 film *Saturday Night Fever* (see entry under 1970s–Film and Theater in volume 4) sold at auction in the mid-1990s for $145,000. Leisure-suit conventions, where men gather for competitions such as "Most Flammable Outfit," have become popular events. A series of computer games created in the late 1990s and early 2000s features Leisure Suit Larry as the hopelessly uncool hero, in adventures with titles like "Land of the Lounge Lizards."

The popular polyester leisure suit. *Lambert/Archive Photos, Inc. Reproduced by permission.*

—*Tina Gianoulis*

For More Information

Adato, Allison, and David Burnett. "A Leisure Suit Convention." *Life* (February 1996): pp. 18–21.

"Leisure Seizure." *People Weekly* (April 20, 1992): p. 136.

"Leisure Suits." *Bad Fads Museum.* http://www.badfads.com/pages/fashion/leisure.html (accessed March 22, 2002).

"Leisure Suits." *Yesterdayland.* http://www.yesterdayland.com/popopedia/shows/fashion/fa1561.php (accessed March 22, 2002).

Mood Rings

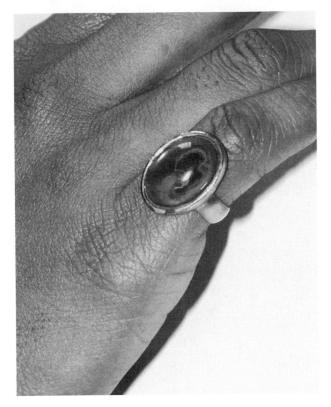

A mood ring, popular in the mid-1970s. *Photograph by Dan Newell. Reproduced by permission of Leitha Etheridge-Sims.*

Mood rings were just that—rings that indicated the mood of the person wearing it. At least that was the promise. Mood rings were one of the many fads that briefly captured people's attentions during the mid-1970s. But more than just a fad, they were a perfect symbol for the decade, a time when people looked inward to their own lives after a decade of social turmoil in the 1960s.

Mood rings were the invention of Joshua Reynolds. In the early 1970s, Reynolds got involved in a number of projects designed to help people discover their true feelings and understand their emotions better. Among these projects were biofeedback, which used a machine to monitor brain waves, and a meditation center called Q-Tran, which used the biofeedback machines. These projects did not work out, so Reynolds hit on the idea of producing small, inexpensive, and portable "mini-biofeedback" machines, which he called mood rings. They worked like this: small crystals in the rings would react to temperature and change colors. Warm temperatures produced bright colors, indicating a bright or happy mood. Cold temperatures caused dark colors, an indication of a dark mood. When Reynolds got the Faberge cosmetic company to back him and a press agent to promote the rings, they sold like crazy in 1975. Many people bought into the idea of mood rings and overlooked the fact that they changed colors based on temperature and not mood. Some celebrities were even seen wearing them, further enhancing their appeal to the public.

By the end of 1975, mood rings, like many fads, faded in popularity. It did not help matters that crystals in the rings turned permanently black after some time. Although they were certainly silly, they reveal the desire among many Americans in the 1970s to get in touch with their inner selves. The 1970s is often called the "Me" decade for this very reason. There were all kinds of personal enrichment programs and therapies designed to help people discover themselves. Mood rings were simply one of the crazier, if harmless, ones.

—Timothy Berg

For More Information

Stern, Jane and Michael. *The Encyclopedia of Bad Taste.* New York: HarperCollins, 1990.

Polyester

Like **nylon** (see entry under 1930s—Fashion in volume 2), polyester heralded a brave new world of fabrics and fashion after World War II (1939–45). Woven in bright colors and strange textures, polyester was the defining fabric of 1960s and 1970s fashion. As a result, when polyester went out of fashion in the late 1970s, it all but disappeared from view. Throughout the 1980s, polyester was something of a joke. Memories of the convenience of "wash and wear," minimal-iron shirts, were tinged with the shame of body odor and fashion tragedy. It was only with the rise of outdoor chic that polyester, in the form of polar fleece, garnered popularity again.

Polyester was the invention of two chemists working for the Calico Printers Association in England. J. T. Dickson and J. R. Winfield worked out a way to spin plastics made from petrochemicals. The DuPont company bought the patents in 1950, and the wonder fabric was launched. As the technology advanced, polyester was blended to make fabrics that looked and felt like cotton or wool. Although these copies were never very good, none of it mattered. In the 1960s and early 1970s, polyester was the height of cool suburban fashion. Flared slacks, knit shirts, and "pantsuits" graced the barbecue party, the workplace, and **malls** (see entry under 1950s—Commerce in volume 3).

By the late 1970s, polyester was everywhere. It flooded the market in such quantities that it lost its fashionable edge. When that happened, people began to notice that polyester made them sweat. Put politely, when everybody wore polyester, the atmosphere could become unpleasant. Polyester's status as the tackiest of fabrics was confirmed in 1981 when director John Waters (1946–) called one of his bad-taste films *Polyester*. In the 1990s, re-engineered and sold under the trade name Polartec, polyester made a comeback. Its light weight, and the fact that it does not absorb water, made polar fleece ideal for skiers, hikers, and other fans of the outdoors. By the late 1990s, top fashion labels such as Tommy Hilfiger (1952–) used it in their fashion ranges. In 2001, polyester has become one of the most comfortable, fashionable, and practical of all synthetic fabrics.

–Chris Routledge

For More Information

Smith, Matthew Boyd. *Polyester: The Indestructible Fashion.* (Schiffer Book for Collectors and Designers). Atglen, PA: Schiffer, 1998.

Stern, Jane, and Michael Stern. *The Encyclopedia of Bad Taste.* New York: HarperCollins, 1990.

1970s
Film and Theater

In the 1970s, the film industry continued to thrive by doing what television could not: telling stories that were more complicated, violent, frightening, or sexy than what could be shown to families sitting at home. Two contrasting trends in movie-making were present in the 1970s. On the one hand, a number of filmmakers, both in the United States and in Europe, began to think of film as an art, and they began to make films that were intellectually challenging. Such films were shown at art-house theaters (theaters that show specialty films thought to have artistic merit) and were seen by few. On the other hand, the major studios continued to back what became known as "blockbusters," spectacular films that drew huge audiences. The amount of money spent on and made by movies grew dramatically in the decade.

The string of 1970s blockbusters started with *The Godfather* (1972), which broke all box-office records. Starring Marlon Brando (1924–) as the boss of a New York mafia family, the film was violent, sexy, and compelling. *The Exorcist* (1973), based on the novel of the same name by William Peter Blatty (1928–), was so disturbing that it drove some viewers to leave the theater—but it also drew in huge audiences.

Special effects and science-fiction themes were no longer used only in "B"-grade movies. In the 1970s, they contributed to two of the biggest pictures of the decade. The star of *Jaws* (1975) was a giant fake shark whose menace was made real by the director who went on to become a giant of twentieth-century filmmaking—Steven Spielberg (1946–). *Star Wars* (1977) used a range of special effects to tell a dramatic space-adventure story. The film—and its sequels, novels, and merchandising—have become a major industry as new films continue to be released in the twenty-first century.

Black performers gained increasing access to movies in the 1970s. They appeared in all-black films, such as the action film *Shaft* (1971), starring Richard Roundtree (1942–), but also in films with major white stars. From the high drama of the decade's many disaster movies to the high camp of such films as *The Rocky Horror Picture Show* (1975), 1970s filmgoers thought they had it all.

A Clockwork Orange

A Clockwork Orange, a 1971 film by Stanley Kubrick (1928–1999), is a grim, futuristic tale of **gang** (see entry under 1980s–The Way We Lived in volume 5) violence and governmental response to it. Ultimately, both are portrayed as equally destructive.

Alex (played by Malcolm McDowell, 1943–) is the teenage leader of a small gang of vicious hoodlums in a near-future England. Their joy in committing "ultra-violence" takes the forms of gang fights, rape, and the brutal beatings of randomly chosen victims. During a home invasion, Alex kills a woman. He is then betrayed by his gang, arrested, convicted, and imprisoned.

Alex gets out of prison by volunteering for a new "behavioral modification" program designed to make him a fit member of society. Through drug injections, Alex is "conditioned" to experience disabling nausea whenever he feels the urge to commit violence of any kind. Thus rendered incapable of hurting anyone, even in self-defense, Alex is paroled. Back on the street, Alex encounters many of his former victims, who pay him back with savage beatings for the pain he inflicted on them. One, a writer whose wife had been raped by Alex's gang, finds a way to drive Alex to a suicidal leap from a third-story window.

Alex survives. Recuperating in a hospital, he is "befriended" by cynical politicians who seek to use his case to drive the current government from power. The fall has broken Alex's conditioning, as well as his body. When recovered, he will be as vicious and brutal as ever. The final scene shows Alex in his hospital bed, his brain full of fantasies of rape and murder. His last, chilling line is: "I was cured, all right."

A Clockwork Orange was based on the 1963 novel by Anthony Burgess (1917–1993). Burgess knew that gang members have their own unique language, so he envisioned Alex and his friends, his "droogs," using slang based on Russian. However, the meaning of the slang, in both the book and the film, is usually clear in context.

Following its 1971 release, the film was associated with several acts of violence committed by young British hoodlums. Director Kubrick then ordered the film pulled from circulation in Great Britain. Into the twenty-first century, *A Clockwork Orange* remains unavailable for viewing in that country.

—*Justin Gustainis*

For More Information

Burgess, Anthony. *A Clockwork Orange.* New York: Norton, 1963.

Hunter, I. Q. *British Science Fiction Cinema.* New York: Routledge, 1999.

Phillips, Gene D., ed. *Stanley Kubrick: Interviews.* Jackson: University Press of Mississippi, 2001.

Disaster Movies

Disaster movies rely heavily on special effects to recreate on-screen violent disasters such as earthquakes, plane crashes, and meteorite storms. The category also includes monster-disaster movies in which an enraged, oversized creature destroys buildings and other large objects. The golden age for disaster movies was the 1970s, but they began to be produced in large numbers in the years after the horrors of World War II (1939–45). This timing may be significant because these films are not just about averting disaster, but surviving it. Old people and pregnant women are rescued, children are lifted from the rubble, and love affairs blossom. Although their plots are often unrealistic, and the acting and special effects unconvincing, disaster movies offer a positive message. It is that through self-belief and the right moral choices, people have the ability to save themselves.

As Hollywood re-embraced the idea of making popular big budget features in the 1970s, the disaster movie became an important format. Although they might seem crude early in the twenty-first century, at the time of their release, films like *The Poseidon Adventure* (1972) and *The Towering Inferno* (1974) highlighted spectacular special effects. They drew in curious audiences to watch destruction on a large scale. The arrival of Computer Generated Images (CGI) in the late 1980s prompted a new wave of disaster movies including *The Abyss* (1989) and *Independence Day* (1996). A large part of the $190 million budget for **Titanic** (1997; see entry under 1910s—The Way We Lived in volume 1), directed by James Cameron (1954–), was spent on ground-breaking special effects.

Characters struggle for balance as their ship sinks in the film *The Poseidon Adventure*. *The Kobal Collection. Reproduced by permission.*

Exactly what appeals to audiences in watching planes crash, ships sink, trains collide, and tall buildings burn will probably never be known for sure. Hard-core disaster-movie fans will argue that they watch for the scenes of destruction and to revel in the special effects. Yet even *Titanic* relies on a human story unfolding alongside the devastation. Whatever the reason for their appeal, disaster movies have been popular ever since early films like **King Kong** (1933; see entry under 1930s–Film and Theater in volume 2) stunned audiences with their special effects. Ironically, films like *The Poseidon Adventure* (1972) and the *Airport* series are credited with rescuing **Hollywood** (see entry under 1930s–Film and Theater in volume 2) from financial disaster in the 1970s.

—*Chris Routledge*

For More Information

Keane, Stephen. *Disaster Movies: The Cinema of Catastrophe.* London: Wallflower Press, 2001.

Keyser, Les. *Hollywood in the Seventies.* San Diego: A. S. Barnes, 1981.

Reeves, Colby. *Disaster Online: The World's Most Comprehensive Disaster Movie Site.* http://disasteronline.tripod.com/ (accessed March 26, 2002).

The Exorcist

The Exorcist was probably the scariest novel published in 1971, and the movie based on it was undeniably the most frightening film of the 1970s. Through new editions and sequels, the story continues to terrify audiences.

William Peter Blatty (1928–) got the idea for his novel from a case he studied while a student at Georgetown University in Washington, D.C. An exorcism is a religious ceremony held to expel an evil spirit or demon from a person. Although exorcisms are rare today, the Catholic Church authorized one in 1949 for a Maryland boy who appeared to be possessed. Blatty turned this account into the story of Regan MacNeil, an innocent girl possessed by a demon and the two Jesuit priests who try to save her. The novel was a huge commercial success, spending more than a year on the **best-seller** (see entry under 1940s–Commerce in volume 3) lists.

The film version was directed by Oscar-winner William Friedkin (1939–). It starred Max von Sydow (1929–), Jason Miller (1939–2001), Ellen Burstyn (1932–), and twelve-year-old Linda Blair (1959–) as Regan. The special effects were startling, with Regan shown levitating, spewing green bile, and rotating her head 360 degrees. The film derives most of its power to frighten from the sheer intensity of the evil represented by the demon, from which the camera does not flinch. The film contains both dialogue and images of shocking ugliness, but they seem entirely justified in light of the subject matter. The film, made for $10 million dollars, earned over $82 million at the box office.

Forgettable sequels followed. *Exorcist II: The Heretic* starred Richard Burton (1925–1984) in 1977. *Exorcist III,* starring George C. Scott (1927–1999), was released in 1990; it was based on Blatty's 1983 novel, *Legion.* A satire, 1990s *Repossessed,* starred Leslie Nielsen (1926–) and a grown-up Linda Blair.

In 2001, Friedkin released a "director's cut" of the original *Exorcist.* Called *The Exorcist: The Version You've Never Seen,* this print contained twelve minutes of footage cut from the original. In mid-2001, director John Frankenheimer (1930–) signed to direct a "prequel" to *The Exorcist.* The new film, *Exorcist: Dominion,* involves an encounter, set in Africa, between a demon and Father Lankester Merrin, the exorcist from Blatty's novel, who was played by Max von Sydow in the original film.

—Justin Gustainis

For More Information

Blatty, William Peter. *The Exorcist*. New York: Harper and Row, 1971.

McCabe, Bob. *The Exorcist: Out of the Shadows*. London: Omnibus Press, 1999.

Newman, Howard. *The Exorcist: The Strange Story behind the Film*. New York: Pinnacle Books, 1974.

Warner Bros. *The Exorcist*. http://theexorcist.warnerbros.com/ (accessed March 26, 2002).

The Godfather

For decades **Hollywood** (see entry under 1930s–Film and Theater in volume 2) had portrayed hoodlums and criminals as solitary figures who rose and fell largely because of their own actions. By the 1970s, however, criminals were more often depicted as part of a complex and impersonal social system dominated by organized **gangs** (see entry under 1980s–The Way We Lived in volume 5), the illegal counterpart to giant corporations. Such is the case in *The Godfather* (1972), based on the best-selling 1969 novel by Mario Puzo (1920–1999). *The Godfather* was the first in a three-film series directed by Francis Ford Coppola (1939–) that depicted the decades-long dramas and inner workings of the fictional Corleones, a ruthlessly powerful organized-crime family.

As portrayed in the trilogy, the Corleones are a family of flourishing **Mafia** (see entry under 1960s–The Way We Lived in volume 4) businessmen whose product is crime. They are like a corporate entity, only they negotiate their deals with bullets and threats of violence. Like any good business organization, the Corleones survive and thrive because they have outwitted (not to mention outkilled) their competitors.

A Corleone might be killed during a gang war; another might die at the hands of a brother, in payment for an act of betrayal. But the loss of one Corleone simply results in the ascension to power of another. For example, even as the aged senior, Vito Corleone (played by Marlon Brando, 1924–, in *The Godfather*), dies a natural death, an offspring is present to replace him. The individual Corleones are separate and distinct characters; the violent, hot-headed Sonny (James Caan, 1939–) may be contrasted to the more calculating, intelligent Michael (Al Pacino, 1940–). Their primary identities are as workers in a criminal empire. At the end of *The Godfather, Part II* (1974), Michael finds himself alone, a victim of his mastering the life of a mob-

ster. The criminal entity he has inherited from his father, however, has reached new heights of prosperity.

The *Godfather* films—rounded out by *The Godfather, Part III* (1990)—portray an America that is neck-deep in corruption. The Corleones mingle with and control crooked law-enforcement officials, politicians, and wildly popular singers whose fame rests on their ties to the mob. Organized crime—not to be confused with individual criminals—thrives in New York, Las Vegas, and Hollywood. Finally, and ironically, in the *Godfather* films, the concept of "family" and "loyalty" has been perversely skewered; it has nothing in common with time-honored concepts of family obligation and ethical values. The initial two films keenly mirror the period in which they were made: the early 1970s, the era of Vietnam War (1954–75) protests and the Watergate political scandal (1972–74). As they depict criminal activity as the offshoot of a certain kind of corporate thinking, they become symbols of the decaying of America.

—*Rob Edelman*

Members of the Corleone family from *The Godfather*: (left to right) Al Pacino, Marlon Brando, James Caan, and John Cazale. *The Kobal Collection. Reproduced by permission.*

For More Information

Bergan, Peter. *Francis Ford Coppola—Close Up: The Making of His Movies.* New York: Thunder's Mouth Press, 1998.

Biskind, Peter. *The Godfather Companion: Everything You Ever Wanted to Know About All Three Godfather Films.* New York: HarperPerennial, 1990.

Coppola, Francis Ford, director. *The Godfather* (film). Paramount, 1972.

Coppola, Francis Ford, director. *The Godfather, Part II* (film). Paramount, 1974.

Coppola, Francis Ford, director. *The Godfather, Part III* (film). Paramount, 1990.

Dirks, Tim. "The Godfather." *Greatest Films.* http://www.filmsite.org/godf.html (accessed March 26, 2002).

Lebo, Harlan. *The Godfather Legacy.* New York, Simon & Schuster, 1997.

Malta, J. Geoff. *The Godfather Trilogy: The Original Unofficial Site.* http://www.jgeoff.com/godfather.html (accessed March 26, 2002).

Jaws

Still one of the highest-grossing films of all time, the 1975 epic *Jaws* helped define the term "summer blockbuster." The bloody story of a shark's assault on a beach community thrilled and frightened moviegoers, establishing the twenty-seven-year-old Steven Spielberg (1946–) as one of the most talented directors in **Hollywood** (see entry under 1930s–Film and Theater in volume 2).

Based on a 1974 novel by Peter Benchley (1940–), *Jaws* tells the story of a series of horrific shark attacks that wrack the placid summertime resort town of Amity. Director Spielberg intercut footage of real sharks with a full-sized mechanical shark (named Bruce) to create the movie's shocking visual effects. Composer John Williams (1932–) crafted the film's menacing score, for which he was awarded an Oscar. *Jaws* also benefited from a top-notch publicity campaign, including classic movie posters featuring the image of a razor-toothed shark about to attack an unsuspecting female swimmer.

Jaws might have been just another blood-and-gore adventure story were it not for its excellent cast. Charlton Heston (1924–) was originally slated to play the role of Chief Brody, the film's lead character, but he backed out, feeling he had already made too many **"disaster" movies** (see entry under 1970s–Film and Theater in volume 4). Actor Roy Scheider (1932–) took his place. Richard Dreyfuss (1946–) played the role

of Matt Hooper, an oceanographer. British actor Robert Shaw (1927–1978) turned in one of the best performances of his career as Quint, the crusty shark hunter.

The script for *Jaws* was largely a collaboration between director Spielberg and novelist Benchley. However, writer John Milius (1944–), who would later pen such acclaimed screenplays as *Apocalypse Now* and *Conan the Barbarian*, was brought in to write one of the film's memorable scenes, in which Quint relates the tale of a grisly shark attack on his vessel during World War II (1939–45).

Jaws made more than $100 million in its initial release, a record that was broken two years later by **Star Wars** (see entry under 1970s–Film and Theater in volume 4). The three *Jaws* sequels failed to match the critical or commercial success of the original. A special twenty-fifth anniversary digital video disc (DVD) of the now-classic sea epic was released in 2000, featuring cut footage (film cut from the original movie) and behind-the-scenes information.

—*Robert E. Schnakenberg*

A scene from Steven Spielberg's classic horror/suspense film *Jaws*. *Archive Photos, Inc. Reproduced by permission.*

For More Information

Brode, Douglas. *The Films of Steven Spielberg*. New York: Citadel Press, 1995.

Gottlieb, Carl. *The Jaws Log*. New York: Dell, 1975.

Gove, Jake. *JAWSmovie.com*. http://www.jawsmovie.com/ (accessed March 26, 2002).

Sanello, Frank. *Spielberg: The Man, the Movies, the Mythology*. Dallas: Taylor, 1996.

Rocky

Everybody loves an underdog. Upon its release to movie theaters, moviegoers fell in love with an unlikely movie: *Rocky* (1976). This feel-good film works on two levels—one fictional, and the other factual—as the saga of an obscure "everyman" who gets his shot at fame and realizes the universal fantasy of achieving one's wildest and most improbable dreams.

The film's title character is Philadelphian Rocky Balboa (Sylvester Stallone, 1946–), an inarticulate, faded boxer who is not so much a has-been as a never-was. During the course of the story, Rocky gets to live out a dream: to fight for the world championship against Apollo Creed, the reigning titleholder. *Rocky* also was the creation of Stallone, an obscure actor who also realized every struggling writer's and actor's fantasy by first penning, then selling, and finally starring in the film.

With *Rocky,* Stallone rose to acclaim and fame in what was, truly, as much of a million-to-one shot as the plight and fate of his character. Prior to *Rocky,* he had appeared in walk-on roles in major movies and starred or had supporting roles in forgettable ones. When he wrote his script, he was living in a shabby apartment in **Hollywood** (see entry under 1930s–Film and Theater in volume 2), and legend has it that his bank account had sunk to $106. United Artists offered to purchase the script for $75,000, and began upping the fee when Stallone refused. The studio wished to cast a more famous—and more bankable—actor in the lead role, but Stallone saw himself in the part. Quite rightly, he paralleled the plight of Rocky Balboa to his own life. Stallone knew that playing the role would offer him the same shot at fame that Rocky had when Apollo Creed selected him as his ring opponent. United Artists finally relented, but on the condition that *Rocky* be filmed on a paltry $1 million budget.

Stallone based the character of Rocky Balboa on Chuck Wepner (1939–), nicknamed "The Bayonne Bleeder," a white boxer selected to oppose **Muhammad Ali** (1942–; see entry under 1960s—Sports and Games in volume 4), who was looking for an easy opponent while preparing for his next major fight. However, Wepner trained hard for the match. What was supposed to be an effortless fight for Ali lasted into the fifteenth and final round. In Round 9, Wepner even knocked Ali off his feet. Stallone had viewed the fight on closed-circuit **television** (see entry under 1940s—TV and Radio in volume 3), and what he saw inspired him to create Rocky Balboa.

Rocky was a critical and commercial hit and went on to win ten Academy Award nominations. Stallone earned two of them, for Best Actor and Best Original Screenplay. The film won for Best Picture, Director (John G. Avildsen, 1935–), and Film Editing. Stallone emerged a bankable Hollywood star, with the film's success inspiring four sequels containing similar feel-good, little-guy-against-the-world scenarios. Most viewers believed all were vastly inferior to the original movie.

The most famous sequence in *Rocky* has become one of the more celebrated in film history. It features Rocky finishing off his rigorous training by jogging up the steps of the Philadelphia Art Museum and triumphantly running in place with his hands raised in the air, all set to the accompaniment of the film's rousing theme music.

—Rob Edelman

For More Information

Daly, Marsha. *Sylvester Stallone*. New York: St. Martin's Press, 1986.
Rocky (film). United Artists, 1976.
Rovin, Jeff. *Stallone! A Hero's Story*. New York: Pocket Books, 1985.
Stallone, Sylvester. *Official Rocky Scrapbook*. New York: Grosset & Dunlap, 1977.
Wright, Adrian. *Sylvester Stallone: A Life in Film*. London: Robert Hale Limited, 1991.

The Rocky Horror Picture Show
• •

The Rocky Horror Picture Show (1975) is a popular-culture phenomenon. Originally a stage musical titled *The Rocky Horror Show* (1973) and conceived by English actor Richard O'Brien (1942–), the project employed an understanding and

appreciation of tacky, low-budget horror and science-fiction films to produce an outlandish satire.

In the film, the setting is the fictional town of Denton, Ohio. Straight-laced sweethearts Brad Majors (Barry Bostwick, 1946–) and Janet Weiss (Susan Sarandon, 1946–), who have set out to get married, are halted by bad weather. They seek refuge in the roadside manor of Dr. Frank-N-Furter (Tim Curry, 1946–), a mad scientist who wears makeup and dresses in women's clothes. Dr. Frank-N-Furter has created Rocky Horror, a model of the perfect male. Other characters include Riff Raff (played

by O'Brien), the doctor's hunchbacked assistant, and a pair of assistants named Magenta (Patricia Quinn, 1944–) and Columbia (Nell Campbell, 1953–).

The stage version, which premiered in the Chelsea district of London, England, was an immediate smash. It eventually played in the United States and then was filmed in London by director Jim Sharman (1945–). The film version flopped at the box office and received mixed-to-negative reviews. "Where the campy hijinks [were] acceptable and even moderately fresh on stage, it only seems labored in celluloid blowup," wrote the critic for *Variety,* the motion-picture-industry trade publication. "Most of the jokes that might have seemed jolly fun on stage now appear obvious and even flat. The sparkle's gone."

Marketing saved *The Rocky Horror Picture Show.* In New York, the film was shown only at midnight. The late-night showing attracted a core audience of fun-seeking younger viewers who were bewitched by the film's outrageousness, sang its praises via word-of-mouth, and kept on returning for repeat screenings. Viewers soon began arriving dressed as their favorite characters; they interacted with the film as it played on-screen, singing along with its musical numbers, speaking its dialogue in unison with the on-screen actors, and commenting on the story's overall triteness. Audience members arrived with rice, which they tossed at the screen during a wedding sequence. When Brad and Janet get caught in a storm, some viewers opened umbrellas, while others shot water pistols.

The Rocky Horror Picture Show cult was born. The film has been screened and enjoyed at midnight showings around the world for years.

—*Rob Edelman*

For More Information

Henkin, Bill. *The Rocky Horror Picture Show Book.* New York: Hawthorn Books, 1979.

Hoberman, J., and Jonathan Rosenbaum. *Midnight Movies.* New York: Da Capo Press, 1991.

Peary, Danny. *Cult Movies.* New York: Delta Books, 1981.

Piro, Sal. *Creatures of the Night: The Rocky Horror Experience.* Redford, MI: Stabur Books, 1990.

Rocky Horror Company Limited. *The Official Rocky Horror Company Web Site.* http://www.rockyhorror.co.uk/ (accessed March 26, 2002.

The Rocky Horror Picture Show. http://www.rockyhorror.com/ (accessed March 26, 2002).

The Rocky Horror Picture Show (film). Twentieth Century-Fox, 1975.

Saturday Night Fever

Saturday Night Fever (1977) was as much an event as a motion picture. It transcended its own astounding popularity and served to define the popular culture of a generation. John Travolta (1954–) became a major movie star playing Tony Manero, a tough but likable nineteen-year-old Italian American street kid from the Bay Ridge area of Brooklyn, New York. By day, Tony is yet another neighborhood minimum-wage slave, toiling as a clerk in a paint store. By night, he comes alive. He is the star attraction at the 2001 Odyssey, a neighborhood discotheque (dance club), where his slick moves on the dance floor to a pulsating **disco** (see entry under 1970s–Music in volume 4) beat have earned him respect. At its core, *Saturday Night Fever* is a coming-of-age story as Tony slowly realizes that the boundaries of his future are way beyond Bay Ridge.

Travolta's star was born the instant he appeared on-screen. In the film, with the Bee Gees' "Stayin' Alive" on the soundtrack, Travolta is captured in different camera angles as he struts down a street with a paint can in his hand, swinging his hips. Later on, to the sound of "Night Fever," he carefully blow-dries and combs his hair as he prepares for an evening at 2001 Odyssey. The club's dance floor is transparent, and lit from underneath. The lights also flash, which makes for a visually dazzling setting as Tony strides out to dance. These sequences, scattered throughout *Saturday Night Fever,* are the film's highlights.

The success of *Saturday Night Fever* signaled the arrival of a new kind of music: disco, yet another phase in the evolution of **rock and roll** (see entry under 1950s–Music in volume 3), to be sure, but an altogether fresh sound with a catchy and highly danceable beat. Back in 1977, disco and Tony Manero, its most celebrated practitioner, were on the cutting edge, and *Saturday Night Fever* was an immediate smash hit. During its first sixteen-plus weeks in movie houses, it grossed over $81 million—and it needed to earn only one-eleventh of that figure to turn a profit. The film was to earn over $400 million worldwide, and its soundtrack album also sold in the millions.

The origins of Tony Manero as a character may be linked to the bad-boy teens of the 1950s, icons (symbols) of their time: **James Dean** (1931–1955; see entry under 1950s–Film and Theater in volume 3) and his adolescent anxiety in *East of Eden* (1955) and *Rebel Without a Cause* (1955); Marlon Brando

John Travolta, as Tony Manero, strikes his famous disco dance pose from the movie *Saturday Night Fever*. *The Kobal Collection. Reproduced by permission.*

(1924–) astride a motorcycle in *The Wild One* (1954); and the hip-swiveling **Elvis Presley** (1935–1977; see entry under 1950s–Music in volume 3) of *Jailhouse Rock* (1957) and *King Creole* (1958). Manero is one of the icons of 1970s popular culture. In *Mr. Holland's Opus* (1995), whose story opens in 1965 and charts thirty years in the life of a high-school music teacher, images of famous personalities and events are used to mark the passage of time. They include President Richard Nixon (1913–1994) and his vice president, Spiro Agnew (1918–1996); Gerald Ford (1913–), who replaced Nixon after the latter's resignation in the wake of the Watergate scandal, stumbling as he exits an airplane; music giant John Lennon (1940–1980), first "imagining" a world at peace, then being assassinated; and, appropriately, John Travolta in *Saturday Night Fever*.

—Rob Edelman

For More Information

Clarkson, Wensley. *John Travolta: Back in Character*. New York: Overlook Press, 1997.

Cohn, Nik. "Another Saturday Night." *Life* (Vol. 8, no. 21, 1998): pp. 48–49.

Edelman, Rob, and Audrey E. Kupferberg. *The John Travolta Scrapbook*. Secaucus, NJ: Carol Publishing, 1997.

Saturday Night Fever (film). Paramount, 1977.

Simpson, Rachel. *John Travolta*. Philadelphia: Chelsea House, 1997.

Shaft

This 1971 feature film, directed by Gordon Parks (1912–), revolutionized the image of African Americans in **Hollywood** (see entry under 1930s–Film and Theater in volume 2). *Shaft* was produced inexpensively by **MGM** (see entry under 1920s–Film and Theater in volume 2). *Shaft*'s star, Richard Roundtree (1942–), was paid only $13,000 to play John Shaft. The gritty private-eye drama proved a huge box-office success and helped create the movie craze known as "blaxploitation" (films in which black characters' lifestyles are often displayed in a fashion that reinforces negative stereotypes).

John Shaft was a private detective hired to locate the kidnapped daughter of an underworld chieftain. With its loner hero, fiendish plot twists, and shady characters, *Shaft* echoed the golden age of Hollywood detective movies like *The Big Sleep* and *The Maltese Falcon*. There was just one twist: For the first time, all the major characters were African Americans. Director Gordon Parks (1912–), a distinguished photographer and cinematographer, succeeded in capturing the look and feel of urban America in the 1970s. The film's funky score by Isaac Hayes (1942–) featured the Academy Award–winning "Theme from Shaft," with its memorable lyrics "Can you dig it?" and "Shut yo' mouth."

Ultimately Shaft triumphs over his enemies and completes his assignment, with little or no help from the white establishment. The plot of *Shaft* was largely secondary to the film's style—and that of its star, however. As Shaft, Roundtree brought an element of cool to his character that few African American actors had brought—or been permitted to bring—to their roles in the past. With his stout Afro hair style, ankle-length leather coat, and quiet manner, Shaft became an icon (a symbol of his time) and a sex symbol to millions of youths, both black and white.

Roundtree returned for two sequels to the moneymaking picture: *Shaft's Big Score!* (1972) and *Shaft in Africa* (1973). Each film placed Shaft in ever more cartoonish situations, and neither sequel made as much money as the groundbreaking original. But *Shaft's* influence was felt in other successful "blaxploitation" classics like *Superfly* (1972) and *The Harder They Come* (1973), each of which featured lead characters clearly modeled on John Shaft. Eventually the blaxploitation genre boom petered out with clunkers like *Blacula* (1972) and *Blackenstein* (1973). *Shaft's* unique impact on American cinema was evident when it was remade in 2000 by director John Singleton (1968–). This time, Samuel L. Jackson (1948–) played the title character, bringing the classic "Shaft cool" to a new generation of filmgoers.

Richard Roundtree starred as the tough, street-wise private detective John Shaft in the film *Shaft*. *AP/Wide World Photos. Reproduced by permission.*

—*Robert E. Schnakenberg*

For More Information

Blaxploitation.com. http://www.blaxploitation.com/ (accessed March 26, 2002).

James, Darius. *That's Blaxploitation: Roots of the Baadasssss 'Tude (Rated X by an All'Whyte Jury).* New York: St. Martin's Press, 1995.

Martinez, Gerald, Diana Martinez, and Andres Chavez. *What It Is . . . What It Was!: The Black Film Explosion of the '70s in Words and Pictures.* New York: Hyperion, 1998.

Shaft Official Movie Web Site. http://www.shaft-themovie.com/ (accessed March 26, 2002).

Star Wars

In 1999, the film *Star Wars: Episode I—The Phantom Menace* opened after years of anticipation, aggressive marketing,

and media hype. Episode I is the fourth *Star Wars* film to be released. The first movie by George Lucas (1944–), *Star Wars* (now often called *Star Wars: Episode IV—A New Hope*) appeared in 1977, starting a box office and merchandising franchise worth billions of dollars. Two sequels, *The Empire Strikes Back* (1980) and *The Return of the Jedi* (1982) followed. By 1999, it was estimated that the trilogy had earned $1.5 billion. All three are in the top ten movies for box-office revenue. The Oscar-winning *Star Wars* theme music by John Williams (1932–) is among the best known of film-theme tunes.

Phrases from the series like "May the Force be with you" have entered the English language. In the 1980s, "Star Wars" was the name given to the controversial Strategic Defense Initiative (SDI) proposed by President Ronald Reagan (1911–). The National Missile Defense system of President George W. Bush (1946–) has been dubbed "Son of Star Wars." The absorption of *Star Wars* into global popular culture is astonishing. Mention "the Force" almost anywhere in the world and people will understand its meaning.

All the *Star Wars* movies are based on the same simple idea that good struggles with evil. Set in a galaxy "far, far away" where peaceful, pioneering people are under threat from a savage Empire, the *Star Wars* movies retell familiar stories of American mythology. The opening scenes and story lines of *A New Hope* are similar to the opening of the 1956 Western *The Searchers* starring **John Wayne** (1907–1979; see entry under 1930s–Film and Theater in volume 2). Both films begin with the killing of a family and the destruction of their homestead. Like *The Searchers,* the initial *Star Wars* is also the story of a search for a missing woman. The success of the first three films can be put down to the simplicity of their message. The *Star Wars* films suggest that people are free to make choices about whether to be good or evil. Although they describe a society struggling against an oppressive regime, the films take the positive view that the human spirit can never be crushed.

Luke Skywalker becomes involved with rebel forces, pursuing the captors of beautiful Princess Leia, confronting the evil Darth Vader, and finally destroying the "Death Star," a huge and deadly artificial planet. *Star Wars* also comments on its own time, reflecting the Cold War (1945–91) between nations of the West and the former Soviet Union. Luke's adventures also include trying to inspire cynical trader Han Solo to join the rebels, dealing with the comical droids C-3PO and R2-D2, as well as learning to control "the Force." With the help of his tutor Obi-Wan Kenobi, Luke begins his training as a Jedi Knight. *The Empire Strikes Back* sees Luke continuing his confrontation with evil, both in the form of the Empire and within himself. Luke also finds out that Darth Vader is actually his father. In this and the third film, *The Return of the Jedi,* Luke learns to control the Force and use it for good. He even succeeds in rescuing his father from the dark side of the Force.

Episode I: The Phantom Menace arrived in 1999 in a whirlwind of hype and excitement. Only the second of the *Star Wars* films to be directed by Lucas himself, it cost well over $100 million. Set thirty or so years before the events of *A New Hope, The Phantom Menace* is the story of Luke Skywalker's father Anakin and his training as a Jedi Knight, and the story of the rise of Emperor Palpatine as well. For those fans old enough to remember the release of the original film, *The Phantom Menace* promised to bring back memories of younger days. Younger fans hoped it would add to a story that was already part of popular mythology. Many even paid to watch other films just so they could see the *Star Wars* trailer (preview). The film itself could never live up to such expectations. Although loaded with impressive special effects, *The Phantom Menace* has been criticized for its lack of humor and clear plot, its weak dialogue, and poor performances by the actors.

When the original film appeared it set new standards in special effects and tapped into a popular need for positive stories about ordinary people struggling against market forces and so-called big government. By 2001, *Star Wars* had become far more than just a science-fiction adventure. It had inspired award-winning computer games, a best-selling series of books, a growing collectors' market in toys, and many Web sites. Blockbuster movies like *Independence Day* (1996) have been inspired by the "look" of the *Star Wars* films. With two further episodes to run, including *Episode II: Attack of the Clones* (2002), Lucas's *Star Wars* empire looks set to continue its domination of popular science fiction well into the twenty-first century.

—*Chris Routledge*

For More Information

Edwards, Ted. *The Unauthorized Star Wars Compendium: The Complete Guide to the Movies, Comic Books, Novels and More.* Boston: Little Brown, 1999.

Jenkins, Garry. *Empire Building: The Remarkable Real-Life Story of Star Wars.* Secaucus, NJ: Carol Publishing Group, 1999.

Sansweet, Stephen J., and Timothy Zahn. *Star Wars Encyclopedia.* New York: Ballantine Publishing Group, 1998.

Slavicsek, Bill. *A Guide to the Star Wars Universe.* New York: Ballantine Publishing Group, 2000.

Star Wars. http://www.starwars.com (accessed on March 26, 2002).

1970s

Music

Musically, the 1970s was a decade of great variety. Hard rock got harder, soft rock got softer, and artists frustrated with standard musical forms tossed them aside and started their own. For fans of such new forms as funk, disco, punk, or new wave music, this innovation was wonderful. But others hated the music. Groups formed to express their hatred of disco. Some thought that punk culture was the sign of the downfall of civilization.

Hard rock had emerged in the 1960s as a way of protecting the angry and rebellious spirit of rock and roll. In the 1970s, musicians like KISS, Led Zeppelin, Black Sabbath, and Alice Cooper (1948–) took hard rock in different directions. KISS was less famous for its music than for its outrageous costumes and explosive stage shows, and they blazed the way for rock as spectacle. Led Zeppelin inspired a cult following, encouraged by the band's hard-living reputation and its almost mystical lyrics. Rock got softer in the 1970s as well, thanks to performers like the Carpenters, Barry Manilow (1946–), the Eagles, Fleetwood Mac, and the Swedish group ABBA, the most successful pop group of the 1970s. Although mocked by youths, their hits were played more widely on adult radio stations.

In punk and new wave music, rock split off in other directions. Punk music was an expression of the punk subculture, which protested the dullness and uniformity of society. Played by bands like the Ramones, the Sex Pistols, and the Clash, the music was loud, fast, and angry. New wave bands like the Talking Heads, the Pretenders, and the Cars also engaged in cultural commentary, but with a wry sense of humor and much more polished playing. New wave music—later called alternative music—grew to be an important if somewhat hard-to-define branch of rock music.

Combining rock, rhythm and blues (R&B), jazz, and soul, funk music was an African American musical form that came to be associated with "Black Pride" and the civil rights movement. Its most famous practitioners were James Brown (1933–),

Sly and the Family Stone, Parliament-Funkadelic, and Curtis Mayfield (1942–1999). Disco emerged out of funk in the late 1970s, as white and black bands combined funk and rock in order to make popular dance music. Like punk, disco was both a music and a culture. Disco featured flashy dance moves, mirror ball lights, and silk shirts. The music and culture of disco were captured in the 1977 hit film *Saturday Night Fever,* starring John Travolta (1954–). Hard-rock fans so hated disco that in Detroit, Michigan, and Chicago, Illinois, they engaged in open protests against disco. Such was the era of the 1970s, where musical styles often clashed.

Disco

Disco holds the distinction of being one of the most popular, and most hated, musical styles in the history of **pop music** (see entry under 1940s–Music in volume 3). When it emerged in dance clubs in the middle of the 1970s, many people could not resist the steady pulse of its beat, and they hit the dance floors in droves. More than just a new kind of music, disco created new styles in fashion and **dancing** (see entry under 1900s–The Way We Lived in volume 1), and it defined the glitzy nightclub life popular in American cities, especially at such clubs as Studio 54 in New York City, in the 1970s. Although many embraced the positive messages in the music, others feared that disco's focus on dancing, and not on the key rock themes of rebellion and personal expression, signaled the death of pop and **rock and roll** (see entry under 1950s–Music in volume 3) music.

The sound of disco emerged in the mid-1970s in such hits as **"The Hustle"** (see entry under 1970s–Music in volume 4) by Van McCoy (c. 1940–1979). "The Hustle," propelled by a prominent bass guitar and a steady drum beat, combined elements of soul and **funk** (see entry under 1970s–Music in volume 4) music. As the sound caught on, both on **radio** (see entry under 1920s–TV and Radio in volume 2) and in dance clubs, disco became more prominent. That sound went hand in hand with changes in dance clubs. Many clubs added lights that flashed along with the beat of the music, mirror balls that sent spots of light spinning around the room, and smoke machines that added a dramatic effect. **Disc jockeys** (see entry under 1950s–Music in volume 3) controlled the music and worked the crowds

A couple disco dancing under a disco ball. *AP/Wide World Photos. Reproduced by permission.*

into a frenzy. Groups such as Kool and the Gang, KC and the Sunshine Band, and The Village People, and individual artists such as Donna Summer (1948–), Gloria Gaynor (1949–), and Alicia Bridges (1953–) had numerous disco hits. Disco's biggest success came with the 1977 film ***Saturday Night Fever*** (see entry under 1970s–Film and Theater in volume 4), starring John Travolta (1954–), and featuring disco music by the Bee Gees and other groups. The Bee Gees had huge hits with "Stayin' Alive," "How Deep Is Your Love," and "Night Fever." The *Saturday Night Fever* songs seemed to be on every radio station in 1977.

Saturday Night Fever was disco's high point, but by 1979 the sound began to grow tiresome in many people's minds. Classic rock sounds began to push more disco music off the airwaves, and new forms of rock music, **punk** (see entry under 1970s–Music in volume 4) and new wave, reenergized the original spirit of rock music that many felt disco ignored. Although disco's popularity was at its height between 1975 and 1979, it continues to enjoy a solid fan base in dance clubs worldwide, a testament to people's love of a good dance beat and a good time.

—Timothy Berg

For More Information

Andriote, John-Manuel. *Hot Stuff : A Brief History of Disco*. New York: Harper, 2001.

Haden-Guest, Anthony. *The Last Party: Studio 54, Disco, and the Culture of the Night*. New York: William Morrow, 1997.

Jones, Alan, and Jussi Kantonen. *Saturday Night Forever: The Story of Disco*. New York: A. Cappella Books, 2000.

Lopez, Bernard F. *Disco Music.com*. http://www.discomusic.com/ (accessed March 26, 2002).

Miller, Jim, ed. *The Rolling Stone Illustrated History of Rock & Roll*. New York: Rolling Stone Press, 1980.

Funk

Funk is a style of music that emerged out of the African American community in the early 1970s. It represents a chapter in the long evolution of black music beginning with **blues** (see entry under 1920s–Music in volume 2) and **jazz** (see entry under 1900s–Music in volume 1) and continuing to gospel, **rhythm and blues** (R&B; see entry under 1940s–Music in volume 3), and soul. Like these other forms of music, funk was an expression of black popular culture that sought to recapture the essentials of the black music experience away from a watered-down version that was marketed more to whites than to blacks.

Funk's immediate predecessor was soul music. As soul music matured in the mid-1960s, some black performers began experimenting with a new sound that relied on heavy bass rhythms and drum beats. The most important of these innovators was James Brown (1933–). Known as the "Godfather of Soul," Brown is also widely acknowledged as the father of funk music. As Brown's style evolved from a more gospel-influenced soul style to a harder-edged rhythmic style, funk was born. The term "funk" was one that he used in such songs as "Funky Drummer" and others. The word referred to sexual activity but also to a general attitude that was both tough and full of style. By the late 1960s, funk was emerging as a tougher, rougher cousin to soul music.

Funk's years of popularity came in the 1970s. Funk, like most great musical styles, proved that it could move in many different directions at once. Parliament/Funkadelic, led by George Clinton (1941–), produced a version of funk that incorporated elements of black science fiction in such albums as *Mothership Connection* with down and dirty funk in such songs as "Tear the Roof Off the Sucker (Give Up the Funk)" and "One Nation Under a Groove." Kool & the Gang produced a more danceable style in songs such as "Jungle Boogie," as did the Commodores with their hit "Brick House." Earth Wind & Fire offered a more polished version of funk. Style was also an important element in funk, with Clinton's outrageous and futuristic costumes and Earth Wind & Fire's mixture of vaguely ancient Egyptian and African styles. Live funk shows were always big productions full of visual spectacles as well as great music. While funk continued as a style throughout the 1980s and 1990s and beyond, its heyday ended with the rise of disco in the late 1970s.

—*Timothy Berg*

For More Information

George, Nelson. *The Death of Rhythm and Blues.* New York: Plume, 1988.

McEwen, Joe. "Funk." In *The Rolling Stone Illustrated History of Rock and Roll.* Edited by Jim Miller. New York: Rolling Stone Press, 1980.

Various Artists. *Millenium Funk Party.* Rhino Records, 1998. CD.

Vincent, Rickey. *Funk: The Music, the People and the Rhythm of the One.* New York: St. Martins/Griffin, 1986.

The Hustle

The Hustle—also commonly known as the Latin Hustle—is an energetic, ballroom-style dance that was wildly popular in the mid- and late-1970s, at the height of the **disco** music (see entry under 1970s–Music in volume 4) craze. The origins of the dance are imprecise, but its evolution can be traced to the sounds of salsa and swing music. The Hustle incorporated the hip motion

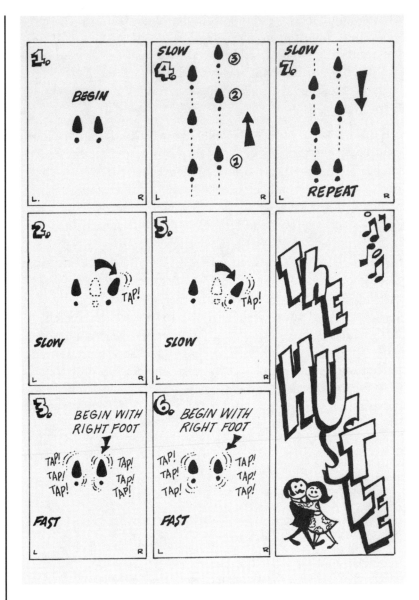

A quick, seven-step instruction on how to dance the Hustle.
Sketch by Jim Hummel. AP/Wide World Photos. Reproduced by permission.

employed in salsa with the footwork of swing music. Ultimately, its movements consisted of plenty of spins and rhythmic footwork, and it was danced to a hard-driving disco beat.

One evening during the mid-1970s, veteran music arranger, writer, and producer Van McCoy (c. 1940–1979) visited Adam's Apple, a New York City disco, where he saw the dance being performed. McCoy was inspired to compose "The Hustle," an instrumental that became one of the era's disco anthems. In July 1975, "The Hustle" hit Number One on the pop music charts.

Eventually, it sold ten million copies, and earned a 1975 Grammy Award as Best Pop Instrumental.

—Rob Edelman

For More Information

"Hustle." *U.S. Swing Dance Server.* http://www.swingcraze.com/ussds/Hustle/hustle.html (accessed March 27, 2002).

Shell, Niel. *Hustle.* Pearl River, NY: Nyemchek's Dance Centre, 1999.

KISS

● ●

With their outlandish costumes, full makeup, and theatrical stage shows, the rock group KISS took **rock and roll** (see entry under 1950s–Music in volume 3) and theater, mixed it together, and sold millions of records and concert tickets. They also took the marketing of rock music to new levels. Along the way, they also made some solid hard-rock records. Among the numerous hard-rock acts in the 1970s, KISS had the most extensive and devoted following.

Formed in 1973, the group consisted of bassist Gene Simmons (1949–), guitarist Paul Stanley (1952–), drummer Peter Criss (1945–), and guitarist Ace Frehley (1951–). Their first album, *KISS,* came out in February 1974. It was reasonably successful, and the band toured constantly and developed their fan base. Their success came mostly from their theatrical stage shows. By the early 1970s, music fans were tiring of going to concerts simply to see their favorite performers in person; now many fans wanted a spectacular stage show. Artists such as Alice Cooper (1948–), David Bowie (1947–), and KISS responded with ever more elaborate stage productions. KISS took this concept the furthest. They never appeared in public without full makeup, and their shows featured dry ice, blood spitting, dramatic lighting, explosions, and fire breathing. At these shows and on their records, KISS played straight-ahead rock and roll. Their songs "Rock and Roll All Nite," "Calling Dr. Love," and "Hard Luck Woman" were minor rock classics. They even scored a top-ten hit in 1976 with their rock ballad "Beth."

KISS capitalized on their success with some clever marketing gimmicks. In the late 1970s, there were KISS dolls, lunch boxes, pinball machines, comic books, and literally hundreds of other items of KISS merchandise. They also had an animated cartoon special, *KISS Meets the Phantom of the Park* (1978).

The rock group KISS poses in its customary eccentric costumes and makeup: (clockwise from upper left) Gene Simmons, Ace Frehley, Peter Criss, and Paul Stanley. *AP/Wide World Photo. Reproduced by permission.*

Their classic period ended in the early 1980s when Peter Criss and Ace Frehley left the band; two drummers followed Criss and three guitarists followed Frehley before both returned to the band in 1996. KISS gave up their makeup in 1983 and continued to tour and make albums; when Criss and Frehley returned, so did the makeup.

—Timothy Berg

For More Information

Bangs, Lester. "Heavy Metal." In *The Rolling Stone Illustrated History of Rock and Roll*. Edited by Jim Miller. New York: Rolling Stone Press, 1980.

KISS. Introduction by Sylvie Simmons. New York: St. Martin's Press, 1997.

KISS On Line. http://www.kissonline.com (accessed March 27, 2002).

Kitts, Jeff. *KISStory*. Los Angeles: KISStory, 1994.

Lendt, C. K. *KISS and Sell: The Making of a Supergroup*. New York: Billboard Books, 1997.

Led Zeppelin

One of the most popular rock groups of the 1970s, Led Zeppelin combined strong roots in **blues** (see entry under 1920s–Music in volume 2) music with a harder-edged **rock and roll** (see entry under 1950s–Music in volume 3) sound. This combination set the stage for the development of **heavy metal** (see entry under 1980s–Music in volume 5) music. More than this, they brought new elements into rock music, including British folk, Celtic mythology, and mysticism. A series of popular albums and phenomenally successful tours made Led Zeppelin a major presence in rock music during the 1970s.

The group's origins were not in the 1970s but in the blues-rock revival in Britain during the late 1960s. Guitarist Jimmy Page (1944–) was a member of the popular group the Yardbirds just before they broke up. He recruited singer Robert Plant (1948–), bassist John Paul Jones (1946–), and drummer John Bonham (1948–1980). Together they recorded their first album *Led Zeppelin* in late 1968 and released it in January 1969. Rooted in blues forms, the album's songs took the blues in new and harder directions, with crunching power chords, hot solos, and Plant's powerful vocals. Songs such as "Communication Breakdown," "Good Times, Bad Times," and "Dazed and Confused" set the tone for a new era in rock. The band continued their success with the albums *Led Zeppelin II, Led Zeppelin III,* and *Led Zeppelin IV.* Songs such as "Whole Lotta Love" and "Rock and Roll" continued their heavy guitar rock, but they also showed a softer side with such songs as "Going to California" and "The Rain Song." They also had a huge hit with their anthem "Stairway to Heaven," a song that quickly became a rock standard.

The death of drummer John Bonham, who choked on his own vomit after a drinking binge in September of 1980, proved the end of the band. The remaining members pursued various solo projects thereafter. They reunited for single shows, including

Live Aid (see entry under 1980s—Music in volume 5) in 1985. In 1994, Page and Plant appeared on *Unplugged,* an **MTV** (see entry under 1980s—Music in volume 5) program featuring acoustic music.

—Timothy Berg

For More Information

Cole, Richard. *Stairway to Heaven: Led Zeppelin Uncensored.* New York: HarperCollins, 1992.

Davis, Stephen. *Hammer of the Gods.* New York: Boulevard Books, 1997.

Led Zeppelin. *Led Zeppelin.* Atlantic Records CD Boxed Set, 1990.

Led-Zeppelin.com: Electric Image. http://www.led-zeppelin.com/index2.html (accessed March 27, 2002).

Miller, Jim. "Led Zeppelin." In *The Rolling Stone Illustrated History of Rock and Roll.* Edited by Jim Miller. New York: Rolling Stone Press, 1980.

Barry Manilow (1946–)

In the 1970s, Barry Manilow (born Barry Alan Pincus) became popular for his melodic romantic songs and intimate singing style. "Serious" music critics mocked him for his audience of middle-aged women. His boy-next-door appearance made him the target of cruel jokes. But Manilow sold records by the millions. Songs such as "Mandy" and "Copacabana" had huge chart success. Never exactly a groundbreaking artist, Manilow always entertained his loyal audience with easy-listening romantic pop.

After attending the New York College of Music and the Juilliard School in the 1960s, Brooklyn-born Manilow proved himself an all-round music professional. He began his career as a composer and arranger of commercials for such products as Dr. Pepper and Band-Aid and also sang on **Broadway** (see entry under 1900s—Film and Theater in volume 1). Since the height of his fame in the late 1970s and early 1980s, he has concentrated on his great passion, the show tunes of the 1930s and 1940s.

—Chris Routledge

For More Information

Barry Net: The Official Site of the Barry Manilow International Fan Club. http://www.barrynet.com (accessed March 26, 2002).

Peters, Richard. *Barry Manilow: An Illustrated Biography.* New York: Delilah Books, 1983.

Punk

In the mid-1970s, at a time when **pop music** (see entry under 1940s—Music in volume 3) was dominated by soft-rock singer-songwriters and **disco** (see entry under 1970s—Music in volume 4), punk rock burst forth with an angry snarl that reawakened the original rebellious spirit of rock and roll. Like **rock and roll** (see entry under 1950s—Music in volume 3) in the mid-1950s, punk in the mid-1970s was more than a musical style. It was a new musical style, a new fashion style, a new attitude of political and cultural awareness and criticism, and a new lifestyle. Like early rock, punk challenged both American and British society. Love it or hate it, punk was not easy to ignore. It was an in-your-face movement that demanded to be heard. Punk influenced music and fashion far beyond its core supporters.

The first punk band was the Ramones, formed in 1974 in New York City. The Ramones reduced rock to its original elements of guitar, bass, drums, and singer. They played fast and furious in short songs such as *I Wanna Be Sedated* and *Gimme Gimme Shock Treatment*. These songs often commented, sometimes in a humorous way, on the darker side of life. Their energy, creativity, and pure power as a group inspired a whole host of punk bands in the United States and in Great Britain. Both New York and Los Angeles were key centers of punk music and style, producing influential punk bands such as Black Flag, X, and The Minutemen.

In Britain, the **Sex Pistols** (see entry under 1970s—Music in volume 4) became the most notorious of punk bands with their antiauthoritarian lyrics, their playing style that bordered on chaotic, and their boisterous live shows. Their personal behavior, including the death of bassist Sid Vicious (1957–1979) from a drug overdose in 1979, added to their notoriety. Although the Sex Pistols folded in 1979, the British punk scene lived on in such bands as the Clash, known for their Marxist politics and for pushing punk in new, more musical directions in such albums as *London Calling* (1979) and *Sandinista* (1980).

The heyday of the punk movement was largely over by the early 1980s. Many of the original punk bands, including the Ramones, carried on the tradition for many years thereafter. Punk music also influenced other musical trends, most notably new wave music in the late 1970s and early 1980s and in later bands such as Sonic Youth and Green Day. Punk also had an influence on fashion trends. Although that impact has largely passed, in most large cities one can usually find punk bands and punk fans sporting the original punk leather jackets, boots, and mohawk hairstyles. (A mohawk is a narrow strip of hair, usually styled to stick straight up, running from the front to the back of the head. It is created by shaving the hair on the sides of the head.) More important than these fashion trends, punk served to energize rock music at a time when many believed it badly needed it.

—Timothy Berg

For More Information

Boot, Adrian, and Chris Salewicz. *Punk: The Illustrated History of a Music Revolution*. New York: Penguin Studio, 1997.

Haimes, Ted, writer, producer, and director. *The History of Rock 'n' Roll: Punk* (video). Burbank, CA: Warner Home Video, 1995.

Laing, Dave. *One-Chord Wonders: Power and Meaning in Punk Rock*. Philadelphia: Open University Press, 1985.

McNeil, Legs, and Gillian McCain. *Please Kill Me: The Uncensored Oral History of Punk*. New York: Grove Press, 1996.

Miller, Jim, ed. *The Rolling Stone Illustrated History of Rock and Roll*. New York: Rolling Stone Press, 1980.

Punkmusic.com. http://www.punkmusic.com/ (accessed March 26, 2002).

Sex Pistols

Although their life as a punk band lasted just a few years in the late 1970s, the Sex Pistols had a lasting impact on both **punk** (see entry under 1970s—Music in volume 4) music and music in general. As a leading group in the British punk scene, the Sex Pistols combined the raw sound of loud guitars, bass, drums, and snarling vocals with an aggressive attitude that challenged conventional society and bordered on anarchy (denial of the authority of a government or an established society).

Formed in late 1975 by boutique owner Malcolm McLaren (1946–), the band consisted of guitarist Steve Jones (1955–), bassist Glen Matlock (1956–), drummer Paul Cook (1956–), and singer John Lydon (1956–), who went by the name Johnny Rotten. Matlock was later replaced on bass by Sid Vicious (John Simon Richie, 1957–1979). In November 1976, they released their first single, "Anarchy in the U.K." Their sound was abrasive. When combined with Rotten's lyrics, which confronted British society, the band attracted immediate attention, not all

Johnny Rotten, lead singer of the influential punk band the Sex Pistols, screams out a song on stage. *AP/Wide World Photos. Reproduced by permission.*

of it positive. The band even attacked the British queen herself in the song "God Save the Queen."

Although they had legions of fans among young people, the Sex Pistols' music was soon banned by British authorities, which only added to their bad reputation and thus their fame. They released only one album, *Never Mind the Bullocks,* in 1977. They toured the United States in January 1978, a tour that lasted only fourteen days. The pressures of stardom and notoriety and their own chaotic behavior proved too much for the group. Bassist Vicious was indicted for the murder of his girlfriend, and he died of a drug overdose in 1979. Rotten, reborn in the form of his real name, John Lydon, formed his own band, Public Image Ltd.

Although the Sex Pistols' time as a band was short, their impact has been long lasting. They were not the best musicians, nor did they produce a great quantity or variety of music, but they inspired countless punk bands to form in Britain. Their one album reduced **rock and roll** (see entry under 1950s–Music in volume 3) to its bare essentials and restored its early spirit of rebellion and youthful anger. More importantly, their attitude of rebellion fit the mood of British youth culture in the late 1970s as good jobs became harder to find. That same attitude proved immensely appealing to many young people in the United States, and the Sex Pistols had a large following there as well. Long gone though they may be, the band's work remains a hallmark in the history of rock and roll.

—Timothy Berg

For More Information

God Save the Sex Pistols. http://www.sex-pistols.net/ (accessed March 26, 2002).

Marcus, Greil. "Anarchy in the U.K." In *The Rolling Stone Illustrated History of Rock and Roll*. Edited by Jim Miller. New York: Rolling Stone Press, 1980.

McNeil, Legs, and Gillian McCain. *Please Kill Me: The Uncensored Oral History of Punk*. New York: Grove Press, 1996.

Savage, John. *England's Dreaming: Anarchy, Sex Pistols, Punk Rock, and Beyond*. New York: St. Martin's Press, 1992.

Temple, Julien, director. *The Filth and the Fury* (video). Los Angeles: New Line Home Video, 2000.

Walkman

The Sony Walkman is one of the most successful electronic products of all time. After the introduction of the Philips compact cassette in 1963, by the 1970s the size of a cassette player had settled at about the size of a trade paperback. The truth was that nobody really saw the need to make it any smaller. So when Sony introduced the pocket-sized Soundabout, later called the Walkman, it seemed a clever concept that would never catch on. Unlike other cassette players in 1979, the Soundabout had no loudspeaker, delivering sound through stereo headphones. Even Sony's marketing department did not expect it to sell. Although the Japanese liked it, in the United States consumers were put off by the $200 price tag.

The Walkman II, introduced in 1981, was smaller, simpler, and much cheaper. Within a couple of years other manufacturers had entered the market. Whatever they called their products officially, competitors' cassette players were known as "Walkman" by the people who bought them. As the 1980s progressed, the machines became smaller and cheaper while sound quality improved. Sony sold more than fifty million units of the Walkman in the first ten years, and almost thirty million every year in the 1990s. By 1990, the range of products offered included waterproof and shock-resistant versions as well as models that were barely bigger than the cassette tape itself.

Portable **compact disc** (CD; see entry under 1980s–Music in volume 5) and Minidisc players continued the Walkman tradition in the late 1990s, but neither has had the impact of the Walkman itself. The Walkman was not only a major technological advancement but a cultural one as well. It broke all the unwritten rules about the size of consumer products and changed the way people listened to music. It spawned a rash of compilation tapes—tapes containing a collection of songs by different artists. The music itself was produced to match the capabilities of the Walkman's tiny in-ear headphones. The Walkman proved an ideal companion for fast-moving modern life. On crowded subways and city streets, the Walkman allowed people to feel they were alone. By adding a soundtrack to everyday life, the Walkman changed the way people experienced the world.

A couple enjoying the convenience of portable music with the Walkman.
Bettmann/Corbis. Reproduced by permission.

—*Chris Routledge*

For More Information

Gould, William. *Sony.* New York: Contemporary Press, 1997.

Millard, Andre. *America on Record: A History of Recorded Sound.* New York: Cambridge University Press, 1995.

"Sony History." *Sony.* http://www.sony.co.jp/en/Fun/SH/1-18/h1.html (accessed March 27, 2002).

1970s
Print Culture

Serious readers in the 1970s had good reason to be confused. Critics surveyed a publishing world that seemed no longer to be producing great works of literature, and they proclaimed that the novel was dead. What they might have said, however, was that the novel was changing and changing fast. No longer were the great novels being produced by white American male writers; in the 1970s, some of the best serious fiction was being produced by minorities, women like Alice Walker (1944–) and Toni Morrison (1931–), and people living outside the United States, such as Gabriel García Marquez (1928–) and Jorge Luis Borges (1899–1986).

The market for popular fiction boomed in the 1970s, as Americans lapped up exciting, fast-paced books by skilled popular novelists. Harold Robbins (1916–1997) and Judith Krantz (1937–) specialized in "trash fiction," with its sensational doses of sex, money, and power. Novels about spying and global political intrigue frequently topped the best-seller lists. The most popular writers of these novels were Robert Ludlum (1927–2001), Irving Wallace (1916–1990), and Leon Uris (1924–). Barbara Cartland (1901–2000) and Phyllis A. Whitney (1903–) were the queens of the romance novel. A new series—called Harlequin Romances—offered a steady stream of romance fiction intended for women. The 1970s also saw the first appearance of the man who would dominate the best-seller list for the rest of the century: horror writer Stephen King (1947–). One of the surprise hits of the decade was a historical account of the life of a black family titled *Roots,* by Alex Haley (1921–1992). *Roots* later became a popular television miniseries.

The American magazine market continued to splinter, with new magazines being created to serve all variety of interests. Three magazines that started in the 1970s provide a taste of this variety. *People* aimed to provide upscale gossip and photos to Americans hungry for any word on celebrities. *Ms.* covered serious issues of interest to feminists, while *Hustler* certainly did not.

Judy Blume (1938–)

Judy Blume is credited with being the first writer for young adults to deal realistically with teenage worries. Her 1970 novel *Are You There God? It's Me, Margaret* addresses the issues of starting a new school in a new neighborhood and finding a religious faith. Its central character, Margaret, also worries about beginning menstruation and buying her first bra. In *Forever* (1975), Katherine has to decide whether to "go all the way" with her boyfriend Michael. These were topics that just a few years before had been forbidden subjects for children's fiction.

Blume's books have sold millions of copies, and several have been adapted for **television** (see entry under 1940s–TV and Radio in volume 3) and film. Refusing to back away from the controversies her books have caused, Blume became an outspoken opponent of censorship and offered her support to other civil-liberties organizations. Critics have recognized that Blume revolutionized the field of realistic children's literature. More importantly, she also informed and encouraged many millions of young women.

—Chris Routledge

For More Information

Judy Blume's Home Base. http://www.judyblume.com/index.html (accessed March 27, 2002).

Lee, Betsy. *Judy Blume's Story.* New York: Scholastic, 1981.

Marcus, Leonard S., ed. *Author Talk.* New York: Simon & Schuster, 2000.

Weidt, Maryann N. *Presenting Judy Blume.* Boston: Twayne, 1990.

Cathy

In November 1976, a new comic-strip hero made her debut in newspapers around the country. Cathy—an energetic and assertive single career woman with a mocking sense of humor—was clearly a product of the women's liberation movement of the early 1970s. As society's expectations of women were beginning to change, Cathy was the woman caught in the middle, trying to be both strong enough and soft enough, to be both clever and capable at her job and thin and fashionable for her dates. Cathy's witty solutions to her problems have caught the attention of readers for over two decades. At the beginning of the twenty-first century she had appeared in fourteen hundred newspapers around the world, twenty books, and several **television** (see entry under 1940s—TV and Radio in volume 3) specials.

Cathy's life is a hectic and goofy whirlwind of work, shopping, dating, dieting, and dealing with her well-meaning but irritating parents. The cast of characters surrounding her represents a generous slice of a modern woman's life: Mr. Pinkley, her bewildered boss; her girlfriend Andrea, a feminist wife and mom; Irving, her maddening on-again-off-again boyfriend; and her mom and dad. Cathy is close to her parents and, though they drive her crazy, she always runs to them when she needs a shoulder to lean on. Although her mother dreams of Cathy's wedding day, Cathy remains happily single. However, she did partly fulfill her parent's desire for a grandchild when she got her puppy, Electra.

Cathy creator Cathy Guisewite (1950–) has won a Reuben Award from the National Cartoonists Society (1993) and an Emmy for Best Animated Television Special (1987) for her work on the comic strip. Guisewite and her plucky heroine have more than their first names in common. After graduating from the University of Michigan in 1972, Guisewite got a job in advertising, where she worked until 1977, working her way up to vice president. She began to draw *Cathy* to express the humor she saw in the contradictions and problems facing young career women. Some have criticized the strip's heroine for being shallow and obsessed with looks and fashion, but *Cathy* continues to provide a laugh for both men and women caught up in the frantic pace of modern life.

—Tina Gianoulis

For More Information

"Cathy." *UComics.com.* http://www.ucomics.com/cathy (accessed March 27, 2002).

"Cathy Lee Guisewite." *Current Biography.* (Vol. 50, no. 2, February 1989): pp. 21–26.

Lapin, Claudia. "Cathy on Cathy." *Savvy* (January 1988): pp. 50–54.

Millner, Cork. "How Cartoonist Cathy Guisewite Makes Us Laugh at Life's Little Frustrations." *Seventeen* (May 1983): pp. 42–44.

Garfield
• •

A creation of cartoonist Jim Davis (1945–), Garfield is a lazy but scheming cat who ranks with **Felix the Cat** (see entry under

Garfield creator Jim Davis pauses after drawing the lazy and always hungry cartoon cat. *Photograph by Michael Conroy. AP/Wide World Photos. Reproduced by permission.*

1910s–Film and Theater in volume 1), Sylvester, and **Krazy Kat** (see entry under 1910s–Print Culture in volume 1) among the most popular feline comic-strip characters of all time. Described by his creator as a "fat, orange couch potato," the cat with the huge saucer eyes first made his appearance on June 19, 1978, in a strip populated with his owner, Jon Arbuckle; his Teddy bear, Pooky; and his sidekick, Odie, a constantly panting dog whose energy contrasts sharply with Garfield's relaxed persona.

Garfield is happiest when indulging in his favorite food, lasagna, or engaging in his preferred pastime, raiding the cookie jar. Next to eating, his favorite deed is sleeping, an activity he describes as a "nap attack." When Jon complains in one strip, "Every time I look at you, you're either eating or sleeping," a perplexed Garfield replies, "I'd be happy to choose one and stick with it." The term "reply" is used figuratively, since Garfield never "speaks" in the same way that his human owner does; the cat's thoughts are always framed in a cloud-shaped balloon with circular "smoke signals," indicating the thoughts of this mysterious creature with his somewhat aloof attitude toward both Jon and Odie, as well as toward life itself.

Davis calls Garfield a "human in a cat suit" when explaining the popular appeal of a cat described on his official Web site as "a wisecracking, nap-taking, coffee-guzzling, lasagna-loving, Monday-hating, dog-punting, spider-whacking, mailman-mauling fat cat." Since the beginning of the *Garfield* comic strip, the cat has appeared in several dozen **comic-book** (see entry under 1930s–Print Culture in volume 2) collections of Davis's strips, in a **television** (see entry under 1940s–TV and Radio in volume 3) cartoon series that ran from 1988 to 1995, in numerous video specials, in a **video game** (see entry under 1970s–Sports & Games in volume 4), and on lunch boxes.

—Edward Moran

For More Information

Official Site for Garfield and Friends. http://www.garfield.com (accessed March 27, 2002).

Rogers, Katharine M. *The Cat and the Human Imagination: Feline Images from Bast to Garfield.* Ann Arbor: University of Michigan Press, 1997.

Harlequin Romances

Though it is often said that money cannot buy love, Harlequin Enterprises seems to have proved that love can make a publisher quite a lot of money. Founded in 1949 as a small publisher of out-of-print novels, Harlequin began to focus on romance novels in the early 1970s. Since then, the publisher has grown to be the leader in a multimillion-dollar romance novel industry. In 1999, the Canadian company published 160 million books in 24 languages, sold them in 100 countries, and earned almost $90 million in profits. Although some people laugh at the flowery writing in Harlequin romances and make fun of the dramatically passionate pictures on their covers, millions of readers eagerly scan the supermarket display stands for the latest romance adventure to whisk them away from the stress and boredom of everyday life.

Harlequin Enterprises gained its huge share of romance novel sales by a clever sales strategy. Realizing that most romance novels were bought by housewives seeking a break from their daily routine, Harlequin began to sell its books at the grocery stores and variety stores where housewives shopped.

They developed their "brand" of romance novel the same way other household product brands are developed, by having an easily remembered brand name and recognizable packaging. With its brightly colored cover art, usually of an attractive couple in a passionate embrace, and prominently displayed brand name, the cover of a Harlequin romance is easily recognized. Inside the cover, readers will find few surprises. Harlequin employs hundreds of writers. Each writer follows strict guidelines for the romances, which always include physically beautiful heroes and heroines as well as happy endings.

With over seventy new titles appearing every month, a Harlequin romance is almost like a magazine. The books are inexpensive—usually costing between three and five dollars each—and short enough to be read in an hour or two. Over the decades, Harlequin has developed several different series of romances, each designed for a different audience. The super-sexy Temptation series is aimed at younger readers. The Star-sign Romances have an astrological twist, and the Love Inspired series features Christian romance stories. In the mid-1990s, the Canadian film company Alliance Communications Corporation joined with Harlequin to make four Harlequin romance films.

—*Robert E. Schnakenberg*

For More Information

Bold, Rudolph. "Trash in the Library: Paperback Romances." *Library Journal* (May 15, 1980): p. 1138.

Harlequin Enterprises. *eHarlequin.com.* http://www.eharlequin.com (accessed March 27, 2002).

Mallet, Gina. "The Greatest Romance on Earth." *Canadian Business* (August 1993): pp. 18–24.

Pollack, Richard. "Romance Slaves of Harlequin." *The Nation* Vol. 254, no. 10 (March 16, 1992): pp. 33–37.

Hustler

At the close of the twentieth century, "sexploitation" magazine publishing had evolved into a $1-billion-a-year business. Leading the field was *Hustler* magazine. Unlike **Playboy** (see entry under 1950s—Print Culture in volume 3), its chief rival during the century's last decades and a publication whose sexual imagery was far less degrading by contemporary standards, *Hustler* printed photographs that are raw, graphic, and sexually explicit. Many sex magazines were available only in shops specializing in XXX-rated material. In comparison, *Hustler* could be found on the magazine racks in all types of bookstores. For better or worse, its initial success in the mid-1970s helped to lift pornography into the mainstream of popular culture. For this reason alone, *Hustler* is one of the most controversial magazines ever published.

Hustler was the brainchild of Larry Flynt (1942–), its publisher and founder. In 1972, Flynt, who owned a chain of bars that featured strippers and go-go dancers, began publishing a sex-oriented newsletter, which he eventually expanded into a glossy magazine. He broke from *Playboy* and *Penthouse,* another of the era's popular "men's magazine," in that he refused to tastefully obstruct his models' "private parts." Nor was Flynt concerned with celebrating the beauty of the female form. He often depicted his models participating in rape or male-domination fantasies, or smeared with excrement. On one of his more infamous covers, he pictured a woman being fed into a meat grinder. In 1975, he raised a furor—and won reams of publicity—by printing a photo of a nude Jackie Onassis (1929–1994), the former first lady and wife of John F. Kennedy (1917–1963), sunbathing in Greece.

Flynt was a shrewd self-promoter. As he became a magnet for controversy, sales of his magazine soared. Through the years, he often was hauled into court on obscenity charges. Moral Majority leader Jerry Falwell (1933–) sued Flynt in the wake of a *Hustler* parody depicting the preacher having sex with his mother in an outhouse. A lower court ruled in Falwell's favor, and the case was argued in the U.S. Supreme Court in 1988. The higher court reversed the decision, endorsing Flynt's right to lampoon a public figure.

Since the mid-1970s, Flynt's legal costs have topped an estimated $50 million. In 1978, outside a courthouse, a would-be

Larry Flynt, publisher and founder of *Hustler* magazine, in front of the U.S. Supreme Court Building. *AP/Wide World Photos. Reproduced by permission.*

assassin shot the publisher twice from close range, using a high-powered rifle. Flynt survived, but permanently lost the use of both his legs. His life story was told in the 1996 film *The People vs. Larry Flynt,* directed by Milos Forman (1932–).

—*Rob Edelman*

For More Information

Flynt, Larry, with Kenneth Ross. *An Unseemly Man.* Los Angeles: Dove Books, 1996.

Hustler Magazine, Inc. et al. v. Jerry Falwell. http://www.bc.edu/bc_org/avp/cas/comm/free_speech/hustler.html (accessed March 27, 2002).

The People vs. Larry Flynt (film). Columbia Pictures, 1996.

Smolla, Rodney A. *Jerry Falwell v. Larry Flynt: The First Amendment on Trial.* New York: St. Martin's, 1988.

Ms.

. . . .

Ms. was the best-known and most widely circulated magazine devoted to the culture of the "liberated woman" that emerged out of the feminist movements of the 1960s and 1970s. *Ms.* made its debut as a monthly in July 1972 with Gloria Steinem (1934–) as editor. Although denounced by some critics for its outspoken attitude, the magazine's preview issue, inserted in *New York* magazine and dated December 20, 1971, sold three hundred thousand copies in eight days, attracted twenty-six thousand subscribers, and twenty thousand letters to the editor.

From the start, *Ms.* tackled such issues as women's economic and psychological oppression, abortion, and lesbianism, positioning itself as a far more radical voice than the established women's magazines, which often focused on homemaking, fashion, cosmetics, cooking, and how to be a dutiful wife. The magazine also helped popularize the use of the title "Ms." (instead of "Mrs." or "Miss") to describe a woman in her own right, regardless of marital status.

The magazine was founded by Gloria Steinem of *New York* magazine and Patricia Carbine (1931–), who wanted to publish a glossy feminist-oriented magazine that would be supported by national advertising. They secured a $1 million investment from Warner Communications and brought together an editorial staff of experienced women journalists.

Ms. tried to support itself with advertising, though some companies were ambivalent about appearing in a magazine that challenged the image they wanted to create for women. When the magazine featured a cover shot of Russian women without makeup, for example, Revlon cosmetics pulled its advertising from the issue. In 1979, the struggling magazine had to seek not-for-profit status to stay alive, and was published as an organ of the Ms. Foundation for Education and Communication until 1987, then sold to an Australian conglomerate, next to two Australian feminists, and finally to Lang Communications.

By the late 1980s, *Ms.* was accused by critics and dissatisfied readers of toning down its radical stance in order to satisfy its advertisers. Circulation dropped from 550,000 to less than 100,000. Lang suspended publication of *Ms.* for nearly six months. It resumed publication in the summer of 1990 as a bimonthly, with feminist writer-activist Robin Morgan (1941–) as editor. The new *Ms.* was fully reader-supported, with no advertising. It was purchased by MacDonald Communications in 1996, which suspended publication again in 1998. In 1999, it was acquired by Liberty Media for Women, a newly formed group that included Steinem as well as younger entrepreneurs and activists. *Ms.* resumed bimonthly publication with the March/April issue.

—Edward Moran

For More Information

Farrell, Amy Erdman. *Yours in Sisterhood: Ms. Magazine and the Promise of Popular Feminism.* Chapel Hill: University of North Carolina Press, 1998.

Ms. Magazine. http://www.msmagazine.com (accessed March 27, 2002).

Thom, Mary. *Inside Ms.: 25 Years of the Magazine and the Feminist Movement.* New York: Henry Holt and Company, 1998.

People ....

Founded in 1974 as part of the Time-Life publishing empire, *People* magazine, a mass-circulation weekly magazine, helped define the way journalists and **television** (see entry under 1940s—TV and Radio in volume 3) talk shows covered celebrities and other prominent figures. It has successfully occupied a position above the more sensational gossip tabloids while

People weekly

March 4, 1974   35 Cents

Mia Farrow
In 'Gatsby,'
the year's next
big movie

Mia Farrow, as Daisy from the movie *The Great Gatsby,* graced the first cover of *People* magazine on March 4, 1974. *AP/Wide World Photos. Reproduced by permission.*

maintaining a lively, graphic image that makes ample use of photographs and exclusive interviews. The magazine has sometimes been criticized for blurring the distinction between hard news and entertainment, but it has established itself as one of the most widely read U.S. magazines.

Time, Inc. originally conceived *People* as a replacement for **Life** (see entry under 1930s—Print Culture in volume 2), which had ceased weekly publication in 1972. Instead of reporting exclusively on the artistic or political achievements of important public figures, *People* focused on their triumphs over personal adversities, such as divorce or addiction, a formula its editors described as "extraordinary people doing ordinary things and ordinary people doing extraordinary things." The

magazine appeared during the unfolding of the Watergate scandal, at a point in American life when the private lives of public figures were no longer considered off-limits to mainstream journalists. Unlike the scandal sheets, which relied on gossip and sensationalism, *People* wrote about the weaknesses of celebrities and politicians in a serious, if informal, manner. It also redefined the boundaries of "celebrity" beyond show business to include business people, politicians, athletes, and even religious leaders.

People followed the lead of the TV industry in treating news as another form of entertainment. Since the magazine was initially sold on newsstands only and not by subscription, its editors devoted special attention each week to finding an attractive cover subject, with an emphasis on youth, beauty, power, and glamorous sex appeal. Some of *People*'s best-selling issues depicted cover shots of John Lennon (1940–1980), Princess Grace (Grace Kelly, 1929–1984), and Princess Diana (1961–1997) just after they had died. *People* is credited with having influenced other mainstream newspapers and magazines to devote more coverage to news items and features about celebrities, and of paving the way for TV shows like *A Current Affair* and *Entertainment Tonight* as well as talk shows by Oprah Winfrey (1954–) and Jerry Springer (1944–).

—*Edward Moran*

For More Information

Braudy, Leo. *The Frenzy of Renown: Fame and its History.* New York: Oxford University Press, 1986.

Kessler, Judy. *Inside People: The Stories Behind the Stories.* New York: Villard Books, 1994.

People.com. http://people.aol.com/people/index.html (accessed March 27, 2002).

1970s
Sports and Games

More than anything else, money changed professional sports during the 1970s. In football and baseball, moneymaking television contracts led to changes in the rules and a lengthening of the season. Playoffs in both sports extended the seasons and brought huge revenues. Players wanted a share of the increased revenues, and players unions organized to demand higher pay and more freedom to move from team to team. In baseball, a policy called "free agency" moved players around and helped a number of players reach salaries at or near $1 million a year.

Professional baseball was dominated by the Cincinnati Reds, led by Pete Rose (1941–), and the Baltimore Orioles, led in 1970 and 1971 by Frank Robinson (1935–), who would become baseball's first black manager in 1975, with the Cleveland Indians. Strong runs by upstart teams like the Oakland A's and the Pittsburgh Pirates made it an exciting decade for baseball. In pro football, the Pittsburgh Steelers were the team to beat, but not many teams did. The Steelers won four Super Bowls. The leading players of the decade included O. J. Simpson (1947–), Roger Staubach (1942–), "Mean" Joe Greene (1946–), and Terry Bradshaw (1948–). Professional basketball was in a bit of a slump during the decade, despite the play of superstar Julius "Dr. J" Erving (1950–) of the Philadelphia 76ers. Pro hockey began to gain in popularity, although it would never challenge the big three sports. College football and basketball also remained hugely popular, and many of the games were shown on TV.

Outside of the major pro and college sports, perhaps the biggest sports story of the decade was the "Battle of the Sexes," a tennis match between women's great Billie Jean King (1943–) and aging men's pro Bobby Riggs (1918–1995). King won the match—and $100,000. Women's tennis advanced rapidly during the decade, thanks to the exciting play of such stars as Chris Evert (1954–) and Tracy Austin (1962–). In car racing, Janet Guthrie (1938–) became the first woman to drive in the Indianapolis 500 in 1977; she came in eighteenth. Black athletes continued to make gains, earning salaries comparable with those of white athletes and establishing important records. No record was more striking than the one Henry Aaron (1934–) set early in 1974 when he topped Babe Ruth (1895–1948) for the all-time home-run record.

Sports and games were not just for the pros, however. In the 1970s, millions of Americans took up jogging or aerobics in order to improve their physical fitness. Both activities produced industries of their own to provide shoes, clothing, and video-tapes for exercising Americans.

Video games became an important new source of entertainment in the 1970s. Pinball machines had been available in pool halls and other areas for years, but the video game brought game play into the home. Millions of Americans purchased the new Atari game system, which allowed them to play a graphically primitive game called "Pong." In "Pong," players used a crude paddle to bounce a ball across a screen. Better games, however, would soon arrive.

Aerobics

The word "aerobic" means "using oxygen." Aerobic exercises are those designed to increase the oxygen content in the blood and pump this oxygen-enriched blood to the muscles, increasing overall health. Aerobic exercise involves performing an active movement, such as **jogging** (see entry under 1970s– Sports and Games in volume 4), biking, or swimming, for an extended period of time. This sustained movement allows the heartbeat to increase and remain at a high level.

When the benefits of prolonged energetic physical activity were first publicized in 1968, only about one hundred thousand Americans jogged for exercise. By 1999, over thirty-four million American were running regularly. Millions more rode stationary bikes or attended classes for aerobics, aerobic dance, **jazz** (see entry under 1900s–Music in volume 1) aerobics, aqua aerobics, step aerobics, and more.

In 1968, Kenneth H. Cooper (1931–), an Air Force surgeon from Dallas, Texas, published a revolutionary new exercise book based on his research with fifty thousand men and women in the Air Force. Cooper designed a program to make the exercise routines used by the military available to everyone, and his ideas caught on quickly. By the 1970s, dance instructors had added various kinds of music to vigorous exercise, creating aerobic **dancing** (see entry under 1900s–The Way We Lived in volume 1), jazzercise, and soul aerobics. These dance-and-exercise combinations were especially popular with women, who flocked to classes that promised to keep them healthy as well as to help them lose weight.

The 1980s, with its focus on personal improvement, saw an increased popularity of private gyms. Many gyms began to offer aerobics classes. Exercise "gurus" like Richard Simmons (1948–) and Jane Fonda (1937–) released videos that taught viewers how to exercise aerobically in their own homes. Movies like *Flashdance* (1983) and *Perfect* (1982) glamorized aerobic exercise. Manufacturers like Reebok and Janzen, who had once made specialty shoes and clothing for sports and dance, now made "aerobic" wear for the everyday exerciser. Aerobics had become a multimillion-dollar business.

The 1990s saw the development of less strenuous forms of aerobics like aqua aerobics, done in swimming pools, which were intended to reduce the chances of injury. The 1990s also brought professionalism to aerobics. Organizations like the Aerobics and Fitness Association of America developed certification programs for instructors, and aerobics athletes competed in national and international championships.

–Tina Gianoulis

For More Information

Cooper, Kenneth H. *The Aerobics Way: New Data on the Worlds Most Popular Exercise Program.* Dallas: M. Evans & Company, 1977.

McNamara, Jo Ann, and Sharon Pendleton. *The ABCs of Aerobics.* Dubuque, IA: Kendall/Hunt, 1990.

Savage, Jeff. *Aerobics.* Parsippany, NJ: Crestwood House, 1995.

Atari

The Atari company started a global phenomenon. For millions of people worldwide, **video games** (see entry under 1970s–Sports and Games in volume 4)–played at home, in arcades, or using portable devices–are an entertaining part of everyday life. In the 1970s, Atari paved the way for the video-game giants of later years, like Nintendo and Sega.

Teens compete for the top score in Asteroids, one of Atari's popular arcade games. *AP/Wide World Photos. Reproduced by permission.*

Atari was founded in 1972 by Nolan Bushnell (1943–), an engineer who believed electronics could be adapted for entertainment. He invented the first video-game machine, **Pong** (see entry under 1970s–Sports and Games in volume 4). The electronic version of ping-pong became a huge hit in bars and arcades. Together with some friends, Bushnell created a company to market it. They called their company "Atari," after a word used in the popular Japanese card game "Go."

Pong was such a hit that Atari created an equally popular home version in 1974. Warner Communications bought Atari from Bushnell and his partners for $28 million the next year. Warner began developing an even more sophisticated home-arcade system that could play a wide variety of games. This system, the Atari Video Computer System, or VCS, was introduced just in time for the Christmas season in 1977. The arcade system and the nine games sold with it proved so popular that people actually lined up to purchase them. Over the next few years, Atari products became an international sensation. Popular software titles, some of which were based on Atari's own arcade games, included Space Invaders, Asteroids, and **Pac-Man** (see entry under 1980s—Sports and Games in volume 5). By 1982, Atari was a $2 billion company.

Eventually, Atari's competitors began to catch up. Atari was slow to upgrade its system, while others, like CBS' Colecovision, started to steal the Atari's market share. In addition, the home video-game market became flooded with too many games. By 1984, the industry was in a deep sales slump, from which Atari never fully recovered. When video-game sales picked up again a couple of years later, new companies like Nintendo and Sega were on hand to take Atari's place. Although still in business into the twenty-first century, Atari possessed little more than nostalgia value for a generation of adults who had grown up playing Pong, Space Invaders, and Asteroids.

—*Robert E. Schnakenberg*

For More Information

Atari. http://www.atari.com (accessed March 27, 2002).

Atari Historical Society. http://www.atari-history.com (accessed March 27, 2002).

Kent, Stephen L. *The First Quarter: A 25-Year History of Video Games.* New York: BWD Press, 2000.

Phillips, Gary, and Jerry White. *The Atari User's Encyclopedia.* Los Angeles: The Book Co., 1984.

Poole, Stephen. *Trigger Happy: Video Games and the Entertainment Revolution.* New York: Arcade Publishing, 2000.

Dungeons and Dragons

The introduction of the game Dungeons and Dragons in 1974 marked a dramatic innovation in board games. Like the interactive computer games that would follow two decades later, Dungeons and Dragons (often known as "D & D") was an active game that required creativity and imagination from its players. Dungeons and Dragons was the first of the "role-playing games." In role-playing games, players imagined themselves in another world, making choices and taking actions that affected the outcome of the play. Millions of people, many of them teenagers, joined in the game. The game allowed them to escape from the limitations of reality to enter a wondrous fantasy world where they could wield supernatural powers.

Invented by Gary Gygax (1938–), a Chicago insurance salesman who had been a childhood chess whiz, Dungeons and

A Dungeons and Dragons instructional handbook and players' pieces. *AP/Wide World Photos. Reproduced by permission.*

Dragons does not require a lot of equipment. A playing board, multisided dice, and a complex rule book make up the entire game. The rest depends on the imagination of the players, who roll the dice to receive their roles and powers. Set in a medieval fantasy world similar to that found in the *Lord of the Rings* by **J. R. R. Tolkien** (1892–1973; see entry under 1950s–Print Culture in volume 3), players may be wizards, thieves, fighters, elves, or dwarves as they rescue princesses or defeat dragons. Games—called campaigns—can last for hours or weeks, depending on the endurance of the players.

After its release in 1974, Dungeons and Dragons caught on quickly, earning Gygax's company, TSR, more than two million dollars by 1978, soaring to $26.7 million by 1983. The game soon gained a cult status. Some religious groups and parents began to worry about their children's obsession with their Dungeons and Dragons campaigns. A 1982 **television** (see entry under 1940s–TV and Radio in volume 3) movie, *Mazes and Monsters,* warned of the dangers of addiction to role-playing games. By the 1990s, Gygax had sold his interests in the game, which is now owned by Wizards of the Coast.

Though the popularity of Dungeons and Dragons faded somewhat with the advent of the **Internet** (see entry under 1990s–The Way We Lived in volume 5) and more advanced computer games in the 1990s, it was estimated that a million gamers still play the game every month. In 2001, a film version of Dungeons and Dragons was released, to mixed reviews. The film could produce far more spectacular special effects than the simple board game, but it could not reproduce the magic found in the imaginations of the players.

–Tina Gianoulis

For More Information

Advanced Dungeons and Dragons: Player's Handbook for the AD&D Game. Lake Geneva, WI: TSR, 1995.

Cardwell, Paul, Jr. "The Attacks on Role-Playing Games." *Skeptical Inquirer* (Winter 1994): pp. 157–66.

"D & D." *Wizards of the Coast.* http://www.wizards.com/dnd/main.asp?x=dnd/welcome,3 (accessed March 27, 2002).

Holmes, John Eric. "Confessions of a Dungeon Master." *Psychology Today* (November 1980): pp. 84–89.

Hacky Sack

The Hacky Sack—also known as a "footbag"—became a popular pastime in the 1970s. The sport was invented in Oregon City, Oregon, in 1972 when two friends, John Stalberger and Mike Marshall, began kicking around a small, handmade bean bag. The friends soon developed a game in which they batted the ball back and forth using their legs and feet; they called the game "Hack the Sack." After Marshall died from a heart attack in 1975 at age twenty-eight, Stalberger continued to promote the two friends' creation. Stalberger sold the idea to Wham-O, which brought the "Hacky Sack" to the mass market in the late 1970s and early 1980s.

Hacky Sack quickly became a fad among teenage boys, who could stand about in a circle and kick their sack back and forth. Most hackers play such informal games. The game has become formalized, however. The International Footbag Committee sanctions competition in "footbag net" (with rules similar to volleyball) and "footbag freestyle," in which single players perform acrobatic moves with their footbag. Perhaps like table tennis and rhythmic gymnastics, Hacky Sack will one day become a sport in the **Olympics** (see entry under 1900s–Sports and Games in volume 1).

—Tom Pendergast

For More Information

Cassidy, John. *Hacky Sack: American Footbag Game.* Palo Alto, CA: Klutz Press, 1983.

Footbag Worldwide. http://www.footbag.org/footbag.html (accessed March 27, 2002).

Jogging

During the 1970s, Americans in general began to be more health conscious. Preventative medicine (taking positive steps to improve health before disease strikes) became a popular approach to health care. One of the key aspects of preventative medicine involves physical activity. For adults, jogging–running at a moderate, sustainable pace–became a preferred method of exercise.

Before the 1970s, physical activity was viewed as a childhood pastime. A school kid or a teenager might partake in school-yard games, or play **Little League** (see entry under 1930s–Sports and Games in volume 2), or run on the high-school track team. Upon entering adulthood, people were expected to put away–or throw away–their sneakers, footballs, and **baseball** (see entry under 1900s–Sports and Games in volume 1) gloves and adopt a more inactive lifestyle. In the 1970s, with an increased awareness of health-related issues, particularly among **baby boomers** (see entry under 1940s–The Way We Lived in volume 3), came a desire to improve one's quality of life and avoid illness. Whereas others previously had advocated running and physical activity for adults, Jim Fixx (1932–1984) became a key figure in the jogging boom when he published *The Complete Book of Running* (1977). The book sold over a million copies and spearheaded the jogging revolution. Fixx made sneakers, jogging shorts, and sweating stylish. He declared that joggers would lose weight, have more energy, enjoy more active sex lives, feel better, and live longer.

Ironically, Fixx was felled by a heart attack at the age of fifty-two while jogging along a country road. His father had died in a similar manner at age forty-three, and Fixx had ignored earlier warnings of heart problems. Yet Fixx's pioneering efforts, and those of other running advocates such as Bill Rodgers (1947–), who won eight Boston and New York marathons between 1975 and 1980, have altered the consciousness of adults with relation to physical activity. They created an industry whose byproducts are adult gyms, **aerobics** (see entry under 1970s–Sports and Games in volume 4) programs, runners' magazines, sports-equipment stores, running clothes and accessories, **television** (see entry under 1940s–TV and Radio in volume 3) exercise shows—and a raised consciousness in relation to exercise and health care.

—*Rob Edelman*

For More Information

Fixx, James F. *The Complete Book of Running.* New York: Random House, 1977.

Glover, Bob, and Jack Shepherd. *The Runner's Handbook.* New York: Penguin, 1985.

Olney, Ross Robert. *The Young Runner.* New York: Lothrop, Lee, & Shepard, 1978.

Monday Night Football

Since 1970, ABC's *Monday Night Football* has been the weekly prime-time **television** (see entry under 1940s–TV and Radio in volume 3) showcase for the **National Football League** (NFL; see entry under 1920s–Sports and Games in volume 2). The telecast has created controversy, fostered technical innovations, and consistently been one of the most-watched shows in prime time.

Monday Night Football debuted on September 21, 1970, with a game between the New York Jets and the Cleveland Browns. Keith Jackson (1928–) provided the play-by-play, with color commentary (background information and stories) from Don Meredith (1938–) and Howard Cosell (1918–1995). Ex-Giants great Frank Gifford (1930–) replaced Jackson in 1971 and it was this team of colorful broadcasters that helped create a media "buzz" that turned the prime-time football experiment into a ratings smash.

Monday Night Football became successful for many reasons. The NFL tried to make sure that only the best teams and most

Monday Night Football anchors (left to right) Don Meredith, Howard Cosell, and Frank Gifford helped make prime-time football ratings a success. *AP/Wide World Photos. Reproduced by permission.*

heated rivals played in the nighttime showcase. In addition, because ABC only covered one game a week—as opposed to the other major networks, which covered several—the network could devote all of its resources to technical innovations that made the telecasts more exciting. These included multiple cameras, handheld cameras, and the use of Goodyear's floating blimp to provide aerial views of the stadiums.

The most popular aspect of the *Monday Night Football* telecast, however, has always been the announcing team. Many viewers hated Cosell, who many viewed as an arrogant, nasal-voiced egotist who often made fun of his colleagues. (He famously dubbed Meredith "Dandy Don.") Nevertheless, even non–football fans tuned in week after week to hear what Cosell would say or do next. When "Humble Howard" quit after the 1983 season, it seemed like the end of an era. The show struggled to maintain its ratings and the "attitude" that had left with the irritating Cosell.

A series of changes were made to the telecast to keep it fresh. In the 1990s, a new theme song, composed by country singer

Hank Williams Jr. (1949–), posed the question, "Are you ready for some footbaaaaaallll?" Although broadcasting veteran Al Michaels (1944–) provided play-by-play stability starting in 1986, his color commentating partners were shuffled in and out in an attempt to recapture some of the Cosell-era magic. Most notable was the presence of comedian Dennis Miller (1953–) for the 2000 and 2001 seasons; his commentary was often laced with bizarre references that few football fans could follow. Excitable coach-turned-announcer John Madden (1936–) was hired in 2002 to sit alongside Michaels.

—*Robert E. Schnakenberg*

For More Information

Cosell, Howard, with Peter Bonventre. *I Never Played the Game.* New York: William Morrow, 1985.

Gunther, Marc, and Bill Carter. *Monday Night Mayhem.* New York: Beech Tree Books, 1988.

Monday Night Football Online. http://www.mondaynightfootballonline. com/ (accessed March 27, 2002).

Pong

Pong was the first **video game** (see entry under 1970s—Sports and Games in volume 4), arriving on the American scene in 1972. Invented by Nolan Bushnell (1943–), Pong was a simple game modeled after tennis. Each player controlled a dial, or paddle, that moved a small electronically formed rectangular block up and down. As an electronic blip (the ball) moved across the screen, each player had to move the paddle to block it and hit it back to his or her opponent. Each time the ball hit the paddle, a beep was heard. The longer the game went on, the more the ball sped up to challenge players. The top of the screen showed the score as the game progressed. Graphically, the paddle was a long, thin rectangle and the ball was a large dot on a contrasting background. It was that simple. After inventing Pong, Bushnell formed the **Atari** (see entry under 1970s—Sports and Games in volume 4) company to produce more Pong games.

Pong was more than a simple video game; it was the start of a whole new era in home entertainment. The first Pong game was played in arcades, but home versions were soon developed that hooked up to people's **television** (see entry under 1940s—TV and Radio in volume 3) sets. When the **Sears, Roebuck, catalog** (see entry under 1900s—Commerce in volume 1) carried the game, it sold 150,000 copies. The basic format was expanded to include other games that involved hitting a ball, including soccer and hockey. These were basically Pong with the screen slightly changed. Although Pong seems primitive by today's standards, it was an exciting addition to many Americans' homes. Soon, other games were released, each with its own game console (the device that controlled the games). Sports-related games, battle games, racing, space adventures, and others followed. Atari adapted many of its arcade games for home use, including Centipede, Asteroids, Missile Command, and others. Before long, more advanced systems such as Nintendo and Sony Playstation took home video gaming to a new level of sophistication, as did computer games in the 1990s and beyond. But before all of these games there was Pong, the start of the video game revolution.

—*Timothy Berg*

For More Information

Atari. http://www.atari.com (accessed March 27, 2002).

Clark, James I. *A Look Inside Video Games.* Milwaukee: Raintree Publishers, 1985.

Koerner, Brendan. "How Pong Invented Geekdom." *U.S. News & World Report* (December 27, 1999): p. 67.

Poole, Steven. *Trigger Happy: Videogames and the Entertainment Revolution.* New York: Arcade Publishers, 2000.

Winter, David. *PONG-Story.* http://www.pong-story.com/intro.htm (accessed March 28, 2002).

Video Games

The idea of interactive games played on a **television** (see entry under 1940s—TV and Radio in volume 3) screen is almost as old as TV itself, and video games have evolved as quickly as TV and computer technology have developed. The industry generated over $100 billion a year worldwide by 2000, as millions of gamers played at home, millions more at arcades, and millions more carried games with them on portable players. Though some parents and teachers complain that video games teach little except violence and inactivity, others insist that the games teach complex problem-solving skills and coordination. All in all, ever since the first game was marketed, video games have proven addictive for many players of all ages.

The first widely popular video game was **Pong** (see entry under 1970s—Sports and Games in volume 4), a simple ping-pong game with two lines, or "paddles," that could be moved to hit a "ball" back and forth across a television screen. Ralph Baer (1922–), a TV technician, first got the idea of adding interactive games to TV in 1966. However, it was Nolan Bushnell (1943–), later the president of Atari, who brought the new game Pong to the public, with a coin-operated arcade version. Pong was instantly popular, and a home version was soon available. By 1978, hundreds of video games were available, including the popular **Pac-Man** (see entry under 1980s—Sports and Games in volume 5). Americans spent $200 million that year on hardware and software for video games.

The mid-1980s saw a slump in video games, as players became bored with repetitive games. Interest picked up when a Japanese playing-card company called Nintendo entered the market with a faster processor that supported faster and more complex games. Their whimsical new game, Donkey Kong, along with other Nintendo offerings brought a new wave of video-game popularity. By 1989, thirty million Americans owned the new game technology. Other companies, like Mattel, Sega, and ID Software introduced competing game systems.

Games have continued to develop complexity, realism, and speed as the processors have grown from Nintendo's early 8-bit to 64-bit. Video games are now often designed for CD-ROM drives on computers or game boxes for TVs. The average age of game players has risen from seven in 1987 to seventeen in 1996. Some adults continue to worry that games take players' energy away from more active pursuits and that they encourage violence, as many games involve fighting and shooting. In 1994, video games began to be rated for content, after a controversy over the graphic violence of the game "Mortal Kombat." Shooting games continue to be popular however, in spite of parental worries about the gruesome fight scenes in games like "Kingpin," where players mow down groups of gangsters with highly realistic gunshots.

Some video games have taken realism a step further and have been made into films, such as 1994's *Mortal Kombat* and 2001's *Tomb Raider*.

—*Tina Gianoulis*

For More Information

Chance, Greg. "History of Home Video Games." *Videogames.org.* http://videogames.org/html (accessed March 28, 2002).

Hart, Sam. "A Brief History of Home Video Games." *Geekcomix.com.* http://www.geekcomix.com/vgh/ (accessed March 28, 2002).

Leland, John, and Devin Gordon, Anne Underwood, Tara Weingarten, and Ana Figueroa. "The Secret Life of Teens: Video Games, Music and Movies Alarm Adults." *Newsweek* (Vol. 133, iss. 19, May 10, 1999): pp. 44–45.

Poole, Steven. *Trigger Happy: Video Games and the Entertainment Revolution.* New York: Arcade Publishing, 2000.

Videotopia. http://www.videotopia.com (accessed March 28, 2002).

1970s
TV and Radio

To the surprise of many, the quality of commercial programming on television improved dramatically in the 1970s. Perhaps programmers were responding to complaints about the poor quality of TV in the 1960s, or they were trying to fill the void left by the decline of political and social activism. For a number of reasons, TV shows in the 1970s tackled some difficult social problems. These shows proved that the medium of television was capable of making a contribution to the national debate about social change. The 1970s also saw the emergence of cable TV, which offered Americans alternatives to the standard programming on the big three networks.

One of the most popular programs of the decade was *All in the Family* (1971–79). Set in a working-class household in the Bronx, the show provided a forum for the discussion of race, sexuality, and generational tensions—all while being laugh-out-loud funny. African Americans gained an increasing presence on TV. One of the most popular shows, *Sanford and Son* (1972–77), focused on the lives of a black junkyard dealer (played by comedian Redd Foxx, 1922–1991) and his son. Other popular shows featuring black actors included *Good Times* (1974–79) and *The Jeffersons* (1975–85). Americans came to terms with feminism and the career woman thanks to *The Mary Tyler Moore Show* (1970–77), whose lovable lead character made working women seem less threatening.

Although there were many quality shows dealing with important issues, TV also offered plenty of light-hearted, mindless entertainment. The networks had something for everyone. *Little House on the Prairie* (1974–83), *The Waltons* (1972–81), *Happy Days* (1974–84), and *Laverne & Shirley* (1976–83) provided a nostalgic look at days gone by. Americans tuned into *Charlie's Angels* (1976–81) and *Hawaii Five-O* (1968–80) for action. For sheer escapism, *Fantasy Island* (1978–84) and *The Love Boat* (1977–86) were the shows to watch. Perhaps the silliest show of the decade was *The Gong Show* (1976–80), hosted by Chuck Barris (1929–). Children also were increasingly offered new programs, including such shows as *The Brady Bunch* (1969–74) and a variety of Saturday morning cartoons.

Radio benefited from advanced technology during the decade. Up until this decade, most radio programs had come over the AM band. But as radio stations increasingly became oriented toward playing music, many stations took their signals to the FM band, which offered much higher sound quality. These FM stations soon became more daring, offering alternative music and more interesting programming. By the end of the decade, the FM band was dominant.

All in the Family
· ·

All in the Family was the most popular and most controversial television **sitcom** (see entry under 1950s–TV and Radio in volume 3) of the 1970s. The show commented on political and social issues never before mentioned in a prime-time sitcom, such as racial conflicts, women's liberation, and the **sexual revolution** (see entry under 1960s–The Way We Lived in volume 4). Produced by Norman Lear (1922–) and starring Carroll O'Connor (1924–2001) as Archie Bunker and Jean Stapleton (1923–) as his wife, Edith, the show debuted on January 12, 1971, and ran until 1979, when the show—with O'Connor only—became known as *Archie Bunker's Place*.

Based on a British sitcom called *Till Death Do Us Part, All in the Family* explored the generational conflicts within a blue-collar household during a period of rapid social change. *All in the Family*'s Archie Bunker was a middle-aged laborer living in a working-class neighborhood in New York City with his dutiful and ever-cheerful wife Edith, whom he nicknamed "dingbat." Edith was not "liberated"; she was a traditional housewife. Archie expected Edith to "stifle" herself—keep her thoughts to herself—and fetch him his nightly can of beer as he relaxed in his armchair. In one memorable episode, she stood her ground and refused to "stifle" herself—a bold statement that was applauded as a victory for the women's movement of the 1970s.

Sharing the house with Archie and Edith were their daughter Gloria, played by Sally Struthers (1948–), and her husband, a long-haired radical named Mike Stivic, played by Rob Reiner (1947–). Mike and Gloria represented the generation of liberal

American **baby boomers** (see entry under 1940s–The Way We Lived in volume 3) who came to maturity during the 1960s listening to **rock and roll** (see entry under 1950s–Music in volume 3) music, protesting the Vietnam War (1954–75), and supporting the **civil rights movement** (see entry under 1960s–The Way We Lived in volume 4) and the women's movement. In every episode, Archie berated his son-in-law for his "communist" or "pinko" sympathies, calling him "Meathead" and casting slurs on his Polish background. Mike would just as fiercely criticize Archie for his bigotry (complete belief in his own opinions and prejudices) and mindless patriotism. Another source of comedy was provided by the Bunkers' next-door neighbors, the Jeffersons, an African American family who were often the brunt of Archie's rants. Part of the show's appeal was that Archie and Edith, in spite of their narrow-mindedness, were never portrayed as purposely cruel characters, just ordinary people cramped by their social class and lack of exposure to the wider world. Indeed, there were occasional scenes that showed Archie's obvious love of and loyalty toward his family.

—*Edward Moran*

For More Information

Adler, Richard P. *All in the Family: A Critical Appraisal.* New York: Praeger, 1979.

Allinthefamilysit.com. http://www.allinthefamilysit.com/ (accessed March 28, 2002).

Marc, David. *Comic Visions: Television Comedy and American Culture.* Boston: Unwin Hyman, 1989.

McCrohan, Donna. *Archie & Edith, Mike & Gloria.* New York: Workman, 1987.

The Brady Bunch

From 1969 to 1974, a large, happy family known as *The Brady Bunch* dropped by millions of American homes one night a week. The popular **sitcom** (situation comedy; see entry under 1950s–TV and Radio in volume 3) about an architect, his wife, and their six children became an even bigger hit in syndicated reruns. An icon (a symbol) of 1970s culture, the "groovy" family comedy inspired two popular movies and numerous TV spin-offs, becoming one of the best-known American **television** (see entry under 1940s–TV and Radio in volume 3) properties worldwide.

Sherwood Schwartz (1916–), the creator of **Gilligan's Island** (1964–67; see entry under 1960s–TV and Radio in volume 4) developed *The Brady Bunch* after reading a newspaper report about the growing **divorce** (see entry under 1970s–The Way We Lived in volume 4) rate in America. Americans would tune in to see a new type of family show where the children were the product of different marriages, he reasoned, and convinced ABC to give the show a chance to crack its prime-time lineup in the fall of 1969. A catchy theme song set up the sitcom's premise: Architect Mike Brady, played by Robert Reed (1932–1992), a widower with three male children, marries Carol, played by Florence Henderson (1934–), a widow with three girls of her own. The family sets up house in the suburbs of Los Angeles, California. The newly constituted "bunch" must learn how to get along as a family and deal with everyday problems, from how to share phone and bathroom time to how to resolve issues of jealousy and competition. A wisecracking housekeeper, Alice, played by Ann B. Davis (1926–), was on hand to keep the active kids under control. The children were played by Barry Williams (1954–), Christopher Knight (1957–),

Mike Lookinland (1960–), Maureen McCormick (1956–), Eve Plumb (1958–), and Susan Olsen (1961–).

While never a ratings smash, *The Brady Bunch* remained on the air for five seasons and proved very popular among teenage viewers. Each of the children—Greg, Peter, Bobby, Marcia, Jan, and Cindy—developed a fan following and several even graced the covers of popular teen magazines. There were Brady lunch boxes, a board game, even a short-lived musical group inspired by the success of **The Partridge Family** (1970–74; see entry under 1970s—TV and Radio in volume 4). Despite its popularity with younger viewers, however, ABC canceled the show in 1974.

Cancellation proved to be a blessing in disguise, as *The Brady Bunch* became a cult favorite in syndication. The show was revived three times in different formats, with each lasting less than a full season—the first as a weirdly compelling variety hour in 1977, the second as a sitcom focusing only on Marcia and Jan in 1981, and the third as an awkward drama in 1990. A highly rated Christmas TV movie ran in 1988. Finally, in 1995 came *The Brady Bunch Movie,* the first of two critically acclaimed films featuring an all-new cast. Many years after its debut, the show continues to attract new viewers worldwide through its regular exposure on the cable nostalgia channels TV Land and Nick at Nite.

—Robert E. Schnakenberg

For More Information

The Brady Bunch Network. http://www.nitscape.com/ (accessed March 27, 2002).

Moran, Elizabeth. *Bradymania! Everything You Always Wanted To Know— and a Few Things You Probably Didn't.* New York: Adams, 1994.

Rubino, Anthony. *Life Lessons from the Bradys.* New York: Penguin, 1995.

Stoddard, Sylvia. *TV Treasures: A Companion Guide to the Brady Bunch.* New York: Forge, 1996.

Williams, Barry. *Growing Up Brady: I Was a Teenage Greg.* New York: Harper Perennial, 1992.

Winans, Wendy. *Brady World.* http://www.bradyworld.com/ (accessed March 27, 2002).

Cable TV

By the early 1950s, **television** (see entry under 1940s—TV and Radio in volume 3) was becoming a major force in the way

Americans spent their leisure time. But there were large areas of the country where TV and **radio** (see entry under 1920s–TV and Radio in volume 2) reception was poor or non-existent. Many people in these mostly rural areas wanted TV. The three big networks—ABC, CBS, and NBC—wanted them to become viewers because the bigger the audience, the more money advertisers would pay for airtime. Cable TV was the answer, but in the 1950s and 1960s, the Federal Communications Commission (FCC) restricted the growth of cable networks. The FCC feared that if the big networks moved in, local TV and radio stations would be forced out of business. When in 1972 the FCC allowed **satellite** (see entry under 1950s–The Way We Lived in volume 3) broadcasts to be distributed on the cable networks, Time Warner's Home Box Office (HBO) was the first on the scene. Within four years, cable TV had become widely available across the country. When the rules were relaxed again in 1992, the big TV networks finally took over. American cable TV in the twenty-first century is controlled by a handful of global media corporations.

Cable TV began with Community Antennae Television (CATV) in the 1950s. The system involved each town building a single large antenna to pick up broadcasts from great distances away. Cables then carried the signal to homes in the local area. In this way, isolated communities could receive nationally broadcast TV shows. Radio was also cabled into homes, where it was heard through the speaker on the TV set. By the mid–1970s, the CATV system could not cope with demand. Cable companies quickly realized that by charging a monthly subscription fee they could cover the cost of laying cable to connect as many homes as possible to the network. People were willing to pay for better picture quality and dozens of channels. The subscription also gave cable companies some freedom to show nudity, violence, and "bad" language.

The effect of cable TV on American culture is difficult to judge. Early cable broadcasts were mainly old **Hollywood** (see entry under 1930s–Film and Theater in volume 2) movies and repeats of shows such as *I Love Lucy* (1951–57; see entry under 1950s–TV and Radio in volume 3) and *Three Stooges* (see entry under 1930s–Film and Theater in volume 2) shorts. This meant that kids growing up in the 1970s were knowledgeable about TV culture of the previous twenty years. Unfortunately, many of them learned very little else. In the 1970s, TV overtook reading as the main source of information for Americans. As it became more dominant, many Americans actually became less informed about the world around them. But not everybody wanted a diet of old TV show reruns and Hollywood movies. By the 1980s, the big cable companies knew they had to create their own shows. They also knew that the best way to attract advertisers was to have specialized channels.

Of all the specialized channels that appeared in the 1980s, **MTV** (see entry under 1980s–Music in volume 5) has probably made the greatest impact. By adding pictures to the music and creating "videos," MTV revolutionized the **pop music** (see entry under 1940s–Music in volume 3) industry and threatened local radio stations. Such stars as **Madonna** (see entry under 1980s–Music in volume 5) owe their iconic status to the non-stop plugging of their music on MTV. Young audiences have followed MTV's lead since it began in 1981. They have become fans of **grunge** and even **Britney Spears** (see these entries under 1990s–Music in volume 5) thanks to MTV. MTV's success was followed by other specialist cable channels such as the Weather Channel, Court TV, the Discovery Channel, and Comedy Central. **CNN** (Cable News Network; see entry under 1980s–TV and Radio in volume 5) has become the world's top twenty-four-hour news source. All of this has been good news for advertisers, but some critics doubt whether viewers have benefitted. Since very few companies own all the channels, the amount of choice is not as great as it seems. Meanwhile, TV news has been accused of avoiding stories that reflect badly on advertisers or the networks themselves.

The arrival of the World Wide Web in the 1990s created another use for the TV cables. Unlike telephone cable, TV cables allow huge amounts of data to be exchanged at high speed. Because the cables were already in place, the United States led the world in home access to the **Internet** (see entry under 1990s–The Way We Lived in volume 5) in the 1990s. In the twenty-first century, cable subscribers can watch TV, surf the Internet, send **e-mail** (see entry under 1990s–The Way We Lived in volume 5), and use the telephone all at the same time. TV itself is changing rapidly. With the right equipment, viewers can pause live TV shows, watch "pay-per-view" sports events or concerts, and even "edit" the broadcasts they watch. Cable TV and its spin-off technologies have brought entertainment, drama, and information into millions of American homes. The big challenge facing cable TV companies in the twenty-first century is how to improve the quality of the shows and services they offer.

—Chris Routledge

For More Information

Baker, William F., and George Dessart. *Down the Tube: An Inside Account of the Failure of American Television.* New York: Basic Books, 1998.

Stark, Steven D. *Glued to the Set: The 60 Television Shows and Events that Made Us Who We Are Today.* New York: Free Press, 1997.

Whittemore, Hank. *CNN: The Inside Story.* Boston: Little, Brown, 1990.

CB Radio

The Citizens Band (CB) **radio** (see entry under 1920s–TV and Radio in volume 2) service was established in 1947 by the Federal Communications Commission (FCC), which in 1958 opened up part of the amateur-radio band to enable anyone to engage in free mobile communication over about a ten-mile radius. A typical CB radio setup included a microphone, a speaker, and a control box that could be easily installed and used without the more sophisticated technical skills of an amateur-radio, or ham, operator. The service did not come into widespread popular use until the mid-1970s, when a CB craze swept the nation, popularized by long-haul truck drivers. The truck drivers used the devices to communicate with fellow drivers about traffic conditions and police activity. A trucker's CB Radio also eased the loneliness of being on the road.

Citizens Band radio became popular during a period of social and political turmoil in the United States. The Vietnam War (1954–75) was ending, the Watergate scandal was at full boil, and the oil boycotts of the Organization of the Petroleum Exporting Countries (OPEC) were driving up the price of gasoline. In this environment, CB radio emerged as a popular grassroots forum, a way for the common people to discuss what was important to them. The CB radio offered an easy way for anonymous users to vent their frustrations with the controversies of the day. It also was a kind of forerunner of **talk radio** (see entry under 1980s–TV and Radio in volume 5), the **cellular telephone** (see entry under 1990s–The Way We Lived in volume 5), and the computer **chat room** (see entry under 1990s–The Way We Lived in volume 5).

CB users typically adopted a handle (a nickname) by which they identified themselves. They quickly developed a colorful language that included words like "Smokey" to describe a highway-patrol officer, "wrapper" to describe an unmarked police

car, "negatory" for "no," and "10-4" for "message received." Foul language and explicit sexual talk was officially prohibited, though conversations were often filled with risqué hints.

The CB radio craze of the 1970s helped popularize a "trucker culture" in the United States, in which the long-haul driver was admired for representing the rugged individualism required for being out on the open road. During the period, films like *Smokey and the Bandit* (1977), *Citizens Band* (1977), and *Convoy* (1978) testified to the CB's popularity. *Convoy* was inspired by a novelty song by C. W. McCall (1928–) that reached number one on the *Billboard* charts in 1976. The song described a truck driver, known by his CB handle of "Rubber Duck," who organizes a nationwide, bumper-to-bumper gathering of tractor-trailers.

—*Edward Moran*

For More Information

Dillis, Lanie. *The "Official" CB Slanguage Language Dictionary, Including Cross References.* New York: L. J. Martin, 1977.

Using the handle (nickname) "Daisy Mae," a woman uses the CB Radio in her car. *Bettmann/Corbis. Reproduced by permission.*

Hicks, David E. *Citizens Band Radio Handbook.* 5th ed. Indianapolis: H. W. Sams, 1976.

Lieberman, Jethro Koller, and Neil S. Rhodes. *The Complete CB Handbook.* New York: D. McCay Co., 1976.

The Truckers Place. http://www.thetruckersplace.com (accessed March 28, 2002.)

Charlie's Angels

Charlie's Angels (1976–81) was a smash-hit **television** (see entry under 1940s—TV and Radio in volume 3) series with a surefire formula. In a nod to the feminism of the era, it featured three tough, no-nonsense women who were anything but submissive in their roles as crime-fighting detectives. Detective roles were then usually played by men on both the big and small screens. At the same time, these Angels were no women's liberation icons. They were glamorous, beautiful sex objects who frequently found themselves garbed in short shorts or bikinis as they headed off to sunny climates to complete their assignments.

Charlie's Angels, broadcast on ABC, won major stardom for its three original leads. Kate Jackson (1948–), the most experienced actress of the trio, was cast as the calm, cool, and intellectual Sabrina Duncan. Farrah Fawcett-Majors (1946–) played athletic Jill Munroe. Jaclyn Smith (1947–) was cast as streetwise Kelly Garrett. Fawcett-Majors quickly emerged as the show's most marketable commodity. America fell in love with her toothy smile and abundant blonde hair, and a poster of her garbed in a bathing suit was a hot seller. Fawcett-Majors left the show in 1977 after just one season, and was followed by Jackson two years later. Their replacements were Cheryl Ladd (1951–), playing Jill's kid sister Kris, and Shelley Hack (1952–), who left in 1980 and was replaced by Tanya Roberts (1955–). John Forsythe (1918–) was heard but not seen as the voice of Charlie Townsend, the Angels' boss, who phoned them their assignment at the start of each episode. David Doyle (1925–1997) played John Bosley, Charlie's aide, who was on hand to assist the Angels.

The Angels usually found themselves working undercover. In order to sniff out a killer, foil a kidnapping plot, or bust a drug-smuggling ring, they might masquerade as military recruits, playmate centerfolds, marathon runners, fashion models, student nurses, or convicts. The titles of quite a few episodes

revealed the locales to which they would be dispatched: "Island Angels"; "Angels at Sea"; "The Mexican Connection"; "The Vegas Connection"; "Angels in Paradise." But the series' underlying lowbrow quality is best exhibited by the titles of other episodes: "Pom Pom Angels"; "Disco Angels"; "Angels on Wheels"; "Angels in Chains."

Charlie's Angels was one of dozens of vintage hit TV series to be recycled into feature films decades after the airings of their final episodes. The *Charlie's Angels* film (2000) featured three attractive young stars of a new generation, Drew Barrymore (1975–), Cameron Diaz (1972–), and Lucy Liu (1967–), and involved them in a scheme to foil a kidnapping plot.

—*Rob Edelman*

Farrah Fawcett-Majors (left), Kate Jackson, and Jaclyn Smith starred as beautiful detectives in the television show *Charlie's Angels. AP/Wide World Photos. Reproduced by permission.*

For More Information

"Charlies' Angels." *Screen Gem Network.* http://www.spe.sony.com/tv/shows/sgn/ca (accessed March 28, 2002).

Hofstede, David, and Jack Condon. *The Charlie's Angels Casebook.* Beverly Hills, CA: Pomegranate Press, 2000.

Pingel, Mike, ed. *Angelic Heaven*. http://www.charliesangels.com (accessed March 28, 2002).

The Dukes of Hazzard

From 1979 through 1985, millions of Americans tuned in to CBS on Friday nights to view a fantasy slice of Southern country life on one of the nation's highest rated shows, *The Dukes of Hazzard*. The comedy featured exaggerated Southern accents, tooth-rattling car chases, and comic stereotypes of good and evil. Sandwiched between *The Incredible Hulk* (1978–82) and **Dallas** (1978–91; see entry under 1980s–TV and Radio in volume 5), *The Dukes of Hazzard* drew huge audiences of loyal fans. Even in 2001, sixteen years after its cancellation, *The Dukes of Hazzard* still thrives in reruns.

With its simple, silly plots and wholesome values, *The Dukes of Hazzard* was a counterpoint to the seriousness of politically radical culture of the late 1960s and 1970s and issue-oriented comedies like **All in the Family** (1971–79; see entry under 1970s–TV and Radio in volume 4). The stars of the show were three young adult cousins, Luke (Tom Wopat, 1951–), Bo (John Schneider, 1960–), and Daisy Duke (Catherine Bach, 1954–). The cousins lived with their crusty old uncle, Jesse (Denver Pyle, 1920–1997). The two Duke boys—described in the show's opening song as "just some good ol' boys, never meanin' no harm"— were hell-raisers who clearly represented the forces of good. Daisy Duke is best remembered for the short-short denim cut-offs she wore on every show. Each show found the Dukes caught up in a good-natured battle with the forces of evil in Georgia's Hazzard County, represented by the corrupt Boss Hogg (Sorrell Booke, 1930–1994) and the hopelessly inept Sheriff Roscoe P. Coltrane (James Best, 1926–). The other major personality on the show was the Duke boys' car, the General Lee, a bright orange 1969 Dodge Charger with a Confederate flag painted on its roof. The hero of at least three dramatic chase scenes each episode, the General Lee has its own fan clubs. Several Web sites offer instructions for building a copy of the car.

CBS has produced two *Dukes of Hazzard* reunion films, one in 1997, and one in 2001. Critics hated the films, but loyal fans tuned in happily to catch up with their old friends in the uncomplicated world of Hazzard County.

—Tina Gianoulis

For More Information

Anderson, Gary. *Gary's Dukes of Hazzard Page*. http://hazzard.simplenet. com (accessed March 28, 2002)

Bigonesse, Ray. *Ray's Dukes of Hazzard Page*. http://www.ghg.net/ rbigoness/hazzard.html (accessed March 28, 2002).

Davidson, Bill. "Crackup in Hazzard County! Here's the Casualty Report." *TV Guide* (December 25, 1982): pp. 12–16.

Gritten, David. "Southern Hospitality (and Politics) Gives *The Dukes of Hazzard* an Old Kentucky Home." *People Weekly* (October 12, 1981): pp. 54–57.

Schneider, John. "Dukes of Hazzard." *John Schneider's Official Website*. http://www.boduke.com/dukes_of_hazzard_contents.htm (accessed March 28, 2002).

ESPN

• •

The Entertainment and Sports Programming Network is more commonly known as ESPN. The popular cable sports-television network has been entertaining viewers with sports highlights, game telecasts, and commentary since 1979. It has grown from a tiny operation based in Bristol, Connecticut, to a worldwide media empire that includes multiple **cable-TV** (see entry under 1970s–TV and Radio in volume 4) channels, a **radio** (see entry under 1920s–TV and Radio in volume 2) network, a Web site, books, a magazine, and even theme restaurants bearing the ESPN logo.

Few believed that ESPN could succeed when it started broadcasting in 1979. In those early days, the network carried little-known sports like lacrosse and Australian football as well as exotic events like tractor pulls and strongman competitions. However, it steadily enlarged its audience throughout the early 1980s. In 1987, ESPN secured the rights to telecast **National Football League** (NFL; see entry under 1920s–Sports and Games in volume 2) games on Sunday nights. The deal allowed the network to bring in much-needed advertising money and increased its standing among hard-core sports fans. Also contributing to ESPN's growth was the popularity of its signature sports-news show *SportsCenter*. The program, which ran several times a day, mixed highlights with humor in the form of wisecracking anchors like Keith Olbermann (1959–) and Dan Patrick (1956–). Those two were among the first anchors to include comical catchphrases in their sports highlight narration: "En fuego" indicated an athlete who was "on fire" and "He put the biscuit in the basket" described a player who had just scored.

By the 1990s, ESPN had become *the* place to catch up on the latest sports developments, especially for young viewers. In addition to football, ESPN began producing live telecasts of major-league **baseball** (see entry under 1900s–Sports and Games in volume 1), college basketball, and professional hockey games. *SportsCenter* introduced a rotating list of hosts, each with his or her own catchphrase, from Stuart Scott (1965–), who barked "Boo ya!" every time something exciting happened, to the sarcastic Craig Kilborn (1962–), who went on to host his own late-night talk show. By 1996, the cable channel had grown so popular that it launched its own magazine, *ESPN the Magazine* to compete with **Sports Illustrated** (see entry under 1950s–Sports and Games in volume 3). New channels, like ESPN2 and ESPN Classic, were added to contain the overflow of sports programming that viewers demanded. Although some critics blamed ESPN for "dumbing down" sports coverage with its fixation on "attitude" and repetitive catchphrases, few could deny that the all-sports network was the dominant force in sports **television** (see entry under 1940s–TV and Radio in volume 3) at the dawn of the new century.

—*Robert E. Schnakenberg*

For More Information

ESPN. http://espn.go.com/main.html (accessed March 28, 2002).

Freeman, Michael. *ESPN: The Uncensored History.* Dallas: Taylor Publishing, 2000.

Olbermann, Keith, and Dan Patrick. *The Big Show.* Garden City, NY: Pocket Books, 1998.

Youngblut, Shelley, ed. *The Quotable ESPN.* New York: Hyperion, 1998.

Fantasy Island

"De plane! De plane!" With those famous words, French actor Hervé Villechaize (1943–1993) announced the arrival of a new planeload of celebrity guest stars each week on ABC's *Fantasy Island.* The imaginative drama series ran from 1978 to 1984. It was briefly revived with an all-new cast in 1998. The show, which mixed elements of romance and the supernatural, was the perfect complement to ABC's other Saturday night ratings powerhouse, **The Love Boat** (1977–86; see entry under 1970s–TV and Radio in volume 4).

Both programs were produced by Aaron Spelling (1923–), the legendary creator of **Charlie's Angels** (1976–81; see entry under

1970s—TV and Radio in volume 4) and *The Mod Squad* (1968–73), who would go on to record hits with *Dynasty* (1981–89) and *Beverly Hills, 90210* (1990–2000). For *Fantasy Island,* Spelling cast Latin actor Ricardo Montalban (1920–) in the lead role of Mr. Roarke, the suave proprietor of a tropical resort where visitors come to have their fantasies made real. Clad in an all-white suit and speaking in riddles, Montalban brought an air of mystery to the juicy part. Joining him for most of the show's run was short-statured Villechaize, in the role of Tattoo, Roarke's faithful, if mischievous, attendant. The strange pair defied all the rules of prime-time stardom, yet their banter became a large part of the show's success. Even with his thick accent and unconventional appearance, Villechaize became a pop icon.

Imaginative plots also contributed to *Fantasy Island's* popularity. Each week, a new set of guest stars would show up on the island wanting to live out their fantasies. A homely woman might long to be beautiful, for instance, or a compulsive gambler might wish for one big jackpot. Most fantasies did not turn out as the people had hoped. They came to realize by the show's end that they should have been content with their life as it was. Like *The Millionaire* and, to a lesser extent, *The Love Boat, Fantasy Island* allowed viewers to live out their own fantasies through the characters on the show. For much of its run, *Fantasy Island* scored among the top twenty-five shows in the TV ratings and helped revive ABC's sagging Saturday night lineup.

The quality of the show declined after Villechaize left to pursue other ventures in 1983 (and to battle his personal demons, often related to health problems associated with his size—he committed suicide in 1993). Canceled by the network in 1984, *Fantasy Island* returned in 1998, this time with British actor Malcolm McDowell (1943–) in the role of Roarke. Darker and more disturbing than the previous version, the new series failed to catch on with viewers and was canceled after one season.

—*Robert E. Schnakenberg*

Ricardo Montalban (left) and Hervé Villechaize in a scene from the television series *Fantasy Island. AP/Wide World Photos. Reproduced by permission.*

For More Information

McNeil, Alex. *Total Television.* New York: Penguin, 1996.
Spelling, Aaron, and Jefferson Graham. *Aaron Spelling: A Prime-Time Life.* New York: St. Martin's Press, 1996.

The Gong Show

The Gong Show, which aired from 1976 until 1980, was one of the most bizarre programs ever to appear on **television** (see entry under 1940s—TV and Radio in volume 3). Created by producer Chuck Barris (1929–), the **game show** (see entry under 1950s—TV and Radio in volume 3) offered viewers a satire on traditional talent competitions. Occasionally, the series was a showcase for legitimate amateur talent, but more often it presented acts that were revolting, intentionally awful, or just plain weird.

During the 1960s, Barris had achieved great success as the executive producer of television's *The Dating Game* and *The Newlywed Game.* These programs drew much of their humor from the embarrassing comments made by contestants. In *The Gong Show,* Barris extended his popular blend of competition and humiliation by having terrible acts perform before celebrities in a talent contest. Each episode followed an established format: amateur entertainers had two minutes to perform before three celebrity judges who could immediately end the performance by banging a huge gong. Often, no winner could be determined as the celebrities "gonged" every act in an episode. Those who did survive the full two minutes were then rated by the panel from zero to ten, for a possible total of thirty points. The act with the highest score would receive a Golden Gong trophy and a check for either $516.32 (in the show's daytime version) or $712.05 (nighttime).

American television viewers had never seen "talent" like the performers who appeared on every episode of *The Gong Show.* Typical acts included "Professor Flamo," a man who sang out in pain while lowering his hand onto a candle flame; a man who broke eggs over his head while making faces through a sheet of Plexiglas; and an assortment of zany singers and dancers. One of the most popular recurring performers was "Gene Gene the Dancing Machine" (Gene Patton), an actual stagehand who danced while the audience threw various items at him. The celebrity panel varied each episode and included

Jaye P. Morgan (1931–), Jamie Farr (1934–), Rip Taylor (1934–), **David Letterman** (1947–; see entry under 1980s–TV and Radio in volume 5), Steve Martin (1945–), Arte Johnson (1929–), and Phyllis Diller (1917–).

NBC canceled *The Gong Show* in 1978 after it had become too risqué and extreme. It continued in syndication until 1980. That same year, Barris directed *The Gong Show Movie,* but audiences had grown tired of Barris and his wacky amateurs. A short-lived revival with Don Bleu as host failed in 1988. Barris's version of the series can still be seen on The Game Show Network. *The Gong Show* was gross, crude, raunchy, lowbrow—and loved by audiences.

—*Charles Coletta*

For More Information

Barris, Chuck. *Confessions of a Dangerous Mind: An Unauthorized Biography.* New York: St. Martin's Press, 1984.

Barris, Chuck. *The Game Show King: A Confession.* New York: Carroll & Graf, 1993.

DeLong, Thomas. *Quiz Craze: America's Infatuation with Game Shows.* New York: Praeger, 1991.

"The Gong Show." *Yesterdayland.* http://www.yesterdayland.com/popopedia/shows/primetime/pt1317.php (accessed March 28, 2002).

Happy Days

The **sitcom** (situation comedy; see entry under 1950s–TV and Radio in volume 3) *Happy Days,* which aired on ABC from 1974 until 1984, offered **television** (see entry under 1940s–TV and Radio in volume 3) viewers a nostalgic look at the 1950s. Created by Garry Marshall (1934–), the series was filled with iconic images (images that become symbols) of that earlier decade. Such images include poodle skirts, leather jackets, and **hot rods** (see entry under 1940s–The Way We Lived in volume 3). **Rock and roll** (see entry under 1950s–Music in volume 3) provided the soundtrack to these images, of course. Originally, *Happy Days* focused on a Milwaukee high-school student named Richie Cunningham (Ron Howard, 1954–) and his family. However, the program's focus shifted over the seasons to concentrate on a previously minor character named Arthur "Fonzie" Fonzarelli (Henry Winkler, 1945–). "The Fonz" was the personification of "cool." He possessed an almost supernatural ability to attract women, was a master mechanic, and hid his sensitive side under a tough-guy exterior.

When *Happy Days* premiered in 1974, in addition to Howard and Winkler, the cast consisted of Tom Bosley (1927–) and Marion Ross (1928–) as Richie's parents, Howard and Marion Cunningham; and Erin Moran (1961–) as Richie's sister, Joanie. Richie had two best friends, Ralph Malph (Donny Most, 1953–), and Potsie Weber (Anson Williams, 1949–). The gang spent most of their time hanging out at Arnold's restaurant. To provide some contrast to his bland, middle-class "white bread" characters, Marshall added Fonzie, a greasy-haired, leather-jacketed, motorcycle-riding dropout, to the cast. Although network executives initially feared Fonzie was too threatening, viewers quickly responded to the character. Henry Winkler became a major celebrity, and The Fonz's trademark thumbs-up gesture and "Aaaaaayyyyyy" sound of approval became symbols of the 1950s culture. Fonzie was such a cultural icon that his leather jacket was enshrined in the Smithsonian Institution.

Happy Days evolved over the years as the characters aged. Richie and his pals moved from high school to college and

"Fonzie" merged into the mainstream. No longer the prototypical hood, "Fonzie" became a businessman and in the show's final seasons was Dean of Boys at the George S. Patton Vocational School. Winkler and the series' writers had transformed "The Fonz" into a good role model for the character's legion of young fans. When "Fonzie" got a library card in one episode, millions of children did likewise the following week.

The success of *Happy Days* made Gary Marshall one of the most prolific TV producers during the 1970s. Two of his other hits included *Laverne & Shirley* and *Mork & Mindy,* both spin-offs of *Happy Days.* In 1982, *Joanie Loves Chachi,* which featured the misadventures of Richie's sister and Fonzie's cousin, was short-lived. *Happy Days* reruns continue to draw viewers who respond to its nostalgic attitude toward the 1950s and the magnetic presence of The Fonz.

—*Charles Coletta*

For More Information

Davidson, Ben. *The Official Fonzie Scrapbook*. New York: Grosset & Dunlap, 1978.

Green, Jonathon. *The Fonz & Henry Winkler*. New York: Castle Books, 1978.

"Happy Days Online." *Sitcoms Online*. http://www.sitcomsonline.com/happydays.html (accessed March 28, 2002).

International Happy Days Fan Club. http://www.happydaysfanclub.com/ (accessed March 28, 2002).

Kramer, Barbara. *Ron Howard: Child Star & Hollywood Director*. Springfield, NJ: Enslow Publishers, 1998.

Mitz, Rick. *The Great TV Sitcom Book*. New York: Marek Publishers, 1983.

Taylor, Ella. *Prime Time Families: Television Culture in Postwar America*. Berkeley: University of California Press, 1989.

Hee Haw

With its mix of country and western music and down-home humor, *Hee Haw* was one of American television's most popular variety series in the 1970s and 1980s. It was the first and most popular show about southern rural America.

Hee Haw debuted on CBS in 1969 as a spin-off of the network's *Jonathan Winters Show*. Producers believed that a variety half-hour centered around southern rural themes would appeal to the same audience that watched *Green Acres* and **The Beverly Hillbillies** (see entry under 1960s–TV and Radio in volume 4). The cohosts of *Hee Haw* were Roy Clark (1933–) and Buck Owens (1929–), both veteran **country music** (see entry under 1940s–Music in volume 3) musicians with comedic experience. An animated donkey appeared on a regular basis to react to the humor and to provide the "hee haw" of the title.

The show featured a regular company of comic actors and musicians, including Louis "Grandpa" Jones (1913–1998), Alvin "Junior" Samples (1926–1983), and George "Goober" Lindsay (1935–). One of the most popular performers on *Hee Haw* was Minnie Pearl (1912–1996), a brassy country matron who always wore a hat with a price tag hanging off it. Her trademark whoop, "How-DEEEEEE," became one of the signatures of *Hee Haw*'s twenty-three-year run.

Pearl and the other regulars provided the comedy in the form of sketches. In addition, some of the biggest names in country music, including Johnny Cash (1932–), Merle Haggard (1937–), Tammy Wynette (1942–1998), and Boxcar Willie (1931–1999), took to the *Hee Haw* stage to perform before national audiences. In this way, *Hee Haw* helped to popularize country music and laid the groundwork for its explosion into mainstream American music in the 1990s. In the later years of *Hee Haw,* many of the genre's new breed of superstars, including Garth Brooks (1962–) and Randy Travis (1959–), made their national TV debuts on the trailblazing program.

A ratings smash from the start, *Hee Haw* nevertheless faced cancellation after only two full seasons, when CBS decided to cancel all its rural programs in favor of urban comedies like *All in the Family* (see entry under 1970s–TV and Radio in volume 4). However, the popularity of *Hee Haw* could not be denied. The show continued to flourish in first-run syndication. It even spun off an all-female version, *Hee Haw Honeys,* in 1978 that costarred Kathy Lee Gifford (1953–). Though declining ratings eventually forced Clark and company to shut down the beloved "Kornfield" in 1992, *Hee Haw* remains popular in reruns. Its unique blend of country-life comedy and good-time music may never be duplicated.

—*Robert E. Schnakenberg*

For More Information

Clark, Roy, and Marc Eliot. *My Life—In Spite of Myself.* New York: Pocket Books, 1995.

Lovullo, Sam, and Marc Eliot. *Life in the Kornfield: My 25 Years at Hee Haw.* New York: Boulevard Books, 1996.

Little House on the Prairie

Most books, films, and **television** (see entry under 1940s–TV and Radio in volume 3) programs set on the nineteenth-century American prairie feature gunfights and conflict, battles between cowboys and Indians, hostility between land barons or cattle rustlers and honest, hard-working settlers. One exception is *Little House on the Prairie* (1974–83), one of the top-rated TV series of the 1970s. As with the equally popular the *Waltons* (1972–81; see entry under 1970s–TV and Radio in volume 4), *Little House on the Prairie* was set during an earlier era in American history. Like *The Waltons,* it centered on a loving, old-fashioned family whose members are forced to struggle for survival in difficult times. Many of its storylines were based on those recounted in a series of books written by Laura Ingalls Wilder (1867–1957), in which she recalled her own experiences coming of age on the American frontier. The books, published

The Ingalls family conquered the American frontier and American audiences on *Little House on the Prairie*. The core cast was (left to right) Melissa Gilbert, Michael Landon, Karen Grassle, and Melissa Sue Anderson. *Fotos International/Archive Photos. Reproduced by permission.*

between 1932 and 1943, are known as the "Little House" books. The series' episodes were told from Laura's point of view and included narration by her character.

The father in *Little House on the Prairie* is Charles Ingalls (Michael Landon, 1937–1991), a homesteader who works his small farm in Walnut Grove, Minnesota. At the outset, he is seen with his wife, Caroline (Karen Grassle, 1944–) and three daughters: Mary (Melissa Sue Anderson, 1962–); Laura (Melissa Gilbert, 1964–); and Carrie (alternately played by twins Lindsay and Sidney Greenbush, 1970–). The Ingalls clan must contend with the ravages of nature, which constantly wreck their crops. They mix with the various Walnut Grove townsfolk. The Ingalls parents also deal with the dilemmas of their growing children. In a contemporary, family-oriented TV program, those problems might involve sex and drugs, but in the wholesome *Little House on the Prairie,* they include Mary's losing her eyesight, and Mary's and Laura's growing up, falling in love, and marrying.

As the series evolved, Charles and Caroline Ingalls take in various orphans and briefly move to the Dakota Territory before returning to Walnut Grove. When Landon—who also was the show's executive producer and sometime writer-director—chose to leave the series in 1982, its title was changed to *Little House: A New Beginning*. It lasted only one season. The series, which had originated as a 1974 made-for-TV movie, was followed by three TV movie sequels: *Little House: Look Back to Yesterday* (1983); *Little House: Bless All the Dear Children* (1983); and *Little House: The Last Farewell* (1984).

—Rob Edelman

For More Information

Anderson, William. *Laura Ingalls Wilder: A Biography.* New York: HarperCollins, 1992.

Anderson, William. *Pioneer Girl: The Story of Laura Ingalls Wilder.* New York: HarperCollins, 1998.

Erisman, Fred. *Laura Ingalls Wilder.* Boise, ID: Boise State University, 1994.

Glasscock, Sarah. *Laura Ingalls Wilder: An Author's Story.* Austin, TX: Steck-Vaughn, 1998.

Hines, Stephen W. *I Remember Laura: Laura Ingalls Wilder.* Nashville: T. Nelson Publishers, 1994.

Miller, John E. *Becoming Laura Ingalls Wilder: The Woman Behind the Legend.* Columbia: University of Missouri Press, 1998.

Raatma, Lucy. *Laura Ingalls Wilder: Teacher and Writer.* Chicago: Ferguson Publishers, 2001.

The Love Boat

The Love Boat, which aired on ABC from 1977 until 1986, offered **television** (see entry under 1940s—TV and Radio in volume 3) viewers a mixture of romance, light comedy, exotic locations, and celebrities. Producer Aaron Spelling (1928–) crafted the hour-long anthology series. Each week, the show interwove three romantic plots occurring on the fictional *Pacific Princess* cruise ship. A cast of recurring actors portrayed the ship's crew while an assortment of Hollywood legends, has-beens, and up-and-comers were featured as the ship's celebrity passengers. Critics dismissed *The Love Boat* as TV at its most average in quality, but audiences enjoyed the fluffy program. They made it a permanent part of their Saturday-night viewing for nearly a decade.

The Love Boat was originally based on a novel by Jeraldine Saunders, a former cruise-ship director. The crew of the *Pacific*

Princess was played by a blend of veteran and younger performers: Gavin MacLeod (1930–) starred as Captain Merrill Stubing; Bernie Kopell (1933–) was the ship's physician, Adam "Doc" Bricker; Lauren Tewes (1954–) was perky cruise director Julie McCoy; Fred Grandy (1948–) played purser "Gopher" Smith, who looked after the comfort and well-being of the passengers; and Ted Lange (1948–) was the bartender, Isaac Washington. Every week the crew welcomed several celebrity guests. Often, legendary Hollywood icons like Lana Turner (1921–1995) and Alice Faye (1915–1998) would be lured onto the show with the promise of a free luxury cruise to one of the series' exotic locations. Artist Andy Warhol (1928–1987), who coined the famous idea that in the future everyone would be famous for fifteen minutes, was the perfect guest for the program's two hundredth episode in 1985.

Plots on *The Love Boat* were simplistic and emphasized amusing comedy rather than engaging storylines. The series' format remained unchanged throughout its run and the cast remained relatively stable. By the mid-1980s, however, the program's luster had begun to fade, and the series was canceled in 1986. Still, *The Love Boat* was not completely sunk. The cast reunited for several TV specials and the series thrives in syndication. In 1998, a new version of the program, *Love Boat: The Next Wave,* was short-lived.

–*Charles Coletta*

For More Information

"The Love Boat." *Yesterdayland.* http://www.yesterdayland.com/popopedia/shows/primetime/pt1196.php (accessed March 28, 2002).

Portes, Rick. *The Love Boat: Unofficial Home Page.* http://www.loveboatonline. com/ (accessed March 28, 2002).

Saunders, Jeraldine. *The Love Boat (Collector's Edition).* St. Paul, MN: Llewellyn Publications, 1998.

Spelling, Aaron, with Jefferson Graham. *Aaron Spelling: A Prime-Time Life.* New York: St. Martin's Press, 1996.

Wallace, David. "Once Slated for Dry Dock, The Love Boat Cruises Boozily into Its Ninth Nautical Season." *People Weekly* (April 15, 1985): p. 130.

The Mary Tyler Moore Show

The Mary Tyler Moore Show (1970–77) was one of the most beloved and enduring television **sitcoms** (situation comedies;

Mary Tyler Moore, shown here with Ted Knight, starred as the independent and eternally optimistic Mary Richards on *The Mary Tyler Moore Show*. *Fotos International/Archive Photos, Inc. Reproduced by permission.*

see entry under 1950s–TV and Radio in volume) of its era. The show, which aired on CBS, was more than just a clever, entertaining hit series. Its popularity paralleled the rise of the feminist movement in the United States during the early and mid-1970s. The show's primary character, Mary Richards, played by star Mary Tyler Moore (1936–), was a popular-culture icon, a symbol for the times. She was a character who had never before been seen on **television** (see entry under 1940s–TV and Radio in volume 3): a single professional woman who was career-oriented and independent-minded. Unlike her predecessors, Mary was not man-hungry. She was not out to wed the first respectable male who asked her. Mary Richards lived on her own and was determined to shape her life on her own.

Prior to *The Mary Tyler Moore Show*, single women on TV sitcoms usually had one goal in life: marriage. *Our Miss Brooks* (1952–56), *Private Secretary* (1953–57), and *The Gale Storm Show* (1956–60; also known as *Oh, Susannah*) featured unmarried women whose lives centered around their boyfriends or potential romantic partners and their quests for wedding rings. Although the wanna-be actress heroine of *That Girl* (1966–71) may have been career-oriented, she also had a regular boyfriend, to whom she became engaged before the series ran its course. Meanwhile, married women, such as Laura Petrie—wife of comedy writer Rob Petrie and the character previously played by Moore on *The Dick Van Dyke Show* (1961–66)—rarely had careers outside the home. They were mothers who never mussed their make-up as they dispensed milk and cookies to their offspring. Their husbands were their household's sole breadwinners. Despite their roles as homemakers and housekeepers, they always were stylishly dressed with their hair beautifully styled when their mates arrived home from work. Or, if they yearned for a career—as did Lucy Ricardo, the heroine of *I Love Lucy* (1951–57; see entry under 1950s–TV and Radio in volume 3)—they had to conspire, against their husband's will and without his "permission," to break into their profession of choice.

Mary Richards' career was not in education, library science, or nursing, all traditional women's professions. This thirty-something character worked as an associate producer in the news department of WJM, the lowest-rated TV station in Minneapolis, Minnesota. Mary was a dedicated and ambitious career woman; as the series progressed, she became increasingly assertive in the workplace and eventually was promoted to producer. Yet Mary was not one-dimensionally bold or unrealistically rendered. She could be intimidated by others, at which point she might stutter and garble her sentences. When bothered at work, her arms would flail about and she would whine the name of her boss. These vulnerabilities made Mary Richards a fully realized, deeply human character.

Mary might eventually wed and start a family, but she was never marriage-hungry. Mary would never be dependent upon a man. For her, a relationship would be a fifty-fifty proposition. Furthermore, unlike her single-woman sitcom-character predecessors, Mary Richards had—and enjoyed—a sex life. She might spend the night with a man, and she did not have to be in love with him to enjoy his company.

However, *The Mary Tyler Moore Show*'s popularity did not just stem from the depiction of its central character. The show was genuinely funny. It featured an array of colorful, carefully drawn supporting characters who gravitated around Mary Richards and served to replace husband, parents, and children as Mary's extended family. They included gruff but lovable news producer Lou Grant (Edward Asner, 1929–); pompous, dim-witted news anchor Ted Baxter (Ted Knight, 1923–1986);

wisecracking nice-guy head news writer Murray Slaughter (Gavin MacLeod, 1931–); Georgette Franklin (Georgia Engel, 1948–), Ted Baxter's sweet, none-too-bright girlfriend, then wife; Phyllis Lindstrom (Cloris Leachman, 1926–), Mary's nosy, insensitive neighbor; Sue Ann Nivens (Betty White, 1924–), scheming hostess of WJM-TV's "Happy Homemaker Show"; and, finally, transplanted New Yorker Rhoda Morgenstern (Valerie Harper, 1940–), Mary's neighbor and best friend, a character who, like Sue Ann Nivens, was more of a traditional, male-hungry single woman. A number of these characters also starred in their own spin-off series: *Rhoda* (1974–78), *Phyllis* (1975–77), and *Lou Grant* (1977–82).

Mary Tyler Moore was not only the star of her show. With then-husband Grant Tinker (1925–), she also produced *The Mary Tyler Moore Show*. The sitcom was still a ratings winner in 1977 when Moore and Tinker decided to end its seven-year run. The final episode featured the selling of WJM-TV to a new owner who summarily fired the entire staff, with one exception: inept Ted Baxter, whose incompetence more than likely was the primary reason for the station's lowly ratings.

The character of Mary Richards served as a meaningful and positive role model for women who were coming of age in the 1970s. She inspired them as they extended the boundaries of their futures beyond marriage, motherhood, and traditional women's roles.

—*Rob Edelman*

For More Information

Alley, Robert S., and Irby B. Brown. *Love Is All Around: The Making of The Mary Tyler Moore Show*. New York: Delta, 1989.

"The Mary Tyler Moore Show." *Tim's TV Showcase*. http://timstvshowcase.com/ (accessed March 28, 2002).

The Mary Tyler Moore Show Online. http://www.mtmshow.com (accessed March 28, 2002).

Meehan, Diana. *Ladies of the Evening: Women Characters of Prime-Time Television*. Metuchen, NJ: The Scarecrow Press, 1983.

Moore, Mary Tyler. *After All*. New York: G. P. Putnam's Sons, 1995.

M*A*S*H

Set during the Korean War (1950–53), *M*A*S*H* was first a smash-hit movie in 1970 and then a groundbreaking and wildly popular **television** (see entry under 1940s—TV and Radio in volume 3) series from 1972 to 1983. The screen version, in no unsubtle terms, actually served as a condemnation of America's controversial involvement in the war in Vietnam (1954–75). The small-screen follow-up—which ran eight years longer than the actual Korean conflict—became one of the funniest and most enduring of all TV **sitcoms** (situation comedies; see entry under 1950s—TV and Radio in volume 3).

The setting of *M*A*S*H* is the 4077th Mobile Army Surgical Hospital, a makeshift medical operation situated right behind the frontline fighting. The doctors and nurses assigned to the unit are entrusted to treat the steady flow of wounded being evacuated by helicopter directly from the battlefield. Given the constant presence of death, the hospital is a morbidly depressing environment; the lone way to keep one's sanity is by injecting as much tomfoolery into the proceedings as possible. So despite their grim settings, both the large- and small-screen versions of *M*A*S*H* are loaded with outlandish humor.

The film version was a career breakthrough for esteemed independent filmmaker Robert Altman (1925–). Its primary characters are Captain Benjamin Franklin "Hawkeye" Pierce, played by Donald Sutherland (1934–), and Captain "Trapper" John McIntyre, played by Elliott Gould (1938–). The captains are surgeons whose fierce individualism and rebellious spirit frequently clash with the stuffy, regimented military lifestyle. Hawkeye's and Trapper John's contempt for the mindlessness of military bureaucracy and the self-important behavior of military bureaucrats, coupled with the film's appropriately gruesome humor and antiwar point of view, endeared the film to youthful audiences.

When the television version of *M*A*S*H* premiered, Sutherland and Gould were replaced by Alan Alda (1936–) and Wayne Rogers (1933–). As in the film, Hawkeye and Trapper John were surrounded by carefully etched supporting characters: Major Margaret "Hot Lips" Houlihan (Loretta Swit, 1937–), the uptight head nurse, whose character was humanized as the series progressed; Major Frank Burns (Larry Linville, 1939–2000), a hypocritical, inept surgeon; Corporal Walter "Radar" O'Reilly (Gary Burghoff, 1940–), the shy, young company clerk; Lieutenant Colonel Henry Blake (McLean Stevenson, 1929–1996), the befuddled commanding officer; Corporal Maxwell Klinger (Jamie Farr, 1934–), who savors wearing women's clothing in the hope of earning a military discharge; and Father Francis

Mulcahy (William Christopher, 1932–), a thoughtful clergyman. Burghoff, by the way, was the lone actor from the screen version to appear in the series. As the years passed, various actors decided to leave the show, or their characters were written out of the series. Rogers, Linville, and Stevenson were respectively replaced by Mike Farrell (1939–), playing Captain B.J. Hunnicut, Hawkeye's equally able partner-in-crime; David Ogden Stiers (1942–), cast as aristocratic Major Charles Emerson Winchester III; and Harry Morgan (1915–), playing wry Colonel Sherman T. Potter.

The series was acclaimed for its unusual storylines, many of which spotlighted the grim reality of life in a M*A*S*H unit. For example, the cheer that accompanies Col. Blake's transfer out of the war zone is followed by heartbreak: the character is killed when his helicopter goes down in the Sea of Japan, just after it departs the M*A*S*H unit. In another episode, Hawkeye suffers a concussion and is taken in by a non-English-speaking Korean family. The dialogue consists only of Hawkeye offering a monologue in which he comments on the evils of war and other topics. Still another episode, titled "The Interview," features the characters commenting to a reporter on their feelings about life in a war zone.

The final original *M*A*S*H* episode, which was two and a half hours long, aired on February 28, 1983. Over fifty million viewers—the largest audience to that date in TV history—watched as the Korean War ended and the members of the 4077th finally went home.

—*Rob Edelman*

For More Information

Kalter, Suzy. *The Complete Book of M*A*S*H*. New York: H. N. Abrams, 1984.

*M*A*S*H*. http://www.mash4077.co.uk/ (accessed March 28, 2002).

Maxwell, Jeff. *Secrets of the M*A*S*H Mess: The Lost Recipes of Private Igor*. Nashville: Cumberland House, 1997.

Monty Python's Flying Circus
....

Monty Python was a British comedy troupe that emerged in the late 1960s with its own **television** (see entry under 1940s–TV and Radio in volume 3) show, *Monty Python's Flying Circus*.

The show developed a huge cult following in the 1970s and beyond. The members of Monty Python also made a number of films which, along with their TV show, brought them great success in Britain and in the United States and had a lasting impact on late twentieth-century comedy.

The members of the group consisted of John Cleese (1939–), Eric Idle (1943–), Graham Chapman (1941–1989), Michael Palin (1943–), Terry Gilliam (1940–), and Terry Jones (1942–). They began their individual careers performing in various comedy troupes in Great Britain where they met and often worked with each other. In 1969, they formed Monty Python, a comedy group who wrote and performed satirical sketches, or skits, that made fun of established authorities, like the British government, the rich, and even television itself. The show also featured animation by Gilliam, an American. Monty Python typically performed absurd routines, including ones that involved singing lumberjacks dressed up as women and an office where people could pay to get into arguments. The show was a success in Great Britain and later in Canada. Monty Python's last season on British television came in 1974. Even before that year, news of the group had spread to the United States, helped by the group's comedy record albums. When the **Public Broadcasting System** (PBS; see entry under 1960s–TV and Radio in volume 4) picked up the show in 1975, Americans could then see the group's absurd humor, and they enjoyed a long run on American TV.

With the end of *Flying Circus,* the group went on to make several films. *Monty Python and the Holy Grail,* a spoof of the Arthurian legends from medieval Britain, in 1975, was the first of these films. It contained some of the same absurd and satirical comedy they featured in *Flying Circus.* In *Life of Brian* (1979), they spoofed Christianity, a controversial move, but one that proved successful at the box office. Their final film, *The Meaning of Life,* came out in 1983 and also proved to be their final group project. Individually, the members of Monty Python went on to their own films and other projects after 1983. Beyond their many fans in the United States and elsewhere, Monty Python proved to be a very important force in American and British comedy, influencing the American sketch comedy show *Saturday Night Live* (see entry under 1970s–TV and Radio in volume 4), the Canadian show *Kids in the Hall,* and others.

—*Timothy Berg*

For More Information

Hewison, Robert. *Monty Python: The Case Against.* London: Methuen, 1981.

Miller, Jeffrey S. *Something Completely Different: British Television and American Culture, 1960–1980.* Minneapolis: University of Minnesota Press, 1999.

Perry, George. *The Life of Python.* Boston: Little Brown, 1983.

PythOnline. http://www.pythonline.com/ (accessed March 28, 2002).

Muppets

Puppetry is an ancient art form that has been practiced for centuries in nearly every culture of the world. In the United States, the Muppets have long been the nation's most successful puppetry organization. Founded in the 1950s by Jim Henson (1936–1990), who had been fascinated by the possibilities of presenting puppets on **television** (see entry under 1940s—TV and Radio in volume 3), the Muppet characters have appeared on hundreds of public and commercial TV programs and recordings; in films and commercials; and as toys and merchandise. Henson coined the term "Muppet" by combining the words marionette and puppet. Muppets, unlike other puppets, have flexible faces that allow for a wide range of expressions that play well on TV. Muppet characters like Kermit the Frog, Miss Piggy, Big Bird, Grover, Fozzie Bear, Bert and Ernie, Oscar the Grouch, and Elmo have captured the world's imagination.

Henson had his first taste of success as a teenager when he created a five-minute-long puppet feature for adults to air immediately before **The Tonight Show** (1954–; see entry under 1950s—TV and Radio in volume 3). The show was such a success that Henson and his Muppets were soon asked to appear on **The Ed Sullivan Show** (1948–71), **Today** (1952–; see these entries under 1950s—TV and Radio in volume 3), and *The Tonight Show.* The first Muppet star was Rowlf the Dog, who appeared for three years on *The Jimmy Dean Show* (1957–66).

In 1969, the Muppets achieved enormous popularity through their appearances on the public television program **Sesame Street** (see entry under 1970s—TV and Radio in volume 4). Children were enthralled by the Muppets' antics as they explained the alphabet, did simple math equations, and discussed social issues. Thanks in part to the Muppets, *Sesame Street* grew to be one of the most popular programs in TV history.

In 1976, Henson got his own show, called simply *The Muppet Show*. It remained on the air until 1981. Each week, a human celebrity would appear in a variety-show format with the Muppets, who were led by Kermit the Frog, one of Henson's 1950s creations. The show was a phenomenon and led to several Muppet films, including *The Muppet Movie* (1979), *The Muppets Take Manhattan* (1984), and *Muppets from Space* (1999).

Henson was constantly seeking methods to expand the art of puppetry. His Muppet success financed such innovative work as two TV series, *Fraggle Rock* (1983-88) and *The Storyteller* (1987), and the film *The Dark Crystal* (1982). Henson died in 1990 after a brief illness. The Muppet team endures and continues to delight audiences with their outrageous humor and advanced puppetry skills.

—*Charles Coletta*

For More Information

Bacon, Matt. *No Strings Attached: The Inside Story of Jim Henson's Creature Shop*. New York: Macmillan, 1997.

Finch, Christopher. *Of Muppets and Men: The Making of the Muppet Show*. New York: Random House, 1981.

Gikow, Louise. *Meet Jim Henson*. New York: Random House, 1993.

Henson, Jim, et al. *The Art of the Muppets*. New York: Bantam, 1980.

Muppet World. http://www.muppetworld.com (accessed March 28, 2002).

Sesame Workshop. http://www.sesameworkshop.org/ (accessed March 28, 2002).

The Partridge Family

The Partridge Family (1970–74) was a popular **television** (see entry under 1940s—TV and Radio in volume 3) **sitcom** (situation comedy; see entry under 1950s—TV and Radio in volume 3) about a musical family that makes it in the record industry. Oscar-winning actress Shirley Jones (1934–) starred as Shirley Partridge, a widowed suburbanite whose children have formed their own **rock and roll** (see entry under 1950s—Music in volume 3) band. Mom and kids come together in their garage to tape a song titled "I Think I Love You." A record company purchases it, and the song becomes a monster hit. Soon the Partridges are touring across the United States, driving from performance to performance in a repainted school bus.

The original cast members of *The Partridge Family:* **Shirley Jones is surrounded by (clockwise from upper left) Susan Dey, David Cassidy, Danny Bonaduce, Suzanne Crough, and Jeremy Gelbwaks.** *UPI/Corbis-Bettman. Reproduced by permission.*

David Cassidy (1950–), Jones's real-life stepson, played sixteen-year-old Keith, the senior Partridge kid. His siblings were fifteen-year-old Laurie (Susan Dey, 1952–), ten-year-old Danny (Danny Bonaduce, 1959–), seven-year-old Christopher (played by Jeremy Gelbwaks, 1961–, for one season and then by Brian Forster, 1960–), and five-year-old Tracy (Suzanne Crough, 1963–). The other primary character was Reuben Kinkaid (Dave Madden, 1933–), the band's manager. Even though none of the actors cast as the Partridges played instruments—professional studio musicians performed the music—Jones and Cassidy sang the Partridge vocals.

"I Think I Love You" transcended being a mere TV theme; it became a top-ten hit record, and for three weeks in 1970 it was number one on the charts. The following year, the Partridges scored another hit with "I Woke Up in Love This Morning." The Partridges were a success on two fronts, with the TV show helping to promote the sale of Partridge Family records while their hits helped hype the series. Meanwhile, super-cute Cassidy became a teen heartthrob. Like other 1970s teen icons, among them John Travolta (1954–) and Leif Garrett (1961–), Cassidy was the love-object of dreamy adolescent and preadolescent girls. He was a constant presence on the cover of teen magazines. David Cassidy posters, pins, **T-shirts** (see entry under 1910s—Fashion in volume 1), and lunch boxes sold by the thousands.

"I Think I Love You" and "I Woke Up in Love This Morning" also are "bubblegum music" classics. In the late 1960s and early to mid-1970s, "bubblegum music" was all the rage among pre-teenagers and young teenagers. Its popularity grew out of the acid rock and introspective pop-folk music that was then attracting older teens and young adults. "Bubblegum" sounds are sweet, bouncy, and dance-oriented, with upbeat, innocent lyrics. Among the late 1960s "bubblegum" hits that preceded "I Think I Love You" were "Sugar, Sugar" by The Archies, "Yummy, Yummy, Yummy" by The Ohio Express, and "Simon Says" by The 1910 Fruitgum Company.

The Partridge Family TV show was based on the experiences of The Cowsills, a real-life musical family who hailed from Newport, Rhode Island. The Cowsills consisted of five brothers, their kid sister, and their mother. Their late 1960s hits included "The Rain, The Park and Other Things," "We Can Fly," and "Indian Lake." Reportedly, The Cowsills were approached to play the Partridges, but the deal never was finalized because Jones already had been signed for the show.

—*Rob Edelman*

For More Information

Cassidy, David. *C'mon, Get Happy: Fear and Loathing on the Partridge Family Bus.* New York: Warner Books, 1994.

Colavolpe, Michael, and Jennifer Futch. *C'mon, Get Happy!: The Unofficial Homepage of the Partridge Family.* http://www.cmongethappy.com/ (accessed March 29, 2002).

Green, Joey. *The Partridge Family Album.* New York: HarperPerennial, 1994.

Roots

Roots (1977) was one of the most illustrious and impressive achievements in the history of **television** (see entry under 1940s—TV and Radio in volume 3). A miniseries twelve hours in length, it was broadcast over eight consecutive evenings on ABC. The series was an adaptation of *Roots: The Saga of an American Family* (1976), by African American writer Alex Haley (1921–1992). Haley's book chronicled his quest to discover his ancestry: to discover where his forefathers and foremothers had hailed from and the manner in which they came to America and lived their lives as slaves.

The United States is a nation of immigrants. Its citizens have come to its shores from across the globe, and mainly they have come freely. All, that is, except for one race: African Americans, who centuries earlier were taken from their homelands across the African continent, chained together and deprived of their freedom, and shipped over as slaves. Haley set out to explore his own family history, an effort that resulted in twelve years of research and writing. Because it would be impossible to verify facts, dates, and the identities of all those involved in his story, he chose to present it in novel form, as a combination of history and fiction, while at the same time contending that it was nonfictional in nature. In any case, *Roots: The Saga of an American Family* became a number-one **best-seller** (see entry under 1940s—Commerce in volume 3) and earned Haley a Pulitzer Prize.

Roots begins with the story of Kunta Kinte (played by LeVar Burton, 1957–), who is born in Gambia, West Africa, in 1750. He passes his childhood in freedom and then, at age seventeen, is captured by white slave traders and brought to America on board a ship. Kunta Kinte remains defiant and resentful over his enslavement. Throughout the rest of his life, he makes several unsuccessful attempts to escape his masters. Among his descendants are Kizzy (Leslie Uggams, 1943–), his daughter, who is raped by her owner; Chicken George (Ben Vereen,

LeVar Burton, as Kunta Kinte, from the groundbreaking miniseries *Roots,* which showed the plight of slaves in America. *Archive Photos. Reproduced by permission.*

1946–), Kizzy's son; and Tom (Georg Stanford Brown, 1943–), Chicken George's son—and Kunta Kinte's great grandson. The story ends well over a century after it begins, in Tennessee after the Civil War (1861–65). Tom now may technically be a free man, but he still exists in a nation in which African Americans are economically exploited, second-class citizens.

When *Roots* premiered, nothing like it had ever been presented on American TV. No program before it featured its combination of length and historical thrust. However, the show was open to controversy. Some historians and critics contended that it overstated the explosive relationships between its black and white characters. Furthermore, the slave trade was allowed to thrive as much because of the willingness of black Africans to sell neighboring tribes into slavery as because of the willingness of white traders to make a profit. Several authors even accused Haley of plagiarism; eventually, the writer admitted that segments of a book titled *The African* (1967), by Harold Courlander (1908–), "found their way" into his own work.

Controversy aside, what *Roots* did accomplish was to give the slave experience in America a human face by chronicling the story of one specific family. The series was a ratings hit, with all of its eight telecasts ranking among the thirteen most widely seen programs up to that date. It was followed by a sequel, *Roots: The Next Generations* (1979), which ran twelve hours and was broadcast over seven evenings. Also known as *Roots II,* the miniseries charted the plights and fates of Kunta Kinte's descendants from 1882 through 1967. *Roots: The Gift* (1988), a made-for-TV movie, came nine years later.

—*Rob Edelman*

For More Information

Courlander, Harold. *The African.* New York: Crown Publishers, 1967.
Gonzales, Doreen. *Alex Haley: Author of Roots.* Hillside, NJ: Enslow Publishers, 1994.
Haley, Alex. *Roots: The Saga of an American Family.* New York: Doubleday, 1976.
Roots (television miniseries). ABC, 1977.
The Roots of Alex Haley (television documentary). British Broadcasting Company, 1997.

Saturday Night Live

Saturday Night Live introduced a new type of comedy to **television** (see entry under 1940s—TV and Radio in volume 3).

Early members of *Saturday Night Live*'s Not Ready for Prime Time Players: (clockwise from far left): John Belushi, Dan Aykroyd, Bill Murray, Laraine Newman, Garrett Morris, Jane Curtin, and Gilda Radner. *AP/Wide World Photos. Reproduced by permission.*

Producer Lorne Michaels (1944–) was inspired to create *Saturday Night Live* by the British comedy show **Monty Python's Flying Circus** (see entry under 1970s–TV and Radio in volume 4). Michaels felt that the unbound energy and creativity found in America's comedy clubs was missing from its TV screens. The show debuted on October 11, 1975, on NBC. Michaels landed an 11:30 P.M. Eastern Standard Time (EST) time slot. At the time, this late hour was TV's graveyard, a time when not many people would be watching. But Michaels' took advantage of the late hour and the accompanying relaxed censorship rules to encourage his performers to push the boundaries of what was previously acceptable on TV. The result was a zany show that quickly became popular with Americans.

To cast *SNL,* Michaels scoured comedy clubs across America to find undiscovered talent. The resulting group was dubbed the "Not Ready For Prime Time Players." The original cast members that first year were Dan Aykroyd (1952–), John Belushi (1949–1982), Chevy Chase (1943–), Jane Curtin (1947–), Garrett Morris (1937–), Laraine Newman (1952–), and Gilda Radner (1946–1989). The show soon became known as a launching pad for some of the country's most popular comedians. Many *SNL* cast members have gone on to movie stardom, including Chase, Bill Murray (1950–), Eddie Murphy (1961–), Mike Myers (1963–), and Adam Sandler (1966–).

The format of the show has remained virtually unchanged. The show opens abruptly with a skit, no credits or titles. At the end of the skit, the players turn to the camera and announce: "Live from New York, it's Saturday Night!" Only then are the show's theme song and opening credits rolled. The celebrity host then does a monologue (a short speech on stage). The only other certainties are "Weekend Update" and the guest musical act. Sometime around midnight "Weekend Update," which parodies the current week's news, will run. The musical act, a different guest or group every week, will play at some point in the show as well. In the skits that sandwich the regular bits, anything can happen. Among the show's popular skits were the "Coneheads"; "Wayne's World"; Radner's "Roseanne Roseannadanna"; the "Church Lady" and George Bush (1924–) impersonation done by Dana Carvey (1955–); the spoof of the clay character Gumby by Eddie Murphy (1961–); and Belushi and Aykroyd's "Blues Brothers," to name just a few.

At the beginning of the twenty-first century, *SNL* is still going strong. The long 2000 presidential campaign (and, then, controversial election) between Al Gore (1948–) and George W. Bush (1946–), for instance, provided unending opportunities for political skewering. No longer just a TV show, *SNL* has become an institution: American television's defining cultural landmark of late-night comedy.

—*Robert Sickels*

For More Information

Beatts, Anne, and John Head, eds. *Saturday Night Live.* New York: Avon Books, 1977.

Bradley, Sean. *Saturday-Night-Live.com.* http://www.saturday-night-live.com/ (accessed March 29, 2002).

Cader, Michael, ed. *Saturday Night Live: The First Twenty Years.* New York: Houghton Mifflin, 1994.

Hill, Doug, and Jeff Weingrad. *Saturday Night: A Backstage History of Saturday Night Live.* New York: Beech Tree, 1986.

Schoolhouse Rock

Schoolhouse Rock was a series of short educational cartoons televised on the ABC network beginning in 1973. The colorful animations, accompanied by catchy songs, taught Saturday morning **television** (see entry under 1940s–TV and Radio in volume 3) viewers all about math, grammar, American history, and science, among other topics. The innovative series won four Emmy Awards and has been regularly rerun, a sign of its lasting popularity.

The brainchild of David McCall (1928–), a New York advertising executive, *Schoolhouse Rock* followed **Sesame Street** (see entry under 1970s–TV and Radio in volume 4) in its use of advertising techniques to teach basic skills to children. McCall marveled at his son's ability to learn when multiplication tables were set to music. He convinced ABC, which was looking for educational content to air during **Saturday morning cartoons** (see entry under 1960s–TV and Radio in volume 3), to let him develop an animated series based on that concept. Veteran musicians and songwriters, like Lynn Ahrens (1948–) and Bob Dorough (1923–), were brought in to write the jingles.

The first set of *Schoolhouse Rock* segments, "Multiplication Rock," began airing in January 1973. Young viewers quickly got caught up in such infectious songs as "Zero, My Hero" and "Three Is a Magic Number." A second series, "Grammar Rock," covered parts of speech like nouns, adjectives, and adverbs. And "America Rock," which debuted in time for America's Bicentennial (two hundredth anniversary) in 1976, surveyed important moments in American history like the signing of the Declaration of Independence.

Many of the animations created for the series were quite clever and became pop-culture icons. "Conjunction Junction," from "Grammar Rock," for example, featured a funky conductor who hooked up "phrases and clauses" like boxcars on a train. "I'm Just a Bill" from "America Rock" told the story of how a bill becomes a law—from the bill's point of view. This segment was later affectionately spoofed on an episode of **The Simpsons** (see entry under 1980s–TV and Radio in volume 4) featuring original vocalist Bob Dorough.

Schoolhouse Rock proved so popular that ABC later commissioned additional segments dealing with science, computers, and money management. A musical stage show, *Schoolhouse Rock Love,* heralded a wave of nostalgia for the series in the late 1990s. A group of rock musicians even recorded their own versions of the *Schoolhouse Rock* songs in 1996. Many years after the series' debut, it is still remembered fondly by a generation of TV viewers who spent a good portion of their Saturday mornings in this hip house of learning.

—Robert E. Schnakenberg

For More Information

Okun, Milton. *The Schoolhouse Rock Songbook*. New York: Cherry Lane Books, 1997.

The Unofficial Schoolhouse Rock Web Site. http://users.aol.com/MRandino/SHRockWWW.html (accessed March 29, 2002).

Yohe, Tom, and George Newall. *Schoolhouse Rock! The Official Guide.* New York: Hyperion, 1996.

Sesame Street

"Can you tell me how to get/how to get to Sesame Street?" Since 1969, those words have beckoned children into the imaginary world of *Sesame Street* on public **television** (see entry under 1940s—TV and Radio in volume 3). The hour-long educational program combines music, fast-paced sketches and cartoons, and the interaction of humans and **"muppets"** (see entry under 1970s—TV and Radio in volume 4) to teach numbers, the alphabet, and values. It has won numerous awards and is broadcast in more than 140 countries around the world.

Sesame Street was first developed by educator Joan Ganz Cooney (1929–) and others at the Children's Television Workshop (CTW). The goal of the show was to use the techniques of TV advertising to teach basic skills to children. The first episode was broadcast in November 1969. Set on a fictional New York City street, the show featured a cast of "neighbors" of various ethnic backgrounds. Maria was a young Latina who worked at a local library. Gordon and Susan were a married African American couple. Mr. Hooper was an elderly white man who ran the local store. Additional cast members were added in later seasons.

The real stars of *Sesame Street,* however, were the colorful Muppets. Created by puppeteer Jim Henson (1936–1990), these furry creatures included Oscar the Grouch, a grimy green complainer who lived in a garbage can; Cookie Monster, a blue beast who subsisted on cookies; and Big Bird, an eight-foot-tall childlike feathered creature who lived in a nest and had an imaginary elephant friend. Big Bird often represented the children in the viewing audience, asking questions that a four- or five-year-old child would ask. When Will Lee (1908–1982) the actor who played Mr. Hooper, died in 1982, for example, *Sesame Street*'s writers had Big Bird struggle to understand the finality of his friend's death.

Sesame Street's Muppets became wildly popular and eventually spun off into their own TV and movie series. New Muppets were added to *Sesame Street* to keep the show fresh and to attract even younger viewers. Elmo, a fuzzy red character added in the 1990s, was an especially popular addition. Elmo was voiced in a falsetto (an artificially high man's voice), by puppeteer Kevin Clash (1960–). The endearing, childlike creature won the hearts of small children—and daytime hostess Rosie O'Donnell (1962–), whose sponsorship of the Tickle Me Elmo doll turned it into the must-have Christmas gift of 1996. Although some critics took issue with *Sesame Street*'s aggressive merchandising strategy, the sale of toys helped keep the show on the air and commercial free during a time when budget cutbacks threatened public television.

Joan Ganz Cooney, creator of *Sesame Street,* stands with Big Bird, Oscar the Grouch, Bert and Ernie, and other Sesame Street characters. *AP/Wide World Photos. Reproduced by permission.*

—*Robert E. Schnakenberg*

For More Information

Borgenucht, David. *Sesame Street Unpaved: Scripts, Stories, Secrets, and Songs.* New York: Hyperion, 1998.

Petrucelli, Rita. *Jim Henson: Creator of the Muppets.* Vero Beach, FL: Rourke Enterprises, 1989.

Muppet World. http://www.muppetworld.com (accessed March 28, 2002).

Sesame Workshop. http://www.sesameworkshop.org/ (accessed March 28, 2002).

Woods, Geraldine. *Jim Henson: From Puppets to Muppets.* Minneapolis: Dillon Press, 1987.

Taxi

One of television's most popular **sitcoms** (situation comedies; see entry under 1950s—TV and Radio in volume 3) during

The blue-collar characters on the series *Taxi* dealt with realistic issues that audiences could relate to. Danny DeVito (center) is surrounded by (clockwise from upper left) Andy Kaufman, Christopher Lloyd, Carol Kane, Judd Hirsch, Marilu Henner, and Tony Danza. *Archive Photos, Inc. Reproduced by permission.*

the late 1970s and early 1980s was *Taxi*. The show depicted the comic antics of the drivers of New York's Sunshine Cab Company. The series aired from 1978 until 1983 and was one of the most critically acclaimed and awarded programs of its era. It boasted superior writing and one of the best ensemble casts on **television** (see entry under 1940s—TV and Radio in volume 3). Unlike on many previous sitcoms, blue-collar characters that struggled to make ends meet populated the sets of *Taxi*.

Taxi was based upon a magazine article by Mark Jacobson (1948–) that had appeared in the June 26, 1976, edition of *New*

York. The lead character of Alex Rieger, a philosophical cabbie who could solve everyone's problems but his own, was written specifically for actor Judd Hirsch (1935–). While Alex was satisfied with his life as a taxi driver, everyone else around him hoped for more. The other cabbies included: Tony Banta (Tony Danza, 1951–), a young prizefighter; Bobby Wheeler (Jeff Conaway, 1950–), a struggling actor; Elaine Nardo (Marilu Henner, 1952–), a single mother; and "Reverend" Jim Ignatowski (Christopher Lloyd, 1938–), a drug-damaged former hippie from a wealthy family. Comedian Andy Kaufman (1949–1984) appeared as mechanic Latka Gravas, a foreigner who spoke his own unique language. Overseeing all the cabbies was the hostile dispatcher Louie DePalma (Danny DeVito, 1944–).

One of *Taxi*'s hallmarks was that it tended to be more realistic than other sitcoms. Most of the characters were fully developed individuals who changed over the seasons. They faced the same financial problems, family issues, and insecurities as their viewers. *Taxi* could also depict absurd storylines and did so generally through the Latka and Reverend Jim characters. Kaufman was known for his often-bizarre humor. The character of Latka allowed him the opportunity to bring his offbeat comedy style to mainstream America.

In its first seasons, *Taxi* was both a critical and popular success. During its fourth season, ratings fell dramatically. The series was canceled by ABC despite its Emmy win that year for Best Comedy Series. The show moved to NBC for its fifth and final season. DeVito appeared in a popular commercial announcing the change of networks. As Louie, he snarled, "Same time, Better network!" Although the series continued to be praised by critics, its ratings continued to slide and it left the air in 1983. In 1999, many of the former *Taxi* cast members reassembled for a cameo appearance in *Man on the Moon,* a biographical film about Kaufman starring Jim Carrey (1962–). *Taxi* continues to thrive in syndication and is remembered as one of television's best comedies.

—Charles Coletta

For More Information

Lovece, Frank, with Jules Franco. *Hailing Taxi.* New York: Prentice Hall, 1988.

Sorenson, Jeff. *The Taxi Book: The Complete Guide to Television's Most Lovable Cabbies.* New York: St. Martin's Press, 1987.

Waldron, Vince. *Classic Sitcoms: A Celebration of the Best in Prime-Time Comedy.* New York: Collier Books, 1987.

Zehme, Bill. *Lost in the Funhouse: The Life and Mind of Andy Kaufman.* New York: Delacourt Press, 1999.

Zmuda, Bob. *Andy Kaufman Revealed!: Best Friend Tells All.* Boston: Little Brown, 1999.

The Waltons

The Waltons, which aired on CBS from 1972 until 1981, was one of television's most successful family dramas. Created by Earl Hamner Jr. (1923–), the series depicted the struggles and successes of the large Walton family during the **Great Depression** (see entry under 1930s–The Way We Lived in volume 2). The series stood in stark contrast to other **television** (see entry under 1940s–TV and Radio in volume 3) programming of the era as it emphasized wholesome family values rather than sexual and violent content. The Waltons were a united family who faced economic and personal hardships together. A vast audience responded to the series and made it one of the most successful programs of the 1970s.

Hamner based *The Waltons* on his own experiences growing up in the rural Blue Ridge Mountains of Schuyler, Virginia. His 1961 novel *Spencer's Mountain* led to a movie of the same name, starring Henry Fonda (1905–1982). In 1970, his novel, *The Homecoming: A Novel about Spencer's Mountain,* which was a collection of tales from his boyhood, was optioned by Lorimar Productions for a television special. The Waltons first came to TV in *Homecoming: A Christmas Story* (1971), which starred Patricia Neal (1926–) and Edgar Bergen (1903–1978). The show's success led to a series the following year. The TV show featured Ralph Waite (1928–) as John Walton, the proprietor of a lumber mill, and Michael Learned (1939–) as Olivia, his homemaker wife. Many of the episodes revolved around the Waltons' seven children: John Jr., Ben, Jason, Mary Ellen, Erin, Jim-Bob, and Elizabeth. The most prominent of the children was John Jr. (called "John Boy"), played by Richard Thomas (1951–). John Boy was an aspiring writer and always served as narrator for the program. The concluding line to most episodes ("Goodnight John Boy") soon became a national catchphrase. Also in the cast were veteran actors Will Geer (1902–1978) and Ellen Corby (1911–1999) as Grandpa Zeb and Grandma Esther Walton.

Some critics dismissed the series as offering a simplistic and unrealistic representation of the 1930s. However, closer examination reveals Hamner was often willing to raise important social issues like racism, sexism, and economic inequality on the show. Many of the strongest episodes dealt with the Waltons facing some personal trauma like death, disease, or debt, as well as other catastrophes. Whatever misfortune befell them, the family members were always honest and loyal to one another. The series also promoted the respectability inherent in hard work. After the series ended in 1981, the cast reunited for numerous reunion specials into the 1990s.

—Charles Coletta

For More Information

Hamner, Earl, Jr. "Coming Home to Walton's Mountain." *TV Guide* (November 20, 1993): pp. 10–14.

Hamner, Earl, Jr. *The Homecoming: A Novel about Spencer's Mountain.* New York: Random House, 1970.

Hamner, Earl, Jr. *Spencer's Mountain.* New York: Dial Press, 1961.

Keets, Heather. "Good Night, Waltons." *Entertainment Weekly* (August 20, 1993): p. 76.

The Waltons Page. http://www.the-waltons.com (accessed March 29, 2002).

1970s

The Way We Lived

In 1976, journalist Tom Wolfe (1931–) coined the term "The Me Decade" to describe the 1970s. It was not a compliment. In the eyes of many, Americans in the 1970s retreated from the political and social changes they had pursued in the 1960s and were happy to focus only on themselves. The reasons why they did this were many. First, the economy slowed dramatically in the early 1970s, and people became more concerned with protecting their families from financial trouble than with changing the world. The youthful baby boomers who had populated the activist movements of the 1960s were settling down. As they did, they looked inward instead of outward. Fewer people protested in the streets, and many more visited therapists or sought to improve their spiritual lives. This quest for individual perfection led to a higher divorce rate, as people found it more acceptable to leave a marriage if it did not make them happy or fulfilled.

Activism did not disappear from American society altogether, however. Feminism gained strength in the 1970s, helped along by the long (but unsuccessful) campaign for the passage of an Equal Rights Amendment to the U.S. Constitution. Women made substantial gains in access to equal opportunity in education and the workplace. They also gained protection for the "right to choose" with the Supreme Court's *Roe v. Wade* decision about abortion rights in 1973. Environmentalism also emerged as an important social issue. The first Earth Day was held in 1970. National legislators passed important environmental legislation in the decade.

The 1970s will also be remembered as the decade of fads. In addition to jogging and aerobics, popular fads of the 1970s included tanning, streaking (running naked in public places, which was most popular on college campuses), and buying pet rocks and mood rings. Though hardly widespread enough to be called a fad, disillusioned Americans also joined cults or fringe religious groups in increasing numbers. Hare Krishnas, Moonies, and other groups attracted a great deal of attention. None attracted greater attention than the American cult members who were involved in the mass suicide in Jonestown, Guyana, in 1978. The sexual openness and freedom of the 1960s continued, although it was tempered in the 1970s by the rising problem of sexually transmitted diseases.

Apple Computer

Apple Computer was founded in 1976 by Steve Wozniak (1950–) and Steve Jobs (1955–) to market the Apple I computer. Released the following year, the Apple II began the **personal computer** (see entry under 1970s—The Way We Lived in volume 4) revolution. It offered speed and computing power at an affordable price. Since then, Apple has gained a reputation for producing well-thought-out, high-quality machines. In 2002, Apple remained the only computer manufacturer using software designed specifically for its own machines.

The success of the Apple II made Apple the leading personal computer company of the early 1980s, but the Macintosh made the personal computer an everyday tool. The "Mac," as it became known, was the first affordable machine to use a Graphical User Interface (GUI). A GUI is a system that allows users to operate programs using small images called "icons" rather than type out commands in computer code. In fact, the first PC to use a GUI was made by Xerox and called the Star. The Star even included the first on-screen icons that could be dragged and double-clicked using a mouse, but in 1981 it cost a whopping $16,000. The Mac introduced similar features in 1984 for $2,495.

In the late 1980s, lawsuits raged among Apple, Xerox, and software giant **Microsoft** (see entry under 1990s—Commerce in volume 5) over which company had invented the GUI. The cases were all dismissed, but with its revolutionary overlapping "windows," the Macintosh would still be familiar to computer users in the twenty-first century. Apple also pioneered hand-held computers, infrared communication between machines, and "plug and play," which allows new hardware to be added to a PC. It has not always had success. Early models of the Apple III are alleged to have been unable to do math, while the Newton handheld was supposed to recognize handwriting but did not. Apple went through a crisis in the late 1980s. By the early 1990s, most new PCs ran Microsoft Windows on Intel processors.

The Apple IIGs personal computer. *Corbis Corporation. Reproduced by permission.*

By the late 1990s, Apple was reviving. Using a new generation of Motorola chips, its machines offered class-leading graphics and sound technology. With Jobs back in charge, Apple began to move back into the home-computer market, aiming once more for reliability, speed, and ease of use. Realizing that consumers like bright colors, Apple ditched the traditional "beige box" image with the introduction of the iMac in 1998. At the start of the twenty-first century, Apple still struggled to gain users amid a computer marketplace dominated by IBM-compatible PCs.

—Chris Routledge

For More Information

Apple. http://www.apple.com (accessed March 29, 2002).

Greenberg, Keith Elliot. *Steven Jobs and Stephen Wozniak: Creating the Apple Computer.* Woodbridge, CT: Blackbirch Press, 1994.

Kendall, Steve. *Steve Wozniak: Inventor of the Apple Computer.* New York: Walker, 1994.

Levy, Stephen. *Insanely Great: The Life and Times of Macintosh, the Computer That Changed Everything.* New York: Viking, 1994.

Linzmayer, Owen W. *The Mac Bathroom Reader*. San Francisco: Sybex, 1994.

Linzmayer, Owen W. *The Macintosh Joker: A Collection of 33 Cruel Mac Tricks*. Indianapolis: Hayden Books, 1993.

Chia Pets

Chia Pets are small ceramic figurines that provide the basis for a thick growth of young plants. As seeds sprout on the ceramic base, the leaves are meant to resemble the fur of an animal or the foliage of a tree. The Chia Pet was "invented" and marketed in 1977 by Joseph Enterprises, Inc., a California-based manufacturer of future novelty goods such as The Clapper (which turns lights off with a clap of the hands) and the VCR Co-Pilot (which helps people program their VCRs).

Chia Pets remain popular into the twenty-first century. Chia fans can buy pet sheep, pigs, bunnies, cows, and so on, as well as Chia heads. No matter the shape, chia seeds (*Salvia columbariae*) are placed in the grooves of the ceramic figures and watered. The ease with which Chia Pets can be tended make them popular among children and young adults, and as novelty gifts. The manufacturer also markets a Chia herb garden. Chia Pets resemble the other low-care fads of the late twentieth century, such as **pet rocks** (see entry under 1970s—The Way We Lived in volume 4) and Tamagotchi electronic pets.

—Tom Pendergast

For More Information

Bellis, Mary. "Inventors: Chia Pet." *About.com*. http://inventors.about.com/library/inventors/blchia.htm (accessed March 29, 2002).

Communes

Communes are communities formed by groups of people who share certain values. Often those values include cooperation in working, growing food, cooking, cleaning, and child rearing. Sometimes the groups develop new and often more liberating roles for women. Some communes even experimented with new sexual arrangements between men and women. American culture has often valued individualism over communal effort, and many people started communes as an alternative to the dominant values of their day. Communes have existed in many societies. Among the first communes in the United States were those started by the Shakers and the Oneidas in the mid-nineteenth century. Both groups had strong religious convictions, although very different ones.

Communes enjoyed a resurgence in the 1960s and 1970s during the youth counterculture movement. Then, groups of young people established utopian communes (their idea of the ideal community) as alternatives to the dominant values of the United States. These groups were widely viewed as wild "**hippies**" (see entry under 1960s–The Way We Lived in volume 4). Many of these groups started out enthusiastically, but many lacked the practical skills necessary to remain successful. Most disbanded by the early 1970s. Despite these failures, some communes still existed at the end of the twentieth century.

–Timothy Berg

For More Information

Communes and You. . . . http://www.lehigh.edu/~inengl2/communes/home.html (accessed March 29, 2002).

Zicklin, Gilbert. *Countercultural Communes: A Sociological Perspective.* Westport, CT: Greenwood Press, 1983.

Cults

"Cult" is not a neutral word in American culture. In common usage, it often refers to a group outside the mainstream—a group with abnormal, crazy, perhaps even sinister ideas or practices. Cults that have gained the most public attention tend to reinforce this image.

Social scientists say that to be labeled a "cult" an organization must meet the criteria of size, doctrine, and time. A cult tends to be small in membership, anywhere from a handful to a few hundred. Cults also tend to have one or more differences in doctrine from established religions—a cult may believe in a different god or may have forms of worship not shared by other churches. Finally, a cult is usually new on the scene, which gives it the status of "outsider."

Christianity was considered a cult by the Romans throughout the first century C.E., until it grew in numbers and attained some longevity. Mormonism was considered cultish by many Americans in the nineteenth century, forcing the church to abandon one of its "deviant" doctrines—polygamy (the practice of having more than one spouse). The Church of Scientology was described as a cult in a *Time* (see entry under 1920s—Print Culture in volume 2) magazine cover story in the 1990s.

The cults most likely to become prominent in popular culture are those that are destructive—whether of their own members, or outsiders, or both. In 1978, charismatic preacher Jim Jones (1931–1978) took the members of his San Francisco, California, church, known as the People's Temple, to an isolated patch of jungle in British Guyana to create a new society, Jonestown. Rumors of Jones brainwashing his followers and keeping some against their will led to a U.S. government investigation. After a violent confrontation between cultists and the investigators, Jones commanded all of his followers to commit suicide by drinking poison. The reluctant were shot. On November 18, 1978, U.S. officials found the bodies of Jones and 913 followers dead on the ground. The incident was the subject of a 1980 made-for-TV movie, *Guyana Tragedy: The Story of Jim Jones*. The U.S. government's twenty-two-day siege of the **Branch Davidian** (see entry under 1990s—The Way We Lived in volume 5) Church's compound in Waco, Texas, in 1993 was the focus of intense news coverage. At the beginning, federal agents trying to serve a warrant were shot at and wounded; by the end the compound burned down, killing those inside, including the group's "Messiah," David Koresh (1959–1993). This tragedy has been the subject of two films: *In the Line of Duty: Ambush in Waco* (a 1993 made-for-TV movie) and *Waco: The Rules of Engagement* (a 1997 documentary that is very critical of the government's actions).

—*Justin Gustainis*

For More Information

Abgrall, Jean-Marie. *Soul Snatchers: The Mechanics of Cults*. New York: Algora Publishers, 2000.

Eyre, Anne. "Religious Cults in Twentieth Century America." *ARNet: On-line Resources for American Studies*. http://www.americansc.org.uk/cults.htm (accessed March 29, 2002).

Lewis, James R. *Odd Gods: New Religions & the Cult Controversy*. Amherst, NY: Prometheus Books, 2001.

Wessinger, Catherine. *How the Millennium Comes Violently: From Jonestown to Heaven's Gate*. New York: Northam Publishers, 2000.

Divorce

• •

The concept of marriage as a union of a man and a woman in lifetime partnership is thousands of years old. But as long as people have been getting married, there have been divorces, or other legal ways to end marriages. Though legal in most societies, divorce has often been frowned upon. Until recent decades, divorce was frequently viewed as abnormal or wrong. Since the 1970s, divorce rates have risen steadily. In 2000, 49 percent of U.S. marriages ended in divorce. Although there were over twenty million divorced people in the United States in 2000, American society still worries about whether divorce is a selfish act of people not willing to try hard enough to create a successful marriage or a positive step to end an unhappy relationship.

In many early cultures, marriage was a civil or a legal contract, and divorce was also purely a matter of law. Ancient Romans, Greeks, and Jews, among others, allowed divorce fairly easily. The Catholic church, which began to gain followers in the fifth and sixth centuries C.E., defined marriage as a religious ritual and forbade divorce. The influence of the church spread, and divorce became more difficult all over Europe. However, even when divorce has been difficult because of legal or religious limitations, people have left unhappy marriages. Sometimes people run away. Sometimes people live separate lives while still remaining legally married.

In past centuries, marriage was a necessity of survival. Women married because they were often not legally allowed to earn or inherit money and they needed men to support them. Men married because they needed women to farm, cook, clean, make clothes, bear and raise children, and do the hundreds of jobs required to run preindustrial households. The marriage was only one part of the extended family unit, with grandparents, aunts, uncles, in-laws, and children supporting each other and sharing in the work of the household.

The romantic idea of marriage as two people in love sharing emotional support and affection developed later, around the nineteenth and early twentieth centuries. In addition, the mid-1900s saw the rise of the nuclear family, which defines a family as mother, father, and children. These two developments put much more pressure on marriages. The couple stood alone now, with husband and wife required to not only share the work of the family but meet each other's emotional needs as well.

It is not coincidental that the largest rises in divorce rates have occurred during the two recent periods of feminism, the struggle for women's rights. In the early 1900s, when American women were fighting to be allowed to vote, earn money, and own property, divorce rates rose from one in twenty-one marriages (1880) to one in nine marriages (1916). Again in the 1970s, following a new women's liberation movement that fought for equal pay and equal rights for women, divorce rates soared. This increase has led some conservative critics to say that it is women's "new" desire for independence that has caused rising divorce rates. However, others point out that before feminists won increased rights for women, they were often trapped within unhappy marriages, because they could not earn enough money to leave. Even after gaining the right to work, women are usually poorer after a divorce than men are.

Society's views of divorce have greatly changed over the years. In 1936, King Edward VIII of England (1894–1972) had to give up the throne before he could marry Wallis Warfield Simpson (1896–1986), an American woman who had been divorced twice. But in 1996, Prince Charles (1948–) divorced his wife, Princess Diana (1961–1997), and still maintained his right to become king of England. In 1980, the American people elected Ronald Reagan (1911–), their first divorced president. Where once divorce was a forbidden subject, hidden in silence, the 2000 *Books in Print* lists over two thousand books on the topic, over seventy of them for children whose parents are divorcing.

Much of the controversy about divorce revolves around its effect on the children in the family. Some critics of divorce, researchers, politicians, and therapists, say that divorce is so harmful to children that parents should stay together even if they are unhappy. Others insist that children suffer more harm from living with parents who are in a bad marriage. In 1983, a divorced mother in Illinois started Rainbows, a peer support group for children dealing with their parents' divorce. Rainbows soon grew to have chapters in cities throughout the United States and Canada.

Film, **television** (see entry under 1940s—TV and Radio in volume 3), and other media also reflect society's changing and contradictory views about divorce. Although early TV featured several shows with single parents, such as the early 1960s' *My Three Sons* (1960–72), those parents were always widowed, not divorced. In 1970, the creators of **The Mary Tyler Moore Show**

(1970–77; see entry under 1970s–TV and Radio in volume 4) changed the lead character from a divorced woman to one who had broken up with her fiancé to make the show more acceptable to conservative audiences. By 1975, Bonnie Franklin (1944–) played the first successful divorced mother of two on CBS' *One Day at a Time* (1975–84). By the 1990s, divorced parents were common on the television screen, in such shows as *Grace Under Fire* (1993–98), about a working-class divorced mom, raising three children, and *Once and Again* (1999–2002), a more serious exploration of the complications of step-families.

However, films like *The Parent Trap,* originally released in 1961 and remade in 1998, may best express American society's underlying feelings that divorce is a mistake. The story is a romantic fantasy of twins, separated by their parents' divorce, who reunite and successfully plot to get their parents back together.

Although rising divorce rates clearly show that many marriages have problems, it will take time for society to replace the romantic image of the happy nuclear family with something that better fulfills the needs of modern society.

—*Tina Gianoulis*

For More Information

Charlish, Anne. *Divorce.* New York: Raintree Steck-Vaughn Publishers, 1999.

Feldman, Ellen. "Till Divorce Do Us Part." *American Heritage* (Vol. 51, iss. 7, November 2000): pp. 38–45.

Griswold, Robert L. "Divorce: Social History in the U.S." In *The Reader's Companion to American History Edition 1991.* New York: Houghton Mifflin, 1991, pp. 287–90.

Johnson, Linda Carlson. *Everything You Need to Know about Your Parents' Divorce.* New York: Rosen Publishing Group, 1998.

"Should You Stay Together for the Kids?" *Time* (Vol. 156, iss. 13, September 25, 2000): pp. 74–7.

Earth Day

Observed for the first time on April 22, 1970, Earth Day was created by environmental activists as an unofficial holiday on which people could reflect on the planet's ecology and engage in pro-environmental activities. The cause was taken up by U.S. senator Gaylord Nelson (1916–) of Wisconsin, whose support helped make Earth Day a reality. It is estimated that some twenty million people across the United States participated in the first Earth Day through demonstrations, exhibits, and teach-ins in more than ten thousand communities.

Images of the Earth as a fragile, blue-green ball hanging in dark space were just beginning to filter into the public's consciousness, especially after the first moon landing in 1969. That year also saw two environmental disasters that captured public attention: the Santa Barbara, California, oil spill and a fire in the Cuyahoga River in Cleveland, Ohio. These graphic portraits helped stimulate support for Earth Day, which is now considered the beginning of the modern **environmentalism** (see entry under 1970s—The Way We Lived in volume 4) movement.

The original Earth Day helped arouse support for several important environmental programs undertaken by the U.S. government: the creation of the Environmental Protection Administration (EPA), the Clean Air Act, and the Clean Water Act, all of which began in the early 1970s. For the rest of the decade, environmental activists, many of them veterans of the antiwar and **civil rights movements** (see entry under 1960s—The Way We Lived in volume 4) of the 1960s, continued to press government, industry, and the American public to pay attention to environmental issues. They appealed to government and industry to end pollution and halt the construction of nuclear power plants. They persuaded the general public to conserve resources and recycle their garbage.

By April 22, 1990, Earth Day was being observed by millions of people in 139 nations around the world. Some two hundred million people reportedly participated in what has been called the largest grass-roots demonstration in history. More than a million people gathered in New York City's Central Park, and two hundred thousand assembled in front of the U.S. Capitol in Washington, D.C., to listen to music and hear speeches. Earth Day is still regarded as the symbolic beginning of a wide-scale popular movement to raise consciousness about the perilous state of the planet's ecology.

—*Edward Moran*

For More Information

Cahn, Robert, and Patricia Cahn. "Did Earth Day Change the World?" *Environment* (September 1990): 16–42.

Earth Day Network. http://www.earthday.net/ (accessed March 29, 2002).

Gilbert, Bil. "Earth Day Plus 20, and Counting." *Smithsonian* (April 1990): 46–52.

Hayes, Denis, "Earth Day 1990: Threshold of the Green Decade." *World Policy Journal* (Vol. 7, no. 2, 1990): 289–304.

U.S. Environmental Protection Agency. http://www.epa.gov/ (accessed March 29, 2002).

Environmentalism

For many decades, Americans have felt they could do whatever they wanted with their air, land, and water. There always seemed to be plenty. It was easy to ignore environmental devastation by moving on to a new place. By 1850, for example, more than one hundred million acres of land had been cleared of trees, an area equal in size to the entire state of California. As the United States became more industrialized in the late nineteenth century, those problems became harder to ignore. More Americans became concerned about these problems, and the environmental movement was started. It continues to the present day.

The creation of national parks marked the first stirrings of environmentalism. As Americans realized the limitations of their natural resources, they wanted to preserve some untouched natural areas from development so that they would always be there for future generations of Americans to enjoy. Yosemite, in California, was created in 1864, followed by Yellowstone in Wyoming, Montana, and Idaho in 1872. More national parks, national wilderness areas, and national monuments were established in the coming decades. President Theodore Roosevelt (1858–1919) made environmental preservation one of his priorities during his term in office (1901–9), preserving millions of acres of land and creating a National Forest Service to help manage wilderness areas. Although battles would often be fought over what to do with these national areas from time to time, the United States has continued to add more of these protected areas.

After World War II (1939–45), environmentalism took on a new direction. While there was still concern for protecting unpolluted natural areas, the environmental movement turned to protecting the environments in which most Americans lived. The 1962 book *Silent Spring* by Rachel Carson (1907–1964) awakened many Americans to the dangers of industrial pollution from chemicals. By the 1960s, it seemed that many of the hazards of the industrial era were beginning to build up to intolerable levels. New environmental groups sprang up to alert Americans and to fight pollution, including Greenpeace and the Natural Resources Defense Council. The U.S. government increased its efforts by creating the Environmental Protection Agency (EPA) in 1969. In 1970, the first Earth Day was held to encourage ordinary Americans to get involved protecting the environment in their own communities.

In the decades since 1970, the environmental movement has continued to push for cleaner air, water, and land, fighting industrial polluters and often government indifference. Because the environment is of such vital importance, its protection has remained an important part of American culture.

—Timothy Berg

For More Information

Dunlap, Riley E., and Angela G. Mertig, eds. *American Environmentalism: The U.S. Environmental Movement, 1970–1990.* Philadelphia: Taylor and Francis, 1992.

Earth Day Network. http://www.earthday.net/ (accessed March 29, 2002).

Fox, Stephen. *The American Conservation Movement.* Madison: University of Wisconsin Press, 1981.

Greenpeace International Homepage. http://www.greenpeace.org/ (accessed March 29, 2002).

National Resources Defense Council. http://www.nrdc.org/ (accessed March 29, 2002).

Rome, Adam Ward. *The Bulldozer in the Countryside: Suburban Sprawl and the Rise of American Environmentalism.* New York: Cambridge University Press, 2001.

Sale, Kirkpatrick. *The Green Revolution.* New York: Hill and Want, 1993.

U.S. Environmental Protection Agency. http://www.epa.gov/ (accessed March 29, 2002).

Equal Rights Amendment

The struggle to add an amendment to the U.S. Constitution guaranteeing equal rights for women was an important, if ultimately unsuccessful, chapter in the history of the women's movement in the United States. Throughout the history of the United States, as well as of the world, women had always had fewer rights than men. For years, they could not own property or run for elective office. They could not even vote in the United States until 1920. Although the status of women in the United

States had gradually improved over time, many glaring inequalities with which they had to suffer still existed. The Equal Rights Amendment (ERA) was an attempt to end those inequalities.

The ERA was first proposed in 1925 by the National Women's Party and introduced into Congress by Alice Paul (1885–1977), the group's president. It was a controversial proposal that did not get far in the legislative process. Part of the controversy centered around what would happen to laws designed to protect women if they must be treated equally under the law. Although the amendment was endorsed by both Democratic and Republican parties in the 1940s, it still went nowhere in Congress. In 1970, U.S. representative Martha Griffiths (1912–) of Michigan reintroduced the amendment. It read simply, "Equality of rights under the law shall not be denied or abridged by the United States or by any state on account of sex." This time, in 1972, it passed both houses of Congress. For an amendment to be passed and added to the Constitution, however, it must be approved by three-fourths of the states within seven years. At the state level, a fierce debate ensued. Supporters of

A woman holds up a sign calling for an end to discrimination at an Equal Rights Amendment rally. *Archive Photos, Inc. Reproduced by permission.*

the ERA argued that women deserved the same rights as men. Opponents of the ERA raised people's fears that equal rights for women meant women in combat, more women in the workplace, and the end to other long-established gender roles. Although thirty-five states approved it, and despite a three-year extension of the time limit, it failed to attract the final votes necessary to pass in 1983. It has been periodically resubmitted to Congress without much success in the years since.

—*Timothy Berg*

For More Information

Becker, Susan D. *The Origins of the Equal Rights Amendment: American Feminism Between the Wars.* Westport, CT: Greenwood Press, 1982.

"Chronology of the Equal Rights Amendment 1923–1996." *National Organization for Women.* http://www.now.org/issues/economic/cea/history.html (accessed March 29, 2002).

Evans, Sarah M. *Born for Liberty: A History of Women in America.* New York: The Free Press, 1989.

National Council of Women's Organizations. *The Equal Rights Amendment.* http://www.equalrightsamendment.org/ (accessed March 29, 2002).

Rowbotham, Sheila. *A Century of Women.* New York: Penguin Books, 1999.

The Joy of Sex •••••••••••••••••••••••••••••••••

Published in 1972, *The Joy of Sex,* by Alex Comfort (1920–2000), became the first mass-market book to treat sexuality in a frank and lighthearted way, complete with illustrations designed to help people understand and enjoy intimate matters that had often been shrouded in secrecy. Its author was a British doctor, poet-novelist, and social activist who researched and wrote the book, though he is described as its editor. *The Joy of Sex* was published at a time when U.S. society was loosening many of the rigid, puritanical attitudes that had prevented open discussions about sex. Although some critics were unhappy at the book's condescending treatment of women and homosexuals, Comfort's book is today regarded as an important breakthrough in the "sexual revolution" of the period.

The full title of the book, published by Crown, was *The Joy of Sex: A Gourmet Guide to Lovemaking.* As the title implies, Comfort believed that good sex was like a delicious meal, with fine ingredients skillfully blended by a chef. The book included more than one hundred line drawings and several pages of paintings in full color by Charles Raymond and Christopher Foss. In *The Joy of Sex,* Comfort rejected strict moralistic attitudes toward sexuality, writing that "one aim of this book is to cure the notion, born of non-discussion, that common sex needs are odd or weird." He added, "There are, after all, only two 'rules' in good sex, apart from the obvious ones of not doing things which are silly, antisocial, or dangerous. One is 'don't do anything you don't really enjoy,' and the other is 'find out your partner's needs and don't balk them if you can help it.'" This attitude was condemned by religious critics, among others, as being too permissive.

In 1977, Charles Silverstein (1935–) and Edmund White (1940–) collaborated as authors of *The Joy of Gay Sex,* written to counter what they considered the homophobic (antigay) bias of Comfort's book. In the wake of the **AIDS** (see entry under 1980s—The Way We Lived in volume 5) crisis of the 1980s, later editions of both books emphasized safe-sex techniques.

—*Edward Moran*

For More Information

Comfort, Alex. *The Joy of Sex: A Gourmet Guide to Lovemaking.* New York: Crown, 1972.

Comfort, Alex. *The New Joy of Sex.* Edited by Julie Rubenstein. New York: Crown, 1992.

Kenner, Hugh. "The Comfort Behind *The Joy of Sex.*" *New York Times Magazine* (October 27, 1974).

Silverstein, Charles, and Edmund White. *The Joy of Gay Sex.* New York: Crown, 1977; revised, New York: HarperCollins, 1992.

Kent State Massacre
● ●

On April 30, 1970, President Richard Nixon (1913–1994) announced to the nation that he had sent American forces into the neutral country of Cambodia. His reason was to "clean out" Communist base camps that were being used for attacks against U.S. troops in Vietnam during the Vietnam War (1954–75). Antiwar sentiment on the college campuses, which had been relatively quiet for months, exploded in response to the news. Although Nixon was emphasizing the protection of American troops and the brief nature of the incursion, outraged opponents of the war focused on the neutrality of Cambodia and

Grief prevailed in the aftermath of the confrontation with the Ohio National Guard on the Kent State University campus, where, on May 4, 1970, four students were killed and fourteen injured during a protest. *UPI/Corbis-Bettmann. Reproduced by permission.*

what seemed to be the expansion of the fighting into yet another country. Marches, rallies, and demonstrations of all sorts erupted on campuses across the nation.

One site of vigorous protest was Kent State University, in the northeastern Ohio town of Kent. Some students broke windows of campus buildings, others damaged businesses downtown, and someone set fire to the campus Reserve Officer Training Corps (ROTC) building. When firefighters arrived, protesting students tried to prevent them from extinguishing the blaze. Governor James Rhodes (1909–2001) forbade any further demonstrations on campus, and sent in National Guard troops to keep order.

On May 4, another rally was held in defiance of the governor's order. Campus security officers told the students to disperse, but they refused. National Guard troops arrived soon thereafter. Some students threw rocks. One guardsman, thinking he heard sniper fire, opened up on the crowd. Others followed suit. When the shooting was over, a total of thirty-five rounds had been fired by national guardsmen. Four students lay dead, and fourteen more were wounded. No sniper fire was ever confirmed. The guardsmen were tried for murder and acquitted.

One of the most memorable photographs taken immediately after the shooting shows a young woman named Mary Ann Vecchio screaming as she kneels over the body of slain student Jeffrey Miller. The photo won photographer John Filo the Pulitzer Prize, has been reproduced countless times, and stands as a tragic icon (symbol) of the Vietnam War era. A month after the shootings, the band Crosby, Stills, Nash and Young lamented the tragedy in their hit song "Ohio."

—Justin Gustainis

For More Information

Davies, Peter. *The Truth About Kent State: A Challenge to the American Conscience.* New York: Farrar, Straus, and Giroux, 1973.

Eszterhas, Joe, and Michael D. Roberts. *Thirteen Seconds: Confrontation at Kent State.* New York: Dood, Mead, 1970.

Hensley, Thomas R., and Jerry M. Lewis. *Kent State and May 4th: A Social Science Perspective.* Dubuque, IA: Kendall/Hunt Publishers, 2000.

Kent State University: Department of Special Collections & Archives. http://www.library.kent.edu/exhibits/4may95/ (accessed March 29, 2002).

Personal Computers

By the late 1990s, personal computers (PCs) had found a place in millions of American homes. They were part of everyday life for office workers, as common as coffee cups and paper clips. Personal computers were used in all aspects of the media, in libraries, schools, and businesses of all kinds. Portable models had become a common sight on city streets, on public transport, and in cafes and bars. Yet barely twenty years earlier, PCs were available only to electronics hobbyists and the very rich. For most people in the 1970s, the personal computer was a device straight out of science fiction.

The PC revolution was made possible by the invention of the microprocessor—a computer chip that contains the entire central processing unit (CPU) of the computer. Before the late 1970s, computers were so large they had special rooms all to themselves. They needed a controlled climate and high levels of cleanliness to protect their sensitive electronics from dust and changes in temperature. Reducing complex electronic circuits to the size of a fingernail, microprocessors were robust enough to withstand normal working conditions and small enough to make computers more manageable in size. They were used in hand-held electronic calculators, wristwatches, and simple game machines. Microprocessors also became the key component in the PC.

Just who invented the PC is open to debate. Companies like **IBM** (see entry under 1980s—Commerce in volume 5), **Apple Computer** (see entry under 1970s—The Way We Lived in volume 4), and **Xerox** (see entry under 1960s—Commerce in volume 3) all have claimed to have done so. But the first PCs probably belonged to computer hobbyists. They bought electronic components and assembled the machines themselves. As the cost of microprocessors fell in the late 1970s, companies like Acorn, Apple, **Atari** (see entry under 1970s—Sports and Games in volume 4), and Tandy started to sell computers that were little more than ready-made hobbyist machines. Users had to be familiar with computer programming to make early PCs work. The machines had tiny amounts of memory by modern standards. A standard Tandy TRS-80 personal computer from 1980 had just eight thousand bytes (8K) of usable memory, with no hard disk. That is enough memory to hold just half a page of a basic word-processing document. Files and software were stored on a standard cassette tape.

The Apple II computer, released in 1977, was the best of the early PCs. It was the first to reach a mass market with speed and real computing power. But it was another seven years before the PC became accessible to users with no previous computing knowledge. In 1984, Apple's Macintosh computer had many of the features familiar on PCs in 2001. It was the first mass-market PC to use "drag and drop" icons, overlapping "windows," and a mouse. Known as Graphical User Interface (GUI), this system of opening files and running programs quickly became the standard.

Apple's major competitor in the early 1980s was IBM. Apple and IBM used different microprocessors, but although Apple computers were superior in terms of speed and computing power, other companies copied IBM's design. Before long, Hewlett Packard, Dell, and other computer makers began to swamp the market with PCs based on the IBM model. Running Windows software made by **Microsoft** (see entry under 1990s—Commerce in volume 5), these computers were cheap and used a GUI that was similar to Apple's. Both Apple and IBM had problems in the late 1980s, but the IBM platform became the standard for the desktop PC in the 1990s.

In the 1990s, major advances in the speed and efficiency of microprocessors changed the way PCs were used. In the 1980s, portable computers were the size and weight of a small well-packed suitcase. By 2001, "laptop" computers are small enough to fit in a briefcase and could be used in much the same way as a "desktop" PC. Smaller still, a fully functional handheld PC, complete with miniaturized keyboard and screen, will fit in the palm of a man's hand. Other handheld computers can recognize handwriting traced on a small screen. These pocket-sized PCs are sometimes known as personal digital assistants (PDAs). All these machines are much more powerful than the first PCs. Many exceed the capabilities of the huge "mainframe" computers of the 1960s and 1970s.

In its short life, the personal computer has grown from a hobbyist's toy into an essential everyday item. Once used mainly for word processing and data storage, the PC at the start of the twenty-first century is also a communication tool, a games machine, a sound and video system, and a place to store the family photographs. Since the advent of the World Wide Web, it has also become a shopping **mall** (see entry under 1950s—Commerce in volume 3), a reference library, and the first place to look for new recipes, cheap airline tickets, and classified advertisements. Personal computers have also made possible the growth in working at home and telecommuting. As new, smaller, more powerful PCs take on functions once performed by other machines, it is possible that the old-fashioned desktop PC will eventually disappear. The PCs of the late twentieth century changed forever the way we think about work and leisure.

—Chris Routledge

For More Information

"Computer History Collection." *Smithsonian National Museum of American History.* http://americanhistory.si.edu/csr/comphist (accessed April 1, 2002).

The Computer Museum History Center. http://www.computerhistory.org (accessed April 1, 2002).

Cringley, Robert X., writer; John Gau, producer. *Triumph of the Nerds* (video). New York: Ambrose Video Publishing, 1996.

Freiberger, Paul, and Michael Swaine. *Fire in the Valley: The Making of the Personal Computer.* New York: McGraw-Hill Professional Publishing, 1999.

Levy, Stephen. *Insanely Great: The Life and Times of Macintosh, the Computer That Changed Everything.* New York: Viking, 1994.

Malone, Michael S. *The Microprocessor: A Biography.* Santa Clara, CA: TELOS, 1995.

The pet rock, a popular gift, came with a carrying case and a care and training instruction book.
AP/Wide World Photos. Reproduced by permission.

Pet Rocks

The pet rock was one of the biggest gift crazes in American history. Introduced in time for the holiday gift buying season in 1975, the humble stones sold for two dollars apiece and came with a special "training manual." The man who "invented" the pet rock became an instant millionaire.

Pet rocks were the brainchild of Gary Dahl (1937?–), a California advertising man who came up with the concept while having dinner with some friends in April 1975. Dahl thought, What if there were a pet that did not require any care or feeding? He quickly set about writing his *Pet Rock Training Manual.* Soon after, he decided to market an *actual* pet rock as well. He bought a bunch of Rosarita beach stones at a building supply store and took them to the annual San Francisco gift show in August 1975. The stones cost him only a penny each, but he packed them in a gift box and attached his training manual and offered them for sale to retailers for two dollars each.

The rocks were the hit of the show and Dahl could barely keep up with the orders that came rolling in. Neiman-Marcus, the giant retail chain, ordered five hundred. By October, Dahl was shipping out some ten thousand pet rocks a day. By Christmas, he had sold over one million of the adorable "creatures." At $3.95 retail, that made for an enormous profit margin. The outgoing, bearded ad man was now a millionaire—and with that came instant celebrity. Dahl appeared on **The Tonight Show** (see entry under 1950s—TV and Radio in volume 3) twice and was profiled in newspapers and magazines across the country, including *Newsweek*.

As quickly as the pet rock craze began, it ended. Soon after Christmas of 1975, demand for pet rocks began to plummet. Imitators rushed their own pet-rock products onto the market in the hopes of cashing in, but the mania had subsided. Dahl himself had to give away thousands of unsold stones to charity. Having earned enough to retire on, however, he was not complaining. He embarked on a lucrative second career giving motivational speeches and writing books about how to make a million dollars fast.

Robert E. Schnakenberg

For More Information

Panati, Charles. *Fads, Follies, and Manias*. New York: Harper Perennial, 1991.

Polson Enterprises. "Pet Rock Page." *Virtual Pet Home Page*. http://www.virtualpet.com/vp/farm/petrock/petrock.htm (accessed March 29, 2002).

Skolnik, Peter L., with Laura Torbet and Nikki Smith. *Fads: America's Crazes, Fevers & Fancies from the 1890's to the 1970's*. New York: Crowell, 1978.

Roe v. Wade

Abortion is a controversial issue in America. Those who are pro-abortion, or "pro-choice," fervently support a woman's right to control her body. Their stance is that, if a woman becomes pregnant, it is her decision—and her decision alone—to abort or not to abort a pregnancy. Those who are against abortion, or "pro-life," just as avidly believe that life begins at conception, rather than at birth, and that the law must protect the unborn. Thus "pro-life" supporters believe that the right of the fetus is more important the right of the mother; for those people, abortion is a crime,

Many protests and rallies took place for both sides of the *Roe v. Wade* case. *AP/Wide World Photos. Reproduced by permission.*

and, for many, a crime just as horrible as cold-blooded murder. In 1973, the U.S. Supreme Court handed down the *Roe v. Wade* decision, which legalized abortion—and formalized the battle lines between "pro-life" and "pro-choice" forces.

The major player in *Roe v. Wade* was Norma McCorvey (1947–), or "Jane Roe" as she was known in the case. McCorvey was a poor pregnant Texas woman who was rejected in her attempts to obtain an abortion; eventually, she gave birth and put the baby up for adoption. Meanwhile, two young lawyers who wished to challenge the state's restrictive abortion law took up her case, which eventually was argued before the Supreme Court. The Court ruled that only a pregnant woman and her doctor should be empowered to make the decision to end a pregnancy, so long as it is within three months of conception. After that time period, each state had the right to limit abortions. The decision was based on the concept of the right to privacy, and the belief that, in America, individuals should be able to make the decisions that affect their lives.

Before *Roe v. Wade,* only four states and Washington, D.C., allowed access to abortion. Otherwise, the procedure was illegal. A woman seeking a legal abortion had to travel to one of the four states or to Washington, D.C., or had to leave the country, thus preventing those with meager financial resources from obtaining abortions. A woman could have one performed illegally, by a back-alley abortionist, often in unsafe (and, occasionally, life-threatening) conditions.

The pro-abortion tide was set in motion less than two decades earlier, when a German measles epidemic and the use of a tranquilizer called Thalidomide resulted in a rash of infants born with severe birth defects. Then, beginning in the early 1970s, the burgeoning women's movement led to an increased awareness of women's reproductive rights. It was this climate that resulted in the *Roe v. Wade* decision. The abortion topic has been a political battleground ever since. A political candidate's view on abortion has been a litmus test (a test decided by one issue or factor) for whether he or she is acceptable to many voters.

Despite the politically conservative climate of the 1980s, which emerged with the election to the U.S. presidency of Ronald Reagan (1911–), the Court reaffirmed its position on *Roe v. Wade*. Meanwhile, a few violent anti-abortion activists began attacking abortion clinics and even murdering the doctors who worked there. The "pro-choice" versus "pro-life" battle rages to this day and remains as heated and as contentious as ever.

—Rob Edelman

For More Information

Craig, Barbara Hinkson, and David M. O'Brien. *Abortion and American Politics*. Chatham, NJ: Chatham House Publishers, 1993.

Faux, Marian. *Roe v. Wade: The Untold Story of the Landmark Supreme Court Decision That Made Abortion Legal*. New York: New American Library, 1988.

Reagan, Leslie J. *When Abortion Was Illegal: Women, Medicine, and Law in the United States, 1867–1973*. Berkeley: University of California Press, 1997.

Serial Killers

Serial killers are hunters, and their prey is human. They seek, stalk, and slay their victim, then start looking for another. Over the past twenty-five years, serial killers—both real and fictional—have assumed a major role in America's nightmares.

David Berkowitz, the notorious serial killer known as "Son of Sam," is transported after his arrest in 1977. *AP/Wide World Photos. Reproduced by permission.*

Although this crime is hardly a modern invention, the term "serial killer" was coined by Federal Bureau of Investigation (FBI) agents in the early 1970s. Criminologists distinguish between the "mass murderer" and the "serial killer." The mass murderer kills a number of victims at once, as part of a single explosion of rage; the serial killer, however, spreads out his butchery over time and territory.

The first serial killer to attract wide popular attention was probably Jack the Ripper, who murdered five London prostitutes in 1888. Perhaps because he was never identified, he has been the subject of hundreds of books and stories and more than a dozen movies, most recently 2001's *From Hell.*

Real-life American serial killers have included David Berkowitz, the "Son of Sam" (1953–); Ted Bundy (1946–1989); Albert DeSalvo, the "Boston Strangler" (1931–1973); John Wayne Gacy (1942–1994); Ed Gein, the inspiration for the fictional characters Norman Bates and Hannibal Lecter (1906–1984); Henry Lee Lucas (1936–); Aileen Wuornos, a rare female serial killer (1956–); and the Zodiac Killer (never caught).

Serial killers have become common villains in American crime fiction. Credit for inventing the genre, or category, of crime fiction is usually given to Thomas Harris (1910–1995). Harris created Hannibal "the Cannibal" Lecter, a serial killer who is also a brilliant psychiatrist. Harris introduced Lecter in *Red Dragon* (1981; filmed as *Manhunter* in 1986) and made him the central character of *The Silence of the Lambs* (1988; filmed in 1991) and *Hannibal* (1999; filmed in 2001).

Master of suspense Alfred Hitchcock (1899–1980) used serial killers as villains in several of his films, such as *The Lodger* (1926), *Shadow of a Doubt* (1943), *Psycho* (1960), and *Frenzy* (1972). More recent films focusing on serial killers include *Henry: Portrait of a Serial Killer* (1986), *Basic Instinct* (1992), *Se7en* (1995), and *American Psycho* (2000).

Several **television** (see entry under 1940s–TV and Radio in volume 3) series featured heroes who specialized in hunting down serial killers. These included *Unsub* (1989), *Twin Peaks* (1990–91), *Millennium* (1996–99), and *Profiler* (1996–2000).

—Justin Gustainis

For More Information

Douglas, John, and Mark Olshaker. *Mindhunter*. New York: Pocket Books, 1995.

Fox, James Alan, and Jack Levin. *Overkill: Mass Murder and Serial Killing Exposed*. New York: Dell Books, 1994.

Leyton, Elliott. *Hunting Humans: Inside the Minds of Mass Murderers*. New York: Pocket Books, 1988.

Ressler, Robert, and Tom Shachtman. *Whoever Fights Monsters*. New York: St. Martin's Press, 1992.

The Serial Killer Info Site. http://www.serialkillers.net/ (accessed March 29, 2002).

Sexually Transmitted Diseases

Sexually transmitted diseases (STDs) are a blanket description for nearly twenty-five diseases that are spread primarily by sexual activity. STDs are called a "hidden" epidemic in the United States and affect nearly sixty-five million people. The Centers for Disease Control (CDC) estimated in 1999 that almost fifteen million new cases of STDs occur each year and that teenagers are the group most often infected.

The spread of STDs has been increasing in the United States for many years. The instance of genital herpes among white teenagers, for instance, increased five times between the 1970s and 1990s. By the end of the 1990s, the CDC reported that more than one in five Americans had genital herpes. The rate of increase is tied to the numbers of people with multiple sexual partners and the number of diseases, such as chlamydia and genital herpes, that an infected person can spread without having any symptoms. Some of the diseases, such as herpes, are bothersome life-long infections; others, such as HIV (human immunodeficiency virus) or **AIDS** (acquired immunodeficiency syndrome; see entry under 1980s–The Way We Lived in volume 5) can be deadly.

Most STDs are widespread throughout different regions of the country and infect people regardless of age, gender, race, or sexual orientation (whether a person is heterosexual or homosexual). Although any sexually active person is at risk to contract an STD, young women are at greater risk than others. The reason young women are at greater risk is because young adults tend to have more sexual partners and many STDs are more easily transmitted from males to females. But this does not diminish the threat to others. Some STDs are more common in males, in those living in southern states, and in those already infected with other diseases, such as HIV or AIDS.

Many STDs—including gonorrhea, syphilis, genital warts, and hepatitis B—have been spread by sex for centuries. Others are relatively new; AIDS, the most deadly STD, was first discovered in 1981. Although STDs have been infecting people for generations, they first became a part of popular culture in the 1970s. The popular attention given to STDs stemmed from the **sexual revolution** (see entry under 1960s—The Way We Lived in volume 4) of the previous decade. The sexual revolution was a time when people began to think differently about sex. More people began having multiple sexual partners, and as a result more people contracted STDs. The dramatic increase in STDs in the 1970s prompted both *Time* (see entry under 1920s—Print Culture in volume 2) and *Newsweek* to feature cover stories about the epidemic.

By the beginning of the twenty-first century, news stories about STDs were common. Attitudes about sexual activity had not changed dramatically since the 1970s. Many people still had multiple sexual partners, but many people also knew about the effects of STDs. Efforts to educate people about safer sexual practices that would slow the spread of STDs had become a prominent activity of the U.S. government and health organizations throughout the country.

—*Sara Pendergast*

For More Information

Byers, Ann. *Sexually Transmitted Diseases: A Hot Issue*. Springfield, NJ: Enslow Publishers, 1999.

Little, Marjorie. *Sexually Transmitted Diseases*. Philadelphia: Chelsea House, 2000.

National Center for HIV, STD and TB Prevention. Division of Sexually Transmitted Diseases. "STD Prevention." *CDC: Safer, Healthier, People*. http://www.cdc.gov/nchstp/dstd/dstdp.html (accessed March 29, 2002).

Smiley Face

The sunshine yellow circle with the smile on it became an American cultural icon (symbol) in 1970. Harvey R. Ball

(1921–2001) of Worcester, Massachusetts, created the smiley face for the State Mutual Life Assurance Companies of America (now Allamerica). Originally, the symbol was used to boost morale at the recently merged insurance companies. But by 1970, two brothers—Bernard and Murray Spain—of Philadelphia, Pennsylvania, recognized the commercial potential of the smiley face and began producing buttons, bumper stickers, shirts, cards, and other novelties with the symbol on them. Within a year, more than fifty million smiley face buttons had been sold.

Ball never applied for a copyright or a trademark for his design and made a total of $45 for it. The Spain brothers made considerably more as they cashed in on the height of the smiley face's popularity. The smiley face continues to be used. It is featured in advertisements for **Wal-Mart** (see entry under 1960s–Commerce in volume 4), and in 1999, the U.S. Postal Service issued a smiley-face stamp.

—Sara Pendergast

For More Information

"Creator of Smiley Face Icon Dies at 79." *Boston.com.* http://www.boston.com/news/daily/13/smiley.htm (accessed April 1, 2002).

"Smiley Face: A Short Documentary by Chris Sheridan." *YouKnow.com.* http://www.youknow.com/smiley/index.html (accessed April 1, 2002).

World Smile Corporation. http://www.worldsmile.com/aboutwsc.htm (accessed April 1, 2002).

Streaking

Back in the 1970s, a truly strange fad briefly captivated the nation: Streaking, the practice of removing one's clothes and running about stark naked in a public place, whether a ballpark or a meeting hall, a college campus, or even an Academy Awards ceremony. Streaking should not be confused with nudism. For nudists, nakedness is a lifestyle; nudists are private in their state of undress and socialize only among themselves. Streaking is an act of exhibitionism. It is meant to shock and amuse and attract attention.

The fad reached its peak in 1974. That March, over six hundred University of Missouri students disrobed and marched across the campus, while being cheered on by fifteen hundred

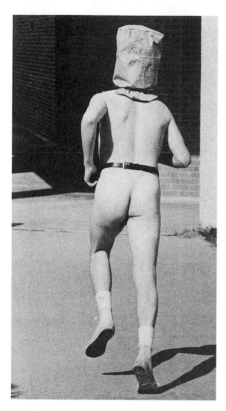

Wearing only socks, tennis shoes, a belt, and a paper bag over his head, this streaker goes for an afternoon jog. *Bettmann/Corbis. Reproduced by permission.*

onlookers. "The Streak," a nonsensical song recorded by singer-composer-comedian Ray Stevens (1939–), then zoomed to the top of the record charts. In it, Stevens captured the essence of the streaker when he sang, "He ain't rude. He ain't rude. He's just in the mood to run in the nude." The "he" is appropriate, given that most streakers were young males. In fact, a University of South Carolina psychology professor who researched the fad concluded that the average streaker was a Protestant male undergraduate who weighed 170 pounds and maintained a B average. He hailed from a town with a population under fifty thousand; his father was a businessman, and his mother was a housewife. Female streakers, meanwhile, tended to be short. They averaged 5 feet 3 inches and weighed approximately 117 pounds.

Some concluded that streaking was a form of nonviolent protest and a way of freeing oneself from one's inhibitions. Most, however, viewed it as a silly pastime, as harmless as a pack of fraternity brothers crowding into a telephone booth. Perhaps the most famous streaking incident occurred in April 1974 at the Academy Awards ceremony. Actor David Niven (1909–1983) was introducing fellow film-star Elizabeth Taylor (1932–) when he was interrupted by a young male streaker who had crashed the proceedings. Niven remained composed. Then he observed, with perfect comedic timing, "The only way he could get a laugh was by showing his shortcomings."

—*Rob Edelman*

For More Information

Pleasant, George. *The Joy of Streaking.* New York: Ballantine, 1974.

Tanning

For many years, suntanned skin symbolized health and sex appeal; a tan first gained status in the 1920s and reached a peak in the 1970s. Movie star Douglas Fairbanks Sr. (1883–1939) was among the first to popularize the suntan when he began appearing in films with gleaming bronzed muscles. His tanned skin became a symbol of his physical fitness. Before this time, creamy white skin had been a mark of high fashion and social

status because those with enough money could stay inside, away from the heat of the day, while field laborers were darkened by the sun. In the early twentieth century, however, more and more laborers moved to the cities and began working long hours indoors. Suntanned skin became a distinction available only to the wealthy with enough leisure time and money to travel to a sunny locale during the dreary winter months. Like Fairbanks, fashion designer Coco Chanel (1882–1971) established a trend for tanned skin in the 1920s. Returning from vacation with a deep, dark tan, Chanel began using tanned models and mannequins for her designs. By 1946, women could wear tiny bikinis to tan as much skin as possible.

Tanning had become a national obsession by the 1970s. Magazines featured articles about achieving the perfect tan. Numerous methods for obtaining a tan were used. People would coat their skin with baby oil, lay on aluminum reflectors, or bake in indoor tanning booths. By the late 1980s, indoor tanning became one of the fastest growing industries in North America, according to *U.S. News and World Report.*

But by the late 1980s, warnings about the risks of sun bathing came to public attention. Incidences of melanoma (a form of skin cancer) had increased more than tenfold from 1930 to the late 1980s. Soon, protective sun lotions were marketed to protect sunbathers from burning. Sunless tanning lotions offered the "look" without the damage. Despite warnings, the numbers of people with the worst form of skin cancer, melanoma, continued to rise at a rate of 7 percent each year since 1981. By the end of the twentieth century, well-known people like U.S. senator John McCain (1936–) of Arizona made public their struggles with skin cancer and warned against overexposure. Appealing public figures, such as Gwyneth Paltrow (1972–) and Nicole Kidman (1967–), were helping to make alabaster skin a sign of sex appeal and status again.

—Sara Pendergast

For More Information

Alder, Jerry, et al. "The Dark Side of the Sun." *Newsweek* (June 9, 1986): pp. 60–64.

"Brown as a . . . " *Newsweek* (August 1, 1966): pp. 58–59.

"Choose Your Cover: Facts and Statistics about Skin Cancer." *National Center for Chronic Disease Prevention and Health Promotion: Cancer Prevention and Control.* http://www.cdc.gov/ChooseYourCover/skin.htm (accessed April 1, 2002).

Levine, Art. "A New Bronze Age for the Tanning Industry: Indoor Tanning Salons Take on Their Critics." *U.S. News and World Report* (September 8, 1997): p. 48.

Sweet, Cheryl A. "'Healthy Tan'—A Fast-Fading Myth." Rockville, MD: U.S. Department of Health and Human Services, Public Health Service, Food and Drug Administration, 1990.

WHERE TO LEARN MORE

The following list of resources focuses on material appropriate for middle school or high school students. Please note that the Web site addresses were verified prior to publication, but are subject to change.

Books

America A to Z: People, Places, Customs and Culture. Pleasantville, NY: Reader's Digest Association, 1997.

Beetz, Kirk H., ed. *Beacham's Encyclopedia of Popular Fiction.* Osprey, FL: Beacham, 1996.

Berke, Sally. *When TV Began: The First TV Shows.* New York: CPI, 1978.

Blum, Daniel; enlarged by John Willis. *A Pictorial History of the American Theatre.* 6th edition. New York: Crown Publishers, 1986.

Brooks, Tim, and Earle Marsh. *The Complete Directory to Prime Time Network and Cable TV Shows.* 7th rev. ed. New York: Ballantine, 1999.

Cashmore, Ellis. *Sports Culture.* New York: Routledge, 2000.

Craddock, Jim. *VideoHound's Golden Movie Retriever.* 2002 ed. Detroit: Gale, 2002.

Gilbert, Adrian. *The Nineties (Look at Life In).* Austin, TX: Raintree Steck-Vaughn, 2000.

Daniel, Clifton, ed. *Chronicle of the Twentieth Century.* Liberty, MO: JL International Pub., 1994.

Dunning, John. *On the Air: The Encyclopedia of Old-Time Radio.* New York: Oxford University Press, 1998.

Dunning, John. *Tune In Yesterday: The Ultimate Encyclopedia of Old-Time Radio 1925–1976.* New York: Oxford University Press, 1998.

Epstein, Dan. *20th C Pop Culture.* Philadelphia: Chelsea House, 2000.

Finkelstein, Norman H. *Sounds of the Air: The Golden Age of Radio.* New York: Charles Scribner's, 1993.

Flowers, Sarah. *Sports in America.* San Diego: Lucent, 1996.

Gilbert, Adrian. *The Eighties (Look at Life In)*. Austin, TX: Raintree Steck-Vaughn, 2000.

Godin, Seth, compiler. *The Encyclopedia of Fictional People: The Most Important Characters of the 20th Century*. New York: Boulevard Books, 1996.

Grant, R. G. *The Seventies (Look at Life In)*. Austin, TX: Raintree Steck-Vaughn, 2000.

Grant, R. G. *The Sixties (Look at Life In)*. Austin, TX: Raintree Steck-Vaughn, 2000.

Green, Joey. *Joey Green's Encyclopedia of Offbeat Uses for Brand-Name Products*. New York: Hyperion, 1998.

Green, Stanley. *Encyclopedia of the Musical Theatre*. New York: Da Capo Press, 1980.

Hischak, Thomas S. *Film It with Music: An Encyclopedic Guide to the American Movie Musical*. Westport, CT: Greenwood Press, 2001.

Katz, Ephraim. *The Film Encyclopedia*. 4th ed. New York: HarperResource, 2001.

Lackmann, Ron. *The Encyclopedia of American Radio: An A–Z Guide to Radio from Jack Benny to Howard Stern*. New York: Facts on File, 2000.

Lebrecht, Norman. *The Companion to 20th-Century Music*. New York: Simon & Schuster, 1992.

Lissauer, Robert. *Lissauer's Encyclopedia of Popular Music in America: 1888 to the Present*. New York: Facts on File, 1996.

Lowe, Denise. *Women and American Television: An Encyclopedia*. ABC-CLIO: Santa Barbara, CA, 1999.

Maltin, Leonard, ed. *Leonard Maltin's Movie Encyclopedia*. New York: Dutton, 1994.

McNeil, Alex. *Total Television: The Comprehensive Guide to Programming from 1948 to the Present*. New York: Penguin, 1996.

Newcomb, Horace, ed. *Encyclopedia of Television*. Chicago: Fitzroy Dearborn Publishers, 1997.

Pendergast, Tom, and Sara Pendergast, eds. *St. James Encyclopedia of Popular Culture*. Detroit: St. James Press, 1999.

Rosen, Roger, and Patra McSharry Sevastiades, eds. *Coca-Cola Culture: Icons of Pop*. New York: Rosen, 1993.

Schwartz, Richard A. *Cold War Culture: Media and the Arts, 1945–1990*. New York: Facts on File, 1997.

Sies, Luther F. *Encyclopedia of American Radio, 1920–1960*. Jefferson, NC: McFarland, 2000.

Slide, Anthony. *Early American Cinema*. Metuchen, NJ: Scarecrow Press, 1994.

Tibbetts, John C., and James M. Welsh. *The Encyclopedia of Novels into Film*. New York: Facts on File, 1998.

Tibbetts, John C., and James M. Welsh. *The Encyclopedia of Stage Plays into Film*. New York: Facts on File, 2001.

Wilson, Charles Reagan, and William Ferris, eds. *Encyclopedia of Southern Culture*. Chapel Hill: University of North Carolina Press, 1989.

Web Sites

Markowitz, Robin. *Cultural Studies Central*. http://www.culturalstudies.net/ (accessed May 13, 2002).

Pop Culture Club. http://www.popcultureclub.org/ (accessed May 13, 2002).

Washington State University, American Studies. *Popular Culture: Resources for Critical Analysis.* http://www.wsu.edu/%7Eamerstu/pop/tvrguide.html (accessed May 13, 2002).

Yesterdayland. http://www.yesterdayland.com/ (accessed May 13, 2002).

Zupko, Sarah. *Popcultures.com: Sarah Zupko's Cultural Studies Center.* http://www.popcultures.com/ (accessed May 13, 2002).

INDEX

Italic type indicates volume number; **boldface** type indicates main entries and then page numbers; "(ill.)" indicates photos and illustrations.